S0-CFC-882

POLICING THE NATIONAL BODY

South End Press
Cambridge, Massachusetts

POLICING THE NATIONAL BODY

Sex, Race, and Criminalization

Edited by Jael Silliman and Anannya Bhattacharjee

A Project of the Committee on Women, Population, and the Environment

South End Press
Cambridge, Massachusetts

Copyright © 2002 by Jael Silliman and Anannya Bhattacharjee

Any properly footnoted quotation of up to 500 sequential words may be used without permission, as long as the total number of words quoted does not exceed 2,000. For longer quotations or for a greater number of total words, please write to South End Press for permission.

Cover design by Ellen Shapiro.
Printed in Canada by Transcontinental Printing.

Library of Congress Control Number: 2002100658

ISBN 0-89608-660-7 (paper)
ISBN 0-89608-661-5 (cloth)

South End Press, 7 Brookline Street, #1, Cambridge, MA 02139-4146
www.southendpress.org

07 06 05 04 03   2 3 4 5 6

Table of Contents

Acknowledgments   viii

Introduction
Policing the National Body:
Sex, Race, and Criminalization
Jael Silliman   ix

1 Private Fists and Public Force:
   Race, Gender, and Surveillance
   Anannya Bhattacharjee   1

2 Killing the Black Community: A Commentary
   on the United States War on Drugs
   Judith A.M. Scully   55

3 Speaking Out Against State Violence: Activist
   HIV-Positive Women Prisoners Redefine Social Justice
   Cynthia Chandler and Carol Kingery   81

4 Abortion in the United States: Barriers to Access
   Marlene Gerber Fried   103

5 Better Dead than Pregnant: The Colonization of
   Native Women's Reproductive Health
   Andrea Smith   123

6 Just Choices: Women of Color, Reproductive
   Health, and Human Rights
   Loretta J. Ross, Sarah L. Brownlee, Dazon Dixon Diallo, Luz
   Rodriquez, and SisterSong Women of
   Color Reproductive Health Project   147

7 The Gendered Assault on Immigrants
   Syd Lindsley   175

8 Put in Harm's Way: The Neglected Health
Consequences of Sex Trafficking in the United States
H. Patricia Hynes and Janice G. Raymond   197

9 Superpredator Meets Teenage Mom: Exploding
the Myth of the Out-of-Control Youth
Anne Hendrixson   231

10 The Changing Faces of Population Control
Betsy Hartmann   259

11 Greening the Swastika: Nativism and Anti-Semitism
in the Population and Environment Debate
Rajani Bhatia   291

Afterword
Reflections on Post-September 11 America:
An Interview with Angela Y. Davis
Anannya Bhattacharjee and Jael Silliman   325

Appendix   329
Index   331
About the Contributors   349
About South End Press   353
Related Titles   354

Acknowledgments

We would like to thank the members of the Committee on Women, Population, and the Environment (CWPE), the contributors to this volume, and our allies and friends for sharing their political analysis and insights with us. A sincere thank you to Lynn Lu, formerly of South End Press, for encouraging us to go ahead with this anthology. We also thank Sonia Shah and Loie Hayes for their work on developing the framework for the book. Tina Beyene, also of South End, served as our key editor and was a wonderful ally to work with to bring this effort to conclusion. Fiona Young, graduate student at the University of Iowa, was very helpful in coordinating the work of the various contributors at the early stages of this project. Melissa Deem, Natasa Durovicova, Maureen McCue, Susan Schechter and Rosemarie Scullion provided critical reading and insights at various phases of the project. Rosalind Petchesky and Melissa Deem were both helpful in brainstorming the title with us. We thank Angela Davis for her contribution to this book, for her courageous commitment, and her long and impressive history of activism to promote civil liberties, and to advance gender, racial, and social justice. Our sincere thanks also go to Amitava Bhattacharjee, Shikha Bhattacharjee, and S. Shankar for the many discussions we had regarding the book and for their readings of the manuscript.

Introduction

Policing the National Body

Sex, Race, and Criminalization

Jael Silliman

A merican politicians, eager to garner support from the large
middle-class, promote "family values," endlessly debate issues of abortion, and outdo each other as champions of "working families" (read "middle-class" families). Popular culture also
reflects middle-class preoccupations. *Traffic* (2000), Academy
Award–winner Steven Soderbergh's hard-hitting movie, portrays the drug war on the United States-Mexico border and
zooms in on the life of Caroline Wakefield, an affluent suburban
high school girl, to examine the devastating impact of drugs on
white America. Caroline's forays into the Black inner city serve
only as a lurid and violent backdrop to show how low she has
sunk to sustain her habit. The audience is sympathetic to the
plight of Caroline and her father, Judge Wakefield, while disen-
gaged and recoiling from the social and personal degradation
that drugs have caused in the inner city.

John Singleton's *Boyz N the Hood* (1991) was anomalous in at-
tracting some public attention to poor Black America. This com-
ing-of-age tale in gang-ravaged Central Los Angeles featured Tre
Styles, caught between the steady guidance of his father, Furious,
and the inescapable violence that surrounds him. Through this rare
movie, the broad public got a glimpse into the systemic violence and
despair that often characterizes life in poor neighborhoods of color.

Essentially, what we have is an America deeply divided across
class and race lines. This makes it possible for mainstream Amer-

ica—its politicians and media—to ignore or rarely address issues of poverty, criminalization, and race that are pressing for communities of color. Incarceration rates for people of color are disproportionately high and assaults and searches by police, the Immigration and Naturalization Service (INS), and border patrol forces are daily occurrences in communities of color. This aggressive law enforcement regime is increasingly accepted by the mainstream as the price to be paid for law and order. A lead article in the February 2001 edition of the *New York Times Magazine* marks this decisive shift in public attitude in New York City from a more libertarian, turbulent, and nonconformist city towards a greater acceptance of aggressive law enforcement.

Though Rudolph Giuliani's two terms as mayor of New York are infamous for discriminatory policing and harsh programs to reduce the crime rate, the "crack epidemic," and "welfare dependency," his policies and programs are widely accepted to facilitate "safety and prosperity." The new wisdom in New York City—one of the bastions of liberalism in the country—is "We no longer believe that to solve crime we have to deal with the root causes of poverty and racism; we now believe that we can reduce crime through good policing."[1]

Aggressive law enforcement policies and actions are devastating women of color and their communities. Though there is a strong and growing law enforcement accountability movement,[2] the women's movement in general has not seen state violence as a critical concern.[3] The mainstream reproductive rights movement, consumed with protecting the right to abortion, has failed to respond adequately to the policing, criminalization, and incarceration of large numbers of poor people and people of color. It has not sufficiently addressed cuts in welfare and immigrant services that have made one of the most fundamental reproductive rights—the right to have a child and to rear a family—most tenuous for a large number of people.

The mainstream reproductive rights movement, largely dominated by white women, is framed around choice: the choice to determine whether or not to have children, the choice to terminate a pregnancy, and the ability to make informed choices about contra-

ceptive and reproductive technologies. This conception of choice
is rooted in the neoliberal tradition that locates individual rights at
its core, and treats the individual's control over her body as central
to liberty and freedom. This emphasis on individual choice, however, obscures the social context in which individuals make
choices, and discounts the ways in which the state regulates populations, disciplines individual bodies, and exercises control over
sexuality, gender, and reproduction.[4]

The state regulates and criminalizes reproduction for many
poor women through mandatory or discriminatory promotion of
long-acting contraceptives and sterilization, and by charging pregnant women on drugs with negligence or child abuse. An examination of the body politics, the state's power of "regulation,
surveillance and control of bodies (individual and collective)," elu-
cidates the scope and venues through which the state regulates its
populations "in reproduction and sexuality, in work and in leisure,
in sickness and other forms of deviance and human difference."[5]

Feminists have challenged narrow and individualistic definitions of rights and have argued that equality must be an essential
tenet in the formulation of rights. As Rosalind Petchesky and Sonia
Correa, feminist reproductive rights theorists and advocates, have
pointed out, "The principle of equality applies to sexual and reproductive rights in two main areas: relations between men and
women (gender divisions), and relations among women (conditions such as class, age, nationality, or ethnicity that divide women
as a group)."[6] A commitment to the notion of equality, thus, promises to address and reduce the differences in power and resources
that divide both men and women and groups of women.

A commitment to diversity also stands as a cornerstone to this
radical, feminist conception of reproductive rights.

> While the equality principle requires the mitigation of inequities
> among women in their access to services or their treatment by
> health providers and policy makers, the diversity principle re-
> quires respect for difference among women—in values, culture,
> religion, sexual orientation, family and medical conditions.[7]

This principle acknowledges that reproductive rights have different meanings and different priorities in different social and cultural contexts. Their framework directly links the rights of the body and the person to social, economic, and political rights.[8]

Women of color have independently articulated a broad reproductive rights agenda embedded in issues of equality and social justice, while keenly tuned to the state's role in the reproduction and regulation of women's bodies. In an effort to protect their reproductive rights, they have challenged coercive population policies, demanded access to safe and accessible birth control, and asserted their right to economic and political resources to maintain healthy children. Through these demands, they move from an emphasis on individual rights to rights that are at once politicized and collectivized. African-American women leaders articulate the barriers to exercising their reproductive rights:

> Hunger and homelessness. Inadequate housing and income to provide for themselves and their children. Family instability. Rape. Incest. Abuse. Too young, too old, too sick, too tired. Emotional, physical, mental, economic, social—the reasons for not carrying a pregnancy to term are endless and varied.[9]

These leaders remind us that a range of individual and social concerns must be engaged to realize reproductive rights for all women.

This anthology places issues of race, class, and gender at the center of the reproductive rights and social justice agendas by focusing on a key concern among women of color and poor communities today: the difficulty of maintaining families and sustaining community in the face of increasing surveillance and criminalization. We discuss the policing of bodies by examining the experiences of women prisoners, women with HIV/AIDS in correctional facilities, women in systems of prostitution, immigrant women, women of color, and young women with a keen awareness of their multiple identities and oppressions. We show how particular communities and women within them are conceived and reproduced as threats to the national body, imagined as white and middle-class. This book explores the various cultural and state preoccupations to reproduce and secure the national body from the threatening forces that emanate from both inside and outside the United States borders.

Anannya Bhattacharjee, in "Private Fists and Public Force," sets the background and political purpose of the anthology. Through extensive research and interviews with activists opposing the repressive power of law enforcement agencies as well as victims of law enforcement, she highlights the ways in which poor women and women of color are criminalized. Bhattacharjee elaborates upon the prison system, police, INS, and border patrol forces to illustrate how they routinely undermine and endanger women's caretaking, caregiving, and reproductive functions. She shows how systemic and frequent abuses of reproductive rights and threats to bodily integrity are often overlooked by narrow definitions of reproductive rights and single-issue movements. She calls for greater coalition-building efforts between the women's movement, the reproductive rights movement, the immigrant rights movement, the violence against women movment, and the enforcement accountability movement, to break down barriers and to ensure the safety and self-determination of women of color. Bhattacharjee concludes with a discussion of the initiatives underway to develop new models for anti-violence work.

Crime and Punishment in the United States

The criminal justice system has become a massive machine for arrest, detention, and incarceration. The events of September 11, 2001 have intensified this trend. Citing "national secutiry" and the "war against terrorism," President Bush has furthered the power of the criminal justice system to arrest noncitizens and to circumvent the court system. Immigrants and communities of color will bear the brunt of the intensified assault on civil liberties. In 1998, on any given day, there were approximately six million people under some form of correctional authority. The number of people in American prisons is expected to surpass two million by late 2001. Federal Judge U.W. Clemon, after a visit to the Morgan County Jail in Alabama, wrote in a blistering ruling, "To say the Morgan County Jail is overcrowded is an understatement. The sardine-can appearance of its cell units more nearly resemble the holding units of slave ships during the Middle Passage of the eighteenth century than anything in the twenty-first century."[10] Imprisonment is the solution currently proffered for drug offenses in minority communities and for the other social problems spawned by poverty. As welfare and service programs are gutted, the only social service available to many of America's poor is jail![11]

Despite this surge in incarceration rates, it is widely accepted that prisons encourage recidivism, transform the occasional offender into a habitual delinquent,[12] fail to eliminate crime, and ignore the social problems that drive individuals to engage in illegal actions. French historian and social critic Michel Foucault explains the political rationale behind what he terms the "production of delinquency," and its usefulness for those in power:

> [T]he existence of a legal prohibition creates around it a field of illegal practices, which one manages to supervise, while extracting from it an illicit profit through elements, themselves illegal, but rendered manipulable by their organization in delinquency.... Delinquency represents a diversion of illegality for the illicit circuits of profit and power of the dominant class.[13]

The building and maintenance of policing and prison systems is politically expedient and highly profitable. Prisons boost local economies. Fremont County, Colorado, home to thirteen prisons, promotes itself as the Corrections Capital of the World. In *Going Up the River*, Joseph Hallinan explains how prisons have become public works projects that require a steady flow of inmates to sustain them.[14] Corporations engage in bidding wars to run prisons, and the federal government boasts about saving money by contracting out prison management to the private sector.

People of color are disproportionately represented in the prison industrial complex. Bureau of Justice statistics indicate that in 1999, 46 percent of prison inmates were Black and 18 percent were Hispanic. In "Killing the Black Community," Judith Scully argues that the war on drugs is used to justify and exercise control over the Black community. She contends that the United States government has historically maintained control over the Black community by selectively enforcing the law, arbitrarily defining criminal behavior and incarceration, and failing to punish white people engaged in lawless acts against the Black community, as exemplified in the infamous Rodney King and Amadou Diallo verdicts. The war on drugs demonstrates how government officials employ legal tools as well as racial rhetoric and criminal theory to criminalize and destroy Black communities. Scully explores how the creation of drug-related crimes such as the "crack baby" demonizes Black motherhood and undermines Black childbearing. Her essay exposes the institutional links between Blackness, suspicion, and criminality.

As strongly as class and race biases determine the criminal justice system, so does gender bias. Since 1980, the number of women in state and federal correctional facilities has tripled.[15] Amnesty International figures indicate that the majority of the over 140,000 women in the American penitentiary system are Black, Latina, and poor women, incarcerated largely for petty crimes.[16] For the same offense, Black and Latina women are respectively eight and four times more likely to be incarcerated than white women. The United Nations special report on violence against women in US state and federal prisons noted the trend in prison management that emphasizes punishment rather than rehabilitation and a widespread reduction in welfare and support services within the criminal justice system. These disturbing trends have led social commentator Barbara Ehrenreich to bluntly state:

> While the government does less and less for us, it does more and more to us. The Right points to the appalling fire-bombing at Waco; we should be just as noisily indignant about the on-going police war against low-income Americans of color, not to mention teenagers, immigrants and other misfits. If there is any handy measure of a government's repressiveness, it is the proportion of citizenry who are incarcerated, and at least by this measure the US leads the world. We don't, in other words have a soft, cuddly government of the kind that could be derided as a "nanny state." We have a huge and heavily armed cop.... Only the helpful functions of government are shrinking.[17]

The criminal justice system works collaboratively with government, corporate, and professional institutions to perform and carry out disciplinary functions deemed necessary to uphold the system of injustice. The recent exposés on racial profiling, discriminatory sentencing, and the compliance of hospitals, medical professionals, and private citizens in administering drug tests or reporting substance abuse among pregnant women are a few examples of the ways in which a range of actors are drawn in (sometimes reluctantly) to the surveillance and disciplinary system. For example, feminist lawyer Lynn Paltrow, executive director of National Advocates for Pregnant Women, describes how the Medical University Hospital in Charleston instituted a policy of reporting and facilitating the arrest of pregnant patients, overwhelmingly African-Americans, who tested positive for cocaine. African-American women were dragged out of the hospital in chains and shackles where the medical staff worked in collaboration with the prosecutor and police to see if the threat of arrest would deter drug use among pregnant women.[18]

Such violations are not going unchallenged. In *Ferguson vs. City of Charleston* (March 2001), a lawsuit engineered by Lynn Paltrow, the US Supreme Court agreed that Americans have the right, when they seek medical help, to expect that their doctor will examine them to provide diagnosis and treatment, and not search them to facilitate their arrest.[19]

Cynthia Chandler and Carol Kingery discuss prison activist strategies to confront state violence. In "Speaking Out Against State Violence," they seek to destabilize dominant social discourses on crime and violence, to develop an anti-violence strategy, and to increase the safety of women prisoners while challenging the foundation upon which the prison industrial complex is built. They argue that the political right has monopolized the discourse on "public safety" to justify the widening net of the criminal justice system. This leaves communities victimized by excessive imprisonment and violence with few alternative frameworks for pursuing safety. Working with three HIV-positive women prison activists, the authors begin imagining alternative modes of safety and justice. They offer several strategies, from acknowledging that violence against women includes institutional violence to opening communication between activists inside and outside prison to effect social change.

It is essential that we do not separate the more blatant forms of policing—videocameras within prisons that track every move of a prisoner, racial profiling, drug tests disproportionately administered in poor communities, and the raids on illegal immigrants crossing over to the United States—from the disciplinary apparatus being deployed across society. The wide use of differential forms of control and discipline is apparent in the ways in which the public has acquiesced to the policing and surveillance increasingly employed in everyday lives.

As a society we are no longer outraged when we hear that public schools in poor neighborhoods are routinely policed and equipped with metal detectors, and that students are hauled away in handcuffs for petty misdemeanors. The bodies being patrolled, segregated by race, determine the form of discipline applied. Perhaps this differential treatment explains why, in response to the spate of shootings in public schools across the country, parents in affluent neighborhoods have rallied and called for greater policing to ensure their children's safety. Middle-class parents invite policing to "protect their children." This contrasts sharply with the policing imposed in schools in poor communities and communities of color that criminalizes rather than protects. Though surveillance and policing differ according to whether they are there to protect or to criminalize, both kinds of interventions further extend state control over individual and collective bodies. The overt and insidious intrusions consolidate power in state and corporate entities.

Biological Control

Women of color have been the target of biological control ideologies since the founding of America. In her book *Killing the Black Body*, Dorothy Roberts traces the history of reproductive rights abuses perpetrated on the Black community from slavery to the present. Roberts shows how control over reproduction is systematically deployed as a form of racial oppression and argues that the denial of Black reproductive autonomy serves the interests of white supremacy.[20] Others have documented the history of sterilization abuse in the Latina and Native American communities, indicating that population control has a long history in the United

States. A Native American reproductive activist reports that on the Pine Ridge reservation today, pregnant women with drinking problems are put in jail, as it is the only holding place for them.[21]

Marlene Fried's essay "Abortion in the United States" situates the attacks on abortion as part of the right wing's efforts to assert ideological control over women and to recriminalize abortion. She explores the gap between the legality of abortion and its inaccessibility through a focus on the abortion experiences of young and low-income women and women of color in America. Fried shows how women's bodies are deployed as cultural and political battlegrounds. Their reproductive options are severely curtailed as part of a broader strategy to criminalize abortion and abortion providers. She examines a range of strategies such as harassment and violence towards abortion providers, stigmatization of young women that have abortions, denial of public funding for abortion rights, and restrictive legislation to undermine abortion rights. Fried argues that eugenicist thinking is behind the anti-abortion onslaught that frames poor women of color as an inherent threat.

In her essay "Better Dead than Pregnant," Andrea Smith traces how Native Americans have traditionally been and continue to be represented as racialized enemies that must be eliminated to ensure the growth of the national body through documenting the history of sterilization abuse in Native communities. Smith frames the attacks on Native American women's capacity to reproduce as the continuation of a long war of domination and control against a people and a culture. Though Native American activists have succeeded in reducing sterilization abuse rates, Smith argues that the state continues to control the reproductive freedom of women of color through the promotion of unsafe, long-acting hormonal contraceptives to women on federal assistance and women with disabilities. Smith contends that the promotion of sterilization and dangerous contraceptives alongside restrictive abortion policies are a contemporary form of genocide waged on Native peoples.

In "Just Choices," Loretta Ross, Sarah Brownlee, Dazon Dixon Diallo, and Luz Rodriquez show how women of color are forging new models of collaboration and organizational techniques to deal with critical issues of concern to them. The SisterSong collective was organized to promote research and action on reproductive issues defined by women of color. Through this collective model, they share experiences of treatment and prevention as well as address medical and societal factors that impact their reproductive health. The SisterSong model works within and across communities of color and represents an important step in broadening the reproductive rights agenda. It increases the capacity of grassroots groups to have a greater impact by building a wide reaching, national collective. By applying a human rights framework to health care problems, SisterSong has helped reconceptualize the human rights agenda, demanding that local, state, and federal governments meet the rights to safe and accessible health care for all.

The potential to extend biological control has expanded exponentially. Advances in data collection and storage through the computer, Internet, and genetic revolutions have made surveillance systems more efficient and invasive. The nineteenth-century "panoptical gaze" made it possible for a prisoner to be seen at all times, and through that process the prisoner internalized surveillance.[22] The new technologies radically expand the ability to collect, process, and encode large amounts of information on ever smaller surfaces. This makes it possible for the human body to be manipulated and controlled in radically new ways—from within the body itself. This intensification takes control from a mental to a physiological realm.

Like policing, corporate intrusion into the private sphere is increasingly naturalized. A great deal of data on individuals is bought, sold, and traded. In this instance, it is information on the rich and middle-class that is particularly coveted. The Internet revolution has made it possible for corporate and security interests to track every move made by an individual on the web to determine a person's consumer preferences, interests, and purchases, in addition to getting credit card information. Such intrusive data collecting techniques regarding an individual's tastes and preferences for corporate niche marketing is rarely framed as a surveillance problem. Critics have discussed it sometimes as a privacy concern, but by and large these incursions are accepted as a market-driven intrusion into our life.

Emerging reproductive technologies, such as cloning, have the potential to blur the distinctions between genetically distinct and genetically determined individuals. This raises ethical questions regarding who would count as fully human with the attendant civil rights and liberties. Valerie Hartouni points to how standards of humanity get "partialized" (making some less human than others) in this process.[23] She fears that, in the current social context, such technologies will be used to manage and contain diversity and the proliferation of difference.[24] Other critics are concerned with the eugenic possibilities of cloning and similar practices that work on humans from the inside out. The commodification of human life and the disruption that such technologies could have on kinship structures and human relations are a source of grave concern.

Surveillance and National (In)Security

Whereas the prison and policing systems are supposed to protect the nation from dangers within, the military, Border Patrols, and INS are ostensibly designed to protect the public from danger and threats that emanate from outside the national body. The discretionary authority and budgets of these institutions have expanded exponentially since September 11, 2001. A group of authors in this collection show how an influx of immigrants, the rhetoric of explosive population growth in the Third World, and angry young men inside and outside the United States are manufactured as a threat to national security.[25]

Immigrants in the United States are constructed as a source of danger. This threat has been used to justify the allocation of billions of dollars to the enforcement programs of the INS that patrol the nation. At present, the INS has more armed agents with arrest power than any other federal law enforcement agency.[26] Mandatory detention provisions have made immigrants the fastest growing incarcerated population in the United States. Stringent controls and border security forces are positioned at strategic places along the United States-Mexico border. Military-style tactics and equipment result in immigrants undertaking more dangerous, isolated routes to cross over where the risks of death, dehydration, and assault are exponentially higher.

Immigrant rights organizations and the press record detailed accounts of immigrants risking their lives to make their way through tortuous terrain to find work in the United States. The Mojave Desert in Southern California with its inhospitable terrain has become one such death trap for immigrants.[27] This dangerous crossing is a dramatic example of the extreme risks that immigrants take to escape INS agents and provide adequately for their families.

Vigilante groups and private citizens in Arizona have taken it upon themselves to "help" patrol ranchers "hunt" Mexican undocumented immigrants. Jose Palafox reports on the roundup of over 3,000 undocumented immigrants on Roger and Don Barnett's 22,000-acre property in Douglas, Arizona, near the United States-Mexico border. Ranchers circulated a leaflet asking for volunteers to help patrol their land while having "Fun in the Sun." Immigrants were considered "fair game."[28]

While border patrol forces and private citizens tighten their grip on illegal immigration and regulate the mobility of poor workers, social services are being slashed for legal immigrants. The latter are often portrayed as a drain on national resources and a direct threat to low-wage workers in the United States, and female immigrants of color are particularly targeted for their family settlement and community building roles.

In "The Gendered Assault on Immigrants," Syd Lindsley situates the anti-immigrant assault in California in the context of the state's regulation of motherhood. She argues that anti-immigrant legislation and propaganda in California is a direct response to the feminization of immigration. Lindsley traces the processes that feminized the majority of the undocumented Mexican immigrant population in the early 1990s and illuminates the critical roles that women immigrants play in integrating their families into American public institutions and in the settlement process. She provides insight into how anti-immigrant legislation and cuts in social services were directed at immigrant women's reproductive and maternal work to disable their attempt to foster the permanent settlement of their families into the United States.

Lindsley's essay touches on the profound racial anxieties that many white Americans are experiencing regarding America's future as a white nation. The realization that nearly half of the nation's 100 largest cities are home to more minorities than whites is most palpable in California. Shaken by the increasing presence of Mexican and non-white immigrant women, they have been cast as undeserving mothers in an attempt to exclude them from welfare while continuing to profit from their labor.

Even though many studies have shown that immigrant labor contributes to the economy, there is a widely held perception that they represent a financial drain. Despite the proverbial anti-immigrant sentiment, the United States economy depends on cheap immigrant labor. Very often undocumented workers perform jobs or are made to engage in activities usually considered too low-paying or too risky for citizens and residents. It has been estimated that 45,000 to 50,000 women and children are trafficked annually into and across the United States for the sex industry, sweatshops, domestic labor, and agricultural work. The INS compares the trafficking in women and children with the drug and weapons smuggling industry. Patricia Hynes and Janice Raymond, in "Put in Harm's Way," draw attention to the ways in which women are trafficked for sexual exploitation and how the trafficked women, not the traffickers, are frequently criminalized in the United States.

Hynes and Raymond examine the global factors that lead to increased sex trafficking, including the economic impacts of globalization on women who are constructed as commodities through the instrumentalization of the body for sex. They argue that trafficking cannot be explained in economic terms alone but must be situated in the global structures of sexual inequality and the male demand for sex through prostitution. In groundbreaking interviews conducted with trafficked women, women in prostitution, social service providers, and activists they present the gender-specific risks that trafficked women face and the health consequences of their exploitation. They put forward a set of policy recommendations to dismantle the sex industry, which exploits trafficked women and children, and propose ways to protect their health and safety.

In "Superpredator Meets Teenage Mom," Anne Hendrixson shows how conservative think tanks, policy-makers, and population control advocates deploy a public discourse on danger and rampant crime to extend the prison industrial complex. In this discursive framework, young men of color in the United States (depicted as superpredators), figure as the internal security threat. John J. DiIulio, Jr., now the director of the White House Office of Faith-Based and Community Initiatives, created a "whole theory around the notion that a new generation of street criminals is upon us—the youngest, biggest and baddest generation any society has ever known" and gave rise to the notion that "America is now home to thickening ranks of superpredators—radically impulsive, brutally remorseless youngsters, including ever more teenage boys, who murder, assault, rape, rob, burglarize, deal deadly drugs, join gun toting gangs and create serious communal disorders."[29]

Though DiIulio regrets having become the intellectual pillar for putting violent juveniles in jail and condemning them as superpredators, and despite the fact that his theories were proved wrong by statistics that showed the rate of juvenile crime dropping by half, the Human Rights Watch as recently as 2000 blamed the superpredator theory for new state initiatives to move juvenile offenders into the adult criminal justice system.[30]

Young women of color, like their counterparts in the Third World, are feared for their fertility. Valerie Hartouni, in her discussion of *The Bell Curve* and the commentary that followed, writes, "the unwed procreating Black body continues to signify the site of the unrestrained wanton breeding of unwanted babies and as the source of social pollution and pathology. It is by definition incorrigible; by definition, a threat to national prosperity; by definition, in need of containment."[31]

Hendrixson demonstrates how the creation, recycling, and deployment of gendered and racist stereotypes of superpredators, angry young men in the Third World, fertile teenagers, and unwed mothers at home and abroad bolster demographic alarmism, population control, militarism, and the prison industrial complex.

In "The Changing Faces of Population Control," Betsy Hartmann reveals the contradictions that shape public policy on population and warns feminists to be vigilant toward population control ideology and its many guises. She unravels the feminist, neoliberal, and population control strains that lie at the heart of current thinking and action on population. She argues that women's health and empowerment agendas cannot be carried forward in a piecemeal way in this period of economic polarization and marginalization. Whereas some of the elements of a women's health agenda may be won, the entire package cannot be realized at a time of downsizing and social program cutbacks. Hartmann challenges women to move outside the safety zone of liberal feminism and speak out against population control, coercion, and racism, and to build alliances with other movements for social and racial justice.

"Greening the Swastika," by Rajani Bhatia, shows how conservative activism and thinking on population and environmental issues in the United States has striking parallels to the nationalist socialist preoccupations with population and the environment exhibited by the Nazis in Germany. Bhatia unravels the way in which the Nationalist Socialist concern for the German environment and the mystical German relationship with land was deeply bound up with its nativist and anti-immigrant scheme. She traces the ideology, actors, and agenda of the right-wing population and environmental lobby in the United States and exposes their ideological connections with Nazi thinking. Bhatia underlines the importance of identifying the ideological underpinnings of mainstream environmental discourse that scapegoats immigrants for population and environmental problems. She unravels a nativist agenda to promote "American" culture and values as part of a concerted campaign against immigrant rights, multiculturalism, reproductive rights, and diversity.

Beyond Analysis: Building a Movement

The writers of this anthology are members or allies of the Committee on Women, Population, and the Environment (CWPE). We are a multiracial alliance of feminist activists, health practitioners, and scholars committed to promoting the social and economic empowerment of women in a context of global peace and justice. We work toward eliminating poverty, inequality, racism, and environmental degradation. A crucial feature of our work, which we carry over into our books, is our identification and cultivation of a political common ground, given our widely ranging ethnic and national identities. These essays complement and extend our ongoing analytical and organizing efforts and allow us to share them with a wider audience.

During the series of United Nations conferences that shaped the 1990s, CWPE focused its efforts to oppose population control and increase the knowledge and support for women's rights and priorities by reaching out to mainstream environmental groups. We worked together to develop the analysis and framework for responding to environment and development linkages that were being forged by mainstream population and environmental groups. This analysis was used for organizing around the conferences and for mobilizing a progressive coalition of women's rights and environmental rights groups. *Dangerous Intersections: Feminist Perspectives on Population and the Environment* brought together our work in the form of a book.[32]

Over the last three years, the composition of the group has evolved to include many more women of color and members working in immigrant rights and enforcement accountability movements. We have challenged environmental groups who have encouraged anti-immigrant rhetoric and portrayed immigrants as threats to the environment, and we continue to work in partnership with immigrant rights and environmental justice advocates to expose the race and class politics behind the anti-immigration movement. We have spoken out against the targeting of women's fertility, and have articulated the connections between the increasing criminalization of people of color and the poor, between prisons and population control.

We underline the critical need for expanding the agenda, constituency, and allies of the pro-choice movement. The dominant neoliberal approach that is focused on expanding the reproductive choices by providing women access to a range of contraceptives and keeping abortion legal does not speak to the realities of broad sections of women. It does not come to grips with the ways in which the rights of low-income women and women of color to have children have been and still are being restricted and their procreation devalued.

Contemporary policies restricting public assistance to low-income women and their families, coercive contraceptive programs and the promotion of long-acting contraceptives and sterilization in people of poor communities, and the prosecution of pregnant women on drug charges are a few examples of the ways in which the right to bear children is systematically undermined. Women of color who promote reproductive rights place reproductive choice in a broader agenda and advocate for women's health, as well as the economic and social rights that are necessary to exercise control over one's life.

CWPE, out of step with the mainstream pro-choice movement, focuses its efforts on challenging abuses of reproductive rights at home and abroad, and builds alliances with other social movements to create the economic, social, and political conditions for all women to be able to exercise real choices regarding when, whether, and with whom to have or not have a child.

CWPE asserts that the oppression of women, not their reproductive capacities, needs to be eliminated and calls for drug treatment for women with substance abuse problems, decent jobs, educational opportunities, and mental health and child-care services. It is the lack of these services that deny human dignity and exacerbate conditions of poverty, social status, and gender discrimination. CWPE continues to work to stop the unethical testing of contraceptives that undermine women's health and well-being.[33]

This anthology is directed at activists, students, policy-makers, and scholars who seek to understand the connections between the criminalization of people of color and the poor, and social and population control. We seek to include the reader in a dialogue that builds collaborations between social movements to move beyond single-issue and identity-based politics towards an inclusive political agenda across progressive movements.

1 Quoting Myron Magnet, editor of *City Journal*.

2 The law enforcement agencies referred to include local and state police agencies; prison systems at the local, state and federal levels; the United States Border Patrol and Interior Enforcement Operations of the Immigration and Naturalization Service (INS); and the rapidly expanding INS detention system. See Anannya Bhattacharjee's essay in this anthology to get an account of the various movements in the United States that challenge the violence and brutality of these enforcement agencies.

3 This is not true in other parts of the world. For example, state violence has been a critical issue for the contemporary women's movement in India. Radha Kumar in *The History of Doing* writes: "The issue of rape has been one that most contemporary feminist movements internationally have focused on, firstly because sexual assault is one of the ugliest and most brutal expressions of masculine violence towards women, because rape and the historical discourse around it reveal a great deal about the social relations of reproduction, and thirdly because of what it shows about the way in which the woman's body is seen as representing the community. In India, it has been the latter reason which has been the most dominant in the taking up of campaigns against rape." (Delhi: Kali for Women, 1993), 128.

4 Foucault, in *The History of Sexuality*, refers to this form of state control as "bio-power."

5 Nancy Scheper-Hughes and Margaret Lock, "The Mindful Body: A Prolegomenon to Future Work in Medical Anthropology," *Medical Anthropology Quarterly*, Vol. 1 (1987), 6–41.

6 For a fuller discussion of a feminist theory of reproductive rights see Rosalind Petchesky and Sonia Correa, "Reproductive And Sexual Rights: A Feminist Perspective," in Gita Sen, Adrienne Germain and Lincoln C. Chen, eds., *Population Policies Reconsidered: Health, Empowerment and Rights* (Cambridge, MA: Harvard University Press, Harvard Series on Population and International Health, 1994), 107–124.

7 Ibid., 117.

8 Rosalind Petchesky and Karen Judd, eds., *Negotiating Reproductive Rights* (New York: Zed Books, 1998), 4.

9 "We Remember: African American Women are for Reproductive Freedom" (1998); statement signed and distributed by leaders in the African-American community including Byllye Avery, Reverend Willie Barro, Donna Brazil, Shirley Chisholm, and Dorothy Heights in support of keeping abortion safe and legal.

10 David Firestone, "Alabama's Packed Jails Draw Ire of Courts, Again," *New York Times*, May 1, 2001, A1.

11 Eve Goldberg and Linda Evans, "The Prison Industrial Complex and the Global Economy," *Political Environments* (Fall 1999/Winter 2000), 47.

12 Dr. James Gilligan, a Harvard psychotherapist who has worked on prisons and recidivism, argues that punishing violence with imprisonment does not stop violence because it continues to replicate the patriarchal code. See *Violence: Reflections on a National Epidemic*, (New York: Vintage, 1997).

13 Michel Foucault, *Discipline and Punish* (New York: Vintage, 1995), 280.

14 Joseph Hallinan, *Going Up The River: Travels in a Prison Nation* (New York: Random House, 2001).

15 Jennifer Yanco, "Breaking the Silence: Women and the Criminal Justice System," *Political Environments,* No. 7 (Fall 1999/Winter 2000), 20.

16 This document, "The UN Special Report on Violence Against Women" by Special Rapporteur Radhika Coomaraswamy, is available from United Nations Publications at www.un.org.

17 Barbara Ehrenreich, "When Government Gets Mean: Confessions of A Recovering Statist," *The Nation* (November 17, 1997).

18 Lynn Paltrow, "Pregnant Drug Users, Fetal Persons, and the Threat to *Roe v. Wade*," *Albany Law Review*, Vol. 62, No. 3 (1999), 1024.

19 This decision affirms the Fourth Amendment to the US Constitution that protects every American, including those who are pregnant and those with substance abuse problems, from warrantless, unreasonable searches.

20 Dorothy Roberts, *Killing the Black Body* (New York: Vintage, 1998).

21 Native American Health Education Resource Center, SisterSong Native Women's Reproductive Health and Rights Roundtable Report (Lake Andes, SD: January 2001), 17.

22 Foucault, *Discipline and Punish*, 195–228.

23 For a rich discussion of this set of issues, see Valerie Hartouni, "Replicating the Singular Self," in *Cultural Conceptions: On Reproductive Technologies and the Remaking of Life* (Minneapolis, MN: University of Minnesota Press, 1997), 110–132.

24 Ibid., 119.

25 For more on the subject see Betsy Hartmann, "Population, Environment, and Security: A New Trinity" in Jael Silliman and Ynestra King, eds., *Dangerous Intersections* (Cambridge, MA: South End Press, 1999), 1–23.

26 Maria Jimenez, "Legalization Then and Now: An Eighty Year History," *Network News*, (Oakland, CA: National Network for Immigrant and Refugee Rights, Summer 2000), 6.

27 Ginger Thompson, "The Desperate Risk of Death in a Desert," *New York Times*, October 31, 2000, A12.

28 Jose Palafox, "Welcome to America: Arizona Ranchers Hunt Mexicans," *Network News* (Summer 2000), 4.

29 Elizabeth Becker, "For an Office with A Heart, a Man With a Change of One," *New York Times*, February 9, 2001, A16.

30 The United States is one of only seven countries in the world that permit the execution of juvenile offenders. The Supreme Court upheld the constitutionality of the death penalty for 16- and 17-year olds by one vote in a landmark ruling written by Justice Antonin Scalia in 1989. The sentencing of juvenile offenders reflects the trend towards treating them as adults that started in the mid-1990s and has continued though the crime rate has been declining. The typical condemned juvenile offender is Southern, Black, poor and male, and his victim was white and female. Sara Rimer and Raymond Bonner, "Whether to Kill Those Who Killed as Youths," *New*

York Times, August 22, 2000, A1, A16.
31   Hartouni, *Cultural Conceptions*, 109.
32   Silliman and King, eds., *Dangerous Intersections*.
33   For further information on CWPE, visit www.cwpe.org.

Chapter 1

Private Fists and Public Force

Race, Gender, and Surveillance

Anannya Bhattacharjee

Over the past thirty years, the entire apparatus of law enforcement in the United States has expanded dramatically, becoming more punitive, highly integrated, heavily funded, and technologically sophisticated. At the same time, a range of public institutions, such as welfare agencies, schools, and hospitals, have become increasingly permeated by what might be described as a culture of law enforcement. In some cases, such institutions have assumed law enforcement functions or integrated law enforcement personnel into their operations.

In response, a broad variety of community-based organizations and advocacy groups have begun to challenge persistent violations of civil, constitutional, and human rights and to press for greater accountability on the part of law enforcement, including local and state police agencies; prison systems at the local, state, and federal levels; the United States Border Patrol and interior enforcement agents of the Immigration and Naturalization Service (INS);[1] and, most recently, the rapidly expanding INS detention system. Such violations have primarily (although not exclusively) affected communities of color, both immigrant and US-born.

Throughout this period, women (again, primarily women of color) have progressively become a more significant presence, both numerically and proportionately, among the populations of prisoners, arrestees, border crossers, undocumented workers, and detainees. Women have also been well represented, both as advocates and as members of affected communities, in the various support and accountability movements mentioned above. Nonetheless, a gender perspective has been weak and sometimes entirely absent in the way these issues have been framed.

A gendered analysis is important not simply for reasons of inclusiveness, but also because it is critical to the development of an analysis of enforcement violence that can sustain cohesive, effective, and strategic social movements. (The term "enforcement violence" is used here to cover violence and the abuse of authority by the full range of law enforcement agencies named above.) Understanding how such violence is experienced by women helps us to go beyond a specific incident, a specific victim, and her or his specific fate, to see how enforcement affects our communities overall.

Such an analysis exposes the impact of law enforcement on issues of basic security such as home life, caregiving, reproduction and sexuality, and paid work, all social arenas in which women are central actors. Finally, a gendered analysis can help illuminate key tendencies in the relationship between the state (that is, the government) and various sectors of the community.

The arenas named—home and family, caregiving, reproduction and sexuality, and paid work—have framed organizing by women's movements over the past generation. Some of these movements have defined themselves as "feminist," while others have not. In either case, a particular thrust of women's organizing has been to challenge violence against women, including domestic violence, sexual assault, and the denial of reproductive freedom.

This broad movement against violence against women has formulated its own strategies regarding law enforcement, and these strategies also need to be evaluated in terms of their effectiveness in promoting safety and self-determination for women, especially women of color, and their communities.

The present analysis of enforcement violence against women considers the practices of different law enforcement agencies, separating them, when relevant, into the broad categories of "policing" (by police agencies, the Border Patrol, and the INS) and "jailing" (including jails and prisons as well as INS detention facilities). However, "immigration" and "criminal justice" are not considered in this discussion as separate issue areas.

For more than a decade, both activists and researchers have noted an increasing integration of these seemingly disparate law enforcement systems, which has been brought about through legislation, funding, institutional restructuring, sharing of technology and personnel, and joint operations. Further, in practice, law enforcement operations do not distinguish among people according to their documentation or citizenship, but rather depend on racial profiling. Reviewing immigration and criminal justice together reveals that their impact at the community level is indistinguishable.

A comprehensive gender analysis of enforcement violence requires an exploration that crosses all of these divisions and can foster a new kind of dialogue and cross-fertilization: between movements for enforcement accountability and those addressing violence against women; between movements based in immigrant and US-born communities; and between advocates concerned with immigration and criminal justice.

While this essay offers a critique of law enforcement, the intention here is not to argue for less government. Contemporary critics of "big government" voice strong opposition to a government role in promoting social welfare, while simultaneously calling for an ever-larger role for every type of law enforcement. It is also not the intention here to negate the reality that some people do commit acts of violence and other offenses, or that every society needs a system for protecting public safety. However, as author and activist Luana Ross has noted in reference to Native Americans and criminal justice, "A thorough analysis of Native criminality must include the full context of the criminal behavior—that is, their victimization and the criminalization of Native rights by the United States government."[2] In the current social order, we believe that the very concepts of criminality and the appropriate state response are heavily shaped by the many injustices and structural inequalities that exist in our society.

The Evolution of Law Enforcement

The Incarceration Explosion

The United States, home to 5 percent of the world's population, incarcerates 25 percent of all prisoners worldwide. While the percentage of women prisoners remains relatively small, it is growing at a much faster rate than the incarcerated population as a whole. Between 1985 and 1996, the population of women in prison increased threefold. According to the Sentencing Project, "African-American women have almost single-handedly expanded the gender-end of the prison industrial complex."[3] Over the last ten years, criminal justice activists have seen a marked increase in the incarceration of younger women between the ages of sixteen and eighteen.[4] Most women are incarcerated for nonviolent crimes (such as passing bad checks or drug violations). The circumstances in which women's behavior is judged to be "criminal" are heavily shaped by social definitions of women's role.

The most rapidly expanding prison system in the United States is the immigration detention system, costing taxpayers millions of dollars a year.[5] The explosive growth of detention is one of many changes that were set in motion by the passage of the Illegal Immigration Reform and Immigrant Responsibility Act (IIRAIRA) of 1996, which imposed very harsh conditions on immigrants. The INS estimated that by the year 2001, it would be detaining 300,000 people annually, an increase of 76 percent from 1997.[6]

Overcrowding, lack of communication with the outside world, lack of access to legal and medical services, and isolation mark life in INS detention centers. Such conditions are worse for women, whose needs are characteristically given the lowest priority. The total number of women in INS detention doubled between 1995 and 1998. Many detainees are held in temporary facilities or moved without warning from one state to another, thus making access to lawyers, translators, and human rights advocates almost impossible. Some INS detainees also face the possibility of arbitrary and indefinite incarceration without any process for determining the length of stay, a condition that clearly violates basic human rights. Some detainees are long-term legal United States residents who have served prison sentences for a broad variety of criminal convictions, including many nonviolent or minor offenses. Under IIRAIRA, they are subject to detention and deportation, even though they may have left their countries of origin as young children and may not have ties there. Prison activist Donna Wilmott, a former political prisoner, reports that some 40 percent of the prisoners at the Federal Correctional Institute in Dublin, California, are foreign-born. Notes Wilmott: "If you are foreign-born and in prison, the unspoken feeling around is that you are inferior," which she believes is a reflection of anti-immigrant prejudice outside.[7]

Policing in the Era of Mass Incarceration

Local and state police agencies are among the most pervasive and mobile law enforcement bodies. They also cooperate with and help gain entry for officials of other agencies, such as the Border Patrol, other INS agents, or drug enforcement agents.

In the 1990s, New York City was credited with inaugurating an unusually violent and abusive style of policing—the so-called "quality of life" policing—under Mayor Giuliani and William Bratton, the police commissioner of the New York Police Department (NYPD).[8]

> In 1997 and 1998, officers with the NYPD's street crimes unit frisked more than 45,000 people thought to be carrying guns, but they arrested fewer than 10,000. This policing strategy allows the police to detain, question, and thus regulate tens of thousands of mostly low-income people of color.[9]

The philosophy and practices employed by the NYPD, one of the largest police forces in the United States, have now made their way across the country. In response, community-based movements nationwide have been challenging the increase of police brutality against communities of color, particularly young people from such communities.

At the federal level, parallel trends are observable in immigration enforcement. In 1998, the INS announced that it employed "more armed agents than any other federal agency, including the FBI."[10] Within the INS, the growth of enforcement operations has dramatically outstripped that of the agency's service operations (processing applications for visas, work permits, citizenship, political asylum, and the like).[11] INS raids, nominally intended to capture undocumented immigrants, can take place in the workplace, home, neighborhood, streets, or parking lots—in short, any place at all. Both border control operations and INS raids invariably target legal residents and citizens as well as undocumented people, with agents using racial profiling.

Social Justice or "Law and Order"?

All of these developments may be understood as manifestations of a broad tendency to redefine profound issues of social inequality as problems of "law and order." From this standpoint, laws mandating more punitive and violent law enforcement are offered up as a substitute for real solutions, which would require a structural transformation of power.[12]

A key example of a social problem that has been reframed as a question of "law and order" is drug trafficking. The redefinition of drug addiction as a legal problem (rather than, for example, a problem of public health) has provided an effective rationale for dramatically expanding the powers and resources of law enforcement agencies. In the words of activist Ethan Nadelmann,

> Police officers, generals, politicians ... qualify as drug czars—but not, to date, a single doctor or public health figure.... [D]rug policies are designed, implemented, and enforced with virtually no input from the millions of Americans they affect most: drug users.[13]

Another example is provided by the contemporary catch phrase "quality of life," which is used to give a humanitarian gloss to the new generation of strategies for urban policing described above. One might well question exactly whose quality of life is being protected. Young people of color are among the most affected by the intensification of policing. According to New York City Police Watch,

> With declines in funding and roughly one in fourteen youths arrested annually by the NYPD, youths aged thirteen to twenty have a greater chance of getting arrested than they do of get-

ting a job after school or having a community youth program
to go to after school. [14]

The two fastest growing incarcerated populations are women
of color and immigrants of color. Women of color have been especially affected by laws imposing mandatory minimum sentences
for all drug offenses, which spread across the nation following the
enactment of the Rockefeller Drug Laws in New York State in
the early 1970s. Federal laws like IIRAIRA and the
Anti-Terrorism and Effective Death Penalty Act, both enacted in
1996, are directly responsible for the huge increases in the numbers of incarcerated immigrants.

In essence, all of these state and federal laws have been posed
as solutions to a broad range of problems associated with poverty
and global economic inequality, for which the US government and
US-based corporations bear a large share of the responsibility.
From this standpoint, one might argue that the primary goal of law
enforcement is to contain those segments of the population that
are most likely to rise up and threaten a public order that protects
the privileged.

Harsher and More Militarized Law Enforcement

The increasingly harsh legal regime described above has been
accompanied by a growing reliance on military-style tactics and
weaponry by law enforcement at every level. This militarization of
domestic law enforcement has been brought about through dramatic increases in funding, increasing use of advanced military
technology, sharing of personnel and equipment with the military,
and promotion of a war-like culture. Long-term women prisoners
report changes such as increasing numbers of guards wearing fa-
tigues and buzz cuts and conducting themselves in military style:
making women march in single file for everything, being more
physically aggressive, using rubber bullets, and generally having
more "toys." [15]

As such trends have progressed, law enforcement itself has intensified dramatically. Advocates report sharply increasing levels
of violence by police and prison guards, overnight stays in local

jails for actions that would have warranted at most a ticket a couple of decades back, and greater criminalization of immigrants and young people, especially from communities of color.

Interagency Collaboration

Over the past two decades, interagency task force efforts have become far more common, whether justified in the name of the "war against drugs" or by concern over undocumented immigration. It is increasingly common for officials of different agencies such as local or state police, the Border Patrol or other INS units, and the county sheriff's department to show up at the same time for law enforcement encounters ranging from traffic stops to house raids. Such developments, initially reported in the United States-Mexico border region, have spread throughout the country.

As communication between agencies increases, one agency can threaten individuals by invoking the powers of another. For example, in New York City, when a woman of Indian origin found herself in the police station with her boyfriend, the latter was threatened with deportation, even though he is a legal immigrant with a work permit and the police do not directly have powers of deportation.[16] In the case of immigrant women caught in situations of domestic violence, the increasing collusion between the police and immigration authorities makes it dangerous to call the police, because they could deport either the woman or the man against the woman's wishes.[17]

Privatization and Profit

As incarceration expands, new opportunities for profit have been created through prison construction contracts, the privatization of health care and food services, and even the privatization of entire institutions. All of these economic arrangements are undergoing rapid expansion, as is the use of prison labor by private corporations. Prisoners, who may be paid next to nothing, also serve as the most controllable workforce, since they cannot unionize.

The INS also serves as a growing source of income for county jails, which are rented out for immigration related detention.

"At an average cost of $58 per day per detainee," according to Human Rights Watch, "the INS spends nearly a half-million dollars each day to house its detainees in local jails. This arrangement provides a source of profit for county governments; in some, county debts have been paid and some taxes eliminated due to revenue from holding immigrants in local jails.[18]

Impact on Other Institutions

The punitive logic of law enforcement has had a pervasive impact on other public agencies, which supposedly serve an entirely distinct mission. For example, welfare recipients increasingly find that welfare services resemble the criminal justice system. Processes like the Eligibility Verification Review, welfare organizers say, reflect the culture of criminalization.[19] Through workfare programs, welfare recipients are obliged to work almost for free and, like prisoners, are not allowed to unionize.[20]

The foster care system and child protective services also increasingly employ punitive measures, especially toward women of color. Investigations by child protective services evoke considerable fear, as they are closely tied to the criminal justice system. Many low-wage workplaces that rely on immigrant labor have also begun to resemble law enforcement institutions. For example, immigrant workers in an Iowa meatpacking factory have been routinely subjected to body searches, restrictive use of and supervision in bathrooms, drug tests, video surveillance, locker searches, and a lack of medical services.[21]

Organizing Against Violence

Enforcement Accountability

Broadly speaking, enforcement accountability movements have focused on confronting the many types of violence and abuse engendered by the unrestrained growth of law enforcement. The constituencies of these movements are diverse, spanning immigrant as well as US-born communities of color (as well as growing numbers of white allies, especially among youth).

The prisoners' rights movement is perhaps the best established of the enforcement accountability movements. Diverse organizations such as Legal Services for Prisoners with Children and Justice Works, among numerous others, work on different aspects of prisoners' lives in all parts of the country. Prison support groups have advocated for various alternatives to incarceration, like community service work, restitution, employment and job training assistance, alcohol and substance abuse treatment, conditional or supervised release, and residential care and counseling.[22]

Also widespread are grassroots police accountability groups, such as Bay Area Police Watch and New York City Police Watch of the Ella Baker Center for Human Rights. There are national networks like the National Coalition on Police Accountability (NCOPA), based in Chicago. The work of all these groups on documenting specific instances of police brutality is crucial in gauging the scope of the issue in different communities.

Similarly, violence and abuse directed against immigrants has been extensively documented by local groups like the Washington Alliance for Immigrant and Refugee Justice. The systematic abuse of human rights at the United States-Mexico border, particularly by the Border Patrol, has been brought to national attention by the American Friends Service Committee's Immigration Law Enforcement Monitoring Project. The National INS Raids Task Force of the National Network for Immigrant and Refugee Rights (NNIRR) has played a key role in publicizing the growing impact of INS raids in interior regions of the country.

The Invisibility of Gender

Among the enforcement accountability movements, the prison movement is the most organized with regard to women, with a range of organizations focusing on sexual violence by guards, medical care, parole, child custody, visitation, and caregivers' programs. It is unusual, however, to find sustained alliances between such organizations and women's anti-violence organizations. The movement against violence toward women has not taken ownership of women prisoners' concerns, and prison groups have not placed themselves in the context of the women's anti-violence effort.

Immigrants' rights organizations have documented and publicized violence inflicted on women by immigration authorities, especially at the United States-Mexico border, where immigration law enforcement has been a focus of community concern for a longer period of time. Nonetheless, documentation and organizing efforts have seldom reflected a sustained focus on how women experience border crossing and associated abuses of their rights. In one case, when immigrants' rights lawyers and advocates organized a campaign around a woman who was raped by a Border Patrol agent, they did so with virtually no links or discussions with women's organizations in the area, because no prior relationships had been established.[23] Further, immigrants' rights groups as well as human rights watchdog groups have often described INS abuse in gender-neutral terms, referring to the impact on "families" and the loss of "wage-earners." Such terms erase the singular hardships that women bear and continue to keep the discussion male-dominated by default, obscuring the considerable leadership women provide in immigrants' rights organizing.

Significant numbers of women of all ages are actively involved in organizing against police brutality. Nevertheless, the focus of such initiatives continues to be disproportionately masculine (although mothers of victims of police brutality, who have created their own organizations, have broadened the discussion).

Recently, a string of cases of police brutality and police killings in New York City sparked broad community outrage, gaining national publicity. During the same time span, the case surfaced of a battered woman who called the police while being beaten by her partner. The police took her to an isolated spot, beat her up brutally, and left her there with the warning that next time they found her, they would kill her.[24] Her case was never taken up by the groups actively protesting the undeniably tragic and unjust deaths of male victims.

The Women's Anti-Violence Movement

Over the past thirty years, women's anti-violence organizations have broken the silence about many types of violence whose existence was previously denied or trivialized. The achievements of the women's anti-violence movement are substantial, involving significant changes in police and court practices and legal standards, as well as a profound transformation of public awareness.

The successes of this movement, however, have come at a price. Women's anti-violence organizations have evolved a considerable distance away from their origins as grassroots, community-based groups; today, most are professionally staffed agencies providing social and legal services. In seeking to hold police agencies accountable for enforcing laws against sexual assault and domestic violence, the women's anti-violence movement has largely sidestepped the problem of the violent and abusive nature of law enforcement in poor communities of color. In the process, it has restricted its focus to the ways in which women may be vulnerable to violence from individual men, overlooking the ways in which women are also subject to violence from authorities of the state.

Over the years, this has resulted in a growing tension between the mainstream anti-violence movement and women of color organizations concerning the posture of women's organizations toward governmental agencies. Fundamentally, this is an issue of how progressive movements understand the role of the state. Does the state apparatus hinder or help women's efforts to ensure the safety and well-being of themselves and their communities?

Reproductive Rights

In the 1960s, women's right to choose safe and legal abortion became a focal demand of the emergent women's movement. Over the years, women of color and poor women have fought to expand the issue, initially by including economic as well as legal barriers to accessing abortion. In the 1970s, the concept of "reproductive rights" was introduced in order to reframe the movement for reproductive freedom by acknowledging and addressing restrictions faced primarily by women of color, beginning with sterilization abuse.

Building on the 1970s critique of sterilization abuse and racist population control policies, progressive scholars and activists have continued to deepen their analysis of the particular character of assaults on the reproductive rights of women of color. Today, the criminal justice system plays an increasingly prominent role in governing reproductive choices for women of color, using the war on drugs as a rationale. In recent years, right-wing opponents of abortion have also found that they could make headway by situating their drive for greater state control of women's bodies within the framework of the war on drugs—beginning, of course, with the bodies of women of color.

In October 1999, the House of Representatives passed a bill that established criminal penalties for anyone who injures a fetus in the commission of another federal offense, which could cover batterers as well as pregnant women themselves.[25] Although the federal bill specifically excludes women who opt for abortions, this type of punitive legislation, justified as an anti-violence measure, is widely considered to be a backdoor strategy to assist right-wing abortion opponents in their drive to secure legal recognition of the "personhood" of the unborn fetus.[26] According to the National Right to Life Committee, similar laws have already passed twenty-four state legislatures.

Long-acting contraceptives like Norplant have also been used as a tool of coercion by the criminal justice system. The safety of Norplant has been challenged by women's health organizations,[27] which have also argued that use of such contraceptives places medical practitioners more in control of women's bodies than the women themselves.

In California's Central Valley, Darlene Johnson, a pregnant African-American welfare recipient, was convicted on charges of child abuse; the judge who sentenced her gave her a "choice" between Norplant and a longer jail sentence.[28] This decision carries several chilling messages: that once women have been convicted, the state has the right to control their reproductive choices, and that the machinery of law enforcement can be invoked to assert such control.

Dorothy Roberts cites a study conducted by Stanford and University of Chicago professors who attributed the drop in crime rates during the 1990s to abortions by poor women of color.[29] The study argues that the rise in abortions by young, poor women of color during the 1970s prevented the birth of unwanted children who would have gone on to commit crimes fifteen to twenty-five years later. On this basis, they argue that legalized abortion can be credited for as much as 50 percent of the substantial drop in crime rates between 1991 and 1997.

Similar sentiments regarding "bad" mothers and their children are manifested toward immigrant communities of color. At the United States-Mexico border, the Border Patrol often accuses pregnant immigrant women of coming to the United States to have children so that they can benefit from the child's automatic American citizenship. This is not unlike a Black welfare mother being told that she is having children to receive larger welfare checks—and only a step away from her being told that she must use Norplant in order to receive the next check.

The contemporary reproductive rights movement has responded unevenly, even weakly, to all these trends toward increasing state repression of women of color: pregnant women being incarcerated for drug use, welfare payments or prison sentences being tied to women's use of birth control, punitive measures to protect fetuses by punishing pregnant women, anti-immigrant scapegoating, and programs that link the dissemination of contraceptives to a population control agenda.

Domestic Violence and Sexual Assault

The growing tension between women of color and the mainstream women's anti-violence movement is not a question of who is "included" in the movement, but rather reflects contradictory understandings of the impact of collaboration with the state. Over time, the efforts of anti-violence organizations to develop working relationships with law enforcement agencies, coupled with their reliance on government funding, have restricted their ability to challenge a repressive state agenda. The demand for more state protection—in essence, more law enforcement—has displaced critical and innovative thinking about alternative community-based strategies for promoting public safety.

In the process, the concerns of women of color, who are far more likely to experience law enforcement as a threat to themselves and their communities, have been marginalized. Some critics have argued that public pressure to increase arrests for domestic violence is inevitably translated into increased arrests of men of color. For undocumented immigrants, police summoned in a case of domestic violence may notify the INS, with the result that both the woman and her male partner may be deported.[30]

No one would dispute that women's safety is fundamental; the issue is rather how it is best achieved. Leni Marin of the Family Violence Prevention Fund in San Francisco, which has fought to improve the responsiveness of the criminal justice system, comments that intervention in domestic violence cases can be dangerous or even fatal to battered women. Achieving protection and safety in such situations is no easy matter. Over the long term, Marin believes that punitive measures cannot change people's behavior and in fact may well cause greater instability in women's lives.[31]

Sue Osthoff of the National Clearinghouse for the Defense of Battered Women emphatically argues that

> unintended consequences are surfacing from over-reliance on the criminal legal system. Twenty-five years ago, women of color were saying that we should not turn to the criminal legal system. But we put all our eggs in one basket without seeking other creative ways of community intervention. The battered women's movement has contributed to the increase in the police state and the increase of men in prisons. We are telling battered women to turn to a system that is classist, sexist, homophobic, arbitrary, and not unlike the batterer.[32]

She asserts that it is impossible to create a just society in a climate of hatred of defendants and with a spirit of vengeance.

Mainstream strategies have many unintended consequences that affect women negatively. Battered women who assault or kill their spouses are detained longer before trial, face higher bails, and receive longer sentences than any other type of defendant. A desperate battered woman may believe she has no alternative but to kill her batterer when he is asleep. The United States legal system considers such a killing only as an isolated incident, disregarding the reality of domestic violence; the woman's act is thus judged not as a desperate measure of self-defense but as premeditated murder. Sociologist Beth Richie has coined the phrase "gender entrapment" to illuminate how survivors of domestic violence are criminalized through a variety of circumstances that stem from their violent lives.[33]

As New York official Sujata Warrier warns, however, there is no clear consensus around the role of law enforcement among women of color anti-violence activists.[34] For example, Lori Humphreys, an attorney with Ayuda (a domestic violence agency in Washington, DC serving immigrants), maintains that mandatory arrests and more policing are needed to protect women of color from domestic violence, although she too agrees that often the survivor has no control over the criminal justice process once it begins.[35] Beckie Masaki of the Asian Women's Shelter in San Francisco observes:

> Domestic violence organizations working with battered immigrant women find themselves in a curious position at the intersection of anti–violence against women work and enforcement accountability work. Remedies through law enforcement are somewhat important but the emphasis is misplaced given the underutilization of this remedy in our communities. It is telling that only five incidents of police intervention in domestic violence calls took place in the Asian community in San Francisco during 1998, although 35 percent of the population is Asian. Women-of-color or immigrant groups will also find that although the issue of cultural specificity is important in ensuring sensitivity, certain monolithic or patriarchal definitions of culture are invariably used by law enforcement in order to excuse violence or to maintain a policy of noninterference."[36]

Masaki notes that training programs for police initiated (and often, provided) by domestic violence organizations have brought about a more friendly relationship between domestic violence organizations and law enforcement as compared to ten or twenty years ago. This has placed domestic violence organizations on a strange footing with organizations that fight against enforcement violence, such as anti–police brutality organizations. The gulf between these two types of organizations has resulted in some lost opportunities as well.

Recently, an African-American police officer in San Francisco with a record of brutality in other situations was also found to be a batterer. When the officer was fired, members of the African-American community came to his defense and the police commissioner ultimately reinstated him. An effective alliance between domestic violence and anti–police brutality groups could have created an occasion to raise crucial issues regarding violence against women *and* police accountability. In the absence of such an alliance, the issues went unexplored.

In summary, the safety and self-determination of women of color and poor women cannot be secured in isolation from the safety and self-determination of their communities as a whole. In the long run, by turning exclusively to law enforcement for protection, without sufficient community organizing and alliance building, the mainstream movement against violence against women has compromised the safety of women of color and their communities. Women of color understand intimately that they cannot demand protection from law enforcement on the one hand and organize around police brutality on the other hand, as if dealing with two separate entities.

A Gender Perspective on Law Enforcement

Although women most definitely face particular gender-related issues in their encounters with law enforcement, by no means can one say that enforcement is fair for men. Our purpose is not to show that women suffer more than men (although significant numbers may) or that more women suffer than men. The point is rather to counter the invisibility of women. Discussions of law enforcement generally center on male images. If, however, we look at enforcement as a community issue, then the experience of women comes into sharper focus. This in turn requires an understanding that encounters with law enforcement do not always leave behind a paper trail, are not always limited to one main victim, and continue well beyond an initial incident.

Common wisdom holds that women have less contact with law enforcement than men. This, however, is a limiting and ultimately distorted view. What remains untold or unrecorded is how deeply women's lives are affected by such encounters or how extensively women become involved in defending or accompanying men—as their wives, girlfriends, sisters, mothers, and caregivers in general. Most men in prison depend primarily on women outside to take care of their survival and legal needs inside and outside the prison.

Women also experience direct encounters with law enforcement, on the street and in their homes. Again, common wisdom holds that law enforcement agents operate mainly on the street. In reality, police and INS agents frequently enter private dwellings, deeply affecting women's home lives. Even in the case of workplace raids, our understanding must be extended beyond the image of male workers being hauled away by the INS—again, an image that obscures the increasingly large numbers of women affected by such operations.

Another way our understanding is distorted is by focusing on the immediate victim of an encounter with law enforcement, echoing the structure of the US legal system. Any such incident, however, is better understood as an experience that involves more than one person—and as a moment in a string of other episodes that precede and follow it. For example, in the case of a police operation, the immediate victim (say, a man) may be in a location (say, the home) where other people (especially women) can be picked up along with him and subjected to similar violence from authorities. Often, the woman is released more quickly and her experience may not leave behind a paper trail, thus erasing it from the official record. After her release, she characteristically faces a daunting burden of responsibility with regard to both the fate of the immediate victim as well as those who are indirectly affected, who may include children and other family members.

Until we make visible these erasures and acknowledge these extensions of women's responsibilities, all of which are part of the impact of law enforcement, we will continue to see law enforcement as mainly a male issue, imposing, as we have argued, serious limitations on the effectiveness and consistency of strategies across movements.

Enforcement Violence Against Women

Denial of Reproductive and Sexual Autonomy

Reproductive Rights

Enforcement violence affects women's reproductive choices in two main ways: through direct intervention in the outcome of a pregnancy, often justified through appeals to the "welfare of the fetus," or through active endangerment or neglect of a pregnant woman, causing adverse results, including termination of her pregnancy. In either case, state intervention results in women losing control over their pregnancies, for whose outcome they may nonetheless be held legally responsible.

Policing

In the name of "fetal protection," women who have tested positive for drugs have been arrested for deciding to carry their pregnancy to full term and may be charged with child abuse or even murder, without any evidence of harm to the fetus. Such operations have focused almost entirely on women of color.[37] In one such case, cited by Lynn Paltrow, "Prosecutors argued that arrest was…justified because evidence of a woman's drug use during pregnancy is predictive of an inability to parent effectively." Paltrow points out that, "fathers identified as drug users are not automatically presumed to be incapable of parenting."[38] Ironically, such women may be sentenced to prison where fully a third of pregnant women are known to miscarry.[39]

By contrast, such ostensible concern for protection of the fetus is nowhere in evidence in INS raids or police stops, during which authorities frequently disregard the consequences of their actions for the outcome of a pregnancy. Under such conditions, a pregnant woman may deliver prematurely, go into early contractions, or lose her fetus. Even if the pregnancy is not compromised, women face enormous physical and mental trauma. The combination of advanced pregnancy and coercive interrogation may provoke a life-threatening condition. One such incident resulted in the death of a woman who was crossing the United States-Mexico border when she was eight and one-half months pregnant:

While being interrogated, [she] showed signs of physical and emotional distress ... difficulty in breathing, spitting up, loss of vision, incoherence, profuse sweating.... She began to lapse into brief periods of unconsciousness.... Despite her critical condition, the officers did not administer rudimentary first aid, nor did they check her eyes, breathing, or pulse.... [She started] exhibiting symptoms of cardiac arrest.[40]

The doctor who eventually attended her later testified that she had suffered a fatal heart attack that was most likely "caused by the coercive interrogation." In ruling on a federal civil suit filed by her husband,[41] the court found that the INS agents' negligence had not caused the woman's death, and no damages were merited—a decision that was upheld on appeal. With redress denied by US courts, the case was forwarded to the Inter-American Commission on Human Rights of the Organization of American States.

The US Customs Service has also received increasing media attention for aggressive searches of women of color, especially African-Americans and Latinas, at various US ports of entry. Women have been held incommunicado for hours, forced to undergo intrusive "body cavity" searches to determine whether they were carrying drugs, and forced to drink laxatives to induce bowel movements. Some have delivered prematurely due to the stress they endured. Documenting and publicizing such abuses is often the first crucial step. Legal challenges to such practices have also been mounted by advocates of immigrants' rights, reproductive rights, and, in the case of the Customs Service, the American Civil Liberties Union.

Jailing

When women are incarcerated, whether by immigration authorities or the criminal justice system, these state institutions frequently disregard their legal and ethical responsibility for providing basic health services. As a result, women's safety during pregnancy is often endangered or neglected, as are other women's health needs. According to Amnesty International,

Many women enter jail and prison pregnant. In 1997–98, more than 2,200 pregnant women were imprisoned and more than 1,300 babies were born in prisons.... In at least 40 states, babies are taken from their imprisoned mothers almost immediately after birth or at the time the mother is discharged from hospital.[42]

In INS detention centers, women face inadequate and uncaring medical services and disrespectful prison officials. The problem is compounded by language barriers, the lack of sanctions for medical neglect, and the lack of female medical staff.[43] Under such conditions, pregnancy and even routine physiological events like menstruation can wreak havoc in a detainee's life. One Haitian detainee described her experience with a miscarriage in these words:

> All the clothing I had on me was soaked in blood, the sheet where I was laying was filled with blood …[they] put chains on my feet and chains on my hands…. I was very, very ill and I started not to see well, my stomach when I was walking felt like it was opening…. Everywhere I went in the hospital I'm in chains, in the surgery room chains are on my feet.[44]

In both detention facilities and prisons, incarcerated women have described the extreme humiliation of having to beg for sanitary pads. A prison activist at the Ohio Reformatory for Women (ORW) writes that:

> Women … bleed all over everything because of no proper sanitary protection for disposal and no tampons are issued, bloody unwrapped sanitaries are in every dorm john, every trash can, and blood on every faucet handle … and everywhere imaginable. This excludes the humiliation factors. We have male staff in housing units.[45]

Those who successfully carry a pregnancy to term may give birth shackled to a hospital bed and surrounded by armed guards.[46] The inadequacy of care for pregnant women reflects the overall lack of services for women prisoners' basic health needs. While health services and other conditions for male prisoners also fail to meet minimal standards, women's needs are consistently accorded an even lower priority.

The prisoners' rights movement has a rich history of fighting for the basic human rights of prisoners, including those of women prisoners. The struggle for adequate medical care inside prisons has been a lengthy one, often spearheaded by women prisoners themselves. Resistance to INS detention is newer, since the dramatic nationwide growth of the detention system is relatively recent. Local grassroots organizations, national watchdog groups like Detention Watch Network, and the Women's Commission for Refugee Women and Children are among the groups in the forefront of this struggle, documenting abuses and raising awareness around the issues. As in every instance we have explored, however, the links among different enforcement accountability movements remain weak or absent, as do links with women's reproductive rights organizations.

Effective strategies for protecting women's reproductive freedom need to be based in a thorough appreciation of the varying mechanisms of restriction, criminalization, and devaluation faced by women—whether they are imposed through legal restrictions on access and funding for abortions, involuntary sterilization, coercive drug tests and coercive uses of contraception, criminalization of immigrant women, or abuse of pregnant women in prison.

Women's Sexual Integrity

Struggles against sexual assault have long been central to the anti–violence against women movement. The focus, however, has mainly been on rape and assault in intimate relationships. Although the use of rape as a weapon of war has been widely denounced in an international context, the women's movement has seldom organized around rape and other forms of sexual assault committed by law enforcement authorities within the borders of the United States. Prison activists and, more recently, immigrants' rights advocates have raised such issues, but, by and large, they have not had organized links with the women's anti-violence movement.

When rapes committed by law enforcement agents become public knowledge, they are generally portrayed as the individual act of a "bad apple," who may be disciplined or even terminated. Rape and other forms of sexual assault committed by law enforcement authorities are better understood as a systemic and deliberate, if unofficial, enforcement practice, whose perpetrators are rarely held accountable for their actions.

Body searches by police, prison guards, or INS agents also

serve as frequent occasions for sexual assault and harassment. Although such searches are supposedly justified for security reasons, their excessive frequency, intrusiveness, and lack of a functional purpose lend credence to the belief of many prisoners and arrestees that the goal is one of control and terror, rather than safety. Finally, women's ability to express their sexuality in positive ways, including through lesbian relationships, is systematically denied in the coercive prison environment.

Policing

The case of a group of tenants in Redwood City, California, who complained to their landlord about deplorable living conditions, became a watershed issue for community organizing locally. The landlord called the INS in retaliation; the INS in turn called local police for assistance and together they raided the apartment building. With both female and male tenants detained in one apartment, the INS agents demanded that some of the women expose their breasts to the agents and the other detainees.[47]

This incident is a clear example of the gendered nature of enforcement violence. It reminds women of their vulnerability to law enforcement, even inside their homes. From the conventional perspective of the men in the community, it reinforces the power of (male) enforcement officers to humiliate male members of the community by dramatizing their inability to protect their female neighbors and family members from abuse by authorities. The sexualizing of this incident is a demonstration of the power of law enforcement authorities to do anything they please, usually without being held accountable.

The raid described here resulted in arrests, deportation, and further human rights abuses for those involved. Ultimately, community outrage over this incident led to a significant victory for enforcement accountability advocates. INS Watch, a collaborative project of the San Francisco–based Ella Baker Center for Human Rights and La Raza Centro Legal, "worked with the tenants to successfully pressure the Redwood City Police Department to establish a 'no collaboration' policy between local police and the INS."[48] In the wake of this victory, community groups are seeking to extend the ban on INS raids to the statewide level.

The seclusion of the United States-Mexico border region makes it especially dangerous for women. AFSC's Immigration Law Enforcement Monitoring Project (ILEMP) reported receipt of 346 abuse reports from ninety-two women between January 1993 and August 1995. The abuses documented included illegal detention, inappropriate interrogation, and sexual assault.[49]

Once a woman has been stopped by authorities, agents have access to her address, leaving her in danger of being stalked and harassed, especially if she is a local resident. In one notable case, a Mexican woman filed a complaint charging Border Patrol agent Luis Santiago Esteves with making sexually explicit, harassing phone calls for days after stopping her and her boyfriend at a border checkpoint. The Border Patrol took no disciplinary action against Esteves, simply transferring him to another inspection station. Later that year he was charged with kidnapping and raping another Mexican woman. Esteves was suspended after this incident, but was reinstated without further disciplinary action when the complaining witness failed to appear in court. When another immigrant accused him of rape two years later, he was arrested and convicted in both cases; his conviction, however, was reversed on appeal. This case illustrates the many difficulties faced by border crossers and border communities in obtaining legal redress, a major reason why human rights advocates at the border believe abuses are seriously underreported.[50]

It is not uncommon for the INS to hide records of agents' past misconduct, such as rape or harassment, which may affect the successful prosecution of rape cases. In a particularly well-known case, a Border Patrol agent, Larry Selders, raped several women over a period of time. When one victim finally sued for damages, it took over three years of legal battle to uncover Selders's previous record. In this case, a sustained effort by ILEMP and its local community partners ultimately ensured his exposure, and the Border Patrol was ordered to pay the plaintiff damages of more than three-quarters of a million dollars.[51] More often, however, the resources for such persistence are not available.

Interrogations can also serve as an occasion for sexual assault. In Encinitas, California, a border enforcement agent who was questioning a woman "asked if she worked as a prostitute"; then he made her pull her shirt up and touched her, while looking around to make sure no one was around. He made her pull her pants and underwear down and penetrated her with his finger.[52]

Sexually humiliating searches can even take place in full view of the public, as in this incident reported to NYC Police Watch:

> I was riding my bike ... when five officers approached me and threw me off.... The officers further proceeded to throw me up against a car and started searching me forcibly for no possible reason ... [the] most degrading experience any civilian can be subjected to.... [One officer] put on rubber gloves and started taking my clothes off in front of the other man officers while [another officer] held me down for the illegal search. Two other officers threw me on the floor on my stomach in the street in front of my building while all my neighbors watched in dismay. The neighbors started to yell, to stop the brutality, and they continued to violate me and pull my pants down, tearing a big hole in my underwear (I have the underwear as evidence) while the other ... officers held me down during the humiliating physical search.[53]

Threats of sexual assault can serve to deter women from challenging law enforcement officers or filing complaints. Mary Powers, coordinator of the National Coalition on Police Accountability, recounts the case of one young woman who wanted to file a complaint about police harassment. The officer involved called her at home to say that if she wanted to file a complaint, then he would come to pick it up.[54]

Shawna Virago of Community United Against Violence in San Francisco observes that it is common for law enforcement officers to assume that transsexual women are sex workers. Transsexuals may thus be arrested and searched anywhere—in a store while shopping, for example—and accused of prostitution even when accompanied by their husbands and carrying their marriage licenses. Groups tracking hate violence against lesbian, gay, bisexual, and transgender (LGBT) people "are particularly concerned with the emerging pattern of police officials targeting transsexual and transgendered people."[55] The National Coalition of Anti-Violence Programs registered a 20 percent increase over just one year (1997–1998) in reports of law enforcement personnel perpetrating anti-LGBT violence.[56]

The nature of sexual harassment and assault by law enforcement does not vary a great deal among different agencies or according to whether they are immigration- or criminal justice–related. Most advocates believe that such abuses are seriously underreported and are frequently covered up. Records of such incidents by police and INS accountability organizations are crucial for uncovering the extent of such abuses. In the United States-Mexico border region, organizations like ILEMP and its local grassroots partners play a crucial role in documenting and investigating such abuses. Missing, however, are the voices of women's organizations and their presence when the community mobilizes.

If women's anti-violence organizations were to join campaigns around such issues, they could promote a stronger understanding of the gendered nature of law enforcement violence. Such links could also help women's organizations to develop an approach to anti-violence work that incorporates a critique of the involvement of the state as a direct perpetrator of violence against women. Similarly, although both immigrant and US-born women of color have very similar experiences of state violence, the opportunities for the cross-fertilization of their organizing experiences are very rare.

Jailing

Women in prisons frequently report rape or harassment by guards and medical practitioners. In an environment characterized by isolation, authoritarian control, and an active philosophy of dehumanization, rape and harassment serve as the ultimate opportunity for guards and others to assert their authority.[57] Needless to say, the predominance of male guards and medical personnel makes women's prisons an especially potent site for use of rape as a tool for reinforcing male control of women's bodies. In federal prisons, for example, 70 percent of guards are men.[58]

Medical care may often serve as an occasion for sexual harassment or rape, for example when doctors subject women prisoners to unnecessary gynecological exams. Involuntary and unnecessary pelvic exams, Pap smears, and similar tests became an issue in the Valley State Prison for Women in Chowchilla, which came to light in a particularly embarrassing fashion for the prison officials. When Ted Koppel in an interview on *Nightline* asked the prison's 71-year-old medical director a question related to this, he replied, "I've heard inmates tell me that they would deliberately like to be examined. It's the only male contact they get."[59] On the other hand, since sexual contact is officially forbidden in prisons, it is difficult for prisoners to obtain accurate information on HIV and other sexually transmitted diseases, and educational materials on such topics may even be banned.[60]

Amnesty International describes "male guards touching prisoners' breasts and genitals during daily pat-down and strip searches, watching women as they shower and dress and, in some cases, selling women to male inmates for sex."[61] A strip search conducted by or in front of men is a frightening experience for any woman; it is all the more so for immigrant women who may come from a culture in which no man has ever seen them naked except their husbands. Additional constraints, such as lack of knowledge of English or of what recourse is available to prisoners, can render the situation even more traumatic. In a report on women asylum seekers incarcerated in an INS detention facility in rural York County, Pennsylvania, the Women's Commission for Refugee Women and Children describes what happened when a Ugandan woman fleeing extreme violence in her country broke down emotionally:

> The prison deemed [her] breakdown a suicide attempt and sent in a "Quick Response Team." The team consisted of four men, three of whom were wearing riot gear. They also brought dogs.... The men, without the presence of a female guard, stripped [her]. She begged them not to remove her bra and panties ... they placed her naked and spread-eagled in four-point restraints on a cot.[62]

Most women prisoners and detainees are survivors of physical and sexual violence. Prisons and detention centers are seldom equipped to support women in recovering from such trauma, and in fact are far more likely to aggravate it with additional sexual violence. According to one analysis of Department of Justice statistics, "48 percent of women in US jails reported being sexually or physically abused prior to their detention; 27 percent reported being raped. Given the general underreporting by women in the area of sexual assault, the actual percentages are likely to be much higher."[63] The INS incarcerates many women asylum seekers who are fleeing gender-based violence in their home countries; such women may be detained for years without outside contact. Both detainees and prisoners receive little support in facing nightmares, depression, suicidal impulses, and other symptoms resulting from severe trauma.

Sexist and patriarchal notions about women affect the way guards respond to women's complaints and infractions of disciplinary rules. Cassandra Shaylor comments that women at Valley State Prison for Women who speak up and fight back are more likely to end up in isolation in the prison's Security Housing Unit (SHU). For example, if a woman is raped by a guard and becomes pregnant but refuses an abortion, she can be sent to SHU. In essence, Shaylor argues, women prisoners become property of the state.[64] At the Women's Correctional Center in Montana, according to Luana Ross, both gender and race are treated as forms of deviance warranting additional punishment. Notes Ross, "Native women are disproportionately represented in maximum security: out of eleven women, six are Native. This ... relates directly to Native prisoners' relationships with white guards."[65]

Homophobic practices are also intensified in the prison environment. Lesbian relationships are interpreted in an exclusive context of violence and victimization, with no recognition of consensual relationships. Some women may be lesbians independently of their incarceration; for others, a lesbian relationship may serve as an adaptation to the prison environment. In either case, homophobic, voyeuristic, and oppressive labeling of lesbian relationships can make intimate relationships difficult or impossible to maintain, even though they may be fundamental to prisoners' sanity. Any expression of affection, whether sexual or not, may be penalized. Lesbian couples identified as such may be separated and beaten. Women perceived as butch may be viewed as always trying to make sexual advances to other prisoners, even though male guards may pose a far greater threat. Books and publications about lesbianism, or a lesbian prison visitor, may be thrown out.[66]

Jackie Walker, AIDS Information Coordinator of the ACLU National Prison Project, comments that lesbian partners of prisoners may be harassed during visitation. Individual wardens may impose arbitrary policies prohibiting women from touching one another or even doing one another's hair.[67] Luana Ross argues that homophobic fantasies, fueled by media stereotypes, "see the imprisoned women as the 'hardened bull-dyke' lurking in the halls, waiting to rape her next victim. Gay women can also be seen as 'unfit mothers' and denied visits with their children, punished excessively, and put in maximum security."[68]

Violence in the Home and Family

The supposedly private space of the home and family is another significant site of enforcement violence against women. The discussion below explores two key concepts: intrusions by law enforcement into the home; and the impact of enforcement violence on women's roles as mothers, and, more generally, caregivers. Both home and family have been pivotal concepts in the development of women's organizing; the present discussion challenges us to rethink our understanding of these social arenas.

Home

As noted in the previous section, the mainstream women's anti-violence movement has sought to protect women from battering by advocating for a more active response from police agencies. The underlying assumption of this strategy is that government intervention is the best way to protect women from intimate violence in their private homes. However, communities of color, both immigrant and US-born, also face a significant threat of violence in the home from state authorities. The supposed privacy and sanctity of the home is a relative concept, whose application is heavily conditioned by racial and economic status.

Police trainings promoted and administered by domestic violence agencies have brought about undeniable improvements in the way police respond to domestic violence calls. In some ways, however, this strategy of reform has backfired. Women who turn to police for protection from battering may still face humiliation or abuse from officers, implicit and sometimes overt encouragement of the batterer, and wrongful arrest of women as the primary aggressors. Such problems may be compounded through deportation of the batterer against the woman's wishes or disproportionate arrests of men of color.

Women—primarily but not exclusively women of color—must also face the intrusion of law enforcement into their homes in the pursuit of drug or immigration raids, often on the flimsiest of legal grounds. Since home is a space where women are often found, either as homemakers or as primary caretakers (in addition to any role they may play as breadwinners), enforcement violence in the home affects women's lives in a central way.

Numerous cases have been documented in which law enforcement authorities have illegally entered private homes, often when it should have been clear that the person they were seeking did not even live there. Women often face the brunt of such raids, either directly or when they come under suspicion of being accomplices or possessing information about the primary suspect. Such raids can lead to the destruction of property, violence, and illegal arrests, as well as to more drastic consequences such as the temporary or permanent separation of mothers from children, deportation, and the breakup of families. Factors that can render home intrusions particularly traumatic for women include the presence of children, pregnancy, state of undress, and the sense of responsibility for the home and everything in it that women carry as primary caregivers.

House raids by immigration authorities are a frequent occurrence in the regions along the United States-Mexico border. Amnesty International has documented cases of homes being invaded and searched without notice and family members being deported if they were unable to produce appropriate identification.[69] Tucson attorney Jesus Romo represented a family subjected to such a raid in Nogales, Arizona. Their complaint against the Border Patrol agents involved notes that the woman of the house and her child are US citizens; her husband is a permanent resident. One evening in 1997, Border Patrol agents "pounded" at their home; when the husband answered the door,

> one of the agents threw the sliding door open and burst in ...
> Once inside, the agents asked [the man] for his papers and then

proceeded to confront the frightened child and mother, screaming for "papers." The agents proceeded to search the house
without ever asking for permission from anyone in the house.
They ... stayed in the household for approximately thirty minutes, causing panic and terror to the occupants.... They never
asked for permission, and during their entire stay ... they acted
as if the Plaintiffs were under arrest and the agents had the absolute right to go through the Plaintiffs' personal property and
rooms without permission. [70]

As a result of the trauma of this incident, the woman of the house,
who was two months pregnant, miscarried within forty-eight
hours. Home invasions by police are similar to those by immigration agents, with frequent reports of the destruction of property or
forced entry. According to one case report,

In New York, a fifty-year-old African American woman was lying in her room and her daughter and dog were in the living
room. The daughter heard a drilling noise and went to the door
to check it. Just then the cops burst in.... The daughter ran out
of the room scared—they shot after her and the bullet went into
the wall. She ran to her mother's door. The cops grabbed and
pulled her back and broke down the bedroom door. Five officers ran in cursing, wearing riot gear with their faces hidden.
They told the woman "to shut the fuck up." They picked up the
bed and said, "there is nothing there." They claimed they had reports of heavy drug activity but the women told them they had
the wrong house. They made the mother and daughter stand in
the hallway in full view of the neighbors while they searched the
house. They took them to the precinct, kept them locked up for
several hours, and gave them a summons for half a joint and a $3
bag of marijuana they said they had found.[71]

Women may be suspected of withholding information if they
are related to a man police are looking for. In other cases, the police
have broken into homes searching for people who did not even
live there.[72] Case reports from police accountability groups paint a
picture of police behavior that includes physical violence, display
of weapons, use of helicopters, wanton destruction of property,

and false arrests. The scale of such actions is entirely disproportionate to any legitimate law enforcement objective.

The aggressiveness displayed in drug and immigration raids is
very much at odds with the behavior of law enforcement when
called upon to defend the rights of those who are vulnerable and
oppressed. In 1999, I received information about a live-in domestic worker, a recent South Asian immigrant working in the home of
a wealthy suburban professional couple. She was working around
the clock for almost no wages and was forbidden to communicate
with the outside world. She was desperate and wanted to escape
but did not know how. As immigrants' rights advocates, my
then-coworker and I knew that if we simply showed up at the
home where the woman was being held, we would be lied to or accused of trespassing. We contacted the police discreetly since she
was undocumented. They said they could not help us communicate
with her employers and that if we approached them we would be
charged with trespassing. In this case, the privacy of these wealthy
employers' home was held to be inviolate, while the plight of an
immigrant worker being held in a condition of involuntary servitude was not serious enough to merit police action.[73]

The types of home intrusions described here have resulted in
numerous community-based campaigns and legal challenges from
legal activists, immigrants' rights organizations, and a variety of
watchdog groups. In particular, house raids have been a major focus for organizations seeking to stop INS raids. As in other instances we have cited, however, there has been little involvement
by women's organizations in such initiatives, while efforts by enforcement accountability groups have reflected little understanding of women's experience of violence, particularly the ways in
which women may be caught in an unbearable double bind when
they face violence from both batterers and law enforcement.

Motherhood and Caregiving

The term "motherhood" has traditionally evoked the experiences of economically secure women living in nuclear families—as
homemakers, or, increasingly, as affluent professionals.
Working-class women and women of color have fought to expand

the discussion of motherhood to include women who are impoverished or working poor, single women, and "physically absent" mothers such as live-in domestic workers or migrant workers. Our understanding of motherhood and caregiving has also expanded to reflect the experiences of lesbian families, extended families (which are more common in communities of color), and other "nontraditional" (that is, non-nuclear) families.

Survivors of enforcement violence challenge us to expand these notions once again to include an understanding of how the caregiving role is shaped for some women by their encounters with the state. The stories presented in this section illuminate how women may be held responsible for parenting even when they have little control over it. We will see how enforcement violence may cause women to be criminalized as "bad" mothers—or to see their lives violently disrupted as they strive to fulfill the responsibilities of motherhood.

Ultimately, violence and other abuses of human rights by law enforcement reconfigure motherhood as a tool for greater state control of women and their communities. As members of extended families—grandmothers, aunts, sisters, and so on—women must also face violent and protracted disruptions of family life caused by enforcement violence, even when authorities did not "come for them."

Such experiences have given rise to organizations led by mothers and caregivers who support each other and organize around enforcement violence and its effects on their families. Examples include Parents Against Police Brutality in New York; Mothers for Freedom in Miami, which focuses on INS detention; and the Boycott Crime Coalition in Newark, New Jersey, a grassroots coalition addressing both police brutality and abusive prison conditions. Legal Services for Prisoners with Children, one of the first organizations to work with prisoners and their children, helped start the Grandparent Caregiver Advocacy Project, in recognition of the role of extended families in prisoners' lives. Locally based grassroots organizations focusing on these issues exist in many parts of the country.

Policing

As women represent an ever-larger proportion of immigrants, increasing numbers of mothers, including single mothers, are affected by INS raids. According to statements compiled by the Washington Alliance for Immigrant and Refugee Justice, a series of INS raids at the Brewster Heights Packing Plant in 1997 and 1998 picked up "lots of women who are single moms with kids in school here in Brewster."[74] One mother described a raid in March 1998 in these words:

> I hid behind a machine.... After they found me the first time, I escaped again and hid in the bathroom. Four agents came in and found me hiding there. They put me in the van and I gave my name and answered other questions they asked. I have five children and I told the agents that I wanted to be with my children. The agents were trying to convince everyone to sign voluntary departure. They said a bus was coming and they could get on it and be in Mexico faster. I, along with another woman, said I would sign voluntary departure if I could get my children to come with me. The agents told us they would get a bus for all of them and they would go get our children. They said this to scare them into signing, thinking we would not want the INS to go get our children. But I told them that was fine with me—I just wanted to be with my children. I called my children and told them to get ready to go.[75]

In addition to the difficulties faced by most mothers in juggling the responsibilities of jobs and parenting, immigrant women face the enormous burden of being continually alert to the possibility of having their family life turned upside down in a matter of hours. Both legally documented as well as undocumented women may be detained and even deported in INS raids.

Immigrant mothers must devise contingency plans for their children in case they are taken away, given that once they are detained, there is little opportunity to make alternative child-care arrangements. Women may need to decide whether or not to take their children with them if they are deported. Children also increase women's vulnerability to coercion by the INS, which may use children as leverage to induce women to sign documents (such as voluntary departure) that they could legally refuse to sign.[76] In Miami, a Mother's Day action in 1998 denounced an abusive and violent workplace raid by the INS the previous month, in which legally documented as well as undocumented women were rounded up.[77]

As primary caregivers, women are often accompanied by their children while running errands. In border towns, being stopped by law enforcement on such everyday occasions is not uncommon. Mothers have been humiliated by being abused by agents in front of their children and have witnessed their children being violently handled while they are helpless to do anything about it. Women who are not directly targeted by INS or Border Patrol agents generally assume responsibility for taking care of the needs of family members who have fallen into the hands of authorities.

US-born women of color face similar anxieties in encounters with police. Mothers may be threatened with major disruptions of family life, including losing their children to the foster care system. In California, "there is no law requiring police officers to allow parents to make arrangements for the care of their children at the time of arrest."[78] The example below is drawn from case reports collected by police watch groups:

> In Stockton [California], a 27-year-old Latina mother was getting her kids ready for school. The police loudly banged on her door, broke it in with guns although she was going to open it, knocked her over bleeding and almost unconscious. Her kids were thrown all over the place. They claimed that they were looking for crack and some man who clearly did not live there.[79]

It is usually women who deal with the aftermath of an encounter with law enforcement, beginning with finding money for bail. Mothers frequently try to ensure fair treatment for their sons at the hands of the police; in the process it not uncommon for them to be assaulted and detained.[80]

A different type of problem is faced by women of color who are arrested or accused of negligence. One well-known case is that of teenage mother Tabitha Walrond of New York, who was unable to obtain adequate medical advice for her newborn due to processing delays and mix-ups by Medicaid and the hospital involved. After the death of her son, she was charged with recklessly causing his death and was convicted of criminally negligent homicide, a verdict that could have drawn a prison sentence of four years. Walrond's case drew a great deal of public attention and she was ultimately sentenced to five years of probation with mandatory counseling.[81]

The attitudes and actions of law enforcement and other agencies of the state reflect a familiar contradiction, in which women of color, both immigrant and US-born, are prevented from caring adequately for their children, while they are simultaneously accused of child abuse and neglect. A white suburban housewife who stays home to care for her children is applauded, while a poor woman of color who seeks state support to do the same is stigmatized as lazy. An undocumented mother who crosses the border in order to be able to provide for her children is seen as negligent for exposing her children to the considerable risks involved—even though such risks have been entirely created by shifts in state policies over recent years.

Jailing

According to Human Rights Watch, "more than two-thirds of all incarcerated women have at least one child under the age of eighteen, and the majority of these are single mothers."[82] Motherhood is a compelling force in the lives of many prisoners, and their children may provide a fundamental motivation to rebuild their lives. Women caught up in the criminal justice system, however, are stigmatized far more harshly than men, resulting in profound suspicion by authorities of their ability to be good mothers.

The rapid rise in the incarceration of women of color has led to situations in which mothers and daughters from the same family, and even grandmothers, may all be incarcerated. In the process, mothers are held solely accountable for society's inability to provide a healthy environment for their children. An overriding issue for incarcerated mothers is the lengthy separation they face from their children, coupled with the diminishing hope of ever getting them back.

Both conventional prisons and INS detention are designed in ways that, rather than aiding women to maintain a bond with their children, instead make it as hard as possible. Women sentenced to federal prison are generally shipped out of state, where they may lose touch with their children and families.[83] Services that do exist to support family reunification owe a great deal to sustained pressure by advocates and affected communities.

If a woman with a child is arrested, she often turns to female relatives—her mother, grandmother, aunt, sister, or older daughter—to act as caregivers until she is released. Relatives are routinely investigated by child welfare authorities, and any past criminal record may lead to the child being placed in foster care. Even when a woman is able to obtain a caregiver or guardian, she still faces serious obstacles in maintaining a relationship with her children, who may be her only lifeline. Factors such as intervention by child welfare authorities, the loss of a caregiver, or the caregiver's lack of commitment to keeping the mother in contact with her child may lead to permanent loss of custody.

Once children are placed in foster care, women prisoners face further obstacles maintaining, not only contact, but also parental rights. The foster care agency may move the child without telling the mother; if the mother does not know where her child is, she may be accused of neglect and abandonment.[84] In California, the Department of Corrections is not required by law to transport women to foster care hearings, yet judges may regard their absence as evidence of the woman's lack of interest.[85]

Donna Wilmott of Legal Services for Prisoners with Children underscores the permanent family destruction caused by the INS detention system.

> The vast majority of immigrants are deported after completing their full sentences.... Even if a woman has lived her entire life in the United States, had children here, and obtained a green card, the chances are high she will be deported.... The present policy of deporting people regardless of where their real community ties are is inhumane.[86]

The Extension of Caregiving

In the case of policing, often there is no clear boundary between the person who is mainly affected by law enforcement and their family members or caregivers. Once someone is incarcerated, however, the sharpest of lines separates those inside prison walls from those outside. Emphasizing the role of women as caregivers for prisoners is not to detract from efforts to support the person who is incarcerated. Rather, it illuminates how women often become invisible when enforcement accountability efforts focus exclusively on the experience of a single (usually male) victim of enforcement violence, and reinforces our understanding of incarceration as a community rather than an individual experience.

Renee Wormack Keels is a member of Silent Warriors, a Massachusetts support group for mothers with sons and daughters in prison. She writes:

> My oldest son is in prison.... I attended the trial every day until the jury was given the case.... my son [was] found guilty AND sentenced, all at the same time. I was overwhelmed.... There was no one with whom I could share my grief and heartache. I closed the door to my room and cried most of the day and into the night.[87]

On death row, a large majority of prisoners are men; like most prisoners, they rely on women outside (mothers or partners) for most aspects of their lives. Guilt by association leaves women caregivers of death row prisoners heavily stigmatized; for some, even buying groceries can become a traumatic experience. When they visit their loved ones, they are treated with contempt and suspicion by prison guards.[88] When released prisoners rejoin their families, everyone in their home may be caught up in the scrutiny and searches of the parole officer. In government-subsidized housing, if a parolee is arrested or anything is found during a search, the family can lose their home.[89]

In immigrant communities, one reflection of the extension of women's caregiving role is the leadership women have taken in challenging abuses of their family members by law enforcement authorities. In early 1999, Mothers for Freedom, a group supporting INS detainees, staged a hunger strike to protest conditions in Florida's notorious Krome Detention Center. The organization played a central role in bringing national attention to the issue of INS detention and in successfully pressuring the INS to change certain policies.

In a very real sense, women caregivers subsidize the United States government by taking care of the largest incarcerated population in the world. Sadly, entrenched patterns of sexism mean that women prisoners may not receive the same level of support from male partners outside; for example, Mary Fitzgerald of Justice Works notes that women prisoners often receive significantly fewer visitors than male prisoners.[90] Nonetheless, whether from inside or outside prison walls, women of color, both immigrant and US-born, struggle valiantly to prevent the state-sponsored destruction of their families and communities.

Violence Against Women in the Workplace

The door is opened to enforcement violence against women in the workplace when the struggle to earn a living is defined as a criminal activity. On the one hand, this criminalization of women's work stems from the heavy reliance of certain economic sectors on undocumented women workers: in service occupations, whether in motels or restaurants or as workers in private households; in agriculture, where women represent an increasing portion of farm workers; and in such industries as meatpacking, canneries, or the garment industry.

In other instances, women's work is criminalized due to the underground nature of certain types of work, such as sex work or drug sales. Anecdotal evidence suggests that women are a major portion of those who survive through a combination of small drug sales and erratic sex work, trapped in cycles of substance abuse, domestic violence, and often both.[91]

A focus on enforcement violence reveals many parallels between these diverse experiences of women's work, even though they are seldom considered together. In both instances, women are subject to harassment, coercion, and outright violence from law enforcement, whether the agency in question is the INS or local police. Although there are important differences in how law enforcement handles workers in these different circumstances, there are also striking similarities.

As "workers on the lowest rung of the occupational ladder," poor immigrant women "are especially vulnerable to exploitation."[92] Their workplaces are frequently targeted by INS raids, at the United States-Mexico border as well as in inland areas of the United States. AFSC's Maria Jimenez points out that the only type of labor regulation that receives plentiful government funding is control of the undocumented workforce, in sharp contrast to the level of government resources devoted to the enforcement of labor laws that protect workers.[93]

Extensive documentation from human rights organizations, labor unions, and immigrants' rights groups verifies that workplace raids frequently affect legally documented workers and US citizens as well as undocumented workers. Immigration raids are frequently used by employers as a tactic to disrupt labor organizing efforts. Far from stopping the inflow of undocumented workers, INS raids serve to intimidate immigrant workers and keep them more vulnerable to exploitation by employers.

While INS raids subject undocumented workers to detention and deportation, "employer sanctions" enacted in 1986 have seldom been enforced. In recognition of this reality, in February 2000 the AFL-CIO reversed its long-standing support for employer sanctions, joining immigrants' rights organizations in calling for a new amnesty for undocumented workers.

The cases cited in previous sections have illustrated the impact of INS workplace raids on women as caregivers, as breadwinners, as mothers-to-be, and as sexual beings. It is important to note as well that current immigration policies favor the immigration of skilled high-tech workers and other highly educated people, most of whom are male, given their greater access to such occupations globally. Women are more often eligible to immigrate legally through family (especially spousal) sponsorship, so that they are dependent on their husbands (or sometimes fathers) to attain legal status.

Women immigrants thus face both class and gender bias in the way immigration policies are structured, which carries over into their interactions with the INS. The Washington Alliance for Immigrant and Refugee Justice reports the experience of a woman detained in an INS raid:

> "Is it true that he is your husband?" he [the INS agent] said and pointed to my husband who was there. "Yes, and he put papers

in for me," I said.... There were others that were trying to tell him that we had papers in process. One woman had some papers to prove that her father had applied for her to get a green card.... This agent ... ripped up her papers. He said we were all liars when we said we had papers in process. I think they don't have the right to rip people's papers. This woman only had two or three years to wait until her papers came through. She's now in Mexico, but all her family is here.[94]

Such an incident could cause a woman's application for legal permanent residence to be jeopardized or revoked.

Domestic work, which is primarily performed by poor women of color, both immigrant and US-born, is another industry that is rife with abuse by employers. Given the lack of decent and affordable child-care, the inexpensive child-care provided by immigrant women makes it possible for many professionals, particularly women, to go to work every day knowing that their homes and children will be safe. Immigrant domestic workers frequently work long hours without any benefits. They are subject to verbal and sometimes sexual abuse and are generally paid well below minimum wage. Many are undocumented, and employers often use the threat of the police and INS to keep them under control.

Sex workers describe many parallel experiences of enforcement violence and its impact on women's efforts to earn a living. The US Prostitutes Collective (USPROS) notes that "many prostitute women are mothers who can't support their children on women's low wages and are being criminalized for finding a way to survive."[95] Sex work, of course, is well known for its constant confrontations with the police. In addition, in cities where immigrant women are increasingly working as prostitutes, police may also work closely with immigration authorities.[96]

Sex workers' encounters with law enforcement frequently entail a range of abuses, from verbal insults to coerced sex, brutal beatings, and rape. If the police know a woman to be a sex worker, they may harass her even when she is not working. Writing in *Gauntlet Magazine,* Jeremy Hay notes:

The most common of police abuses that prostitutes face, requests for sex in lieu of arrest and verbal abuse, are also perhaps the hardest to verify for purposes of complaint. "Blow me and I won't take you in," is an offer that many prostitutes recount having heard and also having turned down. It seems predicated on the assumption that prostitutes don't care who they have sex with and that they will do anything to avoid arrest. In fact, most experienced street prostitutes are resigned to the fact that they will be arrested over and over again, sometimes for questionable charges. What they object to most are the fear and indignities heaped upon them by bad officers who step beyond the line of normal procedure.[97]

In Chicago, Mary Powers describes women prostitutes being picked up by police at bus stops on their way to and from work. The police ask for sexual services in return for favors.[98] In New York City sex parlors, local police may threaten to shut down an establishment if they are not given sexual services. Women picked up in police raids may be taken away in their underwear and have their possessions confiscated.[99]

Transsexual women involved in sex work face abuse in even more complex ways. If the woman is unable to afford a sex-change operation, the legal documentation of her gender does not match her own gender representation, so she is essentially incorrectly documented.[100] In encounters with police, she may then become the victim of cruel jokes and other types of verbal abuse. Transsexuals are also subjected to unnecessary and illegal strip searches, presumably for the unofficial motive of gender identification.

USPROS participated in a Task Force on Prostitution established by the City of San Francisco in 1994, to ensure that the voice of sex workers was heard. The task force found that its costs taxpayers over $7 million a year for the arrest, processing, and jailing of sex workers, even though most voters believe that victimless crimes like sex work should be a low priority for police. Groundbreaking recommendations calling for the decriminalization of sex work have been presented to the city. As USPROS observes, "The police use prostitution and/or suspicion of drugs to profile people they don't like the look of. Anyone they decide looks like a sex worker or hangs out with sex workers, looks transgendered or is Black, Asian, or Latino is stopped on the street, intimidated, questioned, warrants checked, and very likely arrested."[101]

On the street, homelessness, drug addiction, and prostitution can often form a continuum of desperate strategies for economic survival. Many women who need treatment are met instead with enforcement violence. New York City activist Mary Barr was a homeless addict for three years, from 1993 to 1996. Today, she views her substance abuse as an escape from the emotional pain of separation from her children and a reflection of her hopelessness about ever living another kind of life. In two and one-half years on the streets, she was arrested forty-five times, but never once offered the option of treatment. Barr notes that women usually sell drugs to support their habits, not as large-scale drug traffickers. She comments that authorities "didn't have money to treat me. But they had money to take away my children," adding that it costs $750,000 for the state to take care of a child until the age of eighteen, which is thirty times the cost of providing a year of substance abuse treatment.

In recent years, labor and immigrants' rights organizations have increasingly joined in contesting the criminalization of immigrant workers. The lens of enforcement violence permits us to see that in the end, the distinction between "legal" and "illegal" occupations is as limiting as the distinction between "legal" and "illegal" workers. In the case of undocumented labor, enforcement violence serves as one of the principal forces keeping wages low, since workers who live in a state of terror and clandestinity are unlikely to report violations of wage and hour laws or to organize to improve their conditions through collective bargaining. Likewise, although such phenomena are less widely recognized, the underground economy of drug trafficking and sex work, coupled with the lack of "legal" job opportunities, help maintain the cycle of violence, incarceration, and social breakdown that is devastating many urban communities of color.

Although sex workers and undocumented factory or field workers may have markedly different experiences, both reflect the growing criminalization of low-income communities of color, both immigrant and US-born. Both, likewise, form part of an unbreakable continuum of women's strategies for survival, which are an expression of their commitment to themselves, their families, and their communities.

Looking Forward

As I have argued throughout this discussion, until we understand how women experience enforcement violence, we cannot fully understand how such violence affects our communities. Taking this one step forward, a community-centered perspective challenges us to go beyond a more conventional human rights framework, which seeks to hold law enforcement agencies accountable for violating the rights of individuals. Understanding abuse as a community problem permits us to focus on what strategies will best support the safety and self-determination of communities that find themselves under siege from state agencies.

Gender and Enforcement Violence

Home is a location in which women experience both "private" violence (for example, from intimate partners) and "public" violence (from state authorities). The larger project of defending women against violence and abuse urgently requires us to transcend the artificial and damaging divide in which progressive social movements tend to focus on the first type of violence while disregarding the second. By opening up our understanding of violence in the home, we will be able to better understand how law enforcement operates in communities of color, both immigrant and US-born: targeting the home when it comes to raiding it while avoiding or neglecting it when it comes to protecting the people inside, particularly women and children.

The situation is similar with regard to motherhood and, more generally, caregiving. Enforcement violence in poor communities and communities of color disrupts caregivers' ability to fulfill their responsibilities. At the same time, the legal apparatus of the state is used to accuse women of irresponsibility and abuse—with charges sometimes stemming directly from the harm caused by law enforcement or other public agencies.

An even more extreme example is that of the incarceration of women under the banner of "fetal protection," in which a supposed concern for children is hypocritically used to justify the incarceration of women of color, particularly African-American women. In other circumstances, law enforcement authorities treat the outcome of a pregnancy as an unimportant concern, secondary to the imperative to maintain "law and order."

Advocates of women's rights would do well to consider what implications these assaults on the rights of poor women of color, both immigrant and US-born, may have for the rights of women who may not face similar intrusions from law enforcement. The constant erosion of constitutional protections for the rights of poor women of color weakens such protections for everyone. The state's approach to such women—whether they are migrant workers, pregnant defendants with substance addiction, undocumented workers, asylum seekers, or prisoners—may be taken as an indication of the true value accorded by our society to motherhood, family, home, and women's work.

Caregiving and Criminalization

Feminist critiques have highlighted how women, who are the vast majority of caregivers, bear the brunt of economic restructuring—by working for the lowest wages under the most inhumane conditions; by working a double and triple shift as mothers, homemakers, and wage-earners; by taking on new caregiving responsibilities to compensate for the dismantling of social welfare, health care, and pension systems; and by securing the daily survival of their families in conditions of deepening impoverishment and economic dislocation. Today, increasing numbers of women face these challenges as the sole breadwinners for their families.[102] This feminist understanding must be further expanded to take account of how caregivers are affected by enforcement violence. Such violence represents an assault on the integrity and viability of our communities, reflecting broader social processes of criminalization.

Bridging the Immigration–Criminal Justice Divide

Law enforcement is increasingly a seamless web, in which authorities may move without hindrance between a traffic stop and deportation, or a hospital visit and prison, or the airport and a maximum-security cell. This unrestricted integration of law enforcement operations is terrifying to contemplate, let alone to experience. Moreover, according to scholars, such integration, and the accompanying adoption of a national enforcement strategy, is also one of the hallmarks of a totalitarian regime.[103]

At the same time, a variety of regressive legislation enacted in recent years has sharply restricted avenues for legal redress by those who are caught up in the law enforcement net. Reduced access to courts and to legal counsel has affected asylum seekers and other immigrants; prisoners, especially those on death row; and all poor people who rely on legal aid. Protections for due process rights have been seriously eroded by a series of court decisions.

The logic of such policies is similar, whether the specific language refers to "quality of life" policing, drug interdiction, counter-terrorism, or national security. All of these terms extend a false promise of increased safety in exchange for restrictions on constitutional rights. In each case, a comparison of the experiences of immigrant and US-born communities of color reveals many parallels. The major difference is that some of these measures purport to protect the national borders of the United States, while others seek to defend interior borders of institutionalized racism and economic privilege. As long as each type of border is understood separately, however, unexamined beliefs about public safety, on the one hand, and national security, on the other, will continue to foster mutual suspicion and mistrust between immigrant and US-born sectors of the community.

New Alliances, New Strategies

What does it mean in practice to fight violence against women of color while simultaneously addressing the structural violence faced by the larger community? The New York–based Institute on Violence, which focuses on how violence is experienced by African-American women in Central Harlem, is one of several groups around the country seeking to develop a new model for anti-violence work. Working in partnership with Harlem Legal Services and the African-American Task Force, the Institute brought together 300 community members to develop strategies for addressing different levels of violence. The purpose of this project is to strengthen the capacity of different sectors of the community (including residents and business owners as well as health and human services, cultural, religious, and recreational agencies) to respond to violence against women and to affirm the value of African-American women's lives.

In addition to working with community organizations and churches to help strengthen their ability to address violence against women, the Institute is also considering establishing a Community Police Council. As part of this process, it has held meetings with groups of residents to discuss strategies around the criminal justice system. These meetings brought together senior citizens, survivors of domestic violence, people in residential drug treatment programs, and people with disabilities. For everyone involved, the police were a "hot button" issue.[104]

In exploring alternatives to an exclusive reliance on law enforcement for protection in domestic violence situations, the Asian Women's Shelter (AWS) in California is attempting to involve local communities in exploring how domestic violence takes place among their members and how to ensure that battered women are safe and supported. One issue that has come up is how to hold batterers accountable. As organizer Beckie Masaki of AWS observes, a close-knit community is a prerequisite for community-based models of accountability. The more communities of color are affected by multiple forces fostering social breakdown, the more difficult such an effort can be.[105]

In the Boston area, AFSC's Criminal Justice Program, together with the Dimmock Community Health Center, has supported the development of a coalition seeking to work in new ways around issues of women caught up in the criminal justice system. Under the name "Women in Prison, Families in Crisis," this initiative has brought together people with experience in health issues, substance abuse, domestic violence, legal aid, and community organizing. Several members of the coalition are former prisoners or friends and family of prisoners. Using a community circle model, the group discusses how crime might be redefined as "harm," so that the issue becomes how to address the harm caused to everyone involved in a "criminal" action—the victim, the perpetrator, and the community.[106]

The initiatives described above are all important steps toward the development of new alliances and new strategies to address the devastating impact of violence, in all its forms, on low-income communities of color. Organizations and social movements that have come together around such issues as domestic violence, reproductive rights, sexual assault, immigrants' rights, INS detention, police accountability, and prisoners' rights bring sharply different views and experiences to the discussion. It is precisely by working through these differing and sometimes opposing views, however, that we can begin to address the complexities of the relationship between our communities and the state—and the centrality of women to the development of practical strategies for community self-determination.

roduce.

1   Border control operations also include the US Customs Service, which is part of the Treasury Department; some reports of violence and abuse by customs agents are also included in this essay.

2   Luana Ross, *Inventing the Savage: The Social Construction of Native American Criminality* (Austin, TX: University of Texas Press, 1998), 12.

3   The Sentencing Project, briefing sheet (Washington, DC: 1997).

4   Interview with Jana Schroeder, Criminal Justice Program, American Friends Service Committee (Dayton, OH: 1999).

5   Lutheran Immigration and Refugee Service, "Immigration Detention in the United States" (Baltimore, MD: 1998).

6   Deanne M. Pearn, "And Justice for All: Understanding and Addressing Human Rights Abuses Against Women in Immigration Detention Centers," unpublished presentation, Women's Institute for Leadership Development for Human Rights (San Francisco, CA: May 11, 1998).

7   Interview with Donna Willmott, Legal Services for Prisoners with Children (San Francisco, CA: 1999).

8   Amnesty International–USA, "Police Brutality and Excessive Force in the New York City Police Department," AMR Vol. 51, No. 36 (New York: June 1996).

9   Daniel HoSang, "The Economics of the New Brutality," *Colorlines* (Winter 1999-2000).

10   Joel Najar, "The Historical, Political, and Legislative Context for INS Raids," in *Portrait of Injustice: The Impact of Immigration Raids on Families, Workers, and Communities* (Oakland, CA: National INS Raids Task Force, National Network for Immigrant and Refugee Rights, October 1998).

11   Timothy Dunn, *The Militarization of the US-Mexico-Border, 1978-1992: Low-Intensity Conflict Doctrine Comes Home* (Austin, TX: University of Texas Press, 1996), 49 and 63.

12   Interview with Maria Jimenez, Immigration Law Enforcement Monitoring Project, American Friends Service Committee (Houston, TX: 1999).

13   Ethan A. Nadelmann, "Commonsense Drug Policy," *Foreign Affairs*, Vol. 77, No. 1 (January-February 1998).

14   NYC Police Watch, "How to Deal with the Police," resource packet (New York: n.d.).

15   Interview with Cassandra Shaylor, Legal Services for Prisoners with Children (San Francisco, CA: 1999). At the time of this interview, Shaylor was conducting doctoral research about women and solitary confinement at Valley State Prison for Women in Chowchilla, CA.

16   NYC Police Watch, case report (New York: June 1, 1998).

17   Interviews with Gloria Hernandez, Immigrant Women Access Project (Fresno, CA: 1999), and Rebecca Brockman, Las Americas Immigrant Advocacy Center (El Paso, TX: 1999).

18   Human Rights Watch, "Locked Away: Immigration Detainees in Local Jails in the United States," G1001 (New York: September 1998).

19   Eligibility Verification Review is the process to evaluate eligibility for welfare. Elaine Kim, "Women of Color: The Forgotten Members of the

New Economy," unpublished presentation, Community Voices Heard (New York: New York University, March 28–29, 2000).

20 Minerva Delgado, "Women of Color: The Forgotten Members of the New Economy," unpublished presentation, Puerto Rican Legal Defense and Education Fund (New York: New York University, March 28–29, 2000).

21 Deborah Fink, "Workplace Violence: Working to Survive, Invisible and Unregulated," unpublished presentation, "Violence: Shredding Social Fabrics, Destroying Global Health" (Iowa City, IA: University of Iowa, April 14–16, 2000). See also Deborah Fink, *Cutting into the Meat-Packing Line* (Chapel Hill, NC: University of North Carolina Press, 1998).

22 Kristen Flurkey, "Working for Alternatives to Incarceration," *Peace and Freedom* (November-December 1999).

23 Interview with Jesus Romo, attorney and activist (Tucson, AZ: 1999).

24 Greg Smith and Tara George, "Officers Accused of Beating Woman," *The Daily News* (New York), March 2, 2000, 2.

25 This bill failed to clear the 106th Congress, and was reintroduced in February 2001.

26 Noy Thrupkaew, "Republicans Work Overtime for 'Unborn Victims of Violence,' " *Sojourner: The Women's Forum* (November 1999).

27 See National Latina Health Organization, "Essential Principles for Responsible Health Care Reform" (San Francisco, CA: 1993); California Pro-Choice Education Fund, "Norplant: A New Contraceptive with the Potential for Abuse" (San Francisco, CA: 1997).

28 Kathy Holub, "When Worlds Collide," *San Jose Mercury News*, July 7, 1991.

29 John Donohue III and Steven Levitt, "The Impact of Legalized Abortion on Crime," working paper 8004, (Cambridge, MA: National Bureau of Economic Research, November 2000). Dorothy Roberts mentioned press accounts of this study in remarks at a reproductive rights conference at Hampshire College in April 2000.

30 Interviews with Lynn Coyle, Lawyer's Committee for Civil Rights Under the Law of Texas (San Antonio, TX: 1999), and Juanita Genis, Las Americas Immigrant Advocacy Center (El Paso, TX: 1999).

31 Interview with Leni Marin, Family Violence Prevention Fund (San Francisco, CA: 2000).

32 Interview with Sue Osthoff, National Clearinghouse for the Defense of Battered Women (Philadelphia, PA: 2000).

33 Beth Richie, *Compelled to Crime: The Gender Entrapment of Battered Black Women* (New York: Routledge, 1996).

34 Interview with Sujata Warrier, Director, Health Care Bureau, New York State Office for the Prevention of Domestic Violence (New York: 2000).

35 Interview with Lori Humphreys, managing attorney for domestic violence, Ayuda (Washington, DC: 2000).

36 Interview with Beckie Masaki, director, Asian Women's Shelter (San Francisco, CA: 2000).

37 Dorothy Roberts, *Killing the Black Body* (New York: Vintage, 1998), 166.

38 Lynn M. Paltrow, "Prosecution and Prejudice: Judging Drug-Using

Pregnant Women," in Julia E. Hanigsberg and Sara Ruddick, eds., *Mother Troubles: Rethinking Contemporary Maternal Dilemmas* (Boston, MA: Beacon Press, 1999), 71.

39 National Women's Health Network, "The Violation of Incarcerated Women's Reproductive Rights," information packet (Washington, DC: n.d.).

40 Petition to the Inter-American Commission on Human Rights of the Organization of American States, submitted by American Friends Service Committee, four other US and Mexican organizations, and seven individuals (August 12, 1992), 12–13. Although more than a decade old, many of the incidents cited in this document still ring true.

41 *Contreras, et al. vs. Obed Gonzales, et al.* No. B-78-150 (Southern District of Texas).

42 Amnesty International–USA, "Not Part of My Sentence: Violations of the Human Rights of Women in Custody," AMR Vol. 51, No. 1 (New York: March 1999).

43 Pearn, "And Justice for All."

44 Women's Commission for Refugee Women and Children, "Liberty Denied: Women Seeking Asylum Imprisoned in the United States" (New York: April 1997), 18–19.

45 Letter to Diane Malloy from prisoner activist, Ohio Reformatory for Women (Marysville, OH: 1999). Malloy is ombudsman for the Ohio chapter of CURE, a national organization of prisoners' friends and family members.

46 Amnesty International–USA, "Findings of a Visit to Valley State Prison for Women, California," AMR Vol. 51, No. 53 (New York: April 1999).

47 Interview with Renee Saucedo, coordinator, INS Watch, a joint project of La Raza Centro Legal and Ella Baker Center for Human Rights (San Francisco, CA: 2000).

48 Ibid.

49 "US Strategies for Eliminating Sexual Violence Against Women," in Proceedings, "National and International Strategies for the Elimination of Sexual Violence," 5th Annual Symposium, University of Texas School of Law, Austin; published in *Texas Journal of Women and the Law*, Vol. 6, No. 2 (Spring 1997).

50 Human Rights Watch, "Sexual Assault by US Border Patrol Agents," *Global Report on Women's Human Rights*, 01009946, Part 21 (New York: 1995), 183–191.

51 "Arizona Rape Case Challenges Negligence of INS Supervision of Border Patrol Agent," *US Newswire* (Washington, DC: August 13, 1999).

52 Petition to the Inter-American Commission on Human Rights, op. cit., 27.

53 NYC Police Watch, case report (New York: February 9, 1999).

54 Interview with Mary Powers, National Coalition on Police Accountability (Chicago, IL: 1999). Powers coordinates the Chicago-based Citizens Alert and Coalition to End Police Torture and Brutality as well as the National Coalition on Police Accountability.

55 Interview with Shawna Virago, Community United Against Violence (San Francisco, CA: 1999).

56 National Coalition of Anti-Violence Programs, "Anti–Lesbian, Gay, Bisexual and Transgender Violence in 1998" (New York: 1999), 54.

57 Numerous such cases are documented in Human Rights Watch, "All Too Familiar: Sexual Abuse of Women in US State Prisons" (New York: December 1996), and a follow-up report, Human Rights Watch, "Nowhere to Hide: Retaliation Against Women in Michigan State Prisons" (New York: July 1998).

58 Gary Delsohn, "Prison Doctor Loses Post over TV Comment," *The Sacramento Bee*, October 15, 1999.

59 As quoted in Delsohn, ibid.

60 Interview with Jana Schroeder, Criminal Justice Program, American Friends Service Committee (Dayton, OH: 1999).

61 Barbara Vobejda, " 'Abuse of Female Prisoners in US is Routine,' Rights Report Says," *Washington Post*, March 4, 1999, A11.

62 Women's Commission for Refugee Women and Children, "Forgotten Prisoners: A Follow-up Report on Refugee Women Incarcerated in York County, Pennsylvania" (New York: July 1998), 7.

63 Women's Institute for Leadership Development for Human Rights and Legal Services for Prisoners with Children, "Women in California Prisons," information packet (San Francisco, CA: May 1998).

64 Interview with Cassandra Shaylor, Legal Services for Prisoners with Children (San Francisco, CA: 1999).

65 Ross, *Inventing the Savage*, 142.

66 Information provided by Jana Schroeder, Criminal Justice Program, American Friends Service Committee, Dayton, OH, based on presentations at the October 1998 Critical Resistance conference in San Francisco.

67 Interview with Jackie Walker, AIDS Information Coordinator, ACLU National Prison Project (Washington, DC: 2000).

68 Ross, *Inventing the Savage*.

69 Amnesty International–USA, "Human Rights Concerns in the Border Region with Mexico," AMR Vol. 51, No. 3 (New York: May 1998).

70 Complaint filed in US District Court (Tucson, AZ: 1997).

71 NYC Police Watch, case report (New York, February 1, 1999).

72 Bay Area Police Watch, case report (San Francisco, CA: August 30, 1999).

73 Personal experience of Anannya Bhattacharjee as representative of Andolan: Organizing South Asian Workers (New York: 1999).

74 Statements collected by Washington Alliance for Immigrant and Refugee Justice (WAIRJ) (Brewster, WA: 1997). See also WAIRJ and National INS Raids Task Force, "Civil Rights Under Siege: The Impact of Immigration Raids on Washington State" (Oakland, CA: National Network for Immigrant and Refugee Rights, October 1998).

75 Statement by worker at Brewster Heights Packing Plant to WAIRJ (Brewster, WA: 1998).

76 Immigration Law Enforcement Monitoring Project, "Women at the

US-Mexico Border: Violation of Women's Rights as Human Rights in Border Crossings" (Houston, TX: American Friends Service Committee, September 1995).

77 Najar, *Portrait of Injustice*, 21.

78 Thorn Ndaizee Meweh and Dorsey Nunn, "Mass Incarceration and Communities of Color," *Political Environments*, newsletter of Committee on Women, Population, and the Environment, No. 7 (Fall 1999/Winter 2000).

79 Bay Area Police Watch, case report (San Francisco, CA: November 4, 1999).

80 Citizens Alert, case report (Chicago, IL: October 1, 1997).

81 "What Kind of Justice? The Case of Tabitha Walrond," *Sojourner: The Women's Forum* (November 1999), 11.

82 Human Rights Watch, "Nowhere to Hide."

83 Rights for All Campaign, "Impact on Children of Women in Prison," Factsheet No. 3 (New York: Amnesty International–USA, n.d.). See also Amnesty International–USA, "Not Part of My Sentence," *AMR*.

84 Interview with Mary Fitzgerald, Justice Works (New York: 2000).

85 Interview with Cassandra Shaylor, Legal Services for Prisoners with Children (San Francisco, CA: 1999).

86 Donna Willmott, "The War on Immigrants—Behind the Walls," unpublished presentation, Women's Studies Forum (San Francisco: San Francisco State University, October 1998).

87 Renee Wormack Keels, "Me and Other Mothers (MOMS)," a message for Mother's Day, *Loves Herself—Regardless*, Vol. 1, No. 2 (Winter 1997), publication of Women's Theological Center, Newton Center, MA.

88 Interview with Patricia Clark, National Criminal Justice Representative, American Friends Service Committee (Philadelphia, PA: 2000).

89 Interview with Cassie Pierson, Legal Services for Prisoners with Children (San Francisco, CA: 1999).

90 Interview with Mary Fitzgerald, Justice Works (New York: 2000).

91 Interview with Mary Barr, Justice Works (New York: 1999). Barr also works with South 40 Corporation and Motivational Movement, both located in New York.

92 "Women on the Border: Needs and Opportunities," in Rachael Kamel and Anya Hoffman, eds., *The Maquiladora Reader: Cross-Border Organizing Since NAFTA* (Philadelphia, PA: American Friends Service Committee, 1999), 25.

93 Interview with Maria Jimenez, Immigration Law Enforcement Monitoring Project, American Friends Service Committee (Houston, TX: 1999).

94 Statement by worker at Brewster Heights Packing Plant to Washington Alliance for Immigrant and Refugee Justice, Brewster, WA, regarding raid on December 2, 1997. See also WAIRJ and National INS Raids Task Force, "Civil Rights Under Siege."

95 "USPROS: When Police Priorities Change, Attitudes Will Change," statement by the US PROStitutes Collective and Wages Due Lesbians of San Francisco to the Public Hearing on Violence Against Women and Girls

in Prostitution held by the San Francisco Commission on the Status of Women, April 17, 1997. Published in International Prostitutes Collective, *Some Mother's Daughter: The Hidden Movement of Prostitute Women Against Violence* (London: Crossroads Books, June 1999).

96 Interview with Jo Hirschman, Ella Baker Center for Human Rights (San Francisco, CA: 1999). See also US PROStitutes Collective, "Report of Police Harassment of Prostitutes: Statement of the Problems" (San Francisco, CA: August 2, 1994).

97 Jeremy Hay, "Police Abuse of Prostitutes in San Francisco," *Gauntlet Magazine*, Vol. 1, No. 7 (1994).

98 Interview with Mary Powers.

99 Interview with Jane Bai and Hyun Lee, CAAAV: Organizing Asian Communities (formerly Committee Against Anti-Asian Violence) (New York: 1999).

100 Interview with Jo Hirschman, Ella Baker Center for Human Rights (San Francisco, CA: 1999).

101 US PROStitutes Collective, "Are We Not Human? Prostitute Women's Right to Protection and Other Rights—A Human Rights Issue for Everyone," statement presented to San Francisco Human Rights Commission in support of recommendations of San Francisco Task Force on Prostitution (February 11, 1999).

102 While this working paper has focused on conditions inside the United States, the phenomena described here obviously apply on a global level.

103 Dunn, *The Militarization of the US-Mexico-Border, 1978-1992.*

104 Interview with Gail Garfield, Institute on Violence (New York: 2000).

105 Interview with Beckie Masaki, Asian Women's Shelter (San Francisco, CA: 2000).

106 Interview with Jamie Suarez-Potts, Criminal Justice Program, American Friends Service Committee (Cambridge, MA: 2000).

I would like to thank the American Friends Service Committee for their support during the writing of this essay. In particular, I owe much to Rachael Kamel for her unflagging assistance and guidance.

Chapter 2

Killing the Black Community

A Commentary on the United States War on Drugs

Judith A.M. Scully

We live in a country that is deeply rooted in racism. The laws establishing this country were written by white men who did not believe that Black people were full human beings.[1] According to the founding fathers of this nation, Black people were two-fifths property and three-fifths human. Despite our human characteristics, Black people were denied access to all the liberties and rights accorded to white citizens under the United States Constitution and were treated as property for over a hundred years, while slavery was a legally sanctioned institution in this country.

During this period, Black men and women who were enslaved were denied the right to choose sexual partners, to establish families, and to live in communities of their choice without interference from white people.[2] In fact, it was not only impossible for Black people to form their own communities, it was also illegal for more than two or three Black people to congregate together, to learn to read or to assemble to worship.[3] In addition, Black people were beaten, whipped, and subjected to some of the cruelest forms of physical, mental, and emotional humiliation.

When slavery ended, Black people were emancipated without any compensation whatsoever for the century of work that their families had provided free of charge to white people who claimed to "own" them. Many Black families torn apart by slavery were never reunited. The former slaves were therefore "free" to live in social disarray and abject poverty.

Immediately after emancipation, explicit laws called the Black Codes criminalized behavior of Black people even though such conduct was not considered to be criminal if engaged in by white people. For example, vagrancy, unemployment, homelessness, loitering, and "shiftlessness" were deemed crimes worthy of incarceration for Black people but not for whites.[4]

As a result of this criminalization of poverty, prisons previously occupied by only white people became overpopulated with poor Black people.[5] As for the Black people who were not incarcerated in prisons, their freedom was also severely curtailed by white civilians who engaged in acts of terrorism such as maiming, torturing, and lynching. Due to the lack of government concern for Black life, white people who committed these types of inhumane acts were virtually assured that no government action would be taken against them.

By selectively enforcing the law, using their power to define what conduct will be deemed "criminal" and what conduct will not, by incarcerating Black people, and by refusing to punish white people who engaged in lawless acts against Black people, government officials have historically oppressed and maintained social control over the Black community.

This article focuses on the United States government's current war on drugs and its racially disproportionate effect on the Black community. This "war" is an example of how government officials have corruptly employed legal tools and racial rhetoric to continue the criminalization and destruction of Black communities. This type of conduct, after all, is not unusual. It is, in fact, the American way.

Despite its label, the war on drugs is not a war waged on inanimate objects. It is a war waged on Black women, children, and men. It is a war that is destroying our families, our communities, and our image as human beings in the American mind. The war has resulted in massive warehousing of Black men, women, and children in American prisons. The consequences of this war are so severe that if the percentage of Black men in prison continues to increase at the same rate that it did from 1980 to 1993, approximately two-thirds of young Black men between the ages of 18 and 40 will be in prison by the year 2010.[6]

Black women make up approximately one-half of the female prison population. Although there is a lack of data on the effect of the war on drugs on Black women in particular, the massive increase in the incarceration rate of Black women and men has had an undeniable impact on Black families. Nearly 80 percent of women in prisons are mothers.[7] Consequently, many Black children now have at least one and sometimes two incarcerated parents at some time during their lifetimes.

In this article, I examine the historical roots and the rhetorical tactics and propaganda of this country's most recent war on drugs. I also look at the legal arsenal employed in the war on drugs and explore its consequences. My conclusion is that the government's war on drugs is racially unjust, is a violation of international human rights law, and must be stopped in order for the United States justice system to maintain what little integrity it has left.

History and Rhetoric of the War on Drugs

The longest war in United States history has been the war against drugs. In 1909, Dr. Hamilton Wright was appointed by President Theodore Roosevelt to lead a commission on stopping the opium trade in Asia. His report, issued a year later, was most notable for its racist myths and lies about drug use among Black people. The document described, in horrifying detail, the alleged superhuman strength and extreme madness experienced by Blacks who used cocaine. Its central thesis was that cocaine drove Black men to rape.[8] Rumors went so far as to claim that cocaine made Black people bulletproof. In a sensational article entitled "Negro Cocaine 'Fiends' Are A New Southern Menace," the *New York Times* reported that southern sheriffs had switched from .32 caliber guns to .38 caliber pistols to protect themselves from drug-empowered Blacks.[9]

At the same time that the media was portraying all addicts as drug-crazed Blacks, racial fears were running rampant.[10] The image of the dangerous Black drug dealer and crazed drug users was part of a scare tactic used to win national support for programs of law and order and the suppression of Black rights. It was a deceitful but successful strategy that worked in 1910 and is still working today.

More Recent Wars on Drugs

On September 5, 1989 when President Bush released the long-awaited $7.8 billion federal anti-drug plan, the National Drug Control Strategy, he dramatized his speech by holding up a bag of crack he claimed was purchased by government agents in Lafayette Park, near the White House.[11] His attempt to illustrate the pervasiveness of drugs and their easy access backfired.

In the coming days, reporters discovered that there was much more to the story than just a bag of crack purchased by the White House. They discovered that "Keith Timothy Jackson, the eighteen-year-old Black high school senior who sold the three ounces of low-grade crack,"[12] had never heard of Lafayette Park. They discovered that prior to his encounter with government agents, Jackson did not know what the White House was. In fact, Jackson had to be driven to the park by a DEA informant. The journalists also discovered that Bush failed to mention that neither crack, nor any other drugs, had ever been bought in the park until the United States government sent agents out to buy them.[13] Although Jackson was prosecuted for drug distribution, he was eventually found not guilty of charges related to the White House fiasco because the Court ruled that he had been entrapped by government agents.[14]

During this same anti-drug speech, President Bush acknowledged that illegal drugs were available in practically every community in this nation. However, Bush limited the battlefield of the war on drugs to public housing projects, largely inhabited by African-Americans. He claimed:

> [W]hile illegal drug use is found in every community, nowhere is it worse than in our public housing projects. You know, the poor have never had it easy in this world. But in the past, they weren't mugged on the way home from work by crack gangs. And their children didn't have to dodge bullets on the way to school. And that's why I'm targeting $50 million to fight crime in the public housing projects, help restore order and to kick out

the dealers for good.[15]

Journalists also limited the "drug problem" to poor African-Americans living in inner cities in the weeks following the speech.[16] Consistent with this philosophy, the nation's war on drugs has focused almost exclusively on low-level dealers and users in African-American neighborhoods. Police find drugs in these communities because that is where they look for them. Had they pointed the war at college campuses, it is likely that American jails would now be filled overwhelmingly with white university students who are both using and selling drugs.[17] Had the war on drugs been focused on drug users in general, without regard to race, the prison population would be predominantly white since they comprise over 70 percent of all illegal drug users.[18] Even former President Bush's drug policy director, William Bennett, admitted that the typical drug user is "white, male, a high school graduate employed full-time and living in a small metropolitan area or suburb."[19]

Most of the propaganda generated by the war on drugs focused on Black drug users and low-level dealers in the United States. In the early 1990s, for example, the Partnership for a Drug-Free America (PDFA),[20] a nonprofit, private-sector coalition, produced a billion dollars worth of public service messages (a million dollars a day, every day, for three years) to promote the anti-drug message.[21] PDFA created over 250 multimedia messages that warned Americans about drug abuse and drug abusers.[22] Newspapers, magazines, radio stations, television stations, billboard owners, and telephone directories contributed space to "enable millions of Americans to receive PDFA messages."[23]

These messages placed a human face—invariably black or brown—on the "drug problem." In PDFA announcements, people of color are depicted as the "enemy" in the war on drugs. For example, "Snake" depicted an adolescent African-American drug dealer whose face gradually transforms into the head of a cobra, "replete with a forked tongue and accompanying hiss."[24] The message was that enemies in the drug war are not people but vicious animals needing extermination. Another announcement, "Straight

Up," portrayed two black male rappers wearing stereotypical large gold jewelry hanging out in a rundown urban alley. All the drug dealers and users in this advertisement are young black men.[25] The ad, entitled "Addiction is Slavery," also targeted African-Americans by equating illegal drug addiction with slavery.[26] One of these announcements specifically depicted African slaves as ancestors "who never surrendered until they were free" while an announcer warned contemporary African-Americans not to dishonor their ancestors by being a slave to heroin, cocaine, [or] crack." Meanwhile, iron chains and collars were superimposed on addicts lying down in an alley, reiterating the theme that drug abuse was the new slavery. All of these messages suggest that African-Americans are the enemies in the war on drugs and that white people are tangential to this issue of drug abuse. Such propaganda is a disservice not only to African-Americans but also to white Americans by reinforcing the notion that white people do not have drug problems.[27]

The Drugs and Violence Nexus: A Distortion of Crime

At the same time as the media and the government were busy portraying the drug problem as a "Black problem," stories linking violence with drugs were flourishing. As Farai Chideya, a journalist formerly with the *Washington Post* pointed out, "Black people became a symbol of crime."[28] Contrary to the distortions and exaggerations of the media, however, the majority of violent criminals in the United States are white.[29]

In addition to distorting the "face" of violent crime, the media has also distorted the severity of the violent crime problem in America. A study conducted by the *New Orleans Times-Picayune* in 1980 found that although murder and robbery accounted for only 12 percent of actual crimes in New Orleans, they constituted forty 45 percent of crime stories in the newspapers.[30] Similarly, sociologist Mark Fishman found that during a "period in which there was … no documentable evidence of an increase in incidents of violence directed at the elderly in New York City, the three largest daily newspapers and five local television stations reported a surge of such violence."[31] In the January 17, 1994 issue of *US News and*

World Report, the cover story read: "A scary orgy of violent crime is fueling another public call to action."[32] The article focused on a "wave of violence" and the "relentless growth" of crime, when in fact, violent crime had not risen for twenty years. According to Steven Donziger, author of *The Real War On Crime,* the serious violent crime rate for the United States in 1994 stood 16 percent below its peak level in the mid-1970s.[33] The murder rate dropped 9 percent from 1980 to 1992 and in 1996 the murder rate was almost the same as it was in the 1970s. Although most people perceived crime to be rising, the crime rate had remained remarkably stable for many years.

In fact, since 1980 the majority of crime in America has not been violent. In the 1990s, approximately one in ten arrests in the United States was for violent crime; and only three in one hundred arrests were for a violent crime resulting in injury.[34] Currently, when most people think of locking up criminals, they usually have an image of a violent offender—a murderer or rapist. But the vast majority of people filling expensive new prison cells are nonviolent property or drug offenders.[35] From 1980 to 1990, the percentage of individuals sent to prison for violent crimes decreased significantly.[36] In 1992, nonviolent first-time drug offenders outnumbered prisoners convicted of murder by seven to one. According to the federal government, as of 1999, 57 percent of inmates in federal prison were serving time for drug offenses; only 11 percent of the inmates had committed violent offenses. [37]

Despite these facts, the media has created a distorted image of crime in which the issue of violence is intimately linked with drugs and concomitantly with Black people. The creation of the "crack baby" epidemic is a case in point. The term "crack baby" was used by the media to conjure up images of mutant monster infants born to pathetic and despicable drug-addicted mothers who were, according to the media, overwhelmingly Black.

These images help to induce white American fear, disrespect, and disdain for Black women and children. A decade of news reporters fed the American public exaggerated images of cocaine addicted infants and preschoolers. Some reporters went into hospital nurseries and special education schools to "borrow" images of premature, screaming and/or trembling African-American children to illustrate their crack baby stories.[38] An episode of the TV show *60 Minutes* even showed sick babies and gave the impression that their problems were cocaine-related when they were not.[39] At the same time that these images were being projected by the media, doctors and researchers predicted that babies of women who used cocaine would experience permanent learning disabilities and attention and behavior disorders.[40] Some went so far as to claim that crack babies would have to be written off as a "lost generation," a "biological underclass."[41]

Today, there is practically scientific consensus that cocaine does no more damage to infants than cigarette smoking.[42] In one of the first large comprehensive studies to refute the long-held belief that cocaine-exposed babies often suffer major birth defects, University of Florida researchers found that 75 percent of the babies studied had no major problems, the same as a group of babies who were not exposed to cocaine in utero.[43]

Similarly, at Einstein Medical Center, researchers have been tracking the development of more than 200 poor inner-city children since 1989. Although half of these children were exposed to cocaine in the womb, researchers report that there is nothing that distinguishes the cocaine-exposed children from their peers.[44] Claire Coles, a clinical psychologist at Emory University in Atlanta who has studied crack kids, argues:

> There is no evidence of genetic damage, nothing like what was originally supposed. It's astonishing that so much fuss has been raised about cocaine when kids born with fetal alcohol syndrome are so much worse off. The problems suffered by children exposed to cocaine stem from many factors.... But cocaine itself has not been proven to be any more damaging than any other drug used by pregnant women.[45]

The media's deceptive attempts to create public horror regarding Black drug-addicted women was so effective that legislators, judges, and prosecutors across the country were motivated to attempt to criminalize the conduct of pregnant drug-addicted women. In a series of state court cases across the country, prosecutors charged pregnant women with "delivering controlled substances" to their babies in utero.[46] The most infamous of these cases was *Johnson vs. State*,[47] where Jennifer Johnson, a 23-year-old African-American woman, was tried and convicted of delivering cocaine to her child. According to the prosecutor, Jennifer Johnson delivered drugs to her newborn infant through the umbilical cord in the sixty to ninety seconds after birth and before the cord was cut.[48] Although Jennifer's conviction in Florida was overturned on appeal, several other prosecutors across the country attempted to bring similar charges.[49] The majority of these cases were brought against African-American women.

Prosecutors also charged women with child abuse for exposing their unborn children to drugs. Under a South Carolina law, women who tested positive for drug use during their pregnancies or at the time they gave birth were immediately arrested and charged with drug possession, child neglect, or distribution of drugs to a minor.[50] Many of the women who were arrested during their pregnancies wound up giving birth in shackles and chains, bleeding in cold prison cells. All the women arrested under this law were Black with one exception. In the hospital records of the sole white woman arrested, it was noted that her boyfriend was Black.[51]

Similarly, when judges attempted to punish pregnant women by sentencing them to temporary or permanent sterilization, a disproportionate number of the women affected were Black.[52] Legislative initiatives attempting to compel the use of Norplant for all women whose babies were born addicted to drugs also flourished. Luckily, these initiatives did not receive enough support from public officials to become law, but public sentiment articulated in mainstream media seemed to sway in support of these efforts nonetheless.

Eventually, and unfortunately, where the government could not tread, the private sector willingly stepped in. In 1997, Children Requiring a Caring Kommunity (CRACK),[53] a nonprofit organization based in Stanton, California, launched a campaign to promote population control by paying women with substance abuse problems $200 if they could prove that they were permanently sterilized or were using temporary forms of sterilization such as Norplant, Depo-Provera or an IUD.[54] To solicit "clients," CRACK placed large billboards primarily in Black and Latino communities in Los

Angeles.[55] Some of the billboards stated "Don't Let A Pregnancy Ruin Your Drug Habit."[56] Others mimicked Monopoly game cards "If You Are Addicted To Drugs, Get Birth Control—Get $200 Cash."[57]

It is no surprise that Black and Latina women have been disproportionately affected by CRACK's sterilization campaign. Approximately 60 percent of the women who were either temporarily or permanently sterilized were Black or Latina.[58] CRACK's strategy to terminate the reproductive capacity of these women is clearly a result of the war on drugs propaganda targeted at Black women and children.

Pregnant women who use drugs are depicted as primarily Black women addicted to crack who are incapable of rehabilitation and therefore disposable. Black children who are born exposed to drugs are portrayed as being helpless, hopeless, potentially violent, and ultimately not worthy of being born. Programs such as CRACK perpetuate the myth that drug treatment is not an option and that drug-exposed children are permanently damaged. Thus, instead of promoting policies to support drug treatment programs, CRACK is contributing to the dehumanization and demonization of Black women and their children.

Pointing out that the media, and the government, and organizations like CRACK have exaggerated the problem of drug use in Black America is not to suggest that drugs and/or violence are not a problem for the Black community. Drugs and violence clearly are a problem in both Black and white communities throughout the United States, but the media and the government have distorted the reality of crime, drugs, and violence by focusing almost exclusively on images of "violent" Black men, "irresponsible" Black women, and "worthless" Black children.

Jeffrey Reiman, author of *The Rich Get Richer and the Poor Get Prison*, referred to this type of distortion as the "carnival mirror." He argues that the portrayal of crime in America "is like a mirror in which society can see the face of the evil in its midst. Because the system deals with some evil and not with others … the image it throws back at us is distorted like the image in a carnival mirror."[59]

Through the use of a carnival mirror, the media supports the war on drugs and the "get tough on crime" government policies that are terrorizing Black communities. It is the exaggeration of drug abuse and violence that has justified the government's application of war-like military tactics in the Black community. Police officers across the country have literally waged a "war on the Black community" instead of a war on drugs. More importantly, some officers and government officials have used the "carnival mirror" to their advantage and have economically profited from drug distribution in Black communities.[60]

In 1992, Mayor David Dinkins of New York City appointed a commission headed by Judge Milton Mollen to investigate corruption in the police department.[61] The commission found shocking evidence that numerous police officers committed theft, protected drug traffickers, sold and used drugs, falsified police reports, lied in court and treated citizens brutally and violently.[62] One police witness told the commission, "I know of police officers stealing money from drug dealers, police officers stealing drugs from drug dealers, police officers selling stolen drugs back to drug dealers. I also know of police officers stealing guns and selling them."[63]

The commission also identified a former police officer who snorted cocaine off the dashboard of his patrol car regularly and made $8,000 per week as a drug dealer.[64] Another officer set up a system where dealers were required to make regular payments to him for protection. If they fell short on a payment, he would rob them with his service revolver. To cover up the corruption, officers filed false police reports and lied to authorities.[65] The Mollen Commission concluded that the New York Police Department did virtually nothing to address these problems because it was more worried about bad publicity than about the corruption itself.[66]

Similarly, the Philadelphia Police Department was thrown into turmoil in 1995 when a group of rogue officers confessed to planting evidence in drug cases, shaking down drug suspects and pocketing the money, and making false arrests. More than 2,000 criminal cases had to be reopened as a result of the police misconduct.[67] It has also been documented that the Los Angeles Police Department,[68] the Chicago Police Department,[69] and the Pittsburgh Police Department[70] have engaged in similar illegal activities on a regular basis. These illegal police tactics combined with "legal" police maneuvering have trampled the constitutional rights of Black citizens and successfully increased the casualties of Black life in the war on drugs.

New Legal Arsenals: Mandatory Minimums and "Three-Strikes-and-You're-Out" Laws

In the 1980s, state and federal legislatures introduced a series of initiatives that altered the landscape of the criminal punishment system. With the enactment of mandatory minimum sentencing, "three-strikes-and-you're-out" laws, and the elimination of parole in all federal criminal cases and in many state court cases, the prison population began to rise.[71] More and more nonviolent drug offenders were receiving sentences of ten to twenty years for relatively modest offenses. And disproportionately represented were young Black men and women.[72]

Although these laws were allegedly enacted in order to "get tough" on kingpin drug dealers and lock them away for longer periods of time, this has not been the case. The majority of the prisoners serving time for drug offenses are low-level drug offenders. Many of them were first-time, nonviolent offenders with no prior criminal history and were not principal figures in criminal organizations or activities. Nevertheless, they received harsher sentences than "high-level" drug dealers who received leniency in exchange for information about their criminal enterprises.[73] Low-level dealers received longer mandatory minimum sentences because they had no information to bargain with.[74] This drug policy of rewarding "snitches" has a major impact on the long sentences which many low-level African-American drug dealers have received since the enactment of mandatory minimums.[75]

Because of this inequity, 90 percent of federal judges and 75 percent of state judges have indicated that mandatory minimum sentences should be abolished.[76] Even conservative Supreme Court Justices William Rehnquist and Anthony Kennedy have expressed disdain for mandatory minimums.[77] In 2000, President Clinton commuted the prison sentences of several drug offenders who had served a disproportionate amount of time as a result of mandatory minimum sentencing.[78] Despite such dissatisfaction, the mandatory minimum sentences continue to be enforced.

"Three strikes" laws have also resulted in a disproportionate number of nonviolent Black offenders occupying prison cells for extended periods of time. In California, the Los Angeles Public Defender's office revealed that 70 percent of all second- and third-strike cases filed in 1994 were for "nonviolent and nonserious offenses."[79] Only 4 percent of second and third felony convictions prosecuted under the "strike" system were cases of murder, rape, kidnapping, and carjacking.[80] The data also indicates that people of color with roughly the same criminal history as whites were being charged under "three strikes" laws at seventeen times the rate of white people.[81] Similarly, Georgia has a "two strikes and you're out" sentencing scheme that imposes life imprisonment for a second drug offense. In 1995, 98.4 percent of those serving life sentences under this provision were Black.[82]

The Crack/Cocaine Controversy

Another powerful weapon against the Black community in the war on drugs is the 1986 Federal Anti-Drug Abuse Act, which created new penalties for crack cocaine possession and distribution.[83] Under this law, a powder cocaine dealer must possess one hundred times more cocaine than a crack dealing counterpart in order for the two drug dealers to receive the same sentence.[84] Thus, a person convicted of possession with intent to distribute 500 grams of powder cocaine (which represents 2,500 to 5,000 doses with an average retail price of $32,000 to $50,000) receives the same mandatory sentence as someone convicted for possession with intent to distribute 5 grams of crack cocaine (which represents ten to fifty doses with an average retail price of $225 to $750). In addition, the law makes crack cocaine the only drug for which simple possession on a first offense will result in a mandatory minimum sentence of five years in prison.[85]

In 1995, 45.2 percent of defendants sentenced for powder cocaine offenses were white and only 20.7 percent were Black.[86] However, as the US Sentencing Commission report revealed, 92.6 percent of the defendants convicted for crack cocaine offenses were Black and only 4.7 percent were white. Moreover, in seventeen states, not one single white person had ever been prosecuted on federal crack cocaine charges.[87]

By 1999, approximately 85 percent of all crack convictions involved Black defendants, while only 5.4 percent of these convictions involved white defendants.[88] This disparity in conviction rates misleads many people into believing that the majority of crack users in the United States are Black. However, research produced by the National Institute of Drug Abuse (NIDA) has established that most crack users are actually white.[89] Despite this fact, very few white crack users are prosecuted under this incredibly punitive federal law.

The disparity in sentences for crack and powder cocaine becomes even more disturbing when one considers the findings of a study conducted by the Sentencing Commission in 1995, that the physiological and psychoactive effects of crack and powder cocaine were so similar that the discrepancy in punishment could not be justified on any grounds other than race.[90] Accordingly, it recommended that Congress lower the penalties associated with crack cocaine.[91] To this day, Congress has not acted to eliminate this injustice and Black retail crack dealers still receive longer sentences than the wholesale drug suppliers who provide them with the powder cocaine from which the crack is produced.

Like the inequities of mandatory minimums, the adverse racial impact of crack penalties has generated opposition from legal experts and even caused some judges to refrain from enforcing the penalties.[92] Some judges have even resigned in protest,[93] including Federal District Judge Lawrence Irving of San Diego, who believed the guidelines were too harsh. "If I remain on the bench I have no choice but to follow the law," protested Irving, "and I just can't in good conscience continue to do so."[94] Unfortunately, the number of judges who share Judge Irving's sentiment is still too small.

Consequences of the War on Drugs

As a result of the war on drugs, Black men are now incarcerated in state prisons at a rate thirteen times that of white men.[95] Although African-American men make up less than 7 percent of the general population, they comprise almost half of the prison popu-lation in seventeen states.[96] Maryland has the highest percentage of Black inmates, 79 percent, followed by Illinois with 74 percent, Louisiana with 73 percent, and New Jersey with 72 percent.[97]

For Black women, the war on drugs has also been disastrous. The number of Black women in state penitentiaries for drug of-fenses has increased by 888 percent between 1986 and 1996.[98] In the crusade to get tough on crime, policy-makers have gotten particu-larly tough on women, drawing them into prisons and jails in rapidly increasing numbers. Prior to the war on drugs and mandatory sen-tencing schemes, judges were more compassionate regarding a fe-male defendant's need to remain home with her children. Due to mandatory prison statutes and sentencing guidelines, however, this is no longer a valid consideration by the court.[99] In addition, as a re-sult of war on drugs legislation, Black women have experienced the greatest increase in criminal justice supervision[100] (which means that they are either in jail, in prison, on probation, or on parole).

Black youth have been disproportionately affected by the war on drugs. In Baltimore, for example, thirteen white juveniles were arrested on drug charges in 1990 while 1,304 Black juveniles were arrested—a disparity of one hundred to one.[101] As a result of "three strikes" laws, mandatory minimum sentences, and other drug enforcement tools, it is predicted that many young Black drug offenders, both male and female, will spend one-third or more of their lives in prison.[102]

Nationwide, 56 percent of drug offenders in state prisons are African-American.[103] In seven states, African-Americans constitute between 80 and 90 percent of all drug offenders sent to prison.[104] And, once released from prison, the punishment usually continues because former prisoners find it difficult, if not impossible, to obtain a job paying a decent wage capable of supporting a family. This eco-nomic instability inevitably leads to familial disruption. In addition, criminal convictions result in political disempowerment of the Black community because many states disenfranchise ex-felons. It is esti-mated that in some states over 40 percent of the next generation of Black people will permanently lose their right to vote.[105]

For over a decade, the United States war on drugs has been killing the Black community. If the drug laws were enforced against white people with the same level of enthusiasm and commitment as they are enforced against the Black community, the war would at least have an appearance of propriety. Instead, the government ignores the fact that racial disparities have been documented at every stage of the criminal justice system involving drug offenders. It overlooks studies indicating that Black people in similar circumstances with white people are more likely to be stopped by the police, and once stopped, arrested, charged, convicted, and sentenced to the harshest penalties.[106]

Claiming that the war on drugs is not intentionally racially motivated—despite mounting evidence—begs the question, "What is the government's responsibility in this war on drugs?" In criminal law, people who purposely avoid knowledge of certain facts are still deemed to be responsible for their actions.[107] For example, an individual who carries a suitcase full of explosives into an airport will be deemed guilty of possession of the explosives regardless of whether or not he claims that he had no idea what was in the suitcase. A finding of "guilt" is particularly likely when the individual has an opportunity to find out what is in the suitcase but fails to do so. Like the individual carrying the suitcase loaded with explosives, the United States government is also claiming innocence. It is burying its head in the sand and ignoring the fact that its drug policies are killing the Black community.

Government accountability is even more important in light of the fact that willful blindness is not the only "wrong" that this government has committed in its war on drugs. In 1999, two African-American women served as named plaintiffs in a class action suit filed in Los Angeles. The lawsuit, substantiated by three government reports, alleges that the CIA knew that its operatives and contacts were engaged in drug smuggling in Black and Latino communities in South Central Los Angeles and Compton, California, and did nothing to stop it.[108] Although government reports deny direct involvement by the CIA in the drug trade, the reports make it clear that officials at the State and Justice departments, the Drug Enforcement Administration (DEA), and the Immigration and

Naturalization Service (INS), granted special privileges to drug traffickers,[109] including some individuals who were working as CIA contacts. The reports also indicate that government agents even participated in arranging the illegal entery of drug traffickers into the United States.[110]

This type of action suggests that the government not only created drug policies that have had a disproportionate negative impact on the Black community but it suggests that the government knowingly allowed the creation of a drug distribution network in Black and Latino communities in order to fuel their racist war on drugs. Attempts to hold the government accountable for the racially targeted war on drugs such as the Los Angeles class action lawsuit[111] must therefore be supported by those of us who deplore racial injustice. As Human Rights Watch has pointed out,

> The racially disproportionate nature of the war on drugs is not just devastating to Black Americans. It contradicts faith in the principles of justice and equal protection of the laws that should be the bedrock of any constitutional democracy; it exposes and deepens the racial fault lines that continue to weaken the country and belies its promise as a land of equal opportunity.[112]

Although many supporters of the war on drugs have pointed out that the United States Constitution does not prohibit the government from enacting policies that have a disproportionate negative impact on the Black community,[113] international laws recognize that government policies which lead to racial disparities are a violation of human rights. Specifically, the International Convention on the Elimination of All Forms of Racial Discrimination (CERD), requires remedial action whenever there is an unjustifiable disparate impact upon a racial group. Under CERD, the actual intent of the government is irrelevant. What is important is the racial impact of the law. Consequently, CERD requires the United States government to act affirmatively in ending racially disproportionate policies. This is necessary not only because international law requires such action but because a failure to rectify the racial injustice created by the United States government's war on drugs undermines the overall fairness and efficacy of the criminal justice system in this country.[114] The government's claim of blindness to the racial injustice inherent in its drug policies is unacceptable. It is time for the American public to demand an end to this inhumane war based on human rights principles rather than the inadequate provisions of the United States Constitution.

1   John Hope Franklin, *From Slavery To Freedom: A History of African Americans* (New York: McGraw Hill, 1998); Herbert Aptheker, *American Negro Slave Revolts*, 5th ed., and Herbert Aptheker, *And Why Not Every Man: Documentary Story of the Fight Against Slavery in the US* (New York: International Publishers Company, 1983 and 1970, respectively).

2   Ibid.

3   Randall Kennedy, *Race, Crime and the Law* (New York: Pantheon Books, 1997), 30–35, 76–84.

4   Ibid., 82, 91.

5   Ibid., 128.

6   Fox Butterfield, "More in US Are in Prisons Report Says," *New York Times*, August 10, 1995, A14.

7   James Austin and John Irwin, *It's About Time: America's Imprisonment Binge* (Belmont, CA: Wadsworth Publishing Company, 1993), 163.

8   "Opium Problem; Message From the President," (Report to 61st Congress, 1910).

9   Edward Hunting Williams, "Negro Cocaine 'Fiends' Are a New Southern Menace," *New York Times*, February 8, 1914, sec. 5, 12.

10 Lynching had reached an all time high. In 1917, thirty-eight Blacks were lynched. By 1918, the number had risen to fifty-eight and a year later, after the war had ended, more than seventy lynchings were recorded. See Clarence Lusane, *Pipe Dream Blues: Racism and the War on Drugs* (Cambridge, MA: South End Press, 1991), 34–35. In 1919, during the Red Summer, twenty-five race riots exploded across the nation while the Ku Klux Klan grew from a small group of racists in the early 1910s to over 100,000 by the early 1920s.

11 William Elwood, *Rhetoric in the War on Drugs* (Westport, CT: Praeger, 1994), 41.

12 Lusane, *Pipe Dream Blues*, 67.

13 Ibid.

14 Ibid., 68.

15 George Bush, Address to the Nation on the National Drug Control Strategy (September 5, 1989), in *Public Papers of the Presidents of the United States: George Bush, 1989*, Book II (Washington, DC: US Government Printing Office, 1989), 1138.

16 Elwood, *Rhetoric in the War on Drugs*, 60 and 78. Elwood reviewed newspaper and magazine articles using key search words such as crime, drugs, drug use, drug user(s), drug war and narcotics from 1980 through March 1992.

17 Steven Donziger, *The Real War on Crime: The Report of the National Criminal Justice Commission* (New York: HarperPerennial Library, 1996). Also see Paul Butler, "(Color) Blind Faith: The Tragedy Of Race," *Harvard Law Review*, Vol. III (1998), 1270 and 1287, where he states, "People tend to find things for which they look. If the police concentrated their enforcement of drug laws at Harvard Law School (on the theory, say, that law enforcement is a public good and those students should enjoy much of it), the percentage of

Harvard law students under criminal justice supervision would rise appreciably."

18   According to the National Institute for Drug Abuse (NIDA), in 1990, out of the estimated 13 million drug users, 15 percent were African-American, 8 percent were Latino, and 77 percent were white. The percentage of drug use is relatively the same for each race. For African-Americans, Latinos, and whites, the figures are 8.65 percent, 6.2 percent, and 6.6 percent respectively. Despite this fact, 90 percent of prison admissions for drug offenses are African-American or Latino. Similarly, surveys conducted by the National Institute for Drug Abuse have found that African-Americans and whites use cocaine and marijuana at roughly the same rate, yet African-Americans suffer five times the number of arrests as whites for these drugs. Michael Tonry, *Malign Neglect: Race, Crime, and Punishment in America* (New York: Oxford University Press, 1996), 81.

19   Statement made by Drug Policy director William Bennett, appointed by President Bush, in *Intricate Web* (New York: General Board of Global Ministries, The United Methodist Church, 1990), 5.

20   PDFA defines itself as a "Non-profit, private sector coalition of volunteers from the advertising, public relations, production, research, and media industries." Its members consider themselves to be loyal soldiers who are "proud to be doing our part in this war." Partnership for Drug-Free America, informational brochure (New York: 1993), 24. Also see Elwood, *Rhetoric In the War on Drugs*, 83.

21   The most renowned commercial produced by Partnership For a Drug-Free America was the commercial that conveyed the message that drugs fry people's brains. As butter sizzles in a frying pan, the announcer shows an egg and states "This is your brain." After the egg is dropped in the pan and begins to fry, the announcer says, "This is your brain on drugs. Any questions?"

22   Elwood, *Rhetoric In the War on Drugs*, 81. Elwood reviewed a total of forty-five videos, twenty-five print and seventeen radio public service announcements, constituting a 35 percent sample of all public service announcements that the PDFA had produced.

23   Ibid.

24   Ibid., 89.

25   Ibid., 90.

26   K.L. Issokson-Silver, "New Creative: Slaves and Masters," Partnership Newsletter (New York: Partnership for a Drug-Free America, Fall 1990), 5.

27   Elwood, *Rhetoric In the War on Drugs*, 83.

28   Farai Chideya, *Don't Believe the Hype: Fighting Cultural Misinformation about African-Americans* (New York: Plume, 1995), 5.

29   In addition to the fact that nearly two-thirds of those arrested for property crimes were white, and over 50 percent of those arrested for violent crimes were white, over two-thirds (67.6 percent) of those arrested for all crimes in 1992 were white. Concomitantly, less than one-third (30.3 percent) were African-American. Department of Justice, "Crime in the United States,

1992" (Washington, DC: Government Printing Office, 1993), 235, Table 43. In 1999, the government reported that white people accounted for 59.2 percent of all violent crime arrests while Black arrests constituted 38.7 percent of all arrests. See also Samuel Walker, *The Color of Justice: Race, Ethnicity, and Crime in America* (Belmont, CA: Wadsworth Publishing Company, 1996), 39; Farai Chideya, *Don't Believe the Hype*, 198.

30 J. Sheley and C. Askins, "Crime, Crime News, and Crime Views," *Public Opinion Quarterly* (1981), 492.

31 Mark Fishman, "Crime Waves As Ideology," *Social Problems* (June 1978), cited in Jerome G. Miller, *Search and Destroy: African-American Males in the Criminal Justice System* (Cambridge; New York: Cambridge University Press, 1996), 154.

32 Ted Gest, Gordon Witkin, Katia Hetter, and Andrea Wright, "Violence in America," *US News & World Report* (January 17, 1994).

33 Ibid., 3.

34 Donziger, *The Real War on Crime*, 9. See also Sourcebook of Criminal Justice Statistics (Washington, DC: US Department of Justice, 1999), Table 4.10, reporting that only 4 percent of offenders arrested by federal law enforcement agencies were accused of committing violent crime whereas 30 percent of arrests were drug related.

35 Donziger, *The Real War on Crime*, 9.

36 D. Gilliard, *Prisoners in 1992*, NCJ-141874 (Washington, DC: US Department of Justice, 1993), Appendix, Table I, 10.

37 United States Department of Justice, "Federal Criminal Case Processing 1999," NCJ- 186180 (Washington, DC: February 2001), 1.

38 Katherine Greider, "Crackpot Ideas," *Mother Jones* (July/August 1995), 53–56.

39 When *60 Minutes* was called upon to account for these allegations, they claimed that legal considerations precluded them from identifying exactly which babies, if any, were cocaine exposed. Greider, "Crackpot Ideas," 55.

40 Cathy Trost, "Born to Lose: Babies of Crack Users Crowd Hospitals, Break Everybody's Heart," *Wall Street Journal*, July 18, 1989, A1; Rich Connell, "Hidden Devastation of Crack," *Los Angeles Times*, December 18, 1994, A1; Judith Kleinfeld, "Crack-Impaired Children Show Strange Behavior in School," *Anchorage Daily News*, February 20, 1995, B8.

41 Greider, "Crackpot Ideas," 53. See also Susan Fitzgerald, "Crack Baby Fears May Have Been Overstated: Children of Cocaine Abusing Mothers Are No Worse Off Than Others in Urban Poverty Study Says," *Washington Post*, September 16, 1997, Z10.

42 Cocaine increases the risk of low birth weight and premature delivery to roughly the same decrement attributable to cigarette smoking. Greider, "Crackpot Ideas," 54.

43 Melanie Fridl Ross, "UF Researchers: Study Yields New Hope for Cocaine Exposed Babies," *Friday Evening Post* (University of Florida, Health Science Center Communications), May 1, 1998.

44 Fitzgerald, "Crack Baby Fears May Have Been Overstated," Z10.

45   Dana Kennedy, "Crack Babies Catch Up," *Santa Cruz Sentinel,* December 6, 1992.

46   Suzanne D'Amico, "Inherently Female Cases of Child Abuse and Neglect: A Gender-Neutral Analysis, *Fordham Urban Law Journal,* Vol. 28, No. 855 (2001); Dana Hirschenbaum, "When Crack is The Only Choice: The Effect Of a Negative Right of Privacy on Drug Addicted Women, *Berkeley Women's Law Journal,* Vol. 15, No. 327 (2000); Antoinette Clark, "Fins, Pins, Chips & Chins: A Reasoned Approached To the Problem of Drug Use During Pregnancy," *Seton Hall Law Review,* Vol. 29, No. 634 (1998).

47   *Johnson vs. State,* 578 So. 2nd 419 (Florida District Court of Appeals, 1991).

48   *Johnson vs. State,* 578 So. 2nd 422.

49   Dorothy Roberts, *Killing the Black Body* (New York: Pantheon Books, 1997), 167.

50   Ibid., 164–167.

51   Ibid., 166.

52   Dorothy Roberts, "The Future of Reproductive Choice for Poor Women and Women of Color," *Women's Rights Law Reporter,* Vol. 14, No. 305 (Spring-Fall 1992) and *Killing the Black Body,* 194–201.

53   CRACK has reportedly disbanded due to "administrative disputes," but its volunteers have now formed a new organization with the same objectives. This organization is known as Project Prevention. See David Field, "Program Pays the Price of Pregnancy Prevention," *Seattle Post-Intelligencer,* December 4, 2000, www.seattlep-i.nwsource.com/local/preg04.shtml.

54   Judith Scully, "Cracking Open CRACK: Unethical sterilization movement gains momentum," *Different Takes* (Amherst, MA: Population and Development Program at Hampshire College, Spring 2000).

55   Hirschenbaum, "When Crack is the Only Choice."

56   Adam Wolf, "What Money Cannot Buy: A Legislative Response to CRACK," *University of Michigan Journal of Law* (Fall 1999 and Winter 2000).

57   Ibid.

58   See www.cashforbirthcontrol.com (section on statistics).

59   Jeffrey Reiman, *The Rich Get Richer and the Poor Get Prison* (Boston, MA: Allyn and Bacon, 1990), 45.

60   Donziger, *The Real War on Crime,* 167; Human Rights Reports, "Shielded From Justice: Police Brutality and Accountability in the US" (1998), available at www.hrw.org/hrw/reports98/police/toc.htm. See also Erwin Chemerinsky, "An Independent Analysis of the Los Angeles Police Department," www.usc.edu/dept/law/faculty/chemerinsky/rampart_exec summ.html.

61   Eric Pooley, "New York's Untouchables," Special Report, (New York: New York Police Department, 1994), 17, cited in Donziger, *The Real War on Crime,* 164.

62   Donziger, *The Real War on Crime,* 164.

63   Pooley, "New York's Untouchables," 117.

64   Donziger, *The Real War on Crime,* 164.

65   The Mollen Commission found that the most common form of police corruption was the falsification of police records and testimony. Several officers told the Mollen Commission that the practice was so widespread in certain precincts that officers created a name for it: testilying. To explain how they got around the law to make an arrest, officers stated that they simply made up facts. Donziger, *The Real War on Crime*, 36.

66 "Commission to Investigate Allegations of Police Corruption and the Anti-Corruption Procedures for the Police Department," The City of New York, Commission Report 1–2 (1994).

67 Donziger, *The Real War on Crime*, 167.

68 Human Rights Reports, "Shielded From Justice."

69 Ibid.

70 Ibid.; Bill Moushey, Special Report, 10-part series on government misconduct in the name of expedient justice, *Pittsburgh Post Gazette*, www.post-gazette.com/win/.

71 For a detailed discussion of the "get tough on crime" movement see Donziger, *The Real War on Crime*.

72 See Floyd Witherspoon, "The Devastating Impact of the Justice System on the Status of African-American Males: An Overview Perspective," *Capital University Law Review*, Vol. 23., No. 23 (1994). See also Jerome Miller, *Search and Destroy: African American Males in the Criminal Justice System* (Cambridge: Cambridge University Press, 1996).

73 Eric E. Sterling, "Drug Laws and Snitching: A Primer," available at www.pbs.org/wgbh/pages/frontline/shows/snitch/primer; Ofra Bikel, "Snitch," transcript of *Frontline* #1709, air date January 12, 1999, available at www.pbs.org/wgbh/pages/frontline/shows/snitch/etc/script.html; Jane Froyd, "Safety Valve Failure: Low-Level Drug Offenders and the Federal Sentencing Guidelines," *Northwestern University Law Review*, Vol. 99, No. 1471 (Summer 2000).

74 Ibid.

75 Ibid.

76 Chi Chi Sileo, "Sentencing Rules That Shackle Justice," *Insight* (December 6, 1993), 11.

77 "Mandatory Sentencing is Criticized by Justice," *New York Times*, March 10, 1994, A22.

78 William Jefferson Clinton, "My Reasons for the Pardons," *New York Times*, February 18, 2001.

79 California Legislative Analyst's Office, "The Three Strikes and You're Out Law—A Preliminary Assessment" (1995).

80 Ibid.

81 The data presented by the Los Angeles Public Defender's Office was based on the first six months of actual experience with California's "three strikes" law. Vincent Shiraldi and Michael Godfrey, Center on Juvenile and Criminal Justice (government report), "Racial Disparities in the Charging of Los Angeles County's 'Third Strike' Cases" (1994).

82 See David Cole, *No Equal Justice: Race and Class in the American Criminal Justice System* (New York: New Press, 1999), 143–144. In March 1995, the Georgia

Supreme Court ruled in *Stephens vs. State*, that these statistics represented a prima facie case of discrimination and required the prosecutors to explain the disparity. Instead, all forty-six of the state's prosecutors signed a petition asking the Court to reconsider their decision. The petition warned that the Court's approach was a "substantial step toward invalidating" the death penalty and would "paralyze the criminal justice system" because racial disparities in other areas would also have to be explained. Thirteen days later, the Georgia Supreme Court reversed itself, and held that the statistics did not establish discrimination and therefore no justification would be required. *Stephens vs. State*, 456 S.E.2nd 560 (1995).

83   Public Law No. 99–570, Stat. 100, 3207 (1986).

84   Ibid.

85   Kennedy, *Race, Crime and the Law*, 364.

86   Ibid., 364-365.

87   House of Representatives Report Number 104–272, (1995), 335 and 353 (citing US Sentencing Commission study).

88   See 1999 Sourcebook of Federal Sentencing Statistics, Table 34.

89   Of those reporting crack use in the same year, 52 percent were white, 38 percent were black, and 10 percent were Latino. The 1991 NIDA survey indicated that 75 percent of those reporting cocaine use were white, 15 percent black, and 10 percent Latino. See Table 4.4 in "1993 National Household Survey on Drug Abuse: Main Findings," (Substance Abuse and Mental Health Services Adminstration, Department of Health and Human Services Publication No. 93–1980, 1991), 58. Also see "Special Report to Congress and Federal Sentencing Policy," (US Sentencing Commission, February 1995), 38, 39, and 161 (Table 13), indicating that the majority of crack cocaine is consumed by white people. Similarly in 1998, the National Household Survey on Drug Abuse (NHSDA) estimated that almost three times as many whites had ever used crack as blacks. Among those who had used crack at least once in the past year, 462,000 were white and 324,000 were black. US Department of Health and Human Services, Substance Abuse and Mental Health Services Administration (SAMHSA), "Prevalence of Substance Use Among Racial and Ethnic Subgroups in the United States," (Washington, DC, 1998).

90   Dorothy Hatsukami and Marian Fischman, "Crack Cocaine and Cocaine Hydrochloride: Are the Differences Myth or Reality?" *Journal of the American Medical Association* (November 20, 1996), 1580–1588. Also see Christopher Wren, "Study Poses a Medical Challenge to Disparity In Cocaine Sentences," *New York Times*, November 20, 1996, A1.

91   United States Sentencing Commission, "Special Report to the Congress: Cocaine and Federal Sentencing Policy," *Criminal Law Reporter* (Washington, DC: Bureau of National Affairs, May 7, 1997), Vol. 61, No. 6, 2073; Nkechi Taifa, "Reflections from the Front Lines," *Federal Sentencing Reporter*, 10.4 (January/February 1998), 201.

92   *State vs. Russell*, (Minnesota, 1991).

93   Several judges, including Judge Jack B. Weinstein of Brooklyn and Judge

Whitman Knapp of Manhattan, have refused to handle any more drug cases; US District Judge Stanley S. Harris and Circuit Court Judge Audrey Melbourne of Maryland have noted the devastating impact of the mandatory minimums in their sentencing hearings; and Judge Alan Nevas, appointed by President Reagan, remarked that the mandatory minimum sentences for crack cocaine are the "unfairest sentences I have ever had to impose." "Powder Cocaine vs. Crack Cocaine: Balanced Justice?," *USA Today*, May 26, 1993, cited in Donziger, *The Real War on Crime*, 291. Federal Judge Lyle Strom of Omaha ruled that African-Americans convicted in crack cases "are being treated unfairly because they receive substantially longer sentences than Caucasian males who deal primarily in cocaine. *United States vs. Majied* (Nebraska, July 29, 1993).

94   Ibid.
95   Human Rights Watch, "Report on Punishment and Prejudice: Racial Disparities in the War on Drugs" (New York: June 2000).
96   Ibid. at "Section III. Incarceration and Race."
97   Ibid.
98   Ibid., chapter 1. See also Mary Frances Berry, "The Forgotten Prisoners of a Disastrous War," *Essence* (October 1999), 194; Marc Mauer and Tracy Huling, "Young Black Americans and the Criminal Justice System: Five Years Later" (October 1995), 19–20, reporting a 828 percent increase from 1986 until 1991.
99   Barbara Bloom and David Steinhart, "Why Punish the Children?: A Reappraisal of the Children of Incarcerated Mothers in America" (Oakland, CA: National Council on Crime and Delinquency, 1993), 15.
100 John Irwin and James Austin, *It's About Time*," 163.
101 Eric Lotke, Nonanal Center on Institutions and Alternatives, "Hobbling a Generation: Young African American Men in DC's Criminal Justice System of American Cities " (Baltimore, Marylnad: September 1992).
102 The Sentencing Project's Briefing/Fact Sheet, "Why '3 Strikes and You're Out' Won't Reduce Crime," (n.d). Also see "Drug Policy and the Criminal Justice System," available at www.sentencingproject.org/brief/drugs.pdf.
103 Bureau of Justice Statistics, "Prisoners in 1998."
104 Human Rights Watch, "Report on Punishment and Prejudice," 1.
105 In seven states, 25 percent of African-American men are permanently barred from casting a ballot. In two states—Florida and Alabama—nearly one-third of all African-American men cannot vote. See Human Rights Watch and Sentencing Project report, "Losing the Vote: The Impact of Felony Disenfranchisement Laws in the United States" (1998).
106 "Developments in the Law—Race and the Criminal Process," *Harvard Law Review*, Vol. 101, 1473 (1988).
107 See Wayne LaFave and Austin Scott, Jr., "Willful Blindness," *Criminal Law*, (1986), 218–220.
108 *Donna Warren and Berlina M. Doss vs. Central Intelligence Agency, United States Department of Justice, Estate of William Casey, Robert Gates, John Deutch, George Tenet, Estate of William French Smith, Edwin Meese, Richard Thornburgh, Janet*

Reno, and Does I-XXX, Complaint filed in the United States District Court, Central District of California on March 15, 1999.

109 Ibid.

110 Ibid. See also Gary Webb, *Dark Alliance: The CIA, the Contras and the Crack Cocaine Explosion* (New York: Seven Stories Press, 1998).

111 *Donna Warren and Berlina M. Doss vs. Central Intelligence Agency.*

112 Human Rights Watch, "Report on Punishment and Prejudice."

113 The United States Supreme Court has held that racial disparities in law enforcement are constitutional as long as they are not undertaken with discriminatory intent. See *US vs. Armstrong*, (1996); *McClesky vs. Kemp*, (1987).

114 Human Rights Watch, "Report on Punishment and Prejudice."

Chapter 3

Speaking Out Against State Violence

Activist HIV-Positive Women Prisoners Redefine Social Justice

Cynthia Chandler and Carol Kingery

Society works backwards a lot. It lets your dad send you to school with black eyes and your husband lock you up in an institution when you're fourteen because he's leaving town and doesn't trust you. But society wants you to live up to its rules.

> —Rosemary Willeby, prisoner and HIV peer educator, one month before dying of liver disease at the Central California Women's Facility in Chowchilla, California in 1999. She was serving a five-year sentence for a nonviolent crime.

An activist is somebody who will fight and stand against all odds to win rights for others. I have been an activist on the inside. Being positive and being put in a group of people who are labeled unsafe makes me fight harder. I have been treated with prejudice because I question "Why?" I am harassed because of my demands for answers.

> —Theresa Martinez, HIV peer advocate and prisoner activist.

This article documents the opinions and experiences of HIV-positive women prisoner activists in order to develop a progressive anti-violence strategy aimed at increasing the safety of women and to challenge the expansion of the prison industrial complex. Rhetoric of public safety, justice, and victims' rights is regularly used by the political right to justify increasing imprisonment and the widening net of the criminal justice system policies regularly targeted at people of color. As a result, the United States has the highest imprisonment rate in the world,[1] imprisoning a disproportionate number of poor people of color. This disparate policy of imprisonment is resulting in the destruction of families and entire communities.

Yet with the only discourse on safety being offered by the political right, impoverished communities suffering from high crime rates are forced to rely on this same paradigm in their own search for safety. Such communities are plagued both by victimization and community fragmentation that results from increased imprisonment. As a consequence, there is a need for a strategy of social justice that addresses disenfranchised communities' needs for safety, but that does not contribute to their destruction.

The need for such a strategy is particularly pressing when fighting sexist violence against women of color. In order to resist the oppression of women of color, it is essential to acknowledge, resist, and respond to both individual and systemic acts of violence against them. Unless these efforts simultaneously challenge and resist current discriminatory discourses and institutions of safety and justice, they will only serve to strengthen the racism and classism of our current criminal justice system that labels people of color—particularly Latino and African-American men—as criminals. Progressive members of anti-violence movements must develop ways to acknowledge and respond to violence in the lives of women of color without relying upon or strengthening conservative political rhetoric and policies that target and destroy communities of color.[2]

This article is a collaborative effort toward developing an alternative progressive discourse on safety and justice that resists increasing imprisonment and instead offers community-based individualized interventions as positive solutions to crime. As staff of Justice Now,[3] a nonprofit organization based in Oakland, California, providing legal services, community education, and prisoner activist support, we asked HIV-positive women prisoner activists to share their experiences both with surviving violent crime in and out of the prison setting and with the criminal justice system. In particular, we asked women prisoners how they define justice and safety, how and if the current criminal justice system should be included in a strategy of social justice and violence prevention, and what role activism can play in galvanizing social change.

Their experiences and perceptions reveal the particular vulnerability of women to ill health, violence, imprisonment, poverty, racism, and sexism. Further, the pervasive and continuous nature of violence in their lives testifies to the connection between systemic and individual acts of violence and discrimination. They challenge imprisonment as a solution to violence, particularly violence against women, and instead show that state-sanctioned acts of racism, misogyny, and classism within the current paradigm of imprisonment serve to perpetuate violence and enforce the repression and submission of those who try to resist abuses of authority. In their call for positive, individualized, community-based solutions to crime, prisoner activists serve as role models in the fight for a more effective and empowering method of social justice. They challenge those of us in the free world to have the courage to join them in their struggle to resist injustice.

Methodology

This piece relies heavily on the testimony of three HIV-positive women prisoner activists: Brandy, Davara, and Rebecca, clients of Justice Now.[4] Justice Now was created with the goal of ending the suffering of women prisoners and challenging the prison industrial complex. Because it is a legal office, volunteers and staff are able to visit prisoners on legal, rather than social visits. On a legal visit, visitors are allowed to have legal documents, paper, and pens. It is with these allowances that we are able to bring educational and activist materials to prisoners and record women's experiences and thoughts on prison and health care issues. As stronger alliances with particular women prisoners developed, it became clear to us how invaluable their experiences and insights are to a more complete understanding of imprisonment, justice, safety, and health. This piece is an attempt to honor this contribution to a progressive dialogue on violence against women.

Women, Imprisonment, HIV-Infection, and Resistance

The community of HIV-positive women prisoners has been acutely and uniquely affected by both victimization and increasing imprisonment. The dramatic increase in imprisonment in the United States has been accompanied by epidemic rates of HIV among prisoners.[5] Moreover, women currently imprisoned in the United States suffer disproportionately higher rates of HIV infection than free people and male prisoners.[6] Imprisoned women and HIV-positive women share many of the same demographic characteristics.[7] Both are overwhelmingly women of color struggling with poverty and addiction.[8] The vast majority have histories of being abused sexually and in other ways.[9] Linked to all of these risk factors are conditions of disempowerment created through poverty, racism, and sexism that heighten the susceptibility of women to victimization, imprisonment, and life-threatening disease.[10]

The United States has the highest imprisonment rate in the world,[11] with women comprising the fastest growing prison and jail population.[12] While women comprise approximately 17 percent of the prisoner population, the number of women in prison has more than tripled since 1980, nearly double the rate of increase among men.[13] The increase in the women's prison population does not reflect an increase in violent crimes.[14] Rather, it is directly tied to the disenfranchisement of women of color reflected in the war on drugs, poverty, and the abuse of women generally.

The vast majority of women prisoners, 92 percent in federal prison and 68 percent in state prisons, are serving time for nonviolent property or drug offenses.[15] Of the few women who are imprisoned for violent offenses, the vast majority are imprisoned for defensive or retaliatory crimes against abusive partners.[16] Women's own victimization often leads directly to their entanglement in the criminal justice system. Moreover, the increased imprisonment of women, particularly for nonviolent offenses, is directly linked to an increased intolerance for, or outcasting of, poor communities of color.[17] Although women of color comprise only 26.2 percent of the female population in the United States,[18] they comprise nearly two-thirds of imprisoned women.[19] Six out of ten women prisoners had not been employed full-time prior to their arrest.[20]

In addition to facing an increased risk of imprisonment, poor women have extremely limited access to preventive health care in the United States.[21] As a result, it is not surprising that women entering prison have a high incidence of serious heath concerns, including HIV/AIDS. Women prisoners suffer disproportionately high HIV rates as compared to both the general population[22] and male prisoners.[23] The high incidence of HIV among women prisoners can be explained by several factors, many of which are the same factors that put women at risk of imprisonment: being of color in a racist society,[24] poverty, intravenous drug use,[25] and histories of sexual and physical abuse that can also lead to drug dependency as a coping mechanism.[26] Once imprisoned, HIV-positive women face serious medical neglect and discrimination.[27] These abuses reflect the further vulnerability of disenfranchised people within a retributory prison system.

Public health research has shown that the greatest risk factor for HIV infection is belonging to a marginalized and disenfranchised cultural group. Societal discrimination directly undermines and interferes with education, prevention, and care.[28] The current situation in the United States strongly reflects this trend as impoverished women of color who face the additional disenfranchisement of imprisonment are at significantly heightened risk of HIV infection. They are also arguably one of the groups least able to protect themselves against a widening net of imprisonment or human rights abuses within the prison industrial complex.

Reflecting the demographics of HIV-positive women prisoners, the three prisoners featured in this piece are all women of color,[29] all come from poor families, all are survivors of violence as children and adults, and all were sentenced to four or more years of prison time in California for nonviolent crimes. Additionally, just as 80 percent of women prisoners are mothers,[30] all three women are mothers. Through personal experience, they have witnessed how our criminal justice system devastates families and entire communities. Importantly, like many HIV-positive women in California's state prisons, they also self-identify as activists.

Since the late 1980s, HIV-positive women have led organizing efforts among California prisoners resisting human rights abuses within prisons. Despite the fact that organizing among prisoners is prohibited and highly risky, they have courageously fought for their own rights, as well as the rights of other prisoners to access basic medical care and treatment education. Activist HIV-positive women prisoners grapple with disempowerment in the most extreme environment. Prisons function by attempting to reduce individuals to prisoner identification numbers or "inmates." The institutionalization of the individual increases the level and depth of control that the correctional staff can have over the population. Activist prisoners work incessantly to create a space for empowerment in an environment designed to eliminate it. Activist prisoners realize that resistance is essential to survival in prison and eventually on the outside.

Reaching Across Barriers to Find Solutions

When proposing to record women prisoners' experiences and insights, we needed a strategy that would not further exploit the struggles and suffering of women prisoners and that would give the prisoners we worked with a sense of co-ownership over the product we collectively produced. In prison, privacy and choice are rare. As free people, it is easy to use our inherent power to the detriment of the prisoners. And our freedom is not the only divide or privilege separating us from the women we are working with. We (Carol and Cynthia) are both Caucasian, from upper-middle-class backgrounds, and educated at elite institutions. Neither of us has been imprisoned. We are both HIV-negative. Neither of us, at the time of writing this piece, were mothers. We are both under age 35, roughly the same age as Rebecca, but a generation younger than Davara and Brandy.

In order to begin addressing these differences, all parties involved were conscious of, and tried to keep in the foreground, the differences between us. Above all, the differences were respected by all of us since it is precisely the unique, albeit often tragic, experiences of women prisoners with HIV that form the basis of their expertise in discussing criminal justice reforms. The women prisoners were treated as the experts, the educators. We (Carol and Cynthia) were there to learn from them. The women prisoners justifiably had confidence in the fact that their unique experiences informed their understanding and knowledge of the prison industrial complex, and rendered them the experts.

> Being HIV positive is not essential to how I form my views, but there is some influence of HIV on my views on the application of the criminal justice system. It comes to mind when considering the physical aspects of health and degeneration. Oftentimes the severity of a prison term is more magnified because you don't know how your health is going to be maintained—contemplating the effect stress has on the immune system and having the experience of losing 300 T-cells in a thirty-day period and knowing your time could result in a death sentence.[31]

The experience and perspective of HIV-positive women prisoners is unique, and thus deserves attention.

Yet we were all also aware that our differences created barriers to documenting women's histories. Our varied experiences created language gaps and power differentials. Again, we tried to approach these issues openly. At times, we handled our differences with humor. For example, when asked by Carol whether our lack of common backgrounds and experiences affected the way in which we communicated or expressed our thoughts, Brandy replied,

> No. I mean, we've got an age gap, a freedom gap, a race gap, a monetary gap. The only thing we have in common is alcohol and men. I don't even know where your parents got you at. Upon first meeting someone like you, automatically there are defenses that go up. But I also know that if you interact and communicate realistically barriers come down. When you establish lines of communication, there are no more barriers.[32]

Davara also mixed sarcasm with her comments on working with white women with privileges:

> I love white women from privileged backgrounds. This is not my first experience working with white women, you know. I grew up in a community, attended schools of white girls with privileged backgrounds. It pleases me that they take an interest. Motivated with applied energy, intellect, and concerns to make a difference, bridging gaps and challenging inhumane mistreat-

ments, and having concerns for those seemingly in a state of oppression and unjustly condemned.[33]

Despite the awkward humor, in our discussion there was a common theme that it is both valuable and viable to develop respectful
communication across barriers. Cross-racial/class/sex/health collaboration is essential to a broader movement against our current regime of imprisonment and our retributory punishment system.

> Issues of "difference" and "privilege" are very important to me,
> not "academic." It would be nice if people who were in posi-
> tions of power, like police, judges, District Attorneys, people
> who secure society, would help advocate and participate. Why
> can't these people come speak out and advocate? It would have
> an impact if people rallied, got involved. You don't have to tell
> them that it's okay to drink, to do drugs. When the police see
> something that's wrong, an inequality that's just not right, why
> can't they do something about it? Society should not rely only
> on people who are not in the positions of power. Why, when
> you are a police officer and you know something is wrong, why
> can't you advocate for it to be right? Like at Corcoran, why don't
> they say what happened to Tate was wrong?[34] When they do,
> they say they are a "whistle blower." Why don't people say "It's
> Wrong!"? People don't stand up. I don't have a problem with
> people that donate their time and energy, regardless of their race
> or background. I don't think most people would have a problem
> with it. More men should participate. It's usually women who
> get up and stand in the line. Men should stand up. People of
> color should get involved. This will be my next profession.[35]

In order to develop a collaborative process for this history project, we spent many visits devising a publishing contract with the
women involved in the project. The contract includes choices of
pen name, the protection of named individuals, space for prisoners
to acknowledge their affiliations with activist organizations (including prisoner activist organizations that are prohibited under
California law), and the designation of any profits which might ac-
crue from the publishing of any aspect of their life stories.

Each woman also has absolute editorial power over the final
content of any published piece in which they are involved. Addi-

tionally, our editing process was developed to encourage maximum participation and ownership by all participants. We talked with women prisoners about some of the themes we were interested in discussing and got feedback and suggestions. From these discussions, we generated several open-ended questions and gave these questions to the women to think over. Some of the women, such as Rebecca, wrote out lengthy answers to the questions.

Others, such as Brandy, preferred for us to conduct more formal interviews that resembled dictation sessions. The women were also encouraged to decide for themselves whether they wanted to talk about their own lives or about their philosophies or social analysis. In all cases, large amounts of collective editing occurred—we worked with each woman individually to come up with quotes that accurately reflected their ideas. Once we incorporated their quotes into an article, they were given copies of the article and were encouraged to edit the article thoroughly. We worked until a consensus as to the thesis and contents was met, and all women retained the power to withdraw any and all of their ideas and thoughts from any article at any time.

Voice and language choice were also the subjects of much discussion. Women have diverse opinions of, and ownership over, particular titles or labels ascribed to themselves and people in their stories. In particular, most women we interviewed referred to themselves as "prisoners" as opposed to "inmates," viewing "inmate" as connoting submission or institutionalization. However, Rebecca prefers to call herself an inmate rather than a prisoner because she believes it is a more honest depiction of her institutionalized status: "I have been a member of this closed society for most of my life."[36] The appropriation and redefining of institutional language is an important marker of the space women have created in which to represent themselves. "OG" or "original-gangster" and "convict" describe a particular woman and the way she has served her time rather than the criminalization of a person or a gang label. Additionally, there are segments of women's stories that provide examples of violence perpetuating bigotry and hatred by the interviewees. We have not altered the language or context of these accounts, in order to preserve the integrity of the women's voices.

The Normative Nature of Safety and Justice

Before arguing for alternatives to our current system of criminal justice, we first need to understand the extent to which our current system is failing to provide safety and justice to highly vulnerable people, particularly to women of color. The vast majority of women prisoners have been the victims of violent crimes that have gone unpunished and unacknowledged by either their communities or broader society. In contrast, the vast majority of women prisoners are serving prison terms for nonviolent offenses. This discrepancy illustrates how disenfranchised women lack almost any recourse for justice or fairness within our criminal justice system. Moreover, it makes visible the normative power-laden nature of justice.

Women prisoners regularly acknowledge that justice and access to safety are privileges they hardly enjoy. When asked if she could define or give an example of "safety," Rebecca replied with sarcasm, "What is safety? I looked it up in the dictionary because I wasn't exactly sure. I looked up 'justice' too. Webster describes safety as: free from danger, security, protective device or a football back in the deepest position."[37] Davara articulates that disempowerment is perpetuated by this culture, which embraces the inequities of poverty, racism, and sexism in its institutions; and that within this culture, the disenfranchised have no access to safety or justice:

> Not to misappropriate individual responsibility, but we need to recognize the foundation of "Justice for all"—how, why, and what brought about our country. The United States was founded on criminal intent: taking the Native Americans' land; kidnapping, enslaving various groups of people to work and build a nation; the father of our country being the "white male" "fair minded" orchestrator of our government or society, and "other" being a second-class citizen subject to rape, oppression, and capitalism. This criminal hierarchy may be inherently violent depending on the "other's" ability or desire to submit.
>
> I fail to truly accept that our judicial "justice" system is of a solid motivation to protect anyone other than the undisclosed perverted, authoritative, politically disguised, financially secure male. Yes, the criminal justice system could service and understand our (my) needs, if political influences were not the issue.

Today, Justice is bought and sold, fluctuating by economics for those who may or may not be able to afford appetites. Laws are legislated for or by a financially privileged group. Also "who you know" and "money talks" dictate where and what type of incarceration one endures. A corrupt system such as ours is not about safety or justice, especially not for people of color, women, people with HIV or other illnesses.[38]

Our current regime is failing to provide safety and justice to women who arguably have the least access to our democracy. This failure is inextricably linked to the racism, classism, and sexism forming the basis of our institutions of justice. Moreover, this failure highlights the need to create new methods of social justice for addressing the problem of sexist violence, particularly against women of color.

Social Power and the Perpetuation of Individual Acts of Violence

The inequities that underlie both our society's failure to protect the vulnerable and the disproportionate imprisonment of socially disenfranchised people also inform the cycle of individual victimization and participation in acts of violence. As prejudice and discrimination provide vulnerable targets of violence, they also add to the emotions and needs that contribute to individual acts of violence. Our system of justice fails to protect the powerless, and actively aggravates an environment of discrimination that increases the likelihood of victimization and the propensity for violence among the disenfranchised. It is antithetical to the safety of the underprivileged.

The dichotomous relationship between victim and perpetrator disintegrates when we explore the lives of women prisoners. Brandy candidly explains how innumerable experiences of abuse and victimization culminated with one final act of extreme torture that triggered her own violent crimes:

> I picked the same type of men my mom had. Dad held her, controlled her. I said that no one would do that to me. But at eighteen years old, the man gave me heroin. I was in business college. The dope man was the ticket, God, daddy. When I met him, he would say "Why are you in school? You're not learning

anything." He stuck a needle in my arm when things got bad. But soon he was picked up. When he went, so did the supply. A friend said, "You want it, you suck my dick for it." I stole, snatched a purse to pay for it. Eventually I became a prostitute to pay for the dope.

Prostitution was horrible. Pimps taking your money, telling you what to do with it. I wanted to stay loaded in order to keep doing it. I got into cars with strangers. A man picked me up one night and took me home. He had lye in the bathtub. I could either do what he said or try to jump out of his third story window, or he'd burn my face in the lye. He put a coat hanger around my neck and told me to bark like a dog while he sodomized me. He kept me for two or three days before he let me go. Eventually I got to not feel anything.

In 1982 I went to cop some dope in an apartment complex where wetbacks lived. I brought some white women there to turn tricks. I was dressed like a guy, as a pimp, to tell them what they can do. A guy shows me a $100 bill. I go into his apartment. The lights went out, I got hit in the back of the head. Fifteen guys lived there. They hog-tied and blindfolded me and put me in the closet for two weeks. They sodomized me and did everything else for two weeks. I believed they would kill me. A 15-year-old kid from Mexico, the houseboy who didn't work or go to school finally let me go. I stayed in the hospital one month after the boy let me go. I didn't call the cops; I said nothing. I went back two months later. That was my first armed robbery. I did it on my own. It led to a series of fifty robberies. I hurt people, beat them with crowbars. I did it to wetbacks, males. I didn't just take money; I hit somebody. I targeted houses with groups of wetback men. It was my campaign to pay them back for what they did to me. It almost got me killed. The rage.[39]

Brandy did not go to the police; they offered no possibility of relief or safety to her. Her lifestyle and survival as she saw it would discredit her before an institution created for the protection of the privileged. Yet there was no other alternative positive form of social justice on which she could rely. Instead, her pain turned to hatred and rage. Victimization of one member of a dispossessed group perpetuated violence against other minorities.

Brandy took an enormous risk agreeing to expose her own racism and violence. As America has become a society based no longer on social welfare, but on crime control, the criminalization of many populations is needed to explain how unsafe America has become and to justify increased reliance on imprisonment. Admitting that she has played a role in the perpetuation of "un-safety" puts Brandy in a more vulnerable position. She could be used to justify and advance the practice of building bigger and "better" prisons. Brandy risked harsh judgment in order to be part of this histories project as a way to promote positive solutions to violence and to resist further perpetuation of violence and hatred. Her experience illustrates how the cycle of victimization and acts of violence are perpetuated by society's ineffective response to the vulnerable; and how the failure to protect vulnerable individuals in turn contributes to the continued subjugation and abuse of others in their own communities.

Prisons as State Violence Against the Powerless

Many people in the free world view prison as a physical barrier to violence that ensures safety. Yet violence does not cease in prison. Discrimination in the current punishment system is omnipresent and is used to emotionally and physically cripple and brutalize prisoners. Rather than eliminating violence, prisons perpetuate violence against the disenfranchised and serve as state sanctioned venues for violence and discrimination in order to control and subjugate those within their walls.

Women prisoners suffer unique forms of brutality surrounding female sexuality and reproductive capacity, which mirror, yet exaggerate, systemic misogyny in the free world. Our clients often report such forms of state-sanctioned violence or control following the discovery of their HIV-positive status—as if they are being punished for being "dirty," "diseased" women. Rebecca vividly recollects the sexist violence she encountered.

> When I was first tested for HIV, I was in a co-ed county jail. I was tested after my son, Michael, died shortly after birth. When Michael was unplugged from life support machines, I was taken to a mental health unit in the men's ward. They put me in a suicide watch room with a glass wall out to the hallway. They took away my clothes. I had no blankets. They tied me down in

4-point restraints with my hands and legs out—with no clothes.[40] I never said I was suicidal or acted out! They were supposed to ask if I needed to go to the bathroom, but they didn't for 72 hours. I was just quiet and tried to sleep. But I was wet and the air conditioner was on. I was freezing. Everyone going by could see me naked. They would let the male inmates out to work and they could see me naked! I wasn't suicidal; they did this because I had AIDS.[41]

Women prisoners also experience racial and sexual forms of systemic control through abuses of their reproductive rights. One of our white clients was denied access to an abortion while imprisoned and was forced to give birth to a child she did not want. Other women, particularly women of color, have experienced forced sterilization. Davara reports a systemic environment of sexual abuse within women's prisons that reached a crisis for her when she was forced to escape from prison in order to avoid forced sterilization.

Currently, I am sexually assaulted on a daily basis. "Pat Searches" whet the hands and appetites of corrections officers as they fondle my breasts and genitals. I had to escape prison once to avoid being forced to undergo an unnecessary unwanted hysterectomy. In the 1970s I was suffering severe menstrual cramps and a tilted uterus. As a young woman in the criminal justice system serving a life sentence complicated by medical female "disorders" and subject to misdiagnoses by questionable, unprofessional, unethical medical personnel, it was recommended I have a hysterectomy. I was maybe 20 years old. Having some enlightenment about genocide, I felt that the prospect of my being able to have a family was being threatened, so I escaped from prison to have a child. I had a son. He is now 28 years old and I have four grandchildren who I would not have if I had given up my rights. Any imposition upon reproductive rights is an injustice against the well-being of family units—the rights of women, children, and grandchildren, or the promise of the future.[42]

The control of women's bodies and reproduction allows the state the ultimate control and power over disempowered communities—the power to control their destinies.

Resilience in the Face of State Violence

Despite living with long histories of abuse and violence, and surviving in an institution aimed at their repression, the prisoners we work with maintain a sense of dignity that can only inspire those around them to join in their struggle. As activists, they are constantly aware of the mechanisms utilized by the prison to tear down their sense of hope and community. In the face of unceasing adversity, they persevere.

In order to educate others, activist prisoners have to be "out there" to other prisoners and staff. Strength of character is seen as a threat to the security of the institution by most correctional staff. As a result, activist prisoners suffer severe retaliation when speaking out. Rebecca articulates her call to activism and its costs:

> We need to be activists against state violence—stopping misogyny and disagreements between races, stopping prejudice and acts of violence by guards who push or hit inmates or leave them in situations where harm will come to them. We must give factual accounts to people on the outside, those who have voices, thus bringing light to the problems both inside and out.
>
> Being an activist means getting incremental changes in a system, caring more about the rights of others, and having the courage to stand up against a system regardless of the consequences. To be an activist in prison you need to talk to and for people who don't have a voice or the courage to talk in front of others. You have to find out what the problems are, pass on the information to others, yell real loud, and don't be afraid of what might happen to you.
>
> I've been punished for being an activist. I've become close to a lot of people who have died. I have been threatened by a prison's chief medical officer that he'd commit me to a mental hospital and no one could do anything about it. When people think you're crazy, you have no voice at all. I've been put in isolation, and have been forced to take toxic medications that I didn't need. Other people with HIV are not treated like that.[43]

Rebecca has been subjected to many more acts of retaliation by correctional staff since we interviewed her in 1999. She was eventually transferred to a different prison away from her group of peers and outside support. Now at a prison outside of Los Angeles, Rebecca has worked her way into the institution's HIV peer education program where she continues to fight for her fellow prisoners.

Davara also finds that activism within the prison, while essential, is inseparable from the risk of retaliation by staff:

> It is imperative that we speak out against the injustices of our country, our society, that extend to our prisons. As a group, imprisoned women are activist in some category or other—as mothers, singles, wives, minorities, etc. An activist is being open and stimulated to prevail in exposing, enlightening, sharing, and correcting. But when you speak out against the state, you are punished by the paranoid system by being subject to loss of mail (your connection with family and community), broken or defaced property, exploitation, or being lied upon or framed.[44]

Activist prisoners' ability to imagine a better world and inspire hope is a gift to those of us seeking social change and to all who will benefit from it. It is precisely within women prisoners' spirit of collective resistance that one can locate the origins of an alternative model of social justice.

Models of Collective Justice and Safety

Part of women prisoners' resiliency is their ability to imagine alternative modes of safety and justice. While women prisoners recognize the normative nature of, and their inability to access, safety and justice within our current punishment system, they maintain the ability to envision more inclusive alternatives. Interestingly, they do not fall into the ideological trap of relying on our current institutions of punishment in forming these alternatives. From their position of disenfranchisement, they maintain hope that there are methods of obtaining a more inclusive model of safety and justice.

Intrinsic to their proposed alternatives is a sense of community, a community that includes in its "we" both the victim and the offender. Davara articulates this view when asked what could be done to increase safety and justice:

> There should be a correlation between the offense to constructively make up for what was done. Prisoners, "offenders,"

should be mandated and encouraged and taught to give back to the society. Social Justice would be investing the ability of the offender back into the society/the whole. Gaining moral and educational accomplishments meets the needs of both prisoners and society, while meeting economic goals. Any of us may fall short, but Justice should establish maintenance that keeps us from falling again. True safety is the ability to recover and establish boundaries that are selective enough to protect hope. I hope that I may be a blessing of hope in the strategic implementation of care and concern between those of us in need.[45]

Davara emphasizes that we must come together as a community to find justice or safety. She challenges the division between "we," or non-criminal/free people, and "other," or criminals/prisoners, inherent in our current retributive model of social justice. Her vision of justice addresses crimes and criminals within a broader inclusive community structure. This model is in direct contrast to the isolation and ostracism of criminals within the current prison industrial complex.

Similarly, Rebecca offers a positive community-based model of social justice whereby society has both the responsibility and the possibility of being able to heal and strengthen itself by addressing the root causes of individual criminal acts. This model contrasts with the current negative regime of imprisonment that harms socially defined "deviants" in exchange for the harm they have caused recognized victims or the powerful.

The criminal justice system isn't capable of serving society's needs. All the justice system does is lock up people and give minimal attention to rehabilitation. As far as addressing my specific needs, so far they haven't really asked.

A society is only as strong as its members, and ours is in the beginning of destroying itself. People are like links of a chain. When the chain becomes weak and is not repaired, like how the people in prison are not being rehabilitated, it will just fall apart. When enough people are incarcerated, there will come social destruction.

We need to send people to programs, and use prisons only as a place for the most dangerous. By dangerous I mean someone who seriously injures someone else. For most people, we need to reward proper action, including by offering a lot more alternatives to imprisonment. We need to give people incentives to become rehabilitated and offer a wide spectrum of programs and classes to help people with different problems. As it is now, prison is a destroyer of prisoners' self-esteem.[46]

Premised in Rebecca's words is the idea that there is hope both for individuals and for societies to reform, strengthen, and improve. It is through this hope that prisoner activists begin to create a space for a more inclusive reparative model of social justice that offers safety and justice, rather than exclusion and repression, to the disenfranchised.

Conclusion

It's not realistic to say that all crime will ever stop.... But I will advocate until we all feel safe to come forward.[47]

In order to effect social reform, it is imperative that reform efforts intrinsically involve oppressed communities. Without their experience and guidance, activist movements will find their strategies and political rhetoric reappropriated by the systems of oppression they specifically wish to challenge.

The spirit of the collective resistance of activist prisoners should and must be at the heart of any successful attempt at building positive progressive alternatives to our current punishment system. It is their experience that demands the broader movement against sexist violence first acknowledge that violence against women includes institutional violence, and then take responsibility for the movement's role in strengthening punishment institutions that further abuse vulnerable women. They demonstrate how in order to aid women who are most vulnerable to oppression in society, the women's movement must resist punitive strategies against individualized violence that contribute further to the oppression of women by bolstering the institutions that abuse and victimize women and communities of color.

Moreover, it is activist prisoners' inspiration and resiliency that creates a space for imagining alternatives to increasing imprisonment and state-sanctioned violence against the disempowered. In their call for individualized community-based responses to crime, activist prisoners serve as role models for developing an inclusive schema of justice and safety. They challenge all of us to join them in imagining alternatives to our current punishment regime and in resisting abuses of authority.

Women prisoners' words and writings must be incorporated into the broader debate concerning violence prevention and the definition of violence against women. Through correspondence and visits, community activists in the free world can work jointly with prisoner activists to create campaigns and strategies in resistance to violence and oppression both inside and outside prisons. Moreover, those of us with the privilege of freedom must actively work to find ways of creating space for the voices of women inside within social reform efforts—broadcasting and publishing their views to a broader audience. We can begin by opening channels of communication between activists inside and out and working to identify the sources of women prisoners' inspiration as a means of locating solutions and strategy. From women prisoners' inspiration and courage, free activists can find inspiration as well as support women prisoners in their activist efforts.

> I receive inspiration from those of us who fought for equal rights until they could fight no longer and in their deaths brought about the changes that they only hoped for in life—those who in death brought about public awareness of what happens to the people society forgot.[48]

1   Alexander C. Lichtenstein and Michael A. Kroll, "The Fortress Economy: The Economic Role of the US Prison System," in Elihu Rosenblatt, ed., *Criminal Injustice: Confronting the Prison Crisis* (Cambridge, MA: South End Press: 1996), 17.

2   Angela Y. Davis, "The Color of Violence Against Women," *Colorlines* (Fall 2000).

3   Cynthia Chandler and Carol Kingery began working with HIV-postive women prisoners to document their life histories while staff with Women's Positive Legal Action Network (Women's PLAN), a nonprofit founded in 1995 by Cynthia Chandler with the mission of addressing the needs of women prisoners with HIV and other life-threatening illnesses. In September 2000, Women's PLAN merged into Justice Network on Women (Justice Now), a larger nonprofit organization co-founded by Cynthia Chandler. The co-authors' work with women prisoners began through Women's PLAN and has continued under the auspices of Justice Now.

4   For more extensive excerpts taken from the life stories of the three women featured in this article, see Cynthia Chandler and Carol Kingery, "Yell Real Loud: HIV-Positive Women Prisoners Challenge Constructions of Justice," *Social Justice* (Winter 2001). For excerpts from histories of two former prisoners, see Cynthia Chandler et al., "Community-Based Alternative Sentencing for HIV-Positive Women in the Criminal Justice System," *Berkeley Women's Law Journal*, Vol. 14 (1999), 79–84.

5   The rate of HIV infection among prisoners is ten to one hundred times higher than the rate in the general population. See Anne S. DeGroot et al., "Barriers to Care of HIV-Infected Inmates: A Public Health Concern," *AIDS Reader*, (May/June 1996), 79.

6   The rate of HIV infection is higher among women in almost all of correctional systems surveyed (Ibid., 81). 4.2 percent of women prisoners reported testing HIV-positive as compared to 2.5 percent of male prisoners. See Peter M. Brien and Caroline Wolf Harlow, "HIV in Prisons and Jails, 1993," *Bureau of Justice Statistics Bulletin*, NCJ-152765 (Washington, DC: US Department of Justice, 1995), 1.

7   Brenda V. Smith and Cynthia Dailard, "Female Prisoners and AIDS: On the Margins of Public Health and Social Justice," *AIDS and Public Policy Journal*, Vol. 9, No. 2 (1994), 78–85; Sally Zierler and Nancy Krieger, "Reframing Women's Risk: Social Inequalities and HIV Infection," *Annual Review of Public Health*, Vol. 18 (1997), 401–436.

8   Racism, poverty, and drug use put women at increased risk both of contracting HIV and of incarceration. See Smith and Dailard, "Female Prisoners and AIDS," *AIDS and Public Policy*, 78–79.

9   A history of sexual abuse increases women's vulnerability to HIV and to incarceration. See Debi Cuccinelli and Anne S. DeGroot, "Put Her in a Cage: Childhood Sexual Abuse, Incarceration, and HIV Infection," in Nancy Goldstein and Jennifer L. Manlowe, eds., *The Gender Politics of HIV/AIDS in Women: Perspectives on the Pandemic in the United States* (New York: New York University Press, 1997) 225–226. Both incarcerated women and HIV-positive women are likely to have experienced sexual abuse. See DeGroot, et. al, "A Standard of HIV Care for Incarcerated Women," *Journal of Correctional Health Care*, Vol. 5 (1998), 162–163.

10   A significant risk factor for HIV infection is belonging to a group in a culture that is marginalized and disenfranchised. See, "Towards a New Health Strategy for AIDS: A Report of the Global AIDS Policy Coalition," (The Global AIDS Policy Coalition, 1993), 4–6. Social inequities are strongly related to HIV infection among women in the United States. See Zierler and Krieger, "Reframing Women's Risk," *Annual Review*, 401. For a description of links between incarceration and poverty, race, and gender, see Sabina Virgo, "The Criminalization of Poverty," in Rosenblatt, ed., *Criminal Injustice*, 47.

11   Lichtenstein and Kroll, "The Fortress Economy," *Criminal Injustice*, 17.

12   DeGroot, et. al, "Barriers to Care of HIV-Infected Inmates: A Public Helath Concern," *AIDS Reader*, 81. See also Nina Seigel, "Women in Prison: The Number of Women Serving Time Behind Bars has Increased Dramatically. Is this Equality?" *Ms.* (September/October 1998), 65.

13   DeGroot, et. al, "Barriers to Care of HIV-Infected Inmates: A Public Helath Concern," *AIDS Reader*, 81; Seigel, "Women in Prison," *Ms.*, 65, 68.

14   Seigel, "Women in Prison," 68; Nancy Kurshan, "Behind the Walls: The History and Current Reality of Women's Imprisonment," in Rosenblatt, ed., *Criminal Injustice*, 136, 150.

15   Seigel, "Women in Prison," *Ms.*, 68.

16   Ibid.; Kurshan, "Behind the Walls," *Criminal Injustice*, 153.

17   Studies indicate that women of color are "over-arrested, over-indicted, under-defended, and over-sentenced" when compared to white women (Kurshan, "Behind the Walls," *Criminal Injustice*, 152). Impoverished women of color are disproportionately imprisoned (Seigel, "Women in Prison," *Ms.*, 68).

18   Lawrence A. Greenfeld and Tracy L. Snell, "Bureau of Justice Statistics Special Report: Women Offenders" (Washington, DC: US Department of Justice, 1999), 2.

19   Ibid., 7.

20   Ibid., 8.

21   Smith and Dailard, "Female Prisoners and AIDS," *AIDS and Public Policy*, 79-80.

22   DeGroot, et. al, "Barriers to Care of HIV-Infected Inmates: A Public Helath Concern," *AIDS Reader*, 79–81, 82–83.

23   Brien and Harlow, "HIV in Prisons and Jails, 1993," *Bureau of Justice*, 1.

24   Ibid. The disproportionate representation of women of color in prison, combined with the disproportionate impact of HIV on women of color, inherently leads to a high prevalence of HIV among incarcerated women. A US Department of Justice study revealed that, as of 1991, women of color in prison were disproportionately infected with HIV, with an estimated 6.8 percent of Latina/Hispanic women and 3.5 percent of African-American

women testing positive for HIV, as compared to 1.9 percent of white women prisoners.

25 Smith and Dailard, "Female Prisoners and AIDS," *AIDS and Public Policy*, 79; Anne S. DeGroot et al., "A Standard of HIV Care for Incarcerated Women," *AIDS Reader*, 142.

26 Ibid., 143.

27 Cynthia Chandler et al., "Community-Based Alternative Sentencing for HIV-Positive Women in the Criminal Justice System," *Berkeley*, 79–84.

28 The Global AIDS Policy Coalition, "Towards a New Health Strategy for AIDS," 4–5.

29 Brandy and Davara Campbell are African-American and Native American respectively. Rebecca Langley is Latina and Caucasian.

30 Seigel, "Women in Prison," *Ms.*, 70; Kurshan, "Behind the Walls," *Criminal Injustice*, 155.

31 Davara Campbell, interview notes, on file with authors (2000).

32 Brandy, interview notes, on file with authors (2000).

33 Campbell, interview notes, on file with authors (2000).

34 In 1998 the State of California paid $825,000 in damages for the wrongful shooting death of Preston Tate. Correctional Officers were accused of allegedly setting up "cock" fights between prisoners and then shooting them during the "gladiator days" of Corcoran Prison. See Mark Arax and Mark Gladstone, "California in the West: State Agrees to Pay $2.2 Million to Inmate Shot at Corcoran Prison," *Los Angeles Times*, May 16, 1999, A26.

35 Brandy, interview notes, on file with authors (2000).

36 Rebecca Langley, interview notes, on file with authors (1999).

37 Ibid.

38 Campbell, interview notes, on file with authors (1999).

39 Brandy, interview notes, on file with authors (1999).

40 The use of "chaining," or the placement of prisoners in isolation in 4-point restraints, and other human rights abuses against women prisoners identified as suicidal or aggressive is documented in *Scott Segregation Unit* (2000), a documentary produced and directed by Carol Jacobsen, Associate Professor of Art, University of Michigan School of Art and Design.

41 Langley, interview notes, on file with authors (1999).

42 Campbell, interview notes, on file with authors (2000).

43 Langley, interview notes, on file with authors (1999).

44 Campbell, interview notes, on file with authors (1999).

45 Campbell, interview notes, on file with authors (1999).

46 Langley, interview notes, on file with authors (1999).

47 Brandy, interview notes, on file with authors (1999).

48 Langley, interview notes, on file with authors (1999).

Chapter 4

Abortion in the United States

Barriers to Access

Marlene Gerber Fried

A ssessing the current status of abortion rights in the United States is a complex matter. From a public health perspective, if one looks at the statistics comparing maternal mortality in the United States to countries in which abortion remains illegal and unsafe, the situation in the United States looks extremely positive. Abortion has been legal since 1973. There are between 1.2 and 1.4 million abortions annually.[1] There is virtually no mortality from abortions, and the complication rate for first trimester abortion is about the same as for tonsillectomies.

This is a dramatic improvement from maternal deaths in the era before legalization. While we cannot know the exact numbers because the cause of death was not always recorded (even today studies find that 23 percent to 60 percent of maternal deaths are not recorded as such)[2], we do know (from statistics based on death certificates) that there were 1,407 deaths from induced abortion in 1940. That number fell during the 1940s to 200 to 300 per year. Then it rose again in the 1950s and 1960s, and fell sharply after 1970 when the first state legalized abortion. From 1970 to 1980, legal abortion is estimated to have prevented 1,500 pregnancy-related deaths and thousands of other complications. The availability of safe abortion also accounts for much of the decline in infant mortality.[3]

Focusing on abortion experiences, however, especially of young and low-income women, presents a very different picture—one in which reproductive options are severely curtailed. Since legalization, the effort to restrict and ultimately to recriminalize abortion has had a devastating impact on many women's lives.

The case of a 14-year-old girl in the state of Arizona, pregnant, possibly as a result of rape, makes this all too clear.[4] Her case became a political football. As a child in foster care in a state in which abortions are prohibited by law after twenty weeks, she had to receive a court order from her state's Supreme Court allowing her to go out of state to have an abortion. This young girl had to travel 1000 miles away, amid a flurry of anti-choice protests in both her home state and in Kansas where she went in order to obtain the abortion. Her case was leaked to the press even though it is against the law to release confidential information about children who are in the custody of the state. Anti-choice forces followed her to Kansas where they lined the sidewalk outside the clinic in an effort to "persuade" her not to have an abortion.

Sadly, a "normal" day for an abortion patient all too often requires running a gauntlet of protesters, having her confidential medical information made public, traveling long distances, and passing through metal detectors to see her doctor.

Looking at the experience of abortion providers, we may see the extent to which fear and danger permeate their work. In September, 1999, almost exactly one year after provider Dr. Barnett Slepian was shot in his home, clinics in the United States and doctors who perform abortions received an alert warning that extremists had proclaimed September 19 "Anti-Abortion Day."[5] A website with links to the most extreme and violent parts of the movement encouraged anti-choice activists to "celebrate" anti-abortion day "appropriately." Such threats must be taken seriously—to date, there have been seven murders,[6] and over 80 percent of clinics have experienced threats and harassment. The murderer of Dr. Slepian has not been found, nor has the person responsible for the bombing of an abortion clinic in Alabama which killed a security guard and seriously wounded a nurse.

Abortion rights in the United States are literally under siege. Providers operate under constant threat, and many clinics have become secured fortresses. A normal workday for providers includes wearing a bulletproof vest, checking for bombs, and being ever aware of who is around them. There is no other medical service where the dangers to the provider are much greater than those to the patient. There is no other medical service for which violence statistics must be collected.

This article will give a picture of abortion in the United States at the beginning of the twenty-first century from the vantage point of women who bear the brunt of restricted access. This analysis is informed by the author's twenty years of activism, most recently in the National Network of Abortion Funds, a growing network of grassroots groups (currently eighty-four) throughout the United States who raise money for women who want abortions but cannot afford them.

For tens of thousands of women in the United States each year, the lack of access to abortion rights remains a key obstacle to exercising their reproductive rights. Although one cannot deny the substantial gains made in women's health and mortality reduction since the legalization of abortion, access remains a significant issue, as it was in the United States before abortion was legalized, and as it still is for millions of women living in countries where abortion is still illegal or severely restricted.

The barriers to access that will be discussed here—from economic constraints to relentless efforts by anti-choice forces—are not unique to the United States. They are pervasive throughout the world, regardless of the legal status of abortion. Nevertheless, one should not conclude from this that legality is unimportant. The legalization of abortion is necessary but not sufficient to insure the availability of safe abortion to all women who seek it. Women's health advocates are continuing to work against legal restrictions and for funding, training of providers, and access to the range of safe abortion methods.

While battles over abortion tend to dominate reproductive rights politics in the United States, many advocacy groups, especially those organized by women of color, have a broader agenda which includes access to health care, sexuality education, contraception, HIV/AIDS treatment, opposition to coercive contraception and other population control policies, and advocacy for related issues such as housing, education, and employment. Like their counterparts in developing countries, they see abortion rights as part of a larger struggle for all the conditions that will make women's reproductive and sexual freedom a reality.

The Gap Between Legality and Access:
Abortion Experiences of Low-Income Women

There is an extreme dissonance between the legal accessibility of abortion and its practical inaccessibility to women on the social and economic margins. Legal abortion is one of the safest surgical procedures in the United States today, and it is relatively inexpensive compared to other surgeries. At the same time, it remains out of reach for thousands of women each year who find that the expense, location and shortage of services, burdensome legal restrictions, and anti-abortion threats and violence create daunting barriers.

Abortion funds get calls from women all over the United States—women in prison, young women, women who have been raped, undocumented women, and women with few economic resources. The funds repeatedly hear the desperation of girls and women who are faced with an unwanted pregnancy and have no money for an abortion. Women like Ericka, a 19-year-old single parent with two children living on her own without any help from her family. Lacking the money for an abortion, she tried to use a coat hanger, drank an entire bottle of Nyquil and two bottles of tetracycline. Or the 45-year-old woman living in a rural area, in a state, which does not pay for abortions and whose doctor could not perform one for her because his hospital wouldn't allow it[7]. Or the nurse's aid who works for a city government but has no health insurance. Or Denise, who was taking steroids to control her chronic asthma and was not warned that this would make her birth control pills ineffective. Selena, who left her abusive boyfriend and then found out she was pregnant.[8] For these women, it is as if abortion had never been legalized. Their reasons for needing an abortion are the same as any woman's—the difference is that they are poor.

While violence and harassment pose the most visible threat, access to abortion has been even more systematically eroded by other strategies. Since legalization in 1973, there has been a sustained effort by anti-choice forces to undermine abortion rights. As a result, restrictive legislation, judicial decisions, and relentless anti-abortion activity, both legal and illegal, have dangerously limited abortion access, especially for low-income women, women of color, and young women.

Abortion providers are marginalized within the medical profession. Perhaps the most disturbing illustration of this is the lack of outcry from doctors and other health care professionals in response to the violence against abortion providers. Would the profession have remained silent if cardiologists were being shot? Nor has there been an adequate outcry from the general public, the media, or law enforcement officials. After the clinic bombing in Alabama, a headline in a Boston newspaper read: "Innocent officer killed."[9] Clearly those who provide abortions are seen in an alternative category—if not guilty, certainly not "innocent" either.

Similarly, women who have abortions are stigmatized. They are portrayed either as selfish people or hapless victims, incapable of making their own decisions. While one expects to find these negative characterizations in anti-abortion literature, they are, unfortunately, more pervasive. On prime time television and in movies, an unplanned pregnancy is most often resolved by a miscarriage, death of the pregnant woman, or carrying the pregnancy to term.

Not surprisingly in this climate, the experience of abortion continues to be marked by silence and isolation despite the fact that there have been 35 million abortions in the United States since legalization, and millions of illegal abortions prior to that time. While there is a great deal of talk about abortion, there is almost none about real women's abortion experiences. In 2000, the National Network of Abortion Funds released a new video, *Legal But Out of Reach: Six Women's Abortion Stories*, highlighting economic barriers to abortion. However, the project was almost abandoned because it was very difficult to find women who felt they could speak out.

In addition to the direct attacks on clinics and providers, abortion access has been undermined through the denial of public funding for abortion, restrictive legislation such as mandatory waiting periods and parental consent laws that impose burdens on women and on clinics, a shortage of services, and the lack of training for new providers.

Within the system of privatized health care in the United States, a large majority of abortions must be paid for by the patients themselves. About one-third of women lack employment-linked health insurance, one-third of private plans do not cover abortion services (or only cover them for certain medical indications) and at least 37 million Americans have no health care coverage at all, including 9 million women of childbearing age.[10] And Medicaid, the publicly funded program that covers "necessary medical services" for low-income people, prohibits federal abortion coverage.[11] Abortion is the only reproductive health care service that is not paid by Medicaid. In effect, these policies deny low-income women equal access to abortion.

The restrictions on funding came soon after legalization. Federal Medicaid covered abortion from the late 1960s until 1977, four years after *Roe vs. Wade* made abortion legal nationwide. Each year since then, the US Congress has passed different versions of the Hyde Amendment, which prohibits federal funding of abortion. Initially, the only exception was for cases of endangerment of life of the pregnant woman. In 1993, exceptions for rape and incest were added, but only after a long battle. Most states have followed these federal precedents, but even this minimal "liberalization" had to be fought out in court when several states refused to comply.[12]

The impact of the Hyde Amendment has been devastating. Between 1973 and 1977, before Hyde, the federal government paid for about one-third of all abortions. Now it pays for virtually none. Since the average cost of a first-trimester abortion is $296 (nearly two-thirds the amount of the average maximum monthly welfare payment for a family of three),[13] some welfare recipients cannot afford abortions at all. It is estimated that 20 to 35 percent of women eligible for Medicaid who have wanted abortions have instead carried their pregnancies to term because funding has been unavailable.[14] Others are forced to divert money from food, rent, and utilities in order to pay for their abortion.[15] Even when women have been able to raise the money, the time needed to search for funding makes it more likely that they will have a more costly and difficult second-trimester procedure. It is estimated that one in five Medicaid-eligible women who have had second-trimester abortions would have had first-trimester abortions if the lack of public funds had not resulted in delays.[16]

A dramatic example underscores the narrow range of funded abortions under the Hyde restrictions. A Medicaid recipient with a life-threatening heart condition sought an abortion in the first trimester of pregnancy.[17] Although her doctors counseled an abortion, the hospital where she received treatment for her heart condition refused to perform it on the grounds that there was a less than 50 percent chance that she would die from the abortion. Ultimately, she had to be transported by ambulance to another state at a cost of thousands of dollars raised by grassroots Abortion Funds.

These restrictions deny abortion access to all women who rely on the federal government for their heath care, including Native Americans who use the government-funded Indian Health Services, federal employees and their dependents, federal prisoners, Peace Corps volunteers, military personnel and their dependents, teenagers participating in the state Children's Health Insurance Program, and low-income residents of Washington, DC.[18]

Anti-Abortion Intimidation, Violence, and Harassment

Abortion services are severely limited despite the facts that: (1) abortion is legal, (2) there are 40,000 obstetricians and gynecologists practicing in the United States,[19] (3) abortion is the most common obstetrical procedure women undergo (at 1992 rates, one in four American women will have at least one abortion during their lives) and the most commonly performed surgical procedure in the United States,[20] and (4) excellent surgical and medical methods of abortion exist.[21]

The number of abortion providers, however (hospitals, clinics, and physicians' offices), has declined since the 1980s, and services are very unevenly distributed. Nine in ten abortion providers are now located in metropolitan areas; about one-third fewer counties have an abortion provider now than in the late 1970s.[22] Ninety-four percent of non-metropolitan counties have no services (85 percent of rural women live in these underserved counties). One-quarter of women having abortions travel more than 50 miles from home to obtain them.[23]

As older physicians retire, few medical students are being trained in abortion techniques to take their place. Almost half of graduating residents in obstetrics-gynecology have never performed a first-trimester abortion. Many hospitals do so few abortions that they cannot even qualify as appropriate training sites.

Anti-abortion murder, violence, and harassment aimed at doctors and clinic workers contribute to decreased service provision. Clinics and providers have been targets of violence since the early 1980s. Thus far, 1993 was the peak year for anti-choice violence; but levels remain high. These acts included death threats, stalking, chemical attacks (using materials such as with butyric acid), arson, bomb threats, invasions, and blockades.[24] The few remaining independent feminist women's health clinics, already battling for economic survival, have been hit especially hard. An open letter to supporters from Concord Feminist Health Center, the victim of an anti-abortion arson attack in May 2000, reminds us "because our foes have made it so, this work costs—it costs our clients, our community and us materially, psychologically and spiritually."[25]

Anti-abortion activists are also targeting medical students in an effort to cut off the supply of potential providers for the future. Life Dynamics Inc., an anti-abortion organization engaged in a range of activities to intimidate, harass, and ultimately dissuade doctors from providing abortions, produced two anti-abortion comic books which were sent to thousands of medical students and doctors in the United States and Canada. The first, "Bottom Feeder," included "jokes" such as, "What do you do if you find yourself in a room with Hitler, Mussolini, and an abortionist, and you have only two bullets?" Answer: "Shoot the abortionist twice."[26] "Quack the Ripper," the most recent publication, "depicts doctors who perform abortions as zealots, amoral buffoons, and psychotics, and has sparked fears for their safety."[27] The mailing's implicit message is also meant to intimidate. By sending it to students' home addresses, the anti-abortion movement sends a frightening communication: "we know who you are and where to find you."

Because new methods of early abortion will be used by more doctors, be more integrated into obstetrics and gynecology and family practices, and ultimately, perhaps be available in non-clinic settings, many pro-choice advocates believe that they will alleviate the attacks on providers. Indeed, these methods do have the potential to increase abortion services and providers. Many doctors who do not currently do abortions say they would make "medical abortion" available to their patients.

At the same time, the most important factors causing later abortions are not related to the lack of available techniques, but to the barriers to access discussed above. Nor will new methods resolve the political battle. Abortion rights advocates will have to resist efforts to use early abortion as a way of justifying further restrictions on and marginalization of later abortion. Surgical abortion will continue to be necessary, not just as a backup to other methods, but for the vast majority of women who do not make their decisions until after the seventh week of pregnancy. And the opposition will not be daunted. They have already organized Pharmacists for Life, a group committed to refusing to fill prescriptions for mifepristone (a medical abortion method known more commonly as RU486), emergency contraception, and other contraceptive methods.

Young Women's Bodies As Battlegrounds

Controlling young women's sexuality has been a particular concern of the anti-abortion movement; and they have had considerable legislative and ideological success despite the fact that about 40 percent of the one million teens that become pregnant annually choose abortion. Laws requiring minors seeking abortions either to obtain parental consent or notification are enforced in thirty-nine out of fifty-two states and territories.[28] Health care providers face loss of license and, in some cases, criminal penalties for failure to comply.

Although the supporters of such laws claim that they are meant to protect the health and promote the best interests of young women, in fact they are a threat to both health and well-being. Parental involvement laws, even though they include provisions for judicial bypass for young women who cannot or are unwilling to involve their parents, often require travel, extra time, and money. Although most teens who go through the judicial process are ultimately given permission by the court to have an abortion, the experience may be humiliating and traumatizing. The laws require a young woman to discuss her pregnancy and personal details about her life in front of strangers in a courtroom. Although these procedures are supposed to be confidential, in rural areas and small towns a young woman may find that confidentiality is impossible to maintain.[29]

To avoid such laws, many young women are forced to go to a neighboring state for their abortions, often accompanied by a relative. Proposed legislation known as the Child Custody Protection Act would eliminate this alternative. If passed, it would be a crime for anyone other than a parent to transport a minor across state lines for an abortion unless the young woman had already met the obligations of her state's parental involvement law. A grandparent, a close family friend, or a member of the clergy could all be prosecuted and jailed for accompanying a minor to get an abortion if the home state requires parental notification or consent. This legislation would deny the support of caring adults to vulnerable young women who are trying to deal with an unwanted pregnancy. As with campaigns mandating the exclusive teaching of abstinence in sexual education, the intent here is clear—control of young women's sexuality, rather than respecting their rights and health.

Backdoor Efforts to Ban All Abortion: The "Partial Birth Abortion" Strategy

Because direct efforts to ban abortion entirely through amendments to the federal constitution or federal statutes have thus far failed, opponents of abortion have turned to less overt strategies. Laws against so-called partial birth abortion, if successful, could potentially be used to prohibit all abortions. Since 1995, there have been efforts at the federal and state level to ban "partial birth abortions." While opponents claim that this is a specific procedure, "partial birth abortion" is not a medically recognized term. In fact, descriptions of it in legislative bans basically describe what occurs in every abortion procedure.[30] While it has been mistakenly called a Dilation and Extraction (D & X) abortion and often referred to as a late-term abortion, the fact is that the meaning of it has been kept vague in all of the statutes.

Nonetheless, Congress has passed such legislation twice, as have thirty-one states. In June 2000, the US Supreme Court ruled in *Stenberg vs. Carhart* that the ban from the state of Nebraska, and others like it, are unconstitutional.[31] Although this decision was clearly a victory for abortion rights and virtually all the existing bans have the same defect as the Nebraska law, there is still cause for concern. The decision was very close—five to four.

More significant, the ideological battle is being won by the anti-abortion movement. Strategically, these initiatives have enabled them to portray abortion negatively. While battles over the bans and other legal restrictions have weakened and fragmented the pro-choice movement, the anti-abortion movement has been able to use such fights as opportunities to consolidate their movement, to draw in new supporters, and to build support for other restrictions on abortion. And while they have not achieved their ultimate objective, as we have seen, they have won significant victories.

Generating moral disapproval has been a consistent and key strategy in efforts to restrict and recriminalize abortion and to shape public opinion. For example, in the area of public funding for abortion, anti-choice forces argue, "abortion may be legal, but why should we be forced to pay for something that is morally repugnant?" Moral repugnance has been the hallmark of the campaign against "partial birth abortion." The opponents of abortion have been increasingly successful in projecting the idea that there is a universal consensus about the immorality of abortion. Widening the chasm between the moral and the legal status of abortion undermines support for abortion rights. It is difficult to stand up for abortion rights if doing so means that you are standing for immorality at worst, and a necessary evil at best.

The Race and Class Dynamics of Reproductive Control

In order to understand the relationship between restricting abortion rights and other efforts to control reproduction, it is necessary to see the race and class dynamics that underlie both. As this article has argued, the brunt of restrictions on abortion has been borne by young, low-income women and women of color. At the same time, historically, from the oppression of Native American women[32] through slavery to the present, the right of low-income women and women of color to control their own fertility has been severely restricted.[33]

Contemporary eugenicist thinking underlies the scapegoating of young, low-income women of color who are blamed for poverty, child abuse, drug addiction, violence, and general societal deterioration. Proposed solutions also exhibit eugenics. A series of callous, punitive, and coercive measures have been designed to control the lives and reproductive capacity of low-income women. Contemporary policies curtailing public assistance to low-income women and their families, programs of coercive contraception and the promotion of long-acting contraception and sterilization in communities of color, prosecutions of women who use illegal drugs while pregnant, and attempts to bribe poor women not to have babies which are seen as a "drain on society" all aim to control the fertility of those considered unfit for motherhood and to punish them if they become pregnant.

Several provisions of the 1996 welfare law (the Personal Responsibility and Work Opportunity Reconciliation Act), for example, made it easier for states to reduce poor women's reproductive choices through cuts to nutrition programs for children in family day care, and in summer food programs, as well as to child-care, family planning, legal services, foster care, and at-risk youth. Other provisions of the law imposed strict time limits on receiving benefits and required single parents with children to work thirty hours per week and simultaneously cut child-care subsidies. Thus low-income mothers are often forced to choose between inadequate child-care, and losing benefits if they stay home to care for their children.

Under the rubric of "welfare reform," the government uses subsistence benefits to manipulate and coerce poor women's reproductive decisions. For example, a family cap denies increased payments to women who conceive and bear another child while receiving public assistance. The illegitimacy bonus is another such policy. It offers a federal bounty of $20 to $25 million for three years to the five states with the largest decrease in out-of-wedlock birth rates with a simultaneous reduction in abortion rates below 1995 levels.[34] This legislation has ideological implications as well. It revives the stigma of "illegitimacy"[35] by rewarding states that implement policies making it very difficult for poor single women to have children.

The 1996 welfare law has also tried to change the way sex education is taught by earmarking a large amount of money, $88 million, for programs which teach only abstinence as the expected standard, portraying it as the only way to avoid out-of-wedlock pregnancy and stating that extra-marital sexual activity is likely to have harmful psychological and physical effects.[36]

Welfare time limits now force recipients around the country to face a future without a safety net and often without child-care and the other supports necessary to obtain decent paying, stable jobs. Little attention and less money are directed toward supporting young motherhood or enhancing educational and job opportunities for young, low-income women. Instead, the punitive ideological and legislative policies championed by conservatives emphasize the connection between illegitimacy, poverty, and social decay.[37]

New academic work, such as "Legalized Abortion and Crime," reinforces the ideology. This recent study by economists Steven Levitt and John Donohue,[38] purports to show a relationship between legalized abortion and a decline in the crime rate. They argue that women who have higher rates of abortion—most commonly teenagers, minorities, and the poor—are also those at greatest risk for bearing children who would have been likely to commit crimes as young adults.[39] The assumption here is that the children of poor and minority women are more likely to be criminals. Using this theory to provide legitimacy for restricting the reproduction of undesirables is a distortion of reproductive freedom.

The Invisibility of Inaccessibility: Closing the Gap

Although restricted access shapes the reproductive experiences of women who are young, low-income, and women of color, many people in the United States, even those who support abortion rights, are unaware of the extent to which abortion access has been diminished. They fail to see the link between controlling the fertility of "undesirable" women and maintaining their own rights. For example, there is growing support among young people for restrictions on abortion. A 1998 study by the University of California showed that support for legal abortion among young women has dropped every year for the last nine, from 65.5 percent in 1989, to a low of 49.5 percent.[40]

Research with the same age group done by the Pro-Choice Public Education Project[41] uncovered similar opinions. Young people think that abortion is overused and that their peers are irresponsible. Therefore, although young women are frequent targets of restrictive policies, they support them. Narrowing access to abortion services does not dismay them; they think that "choice" will always be there for those who really need and deserve it. Polls conducted by Choice USA in June 1997 and March 1999 reveal quite a bit of confusion and misinformation among 15 to 22-year-olds about when most abortions occur, the rate of complications, and psychological problems following abortion.[42] If lack of information accounts for young people's attitudes about abortion, this must be addressed by advocates of abortion rights.

But a shift in perspective is also required to change these attitudes. There is a tremendous gap between the perception that abortion is too accessible and the reproductive experiences of low-income women, young women, and women of color. The disparity was noticeably acute during the 2000 presidential campaigns that were so determined to project the politics of well-being and prosperity. At the Republican convention, only the demonstrators talked about poverty, inequality, and restrictions on reproductive rights and social justice. And while the Democrats talked a good deal about their support of reproductive choice, they also touted the economy as their crowning achievement and proudly proclaimed that they ended welfare as we knew it. The disconnect between this picture and the lives of the women discussed in this article is profound. It makes poor women invisible and frustrates advocacy efforts.

As part of a strategy to expand reproductive options, the notion of "choice" itself must be expanded to take into account the experiences of low-income women. Women who face obstacles to having children, or to having an abortion, do not see themselves as having choices. Having an abortion because one cannot afford a child in a society that privatizes childrearing is not an expression of reproductive freedom. Historically, movements for reproductive choice in the United States have not advocated for the right to have children. By focusing on women's efforts not to have children, the pro-choice movement has neglected the right to have them.

Traditionally, women of color groups have taken the lead in placing abortion rights within a broader agenda that includes advocacy not only for women's health, but for all of the other economic and social rights needed to have real control over one's life. Younger activists too, who have been negotiating their sexual and reproductive lives through the terrain of HIV/AIDS and other sexually transmitted diseases, sexual abuse and violence against women, and the demonization of lesbians and gay men, also have a broader vision of reproductive rights.

Underlying these important corrections and critiques is the need to challenge the market model of choice. The availability of a product for sale does not in itself constitute the sort of choice that reproductive rights advocates seek. At a recent meeting of abortion providers, a dedicated female physician responded sharply to criticism of quinacrine sterilization—a method of chemical sterilization which has not been properly or adequately tested. She argued that this new method was an expansion of women's reproductive "choices." The race and class dimensions of its use were invisible to her.[43] In this view, quinacrine sterilization without appropriate testing is welcomed because it is cheap and thus affordable to women who lack other reproductive options.

To halt the erosion of abortion access, to counteract other threats to reproductive rights, and to expand women's rights and access to meaningful reproductive choice, the fragility of existing rights must be grasped, and the vision of reproductive rights must be broadened. Members of the movement in the United States can learn from our allies in other countries. While the abortion rights battle has been politically isolated in the Unites States, internationally, especially in the developing world, the women's agenda integrates a wide range of issues. We see this in the platforms for action of both the International Conference on Population and Development in Cairo, and the Beijing Women's Conference. Advocates for women's rights and health placed abortion in a broad human rights framework, which included concerns about maternal and infant mortality, population control, economic rights, violence against women, and environmental destruction.

Battles over restricting abortion are fundamentally about women's power and who will control women's fertility. It is hoped that the abortion rights movement in the United States will strengthen its ties to those fighting for the range of rights necessary to have genuine reproductive freedom. There is a need to re-shape the opinions of pro-choice supporters, the general public, and especially young people to affirm the links between abortion rights, human rights, and social justice.

1   Allan Rosenfield in Maureen E. Paul, Steve Lichtenberg, Lynn Borgatta, David A. Grimes, and Phillip G. Stubblefield, eds., *A Clinician's Guide to Medical and Surgical Abortion* (Worcester, MA: Churchill Livingstone, 1999), xiv.

2   Stanley Henshaw in Paul et al., 19.

3   Ibid.

4   The Henry J. Kaiser Family Foundation, *Kaiser Daily Reproductive Health Report* (September 2–3, 9, 1999). See http://report.kff.org/repro/.

5   The National Abortion Federation Member Alert (September 14, 1999).

6   Dr. David Gunn, March 10, 1993, Pensacola, Florida; Dr. John Britton, July 29, 1994, Pensacola, Florida; James Barrett, clinic escort, July 29, 1994, Pensacola, Florida; Shannon Lowney, clinic worker, December 30, 1994, Boston, Massachusetts; LeeAnn Nichols, clinic worker, December 30, 1994, Boston, Massachusetts; Officer Robert Sanderson, clinic security officer, January 29, 1998, Atlanta, Georgia; Dr. Barnett Slepian, October 23, 1998. Dr. Slepian was murdered at his home; the others were all murdered at their clinics.

7   *Legal But Out of Reach: Experiences from the National Network of Abortion Funds*, Third ed., (Amherst, MA: National Network of Abortion Funds, 1998). See http://hamp.hampshire.edu/~clpp/nnaf.

8   These examples are from the Greater Philadelphia Women's Medical Fund, notes from their files (January to June 2000). Only the names have been changed.

9   *The Boston Globe*, January 2, 1998.

10   Sharon Lerner and Janet Freedman, "Abortion and Health Care Reform," *Journal of the American Medical Women's Association*, 49.5 (1994), 144.

11   Patricia Donovan, *The Politics of Blame: Family Planning, Abortion and the Poor* (New York: Alan Guttmacher Institute, 1995). Donovan points out that even before the Hyde Amendment, not all women in need of subsidized abortion services were able to obtain them either because the services were not available or accessible to them—because the eligibility ceilings are set so low, Medicaid itself covers fewer than half of those who live in poverty—or because the states had policies prohibiting coverage.

12   As of April 2000, sixteen states pay for all or most medically necessary abortions—those necessary to protect a woman's health under the broad definition of *Doe vs. Bolton*, the companion case to *Roe vs. Wade*. The list has fluctuated substantially over the years. See Heather Boonstra and Adam Sonfield, "Rights Without Access: Revisiting Public Funding of Abortion for Poor Women," *The Guttmacher Report on Public Policy*, 3.2 (April 2000), 9. Of the remaining thirty-four states, most pay for abortions in those circumstances permitted under the federal Hyde Amendment.

13   Donovan, *The Politics of Blame*. Costs of abortion go up approximately $100 per week of pregnancy and also vary according to the type of procedure and the type of facility. Abortions in hospitals are more costly. At the same time, hospitals have federal money for free care which can sometimes be accessed for abortions. Medical abortion with mifepristone is expected to

cost the same as surgical abortion. National Abortion Federation Fact Sheet.

14   Stanley Henshaw, "Factors Hindering Access to Abortion Services" *Family Planning Perspectives*, Vol. 27, No. 2 (1995): 54–59, 87.

15   Boonstra and Sonfield, "Rights Without Access," *Guttmacher Report*, 10.

16   *Abortion Delivery in the United States: What Do Current Trends and Non-Surgical Alternatives Mean for the Future?* (Alan Guttmacher Institute, 1995).

17   Amy Goldstein, "A Life At Risk, An Abortion Denied: Ailing Louisiana Woman at Center of a Debate Over Access," *Washington Post*, October 20, 1998, A1.

18   Boonstra and Sonfield, "Rights Without Access," *Guttmacher Report*, 9.

19   Rosenfield in Paul, et al., *A Clinician's Guide to Medical and Surgical Abortion*, xv.

20   Jerry Edwards, Phillip Daney, and Paul in Paul, et al., *A Clinician's Guide to Medical and Surgical Abortion*, 107.

21   Malcolm Potts in Paul, et al., *A Clinician's Guide to Medical and Surgical Abortion*, xi.

22   *Abortion Providers Decreased 14 Percent Between 1992 and 1996*, (The Alan Guttmacher Institute, December 11, 1998).

23   Ibid.

24   Regularly updated statistics on clinic violence and harassment can be obtained from the National Abortion Federation and the Feminist Majority Foundation (www.prochoice.org) which issues an annual Clinic Violence Survey Report (www.feminist.org).

25   Open Letter to Supporters, Concord Feminist Health Center (May 2000), distributed via email.

26   "Bottom Feeder," 1993, Life Dynamics Inc., PO Box 185, Lewisville, Texas 75067.

27   *Pro-Choice Press* (a publication of Pro-Choice Action Network, Spring 1999), "Abusive Comic Book Mailed to Canadian Doctors," found at www.prochoiceconnection.com/pro-can/99spring.html#comic

28   Kathryn Kolbert, et al., "Legal Issues Related to Abortion in the United States," in Paul, et al., *A Clinician's Guide to Medical and Surgical Abortion*, 237.

29   Ann Farmer, "Tell It to The Judge," *Reproductive Freedom News*, Vol. 8 (September 1999).

30   This is a method in which the fetus is given an injection so that it dies in the womb. Fluid is then removed from the cranium as this is the only way to bring the head out without causing tears or bleeding in the woman's cervix, and the fetus is removed intact. This method is rare to the extent that the overwhelming majority of abortions are performed in the first trimester. It is used in the third trimester when the life of the pregnant woman is at risk, or in cases of serious fetal anomaly. It may also be used from twenty to twenty-four weeks of pregnancy if the doctor determines that it is the best procedure to use in the circumstances. This procedure is also referred to as D and X. Sometimes, the anti-abortion movement uses "Partial Birth Abortion" to refer to this procedure. Note that the term "partial birth abortion" is a political, not a medical term. Opponents have portrayed it as infanticide. Most courts in the US have continued to rule that determinations of appropriate medical procedures may not be made by legislatures, but must be left to the physician attending a woman. See Kolbert, et al., in Paul, et al., *A Clinician's Guide to Medical and Surgical Abortion*, 234.

31 On June 28, 2000, the US Supreme Court in *Stenberg vs. Carhart* struck down Nebraska's ban on so-called "partial-birth abortions." The case was argued by Simon Heller from the Center for Reproductive Law and Policy. For more information, contact them at 120 Wall St., 14th Floor, New York, NY 10005, or find them online at www.crlp.org.

32 See Andrea Smith, "Better Dead than Pregnant," in this anthology.

33 For example, Dorothy Roberts points out that African-American women are five times more likely to live in poverty, five times more likely to be on welfare, and three times more likely to be unemployed than are white women. See Dorothy Roberts, "Punishing Drug Addicts Who Have Babies: Women of Color, Equality, and the Right of Privacy," in R. Solinger, ed., *Abortion Wars: A Half Century of Struggle, 1950–2000* (Berkeley, CA: University of California Press, 1998), 152.

34 NOW Legal Defense and Education Fund, "The Illegitimacy Ratio," Q & A on Women and Welfare and Reproductive Rights.

35 Karen Judd with Susan Buttenweiser, "Welfare Reform Update" (Port Chester, NY: ProChoice Resource Center, Inc., 1999).

36 Draft Block Grant Application Guidance, Abstinence Education Provision of the 1996 Welfare Law, found in Judd with Buttenweiser, "Welfare Reform Update," 6–28.

37 Charles Murray described illegitimacy as "the single most important social problem of our time—more important than crime, drugs, poverty, illiteracy, welfare or homelessness because it drives everything else." ("The Coming White Underclass," *Wall Street Journal*, October 29, 1993). Despite the fact that young African-American women bear the brunt of the demonization in the furor surrounding illegitimacy, Murray's focus is on white teenagers. Some critics argue that his real concern is the breakdown of white families and white male authority.

38 While the results of this study were published in the press, the study itself appears only on a website, JCPR Working Paper, No. 1 (August 1999), www.jcpr.org/levitt.html.

39 Karen Brandon, *Chicago Tribune*, August 8, 1999.

40 Linda J. Sax, Alexander W. Astin, W.S. Korn, and K.M. Mahoney, *The American College Freshman: National Norms for Fall 1998* (Los Angeles, CA: Higher Education Research Institute, 1998).

41 In March 1997, the Pro-Choice Public Education project conducted, "An Exploration of Young Women's Attitudes Toward Pro-Choice," a qualitative research project to explore the attitudes of the young women born after *Roe vs. Wade*.

42   These polls were never published. The information cited here was released
     to the press by Choice USA.
43   Marlene Fried's notes from National Abortion Federation Meeting (April
     1999).

Chapter 5

Better Dead than Pregnant

The Colonization of Native Women's Reproductive Health

Andrea Smith

A nn Stoler argues in *Race and the Education of Desire* that racism, far from being a reaction to crisis in which racial others are scapegoated for social ills, is a permanent part of the social fabric. "[R]acism is not an effect but a tactic in the internal fission of society into binary opposition, a means of creating 'biologized' internal enemies, against whom society must defend itself."[1] She argues that it is the constant purification and elimination of racialized enemies within the state that ensures the growth of the national body. "Racism does not merely arise in moments of crisis, in sporadic cleansings. It is internal to the biopolitical state, woven into the web of the social body, threaded through its fabric." Thus, communities of color become pollution from which the state must constantly purify itself. Women of color become particularly dangerous to the world order as they have the ability to reproduce the next generations of communities of color. Consequently, it is not surprising that control over the reproductive abilities of women of color becomes seen as a national security issue.

Native women in particular, whose ability to reproduce stands in the way of the continual conquest of Native lands, threaten the continued success of colonization. As Ines Hernandez-Avila notes, Native women have been particularly targeted for abuse because of their capacity to give birth. "It is because of a Native American woman's sex that she is hunted down and slaughtered, in fact, singled out, because she has the potential through childbirth to assure the continuance of the people."[2]

David Stannard points out that control over women's reproductive abilities and destruction of women and children are essential in destroying a people. If the women of a nation are not disproportionately killed, then that nation's population will not be severely affected. He argues that Native women and children were targeted for wholesale killing in order to destroy the Indian nations.[3] Colonizers such as Andrew Jackson recommended that troops systematically kill Indian women and children after massacres in order to complete extermination.

The notion that communities of color, including Native communities, are "polluting" to the body politic continues to inform the contemporary population control movement. People of color are scapegoated for everything from environmental destruction, to poverty, to war. The so-called overpopulation of people of color is "the single greatest threat to the health of the planet."[4] "They" are destroying "our" environment; "they" are crowding "us" out. The Population Institute even went so far as to blame the Persian Gulf War on overpopulation rather than on US military and economic imperialism and our ravenous appetite for foreign oil.[5] Consequently, Native women and women of color deserve no bodily integrity—any form of dangerous contraception is appropriate for them so long as it stops them from reproducing. Or, as Chicago-based reproductive rights activist Sharon Powell describes it, women of color are "better dead than pregnant."

Sterilization Abuse

During the 1970s, the growth of non-whites in the Third World and in the United States was viewed by elites as a national security risk. As many Third World countries began to resist the neocolonial economic policies imposed by the World Bank and the International Monetary Fund (IMF), the United States government and business interests blamed the unrest on the Third World's "overpopulation problem." In 1977, R.T. Ravenholt from the US Agency for International Development (USAID),

announced a plan to sterilize a quarter of the world's women because, as he put it:

> Population control is necessary to maintain the normal opera-
> tion of US commercial interests around the world. Without our
> trying to help these countries with their economic and social de-
> velopment, the world would rebel against the strong US com-
> mercial presence.[6]

Patricia Hill Collins notes that the state's interest in limiting the
growth of the Black population coincided with the expansion of
post-World War II welfare provisions that have allowed many African-Americans to leave exploitative jobs. As a result, the growing
unemployment rate among people of color means that non-white
America is no longer simply a reservoir of cheap labor; it is therefore considered "surplus" population.[7] One recently declassified
federal document, National Security Study Memorandum 200, revealed that even in 1976 the United States government regarded
the growth of the non-white population as a threat to national security.[8] The equation between people of color and pollution is evident in the statement of one doctor justifying mass sterilization:

> People pollute, and too many people crowded too close to-
> gether cause many of our social and economic problems. These
> in turn are aggravated by involuntary and irresponsible parent-
> hood.... We also have obligations to the society of which we are
> part. The welfare mess, as it has been called, cries out for solu-
> tions, one of which is fertility control.[9]

Contemporary Ob/Gyn

In 1970, the Department of Health, Education, and Welfare
(DHEW) accelerated programs that paid for the majority of costs
to sterilize Medicaid recipients.[10] In 1979, it was discovered that
seven in ten US hospitals that performed voluntary sterilizations
for Medicaid recipients violated 1974 DHEW guidelines by disregarding sterilization consent procedures and by sterilizing women
through "elective" hysterectomies.[11]

Native people do not constitute a relatively sizable workforce.
However, because the majority of the energy resources in this

country are on Indian lands, the continued existence of Indian people is a threat to capitalist operations. Evidence of this fact is the Senate testimony offered by Scott M. Matheson on behalf of various mining associations in opposing the protection of Indian sacred sites. He argued:

> [M]uch of the country's natural resources are located on federal land. For example, federal lands contain 85% of the nation's crude oil, 40% of the natural gas, 40% of the uranium, 85% of the coal reserves …. Thus it is obvious that [federal protection of sacred sites] by creating a Native American veto over federal land use decisions, will … severely interfere with the orderly use and development of the country's natural resources.[12]

Because Native peoples live on lands that multinational corporations still want, both covert and overt genocidal practices against Native peoples continue. Thus, it is not surprising that Native women were targets of the population craze when Indian Health Services initiated a fully federally funded sterilization campaign in 1970.[13] Dr. Connie Uri, a Cherokee/Choctaw doctor, was one of the first people to uncover the mass sterilization of Native women in the 1970s. A young Indian woman entered her office in Los Angeles in 1972 and requested a "womb transplant." Upon further investigation, Dr. Uri discovered that this woman had been given a complete hysterectomy for birth control purposes when she was only 20 years old without being informed of the irreversibility of the operation. The woman was otherwise completely healthy. At first, Dr. Uri thought she had suffered an isolated case of malpractice until she continued to hear from Indian women who had been sterilized either under duress or without full information on the irreversibility of the procedure. Dr. Uri pressured Congress to investigate, and eventually Senator James Abourezk requested a study of United States Indian Health Service (IHS) sterilization policies.[14]

The General Accounting Office (GAO) released a report in 1976, which studied four of the twelve areas serviced by IHS (Albuquerque, Phoenix, Aberdeen, and Oklahoma City). According to this report, 3001 Native women of childbearing age, or approximately 5 percent of total Native women of childbearing age in these areas, were sterilized between 1973 and 1976.[15] A total of

3,406 sterilizations were performed during this time. Of these sterilizations, thirty-six were performed on women under the age of 21, despite a court-ordered moratorium on such procedures.[16]

Native activists have contested these numbers, arguing that the percentage of Native women sterilized is much higher. Dr. Connie Uri conducted an investigation of sterilization policies in Claremore, Oklahoma, and charged that Claremore was sterilizing one woman for every seven births that occurred in the hospital. She claimed that 132 women had been sterilized in 1973, 100 of them non-therapeutic. And in July 1974, forty-eight Native women had been sterilized in Claremore, most of them in their twenties. Her investigation did not rest only on hospital records (as did the GAO report), but on interviews with women who had been sterilized. Consequently, her numbers are much higher than the GAO's report of Native women sterilized in the Oklahoma City IHS area.[17] Her investigations led her to conclude that 25 percent of Native women had been sterilized without their informed consent.[18] She further charged that "all the pureblood women of the Kaw tribe of Oklahoma have now been sterilized."[19] Other activists report even higher numbers. Women of All Red Nations (WARN) estimated that close to 50 percent of Indian women had been sterilized in the 1970s. Native rights activist Lehman Brightman asserts that 40 percent of Native women and 10 percent of Native men were sterilized in this decade.[20] Pat Bellanger of WARN contends that sterilization rates are as high as 80 percent on some reservations.[21]

One study of sterilization rates in Montana, which focused on the Blackfeet reservation and the urban Indian population of Great Falls, found that Indian women were twice as likely as white women to be sterilized.[22] Another study of sterilization rates on the Navajo reservation found that tubal ligations[23] (the author did not give information on hysterectomies) increased by approximately 61 percent from 1972 to 1977.[24] As mentioned previously, for the population of a community to decline, the women have to be targeted for sterilization purposes. Thus, it is interesting that the Montana study found that no Native men had been sterilized in the

populations it studied, whereas 10 percent of white males are sterilized in the general US population.[25]

It is difficult to ascertain the accuracy of these numbers, however, because these citations often do not specify whether the
women are of childbearing age (even white women who are past
childbearing age have high sterilization rates). For instance, many
articles which cite the GAO report mention that 3,400 women
were sterilized without mentioning that 3,000 of them were of
childbearing age.[26]

Also, most of these numbers, such as Dr. Uri's, are based on
one or two IHS hospitals, from which activists generalize what
they believe sterilization rates are for the United States as a whole.
However, it is difficult to make generalizations, because IHS did
not have a uniform protocol for sterilization procedures until after
the uproar over sterilization abuses forced them to adopt one. As a
result, sterilization policies could fluctuate greatly depending on
the particular philosophies of the administrators at various IHS areas (as is the case with Depo-Provera and Norplant policies today,
which I will discuss later in this essay).

In addition, the basis for the numbers given by many of these
individuals is not clearly explained. Given that the Native population did increase in this period, it might seem unlikely that 50 percent of Native women of childbearing age were sterilized.
However, the study of sterilization rates in Montana found that on
average, Native women who were sterilized had three to four children, which might explain how high sterilization rates would not
necessarily lead to a population decrease in Native communities.[27]

Nevertheless, the widespread data we do have of stories of Native women who were sterilized strongly suggests that Indian
women were targeted for sterilization without their informed consent. Dr. Uri discovered that many of the women sterilized at
Claremore were sterilized within a day or two after giving birth.[28]
Such policies would violate federal regulations requiring a 72-hour
waiting period between consenting to the operation and having it.
One woman informed Dr. Uri that she was advised to get a sterilization for headaches. "The doctor told the woman her head hurt
because she was afraid of becoming pregnant, and advised steriliza-

tion. The woman agreed, but the headaches persisted. She later learned she had a brain tumor."[29] Another woman went to a doctor for stomach problems. The doctor assumed she was ill because she was pregnant and yelled, "Why the hell don't you get your tubes tied so you won't get sick any more?"[30] In addition to the stories reported by Dr. Uri, Maria Sanchez, former chief tribal judge of the Northern Cheyenne, reported that two 15-year-old girls were sterilized during what they were told were tonsillectomy operations.[31]

In another story, Norma Jean Serena (Creek/Shawnee) was pressured to undergo a tubal ligation by welfare caseworkers after the birth of her third child. These caseworkers also removed all her children into foster care because she was an "unfit mother." Three years later, she sued Armstrong County for damages from the sterilization and to have her children returned to her. The jury found that the children had been taken away under false pretenses, but did not support her claim that her civil rights had been violated through the sterilization procedure. During the court proceedings, the major complaint against Serena was that she was "dirty and unkempt" and that she had Black friends who, in the minds of the social workers, were also inherently polluting to the body politic.[32]

Interestingly, the GAO report sidesteps the issue of informed consent. The government refused to interview women to determine if they been had given informed consent because "we believe such an effort would not be productive."[33] According to the GAO report, Native women would not be able to remember if they had given informed consent. Of course, how informed could their consent have been if they did not remember anything they were told? True informed consent for sterilization should require lengthy counseling so that women fully understand the finality of the operation. If women do not remember whether they consented, they probably did not receive this kind of counseling.

However, the GAO did note that IHS was "generally not in compliance with IHS regulations. Although there were consent forms in the medical files, most of these forms did not comply with IHS requirements."[34] These consent forms did not: (1) indicate that the basic elements of informed consent had been presented orally to the patient; (2) contain written summaries of the oral presentation; and (3) contain a statement at the top of the form, notifying subjects of their right to withdraw consent. One consent form document did meet the Indian Health Service requirements, but when used was filled out incorrectly.[35] In response to a US District Court order, DHEW had issued regulations which continued a moratorium on sterilization for persons under 21 years of age or who are mentally incompetent. Despite these regulations, thirty-six women under 21 were sterilized during this time period.[36]

Not only was IHS not in compliance with DHEW regulations, but these regulations were also problematic. The DHEW had ended a requirement at this time that "individuals seeking sterilization be orally informed at the outset that no Federal benefits can be withdrawn because of failure to accept sterilizations."[37] Further, it did not require that the signature of the patient appear on the consent forms; thus we are relying solely upon the word of the doctors that informed consent was given.[38] In addition, the informed consent sheet is highly technical, and would not necessarily be understandable by someone who was not fluent in English. Further complicating matters, over half of the sterilizations were performed by contract facilities which do not have to abide by federal procedures regarding informed consent.[39]

As a result of the uproar over these violations, IHS strengthened its sterilization policies. Now sterilization procedures must meet "regulatory policy and legal requirements for informed consent and performance of sterilization procedures."[40] Additionally, the Area/Program Director has to dispatch all data and statistics to Headquarters on time.[41] The current IHS policy regarding sterilization is:

> IHS will neither promote nor discourage sterilization or fertility of the population it serves. Its overall policy is geared to the enhancement of life through assuring the availability of legally, ethically and medically acceptable information and services that afford families and individuals the opportunity to assure that each child is a wanted one. In addition, before discharge following delivery the mother will be offered an opportunity for counseling, guidance and/or services for family planning.[42]

Sterilization abuse, while curbed, is certainly not dead in IHS or society at large. One woman I know went into IHS in the 1990s for back surgery, and came out with a hysterectomy. In the larger society, Barbara Harris started an organization called CRACK (Children Requiring a Caring Kommunity) in Anaheim, California, which gives women $200 to have sterilizations.[43]

Long-Acting Hormonal Contraceptive Abuse

While sterilization abuse in the United States has ebbed since the 1970s, state control over reproductive freedom continues through the promotion of unsafe, long-acting hormonal contraceptives like Depo-Provera and Norplant for women of color, women on federal assistance, and women with disabilities.

As the population scare and the demonization of poverty have moved to the mainstream of the dominant culture in the United States, Norplant and Depo-Provera have become frontline weapons in the war against the poor and populations of color. State legislatures have considered bills that would give women on public assistance bonuses if they used Norplant.[44] In California, a Black single mother convicted of child abuse was given the "choice" of using Norplant or being sentenced to four years in prison.[45] The *Philadelphia Inquirer* also ran an editorial suggesting that Norplant could be a useful tool in "reducing the underclass."[46] Over 87 percent of all Norplant implants are government funded, indicating that poor women are being targeted for Norplant.[47]

Both Depo and Norplant have been approved for contraceptive use by the FDA. However, as the National Women's Health Network points out, FDA approval does not necessarily mean that a drug is safe.[48] Among many of the problems with the FDA approval process is the FDA's reliance upon the manufacturer's data regarding animal and human testing and its failure to double-check the manufacturer's data.

The FDA does not allow consumer groups to verify research studies. Data is prepared by researchers who are often funded directly or indirectly by manufacturers. FDA advisory committees are not constituted by a balance of experts who would be knowledgeable about the wide variety of side effects resulting from drugs. The FDA relies upon the manufacturer for information on adverse effects. Physicians are not required to report adverse drug reactions to the FDA, and the FDA seldom follows up on adverse reaction reports by consumers.[49] In fact, FDA Commissioner Jaime Goddard estimates that "one percent or less" of the adverse reactions to any drug are ever reported to the FDA by doctors.[50]

Depo-Provera is a long-acting injectable contraceptive made by Upjohn Company. This injection prevents pregnancy by stopping the production of progesterone and estrogen, which in turn inhibits ovulation and prevents the lining of the uterus from being prepared to accept a fertilized egg. Also, the drug can cause a mucus surplus to form in the cervix, preventing contact between the sperm and ovum.[51] Side effects that have been linked to Depo-Provera include: irregular bleeding (and this symptom can mask symptoms of uterine cancer), depression (sometimes suicidal depression), weight gain, osteoporosis, loss of sex drive, breast cancer, sterility, cervical cancer, headaches, and many others.[52]

Upjohn, not surprisingly, denies the link between the more extreme symptoms and Depo-Provera. The National Women's Health Network maintained a registry of reported Depo-Provera side effects and has recorded over one hundred related effects.[53] *The Ultimate Test Animal,* a documentary on Depo-Provera, showed interviews with several women who began to suffer from blood clots in the lungs, extreme bleeding requiring a hysterectomy, and cervical cancer after receiving Depo. Depo-Provera is provider-dependent. If a woman has adverse side effects to Depo, she must wait until the Depo leaves her system.

In beagle and rhesus monkey tests initiated in 1968, Depo-Provera was linked to increased risk for breast and uterine cancer.[54] The FDA Public Board of Inquiry stated in 1982, "Never has a drug whose target population is entirely healthy people been shown to be so pervasively carcinogenic in animals as has Depo-Provera."[55] Many health care activists have argued that Upjohn has suppressed much of the information from these animal tests, and that these tests indicate that Depo is even more carcinogenic than reported.[56] Upjohn argued that beagles were not an appropriate test for Depo-Provera because they are very susceptible to breast cancer. Dr. Solomon Sobel of the FDA, however, testified that there are no contraceptives which are carcinogenic in beagles which have reached the United States market.

The largest test on humans was conducted for eleven years beginning in 1967, through the Grady Clinic, affiliated with Emory University in Atlanta. *The Ultimate Test Animal* documents the widespread abuses in this clinical trial. Robert Hatcher, who directed the study, admits that there was no established protocol for the study. In 1978, the FDA sent investigators to Grady. They found that many women were not told they were part of an experiment or that there were side effects associated with Depo.

Several women got cancer and/or died during the trials, but these cases were not reported to the FDA as was required. Hatcher did not send one legally required annual report during the entire study. Women with medically contraindicated conditions, such as cancer, were still given the shot. Record keeping on the clients was sloppy; over 13,000 women were lost to follow-up. Hatcher's response to the critiques of his clinical trial is that these mistakes "did not have any detrimental impact on patients."[57]

However, the National Black Women's Health Project attempted to track some of the women who had been lost in Grady's records and found that these women were suffering from extreme adverse effects.[58] Many young women had double mastectomies, uterine and cervical cancer, or hysterectomies as a result of hemorrhaging. Several women also became clinically depressed from Depo, attempting suicide as a result. Upjohn's response to this side effect is: "headaches, depression and loss of libido mostly require reassurance from a trusted and respected friend or counselor."[59] Dr. Sobel notes of the Grady study:

> [It was] not a carefully controlled trial, but rather, it was a treatment program in which the drug was dispensed without the usual care and monitoring that we associate with a controlled clinical trial. The follow up of patients, etc., was not good, and the FDA could not really accept this as a study of the quality that we require in the drug approval process.[60]

Because of these extreme side effects, several national women's health organizations, including the National Women's Health Network, the Native American Women's Health Education Resource Center, the National Latina Health Organization, and the Black Women's Health Project, have all condemned Depo-Provera as an inappropriate form of contraception.

In 1978, the FDA denied approval for Depo-Provera as contraception on the grounds that: (1) dog studies confirmed an elevated rate of breast cancer; (2) there appeared to be an increased risk of birth defects in human fetuses exposed to the drug; and (3) there was no pressing need shown for use of the drug as a contraceptive.[61] In 1987, the FDA changed its regulations and began to require cancer testing in rats and mice instead of dogs and monkeys; Depo did not cause cancer in these animals.[62] Also, the World Health Organization reported in 1991 that after a nine-year study in three countries, there was no "evidence for increased risk of breast cancer with long duration of use."[63]

It is important to note, however, that nine years do not constitute a long duration of use, and there are no tests to show the long-term safety of either Norplant or Depo-Provera. These studies are also controversial. One study in New Zealand did indicate a higher incident of breast cancer among women under 34.[64] As the Women's Health Education Project points out, all of these studies are conducted by Upjohn, who controls all the data. As with animal studies and the Grady study, there are similar reports of women with extreme side effects being eliminated from the data, and some of the trials were conducted on sample sizes that are too small to be statistically significant.[65] Nevertheless, Depo-Provera was approved by the FDA in 1992.

Even before Depo was approved by the FDA, it was frequently used off-label by IHS, particularly on Native women with difficulties. The reason given was hygienics. Depo-Provera prevents Native women with disabilities from having their periods, keeping them "cleaner" for their caretakers. Once again, Native women's bodies are viewed as inherently dirty, in need of cleansing and purification. Patrick Gideon of the Oklahoma City IHS area said that IHS would not use a non–FDA approved drug except as a final option. However, "It is used in women who are unable to care for themselves. For hygienic reasons, we will go ahead and give it."[66] Apparently, keeping Native women "clean" by sterilizing them is more important than protecting Native women's health.

The Phoenix IHS policy in the 1980s, according to area director Burton Attico, was to substitute Depo for sterilization because sterilization was no longer allowed on patients with mental disabilities. "We use it to stop their periods. There is nothing else that will do it. To have to change a pad on someone developmentally disabled, you've got major problems. The fact that they become infertile while on it is a side benefit."[67] Raymond Jannett of Phoenix IHS argues that Depo-Provera helps girls avoid emotions from their periods. "Depo-Provera turned them back into their sweet, poor handicapped selves. I take some pride in being a pioneer in that regard."[68] But, he said, while he has no problems using it on Indian women, "I will not be going out and using it on attractive 16-year-old girls who one day hope to be mothers." Even Upjohn, the manufacturer of Depo-Provera stated that use of Depo-Provera is inappropriate for promoting hygienics.[69]

Depo-Provera has been largely distributed without the informed consent of either patients or their caretakers. Attico claimed that doctors obtained oral consent, but admits they did not use written consent forms. Cecile Balone, executive director of A School for Me, a Navajo reservation facility, reports that Depo-Provera was used for two years before written consent forms were developed. After they were developed, none of them ever reached the parents or guardians of the girls receiving Depo-Provera. Jannett similarly asserted that he has never offered consent forms to his patients or explained the potential risks or side effects of Depo-Provera. "I don't tell them that rhesus monkeys did strange things, no. Most parents don't have rhesus monkey children. I have a veterinarian son. I'll let him worry about the beagle dogs." Jarret further states, "I don't go into a great deal that it's carcinogenic.... Instead, I tell them it's a drug that helps combat cancer."[70]

Norplant is also a progesterone (a hormone that helps maintain pregnancy), but it is implanted through five rods into a woman's arm, where it prevents pregnancy for five years. This implant injects low-level doses of progestin into the system, suppressing ovulation and thickening the cervical mucus so that it is impervious to sperm. As with Depo, there are no studies demonstrating the long-term safety of Norplant. Norplant is correlated with a number of side effects, the most common being constant bleeding, sometimes for more than ninety days. About 82 percent of Norplant users experience irregular, usually heavy, bleeding the first year.[71]

In addition, irregular bleeding is also a symptom of endometrial and cervical cancer and thus can mask those symptoms. This side effect is particularly problematic for Native women, since women are often excluded from ceremonies while they are bleeding. Other reported side effects include blindness, hair loss, dizziness, nausea, headaches, strokes, heart attacks, tumors, and sterility.[72] Another significant problem with both Norplant and Depo is that they do not protect against STDs. It is problematic to promote these non-barrier methods of contraception in this time of AIDS. One study found that 48 percent of all women who used condoms prior to receiving Norplant stopped using condoms afterwards.[73]

Because of the extreme side effects, approximately 30 percent of women on Norplant want it removed within one year,[74] and the majority want it out within three years.[75] To date, over 50,000 women have sued Wyeth-Ayerst Laboratories for Norplant-related side effects. Norplant sales, as a result, have dropped from 800 per day to less than one hundred per day.[76] Consequently, Depo-Provera, which most women's health organizations believe to be more dangerous than Norplant, ironically is increasing its sales where Norplant sales are dropping off.

As with Depo-Provera, Norplant is provider-dependent. When I was involved in organizing against Norplant in Chicago, I found that women who do not want Norplant have difficulty finding a provider who is willing to take it out. Many doctors know how to insert Norplant, but do not know how to remove it. Doctors also often ignore women's requests for removal. Medicaid typically pays for Norplant insertion but not for its removal.[77]

Norplant was approved for distribution in 1990. Prior to its approval it had been tested in several Third World countries. *The*

Human Laboratory documents how women receiving Norplant in Bangladesh without their informed consent were not able to have it removed when they developed side effects. Further, when they attempted to report side effects, doctors scolded them and refused to record the information. One woman attempting to get it removed told her doctor, " 'I'm dying, please help me get it out.' They said 'OK, when you die you inform us, we'll get it out of your dead body.' "[78] Similar stories are reported in Haiti, India, and many other Third World countries.[79] From these unethical tests, Wyeth-Ayerst reported that "Norplant is a highly effective, safe and acceptable method among Bangladeshi women."[80]

The Native American Women's Health Education Resource Center (NAWHERC) conducted a study of IHS policies regarding Depo-Provera and Norplant because it was finding that they were being aggressively promoted in many Native communities. NAWHERC found that IHS policies vary widely depending on the geographic area. This is similar to IHS's sterilization policies in the 1970s before uniform policies and procedures were instituted.

Prior to FDA approval in 1992, IHS maintained a registry of women on Depo-Provera. This practice was discontinued after its approval, and now women on Depo or Norplant are not monitored or tracked in a systematic manner.[81] This practice is problematic given the high turnover of staff within IHS because Norplant *must* be removed after five years to avoid life-threatening ectopic pregnancies, and Depo must be administered quarterly to be effective. Thus Native women may face similar circumstances as women in India who were not tracked during clinical trials of Norplant to ensure its prompt removal.[82]

Each IHS area has a designated Area Program Maternal Child Health Chief (MCH) who administers IHS family planning policies. Because the system is so decentralized, the range of contraceptives, the training provided, and tracking systems required vary widely depending upon the area.[83] Consequently, some areas do not make Depo or Norplant available at all, some encourage the use of both methods, and some make one or the other available.

NAWHERC found that not all IHS areas were lax in their protocol regarding Norplant and Depo-Provera distribution. It applauds the Crow Service Unit for its detailed protocol which ensures that "the more complex tasks of counseling and documentation are extensively supervised, and that the counseling is performed by each provider in a standardized, acceptable fashion."[84] However, they note that IHS should have a uniform policy on Depo/Norplant to ensure that all women receiving these services receive informed consent and are monitored to ensure that any side effects they suffer from these drugs are addressed promptly.

One shortcoming of NAWHERC's study is that it is limited to questioning the providers, and not the recipients, of Norplant and Depo-Provera. A study focusing on the recipients of these contraceptives might reveal another story about IHS policies regarding informed consent. When I worked with WARN in Chicago (which provided much educational material on these contraceptives to the Native community), I routinely heard from women who said they were pressured by either their caseworkers or IHS doctors to take Norplant, and that they were not told of its side effects. I talked to one health care worker who told me that IHS on her reservation did not even inform women that forms of contraception exist other than Norplant or Depo-Provera.

NAWHERC held a conference on reproductive rights in Rapid City, South Dakota, which I attended in 1996. At the workshop on Depo-Provera, the room was filled with distraught Native women who were first hearing about the side effects of the Depo-Provera injections they had been receiving. I have also heard from Native women in one IHS area who were told that Norplant has no side effects, and yet women receiving Norplant were suffering from effects such as hair loss, tumors, depression, and constant bleeding. In the film *The Ultimate Test Animal*, a Native woman enters an urban clinic with a hidden camera pretending to seek contraceptive counseling. The following is a transcription of the information she received:

> Your body gets mixed up when it's on Depo-Provera so your monthly period may not return right away. Another thing you need to know about this shot is that it is not approved for birth control by the FDA, which we think is stupid.... There was this one study that was done on beagle dogs and they gave a bunch

of beagle dogs this medicine, though in much higher dosages than you will be getting, and some of the dogs developed breast cancer. Now, this study was not a good one because beagles are susceptible to breast cancer anyway. You're obviously not a beagle dog; you're obviously not going to get as high dosage, but we're obligated to tell you this anyway.[85]

This transcription demonstrates that it is possible for health care providers to provide information that, while technically providing clients with all the necessary information, conveys a misleading sense of the issues involved with these contraceptives. Furthermore, even when women receive information on the side effects of contraceptives, they assume that their doctors will not provide them with drugs that could be unsafe. As one Grady trial victim stated in *The Ultimate Test Animal*: "I felt anything Grady would give me would be for my better, and not experimental."

Abortion and Sterilization

Government policies couple the promotion of sterilization or dangerous contraceptives with restrictive abortion policies. As a result of the Hyde Amendment, which denies federal funding for abortion services, IHS (a federal agency) cannot provide abortions to women unless the mother's life is in danger. Since Native women largely access services through IHS, their access to abortion services is disproportionately affected by the Hyde Amendment.

There appears to be some dispute because of vagueness in the language of the legislation as to whether IHS can provide abortions in cases of rape and incest. One domestic violence advocate informed me that a client on her reservation was seeking an abortion for a pregnancy resulting from a rape. At first IHS turned down her request. The advocate sought legal assistance and was informed that there might be cause to sue IHS, at which point the clinic reversed its position and provided the abortion.

Abortion policies then become another strategy to coerce Native women to pursue sterilization or long-acting hormonal contraceptives in order to avoid the trauma of unwanted pregnancy. The strategy of coupling restrictive abortion with sterilization policies is evident within North Carolina's General Assembly HB 1430 which states: "The Department of Human Resources shall ensure that all women who receive an abortion funded through the State Abortion Fund receive Norplant implantation and do not remove it unless the procedure is medically contraindicated."[86] This legislation targets women during a vulnerable period while they are facing an unwanted pregnancy to pressure them into accepting long-acting hormonal contraceptives.

Similarly, in the Northwest Territories of Canada, the Status of Women Council uncovered punitive abortion policies at the Stanton Yellowknife Hospital, which services Inuit women. Women were denied anesthesia during abortion services as punishment for seeking abortions. One woman was told by her doctor: "This really hurt, didn't it? But let that be a lesson before you get yourself in this situation again."[87]

This controversy was uncovered when a rape victim, Ellen Hamilton, went to the media saying that her abortion had been worse than the rape: she was given no counseling, pinned down, and given no anesthesia during the procedure. Hamilton's comments were publicized in the Northwest Territories, prompting a flood of responses from women who had suffered similar fates. The response from the hospital was that they provided all the women with aspirin, making them the only hospital in Canada to provide only aspirin for pain relief during abortion procedures.[88] The Canadian government ordered an inquiry into the hospital's procedures, forcing the hospital to issue a statement that it had developed a new plan "for providing patients with choices in pain control during abortion procedures."[89]

The general rationale for this policy appears to be to punish the women for having abortions. One woman who went in for an abortion and a tubal ligation the same day reported that she was told, "The anesthesiologist does not believe in abortions, we will administer the anesthetic following the abortion, for the tubal ligation." By increasing the pain and trauma associated with abortion, or by making it inaccessible, Native women feel even more pressure to agree to sterilizations or dangerous contraceptives to avoid the traumas of unwanted pregnancies. Although the majority of Native women are "pro-choice" to some extent,[90] some Native women activists do not support abortion rights because they see abortion as a genocidal policy. However, it is equally clear that restrictive abortion policies combined with lenient sterilization policies are also genocidal to Native communities.

Consequently, many Native women's organizations, such as Women of All Red Nations, the Indigenous Women's Network, and the Native American Women's Health and Education Resource Center, have formed to develop a truly comprehensive reproductive rights agenda for Native women. Organized beyond the simple binary of "pro-choice" vs. "pro-life" positions on abortion rights, these organizations attempt to address the underlying causes of Native women's reproductive un/freedom—colonialism, racism, economic exploitation, and so on. As Native activist Justine Smith states:

> The reproductive rights movement frames the issues around individual "choice"—does the woman have the choice to have or not to have an abortion. This analysis obscures all the social conditions that prevent women from having and making real choices—lack of health care, poverty, lack of social services, etc. In the Native context, where women often find the only contraceptives available to them are dangerous... where they live in communities in which unemployment rates can run as high as 80 percent, and where their life expectancy can be as low as 47 years, reproductive "choice" defined so narrowly is a meaningless concept. Instead, Native women and men must fight for community self-determination and sovereignty over their health care.[91]

Conclusion

The attacks on the reproductive rights of Native women are frontline strategies in the continuing wars against Native nations. Native people become metaphorically transformed into pollution or dirt from which the body politic must constantly purify itself of to ensure its growth. Herbert Aptheker describes the logical consequences of these population control movements:

> The ultimate logic of this is crematoria; people are themselves constituting the pollution, and inferior people in particular, then crematoria become really vast sewerage projects. Only so may

one understand those who attend the ovens and concocted and conducted the entire enterprise; those "wasted"—to use US army jargon reserved for colonial hostilities—are not really, not fully people.[92]

Consequently, attacks against the reproductive rights of Native women can be seen as having less to do with a denial of reproductive "choices" and more to do with the history of genocide against Native communities. As the ability of Native women to reproduce the next generations of Native people continues to stand in the way of government and corporate takeovers of Indian land, Native women become seen as little more than pollutants which threaten the well-being of the colonial body. In the colonial imagination, Native women are indeed "better dead than pregnant."

1   Ann Stoler, *Race and the Education of Desire* (Chapel Hill, NC: Duke University Press, 1997), 59.

2   Ines Hernandez-Avila, "In Praise of Insubordination, or What Makes a Good Woman Go Bad?," in Emilie Buchwald, Pamela R. Fletcher, and Martha Roth, ed., *Transforming a Rape Culture* (Minneapolis, MN: Milkweed, 1993), 386.

3   David Stannard, *American Holocaust* (Oxford: Oxford University Press, 1992), 121.

4   Population Institute, Annual Report (1991). See also Zero Population Growth's fundraising appeal, (n.d.); "Population Stabilization: The Real Solution," pamphlet from the Los Angeles chapter of the Sierra Club's Population Committee; Population Institute fundraising appeal which states that population growth is the root cause of poverty, hunger and environmental destruction.

5   Population Institute, Annual Report (1991).

6   Paul Wagman, "US Goal: Sterilizations of Millions of World's Women," *St. Louis Post-Dispatch*, April 22, 1977.

7   Patricia Hill Collins, *Black Feminist Thought* (London: Routledge, 1991), 51.

8   Debra Hanania-Freeman, "Norplant: Freedom of Choice or a Plan for Genocide?" *EIR* (May 14, 1993), 18–23.

9   "Oklahoma: Sterilization of Women Charged to I.H.S.," *Akwesasne Notes* (Winter 1989), 11.

10   Bruce Johansen, "Reprise/Forced Sterilizations: Native Americans and the Last Gasp of Eugenics," *Native Americas*, No. 15:4 (Winter 1998), 45.

11   "Survey Finds Seven in 10 Hospitals Violate DHEW Guidelines on Informed Consent for Sterilization," *Family Planning Perspectives*, No. 11, (November/December 1979), 366; Claudia Dreifus, "Sterilizing the Poor," in Claudia Dreifus, ed., *Seizing Our Bodies* (Toronto: Vintage Press, 1977), 105–120.

12   Andrea Smith, *Sacred Sites, Sacred Rites* (New York: National Council of Churches, 1998), 14.

13   Johansen, "Reprise/Forced Sterilizations," *Native Americas*, 45.

14   Gayle Mark Jarvis, "The Theft of Life," *WARN Report* (n.d.), 14.

15   "Investigation of Allegations Concerning Indian Health Services B-164031(5); HRD-77-3," (Washington, DC: General Accounting Office, 1976), 28.

16   Ibid., 21.

17   "Oklahoma: Sterilization of Women Charged to I.H.S.," *Akwesasne*, 11-12.

18   Jarvis, "The Theft of Life," *WARN*, 14.

19   Dorothy Roberts, *Killing the Black Body* (New York: Pantheon Books, 1997), 45.

20   Johansen, "Reprise/Forced Sterilizations," *Native Americas*, 44.

21   Pat Bellanger, "Native American Women, Forced Sterilization, and the Family," in Gayla Wadnizak Ellis, ed., *Every Woman Has a Story* (Minneapolis, MN: Midwest Villages and Voices, 1982), 31.

22   Charles Warren, et al., "Assessing the Reproductive Behavior of On- and Off-Reservation American Indian Females: Characteristics of Two Groups in Montana," *Social Biology*, Vol. 37, (Spring/Summer 1990), 77.

23   Tubal ligations are a form of sterilization where a woman's fallopian tubes are surgically blocked through burning them or cutting them and tying them, thus preventing her eggs from travelling to her uterus. The process results in generally irreversible sterilization.

24   Helena Temkin-Greener, Stephen Kunitz, David Broudy, and Marlene Haffner, "Surgical Fertility Regulation among Women on the Navajo Indian Reservation, 1972- 1978," *American Journal of Public Health*, Vol. 71, No. 4 (1981), 40.

25   Warren et al., "Assessing the Reproductive Behavior of On- and Off-Reservation American Indian Females," *Social Biology*, 77.

26   Johansen, "Reprise/Forced Sterilizations," *Native Americas*, 44-47.

27   Warren et al., "Assessing the Reproductive Behavior of On- and Off-Reservation American Indian Females," *Social Biology*, 78.

28   Jarvis, "The Theft of Life," *WARN*, 14.

29   Ibid.

30   Ibid.

31   Johansen, "Reprise/Forced Sterilizations," *Native Americas*, 47.

32   Ibid.

33   "Investigation of Allegations Concerning Indian Health Services B-164031(5); HRD-77-3," 24.

34   Ibid.

35   Ibid., 4.

36   Ibid., 21.

37   Ibid., 4.

38   Ibid., 5.

39   Ibid., 4.

40   Federal Register 42 CFR, Parts 50 and 441, Sterilization and Abortions (November 8, 1978).

41   Lin Krust and Charon Assetoyer, "A Study of the Use of Depo-Provera and Norplant by the Indian Health Services" (Lake Andes, SD: Native American Women's Health Education Resource Center, 1993), 15.

42   Ibid., 12.

43   Luis Sinco, "Sterilization Plan Fuels Controversy," *Detroit News*, (1998) Available from www.detroitnews.com/1998/nation/9804/17/04170085.htm.

44   Roberts, *Killing the Black Body*, 104–110.

45   Gretchen Long, "Norplant: A Victory, Not a Panacea for Poverty," *The National Lawyers Guild Practitioner*, Vol. 50, No. 1 (n.d.), 11.

46   Hanania-Freeman, "Norplant," *EIR*, 18–20.

47   Ibid., 21.

48   For example, the Dalkon Shield was approved for use by the FDA, and was then later implicated in the deaths and sterility of several women afterwards. Dowie and Johnston describe the manufacturer's suppression of data that indicated its health hazards in order to assure its FDA approval.

Mark Dowie and Tracy Johnston, "A Case of Corporate Malpractice and the Dalkon Shield," in Dreifus, ed., *Seizing Our Bodies*, 105–120.

49 Doris Haire, "How the F.D.A. Determines the 'Safety' of Drugs– Just How Safe is 'Safe?'" (Washington, DC: National Women's Health Network, 1982).

50 Mike Masterson and Patricia Guthrie, "Taking the Shot," *The Arizona Republic*, 1986.

51 Krust and Assetoyer, "A Study of the Use of Depo-Provera and Norplant by the Indian Health Services," 5.

52 Feminist Women's Health Centers, "Depo-Provera (The Shot)" (1997), www.fwhc.org/bcdepo.htm; Gena Corea, "Testimony: Board of Public Inquiry on Depo-Provera" (unpublished document, 1993).

53 Masterson and Guthrie, "Taking the Shot," *Arizona*.

54 Ibid.

55 Krust and Assetoyer, "A Study of the Use of Depo-Provera and Norplant by the Indian Health Services," 4.

56 Stephen Minkin, "Depo-Provera: A Critical Analysis" (San Francisco: Institute for Food and Development, n.d.); Corea, "Testimony: Board of Public Inquiry on Depo-Provera," op. cit.

57 Karan Branan and Bill Turnley, *The Ultimate Test Animal* (Film, The Cinema Guild), 1984.

58 Ibid.

59 Corea, "Testimony: Board of Public Inquiry on Depo-Provera," 5.

60 Solomon Sobel, "Testimony Before Public Board of Inquiry Regarding Depo Provera. Department of Health and Human Services; Food and Drug Administration, Docket No. 78N" (unpublished document, 1982): 13.

61 Masterson and Guthrie, "Taking the Shot," *Arizona*.

62 Feminist Women's Health Centers.

63 Mildred Hanson, "Injectable Contraceptive Arouses Controversy. Yes, Depo-Provera at Last!," *WomanWise* (Fall 1993), 6.

64 Luz Alvarez Martinez, "Injectable Contraceptive Arouses Controversy. No, We Have to Say No More!," *WomanWise* (Fall 1993), 6–10.

65 Sharon Todd, "New Reproductive Technologies: Norplant, Depo-Provera and RU486/PG," *Womanist Health Newsletter* (n.d.).

66 Masterson and Guthrie., "Taking the Shot," *Arizona*.

67 Ibid.

68 Ibid.

69 Ibid.

70 Ibid.

71 Hanania-Freeman, "Norplant," *EIR*, 18–23.

72 Ibid.; Deborah Cadbury, *The Human Laboratory* (Film, BBC), 1995; Sharon Cohen, "Norplant Lawsuits Flourish Along with Women's Reports of Problems," *Associated Press*, 1997, www.africa2000.com/SNDX/norplant.htm(1997).

73 Judith Scully, "Norplant: Is It Just a New Form of Birth Control or a Genocidal Tool?" (unpublished document, 1993).

74 Hanania-Freeman, "Norplant," *EIR*, 18–23; James Talan, "Women Tell of Norplant Nightmares," *Chicago Sun Times*, September 4, 1994, 25.

75 Roberts, *Killing the Black Body*, 123.

76 Cohen, "Norplant Lawsuits Flourish Along with Women's Reports of Problems," *AP*; Kim Painter, "Bad Image, Sales Plague Norplant Birth Control," *Detroit News*, August 27, 1995. Available from www.detnews.com/menu/stories/14655.htm.

77 Hanania-Freeman, "Norplant," *EIR*, 18–23.

78 Cadbury, *The Human Laboratory*.

79 Ammu Joseph, "India's Population 'Bomb' Explodes Over Women," *Ms.* (1992), 12–15; Kalpana Mehta, "Science and Ethics in the Norplant Trials," *Third World Resurgence*, No. 42/43, 26–28.

80 Cadbury, *The Human Laboratory*.

81 Krust and Assetoyer, "A Study of the Use of Depo-Provera and Norplant by the Indian Health Services," 13–14.

82 Joseph, "India's Population 'Bomb' Explodes Over Women," *Ms.*; Mehta, "Science and Ethics in the Norplant Trials," *TWR*, 27.

83 Krust and Assetoyer, "A Study of the Use of Depo-Provera and Norplant by the Indian Health Services," 14.

84 Ibid., 21.

85 Branan and Turnley, *The Ultimate Test Animal*.

86 State Congress of North Carolina, "House Bill 1430, Norplant Requirement/Funds. General Assembly of North Carolina." (1993).

87 Mary Williams Walsh, "Abortion Horror Stories Spur Inquiry," *Los Angeles Times*, April 3, 1992, A5.

88 Ibid.

89 Ibid.

90 According the 1991–1992 Women of Color Reproductive Health Poll, 80 percent of Native women agree with the statement that "the decision to have or not to have an abortion is one that every woman must make for herself." (Incidentally, the results were 80 percent for African American women, 55 percent for Latinas and 81 percent for Asians). Prepared by the National Council of Negro Women, Washington, DC.

91 Justine Smith, "Native Sovereignty and Social Justice: Moving Toward an Inclusive Social Justice Framework," in Jael Silliman and Ynestra King, eds., *Dangerous Intersections: Feminist Perspectives on Population, Environment and Development* (Cambridge, MA: South End Press, 1999), 211.

92 Herbert Aptheker, *Racism, Imperialism, and Peace* (Minneapolis, MN: MEP Press, n.d.), 144.

Chapter 6

Just Choices

Women of Color, Reproductive Health and Human Rights

Loretta J. Ross, Sarah L. Brownlee, Dazon Dixon Diallo, Luz Rodriquez, and SisterSong Women of Color Reproductive Health Project

Making just choices around reproductive health is difficult for women of color. Just choices are not simply a range of options, but of options that make sense in order to optimize our reproductive health. We don't expect perfect choices, but we want choices that don't violate our sense of dignity, fairness, and justice. Our ability to control what happens to our bodies is constantly challenged by poverty, racism, sexism, homophobia, and injustice in the United States.

We face political regimes that seek to restrict our migration, to punish us for poverty, and to incarcerate us for behaviors politicians have criminalized. We are subject to various population control schemes, carriers of our own internalized oppression, and objects of unprincipled medical research. The race, gender, and class discrimination faced by women of color interferes with our ability to acquire services or culturally appropriate reproductive health information, particularly information on reproductive tract infections (RTIs). Mental health issues—such as oppression, depression, substance abuse, physical and sexual violence, lack of education, the lack of availability of services, and poverty—are related to racial, gender, and economic inequalities that specifically limit the potential of women of color to live healthy lives.

Women of color have not been passive victims in the face of this onslaught. In the words of Francesca Miller, we are "repressed but not resigned."[1] Yet organizing around reproductive health issues for women of color has not been easy. As women of color, we have always sought to protect our reproductive freedom, but issues of power and subordination complicate our efforts to bring attention to the reproductive health issues that threaten our lives.

Sometimes we work with predominantly white organizations that marginalize issues of race and class, and privilege abortion rights over other issues of reproductive justice. In 1987, the Women of Color Program of the National Organization for Women (NOW) organized the first national conference for 400 women of color on reproductive rights. Similar conferences were organized in the late 1980s, also by predominantly white organizations such as the Religious Coalition for Abortion Rights, Planned Parenthood, the National Abortion Rights Action League (NARAL), and the Reproductive Freedom Project of the American Civil Liberties Union (ACLU). Each of these events brought together women of color to discuss reproductive health issues, but they also highlighted the problems of race and class besetting many white organizations. Women of color did not have significant influence on these organizations' agendas.

Some of us work with people of color organizations that marginalize gender and class issues, and where women's reproductive health issues are tangential to struggles against racism. Occasionally, women's reproductive health issues reach the agenda of these organizations, particularly in the areas of sterilization abuse and population control, but they rarely sustain any long-term momentum.

A number of women of color work with anti-poverty organizations that sometimes neglect race and gender issues altogether, assuming that class issues subsume concerns about reproductive health. Women of color numerically dominate organizations that work on poverty, homelessness, and welfare reform, but rarely do these organizations address the reproductive health needs of women of color. Similarly, programs that address violence against women of color sometimes highlight the connection between violence and poor health, but again, reproductive health issues are not their primary concern.

Few women of color organizations have significant programs that focus on reproductive health issues. Most women of color organizations address gender and racial discrimination, but many of these organizations believe that reproductive rights, particularly abortion rights, are too controversial in their communities. The exceptions are a handful of national groups formed in the early 1980s.

The first national conference on reproductive health for African-American women was held in 1990 and sponsored by the National Black Women's Health Project (NBWHP), founded in 1984. The National Latina Health Organization was based on the NBWHP model, as was the National Asian Women's Health Organization, and the Native American Women's Health Education Resource Center. For a brief period, a coalition of these organizations came together to participate in the International Conference on Population and Development held in Cairo, Egypt in 1994 and the Fourth World Conference for Women in Beijing, China in 1995. The coalition unfortunately dissolved after 1995 due to inadequate funding.

In the early part of the 1980s, women of color increased their visibility and numbers by reaching out to women and men in non-feminist circles. For example, strong relationships were developed with activists in anti-poverty and nationalist movements, like the National Welfare Rights Organization and the National Black United Front. Other efforts reached out to sororities, or to civic associations. The efforts were necessary because, without them, the small number of women of color in the feminist organizations could not exert influence and promote their agenda. Only by sponsoring dialogues and trainings among a wider audience were women of color able to build greater strength.

By the 1990s, women of color working on reproductive rights shifted their strategy from that of grassroots organizations to direct involvement in public policy debates. This shift in strategy was in response to external events, such as the hostility of the Supreme

Court, the vigor of attacks by federal and state legislatures, and the resurgence of population control propaganda. The historical focus on grassroots organizing was replaced by participation in public policy debates on abortion restrictions, contraceptive development and approval, the criminalization of pregnant women, and the linkage between population control and environmental degradation.

Among women of color, the more established national organizations made this shift either by establishing separate public policy offices, or by enlarging the percentage of time they spent in trying to influence state, federal, or judicial policies. The results of this change were immediately apparent. More publications by women of color on reproductive health issues began to emerge, and a few women of color organizations were frequently involved in public policy campaigns by mainstream groups.

The most painful consequence of this strategic change has been the de-emphasis on grassroots mobilizing of women of color. It has been more than a decade since the last national conference on reproductive health was organized by women of color because several large women of color organizations are estranged from their grassroots base. For example, after building more than 120 local chapters in the 1980s with thousands of members, the National Black Women's Health Project saw its membership base dwindle to less than ten chapters in the 1990s after opening a public policy office in Washington, DC and closing their Atlanta community organizing office.

Women of color were represented by a few women speaking on behalf of the many rather than the many speaking for themselves. The preoccupation of national organizations to secure seats at the tables of power for themselves meant that aggressive strategies of the past that once recruited new allies into reproductive health activism were abandoned. Instead of controlling the debate on issues prioritized by grassroots women, women of color became reactive to issues promulgated by Congress and the Supreme Court. Instead of staying focused on mobilizing large numbers of women of color to achieve a critical mass, national organizations chose to place a few women in influential positions. While the abandonment of grassroots mobilizing was not deliberate, ten years later, we can see the cost. This strategic shift left the terrain open for other organizations—namely, white women's organizations and organizations controlled by the religious right—to mobilize women of color.

White women's organizations increasingly attempt to mobilize women of color in order to advance their political agenda and broaden their funding options. Organizations such as Planned Parenthood and NARAL want to present a picture of a diverse, inclusive movement and, at the same time, convince funders that they are capable of organizing women of color. While these efforts may be well intentioned, they are inadequate for including significant numbers of women of color. Moreover, these efforts are prone to the same issues of racism, classism, and homophobia that beset previous attempts to engage women of color in white organizations. We repeatedly witness younger women of color hired at white organizations to launch a "Women of Color Project," such as was done in 2001 at the National Abortion Federation. This is an unoriginal strategy from the 1980s that produced only limited results. Almost inevitably, these young recruits are in untenable positions. They are largely unaware of the efforts of women of color who preceded them, and they are marginalized within their organizations. Isolated from the work of other women of color organizations, they rarely last more than two or three years before they give up in frustration.

The funding issues are also problematic because of their racial implications. While many women of color organizations suffer from a lack of sufficient funding to achieve organizational stability, many white women's organizations are provided with generous funding for their "women of color" projects, without a visible track record. This trend has several implications for women of color: the funding we desperately need to organize in our own communities is diverted to outside groups and we are forced to compete for funding on the terms set by the agencies with access to more resources. If funders prefer public policy strategies, for example, we have to produce policy papers in order to secure support.

Another consequence of funding white organizations to work on reproductive rights in communities of color is that such efforts often poison the soil, because racism is synonymous with genocide in the minds of many people of color. If issues of white supremacy, racism, or classism are not addressed by the white organizations, these defects contaminate efforts by women of color, making it difficult to avoid the stigmas left in the wake of more visible and better funded organizations. For example, it is difficult to counter charges that abortion is genocide when a white pro-choice organization displays racist or insensitive behavior in a community of color. A clear example was during the debate over immigration reform in 1996. Several pro-choice organizations actually agreed with the white majority in limiting the rights of immigrants, making it harder for women of color to join with them in solidarity in efforts to stop the "partial birth abortion" bills in Congress.

Even more problematic than the efforts of white pro-choice organizations are the inroads made by the religious right in communities of color. Among the religious right organizations that have increased their appeal to women of color are the Christian Coalition, Operation Rescue, Blacks for Life, and other groups opposed to abortion. Many people of color are drawn into supporting the ambitions of the religious right because those groups do not use open racism to promote their agenda. Because religiously cloaked bigotry is well disguised, it is difficult for most people to identify and challenge.

The religious right opposes women's reproductive freedom by cloaking itself in the moral mantle of the civil rights movement, for example by comparing the rights of unborn fetuses to the rights of African-Americans. It is not uncommon for anti-abortionists like Operation Rescue to use imagery of Martin Luther King, Jr. in their opposition to abortion, even though King was pro-choice. Such appropriation of civil rights language and symbols mocks the integrity of the civil rights movement's struggle for equality and freedom.

Strategists of the religious right use money to appeal to many religious leaders, by providing the funding that progressives fail to supply. In the 1990s, many anti-poverty programs in communities of color were funded by the religious right, often with several caveats such as mandates for organizations to embrace "abstinence only" language for sex education, and calls for the termination of abortion and contraceptive support. Anti-poverty organizations applying for funds from Catholic Charities in the 1990s were forced to sign an agreement that they would not work with pro-choice organizations in their communities, as was reported by anti-poverty groups like the Georgia Citizens' Coalition on Hunger and the Up and Out of Poverty Network. This coercive strategy was lamentably successful as alternative funding from progressive organizations was not available.

This situation is guaranteed to worsen under President George W. Bush, who has already established several faith-based initiatives to provide government funds to religious institutions. Even if one disregards the blurring line between church and state, it is impossible to overlook the fact that such funding will effectively promulgate the president's anti-choice agenda. Not only are women's health issues jeopardized by the president's personal agenda, but increased spending on the military and anti-terrorist campaigns in the wake of the September 11, 2001 attack on the United States will most likely divert significant funds away from addressing all domestic health care concerns.

These attempts to organize women of color demonstrate that much work remains to be done in order to formulate a collaborative, global reproductive health movement that tackles the lack of just choices for women of color. In the twenty-first century, women of color need to examine their previous organizing efforts. For the past decade, women of color working on reproductive health issues have attempted a dual strategy: working within our own communities to advance issues of reproductive health, while also working with the mainstream women's health movement to advance issues for women of color. This dual focus is critical and necessary, but after ten years of making relatively little progress on either front, it is now time to question the splitting of our energies.

Thus, it is critical that women of color again mobilize to defend our reproductive freedom. We are fighting battles on many fronts, and the health of our communities is at stake. We have to use new organizing strategies that do not create an artificial division between public policy advocacy and grassroots mobilizing, and we have to resist the blandishments of the religious right and the mainstream pro-choice movement if they do not truly represent our own agendas.

A New Organizing Strategy

This essay will address issues of reproductive health for women of color in the United States and offer a case study of the SisterSong Women of Color Reproductive Health Project, a collective that seeks to advocate for the reproductive health rights of women of color. SisterSong was founded to organize women of color and establish a plan of action for addressing the reproductive health needs of our communities. SisterSong works to secure adequate funding in order to mobilize significant numbers of grassroots women; it also aims to develop a public policy advocacy agenda and to cooperate rather than compete with other pro-choice and women's health organizations. While interested in broad reproductive health issues, SisterSong focuses mainly on reproductive tract infections (RTIs). This focus on RTIs is a response to the failure of mainstream reproduction rights organizations to pay attention to the impact they have had on women of color.

The sixteen organizations involved in SisterSong are using their histories and experiences in organizing their communities. Their goal is to develop and apply human rights standards to reproductive health education and services for women of color. SisterSong strongly advocates for the reframing of the reproductive health movement in terms of human rights. It defines the right to health, including the right to reproductive health, as a human right that should be protected in the United States.

Reproductive Tract Infections

In 1987, the International Women's Health Coalition (IWHC) formulated the concept of "reproductive tract infections" (RTIs) to draw attention to a serious, neglected aspect of women's sexual and reproductive health, and to stimulate development of the necessary health services and technologies, information dissemination, and wider program efforts. RTIs affect the ovaries, fallopian tubes, uterus, cervix, vagina, and external genitalia. They affect both men and women, but are more common among women.[2]

There are three known types of RTIs that are grouped by cause of infection:

1. Sexually transmitted diseases (STDs) are caused by bacterial or viral infections such as gonorrhea, genital warts, chlamydia, syphilis, and HIV.

2. Endogenous infections result from an overgrowth of microorganisms (bacteria, yeast) that are normally present in the reproductive tract and are not normally transmitted sexually.

3. Iatrogenic infections result from medical procedures such as improper insertion of an IUD, unsafe childbirth/obstetric practices, and unsafe abortions.[3]

There is a culture of silence about reproductive tract infections that affect women around the world because many diseases can be transmitted through sexual intercourse, which is often considered a taboo subject that is also complicated by the subordination of women in nearly every culture. The taboo of non-heterosexual intercourse also makes addressing RTIs in communities of color a challenge. Many women spend years suffering in silence:

> [R]eproductive ill health is different from other forms of ill health because of the centrality of intimate human behaviors. Human sexual and reproductive behaviors are heavily dependent on social relationships, on custom, tradition, and taboo. It is therefore inevitable that social groups and individuals with the least power, with the most limited ability to make decisions, with the most constrained capacities for choice, will suffer the major portion of the burden of ill health results from these behaviors and relationships.[4]

These diseases include viral infections (genital herpes and warts), other diseases related to bacteria or similar organisms (syphilis, gonorrhea, chlamydia, vaginosis), or fungal or protozeal infections (candiasis or trichomoniasis). Women can also be infected by the insertion of unclean materials into the vagina to prevent pregnancy or induce abortion, by unsafe childbirth techniques, and by female circumcision. However, there is growing awareness about the importance of RTIs because of the discovery that RTIs increase the risk of HIV transmission.[5]

RTIs kill thousands of women each year through their association with cervical cancer, unsafe deliveries, and septic abortions.[6] They can cause emotional distress, pain, and marital discord. The economic costs to society include the loss of women's productivity and the expense of treating the severest consequences of RTIs, such as pelvic inflammatory disease (PID). RTIs received the greatest media attention with the advent of AIDS. Each year, 12 million people in the United States become infected with a sexually transmitted disease.[7] Roughly a quarter of infections occur among young people, between the ages of 15 to 19 years.[8]

The high rate of RTIs among women is associated with a number of interrelated sociocultural, biological, and economic factors, including poverty, the low social status of women, low educational levels, racism, rapid urbanization, and local customs.[9] These multiple factors often reduce women's decision-making power over their own sexuality, and constrain their ability to seek quality reproductive health care.

Women's health advocates around the world have been addressing some of these issues, and identifying what can be done locally, nationally, and globally to bring awareness and action to improving women's reproductive health. To the extent that RTIs have been recognized as a public health issue, they have been approached as diseases to be mapped by epidemiologists, prevented through public education, and cured by health professionals. Yet these conventional approaches are not working; RTIs are rampant in many countries, and their prevalence is increasing.

Women of color have raised a number of new questions regarding RTIs, including the ways in which women of color are vulnerable to them, and how they experience their infections personally and culturally. They have also begun to question how they can protect their sexual and reproductive health in the context of power imbalances in their private lives and in their public encounters.

Appropriate health services for women, particularly marginalized women (such as poor women, women of color, rural women, and lesbians) have always posed a challenge for modern Western medicine. Typically, medical approaches within the

United States cling to the assumption that there exists a universal treatment for all women in all cases for reproductive health problems.[10] Rarely is enough priority given to individually tailored health care which takes into account the environment in which women live, although there has been a recent resurgence of health care that does not strictly adhere to Western medical models.

US studies estimate that of 36 million women of color, almost a fourth are uninsured, with limited or no access to quality health care.[11] These 36 million women of color are 46 percent Black, 38 percent Hispanic, 13 percent Asian and Pacific Islander, and 3 percent American Indian/Alaska Native women. Women of color are more than a fourth (27 percent) of all American women.[12] Studies also show that many women of color do not have preventive health screenings tests such as Pap smears, which are critical in early detection of RTIs.[13] While researchers attribute these findings to financial, cultural, and informational causes, the absence of data on women of color has produced inadequate and sometimes inappropriate policies and programs as reported by the Office of Research on Women's Health at the National Institutes of Health.

The SisterSong Model

In an attempt to promote research and advocacy on reproductive health issues faced by women of color, and to ensure appropriate medical treatment of women of color, women of color organizations in the United States, including Puerto Rico and Hawaii, collaborated in collecting reproductive health data, sharing experiences in treatment and prevention, and addressing societal factors that impact the reproductive health of women of color. In 1997 and 1998, the Latina Roundtable on Health and Reproductive Rights convened meetings for sixteen women of color organizations (four Native American, four African-American, four Latina/Hispanic, four Asian-American/Pacific Islander) and eventually formed the SisterSong: Women of Color Reproductive Health Project, with Ford Foundation funding.[14]

The foundation selected the participating organizations with input and advice from organizers who work on reproductive health issues. The meetings and continued consultations identified common concerns and needs in reproductive health, and served as the catalyst for each of the sixteen groups to formulate a plan on prevention and early treatment of RTIs in their respective communities. The groups also recognized the lack of coordinated and effective efforts among women's and children's health initiatives in their communities, and the impact of biased health policies on poor women.

The collective includes a diverse set of organizations working on reproductive health issues as direct services providers and/or as advocates. Among the reproductive health issues addressed by the collective are midwifery, AIDS services, abortion and contraceptive services, clinical research, health rights advocacy, sexually transmitted diseases, and reproductive tract infections.

In order to address identified concerns and achieve its goals, SisterSong formed four mini-communities within the main body of the collective. Each mini-community was established in order to maintain the representation of the cultural experience and sensitivity of each ethnic group. Each mini-community consists of four grassroots organizations, including at least one national, one state, and two local organizations from that ethnic group. This format maintains commitment to the ability of grassroots organizations to effectively reach a diverse group of women.

One organization from each mini-community was chosen to perform as the "anchor organization" in order to facilitate and coordinate the communications, efforts, and contributions of the respective mini-community. Together the four anchor organizations formed the collective coordinating body assuming the administrative duties of the collective. Their responsibilities include maintaining cohesion between the mini-communities and the main body of the collective as well as advancing the organization's overall agenda—the reduction of RTIs among women of color and thereby the improvement of reproductive health.

The process for planning and implementing a three-year program included the development of a collective vision, which identified basic needs, leadership issues, resources, and common ground within the collective. Several themes emerged during the process. There is a general deficiency of knowledge in communities of color across the country about RTIs and there is a dearth of current, accurate, and culturally sensitive research. In addition, there is a lack of funding to institute programs and increase awareness about RTIs. Linguistic and attitudinal issues usually create barriers to accessing information and services. Women often experience challenges in communicating health needs and concerns to sex partners. Traditional medical analyses fail to include the social and economic conditions—often experienced as human rights violations—that inhibit women from obtaining adequate health care.

Initial Program Findings

At a 1998 symposium in Savannah, Georgia, members of SisterSong identified various barriers which impede their work on RTIs in communities of color. Many programs providing physical and mental health care to women are inappropriate and discriminatory. For example, Asian-Americans have been documented to underuse mental health services. The trauma due to war (for example, torture, starvation, rape, forced labor, and witnessing murder), leaving one's homeland, and resettling in another land often results in unique medical conditions, such as psychosomatic or non-organic blindness reported among Cambodian women 40 years of age or older.[15]

In addition, many providers lack the cultural competency to provide a safe and accessible environment for women of color to pursue good health care and make sound health decisions. Another barrier addressed was the overall lack of awareness and sensitivity of heath care providers and consumers of all their human rights, and the lack of adequate information concerning contraceptive choices, reproductive tract infections, and specific behavioral patterns that increase risk.

SisterSong's first step was to create an opportunity for shared learning through the mutual exchange of health information from each ethnic group. For example, data available from the Centers for Disease Control was frequently incomplete and/or inconsistent in meeting the needs of the women in the collective. The aggregated data frequently failed to identity the particular details of population subsets, like indigenous Pacific Islanders or grouping immigrant Black women with African-Americans. By working with researchers from the Centers for Disease Control, the Office of Minority Health, and the National Institutes of Health, SisterSong began the process of identifying the research and advocacy needs of women of color.

The outcome of the symposium has allowed SisterSong to develop education, outreach, and advocacy strategies that increase awareness of reproductive health issues among women of color, inform practitioners of more appropriate treatment, and advocate for more effective legislation regarding women's health. Other findings include the following:

• Approximately 77 percent of women with HIV/AIDS are women of color. In 1996, African-American women were 56 percent of reported US female AIDS cases; another 20 percent were Hispanic women. HIV infection is the third leading cause of death among all women age 25–44, and the leading cause among African-American women of that age group. These women tend to be young, poor, and tend to live in distressed urban neighborhoods.[16]

• The Public Health Service's Office on Women's Health reported that less than 1 percent of Asian/Pacific Islanders and American Indian/Alaska Native women have HIV/AIDS, but the highest rate of increase in new HIV/AIDS cases in recent years occurred among these two groups of women.[17]

• Occupational hazards pose a significant health threat to women of color. Disproportionate numbers of Latina and Asian/Pacific Islanders are employed in farming, forestry, fishing, and service occupations that hold higher risk for occupational diseases and injuries. Inhalation, absorption, ingestion, and repetitive movements of assembly-type activities may cause these illnesses.[18]

• Asian/Pacific Islander women have the lowest screening rate for cervical cancer, second only to American Indian women. Fifty-five percent of Asian Pacific Islanders, compared to 43 percent of Latinas, and 37 percent of African-Americans were unscreened in 1995.[19]

While these are collective problems across the board, each ethnic group also discovered a number of issues that plague its particular community.

Native American/Indigenous Community

According to the Indian Health Service (IHS), Native American women account for 15 percent of AIDS cases in the United States, compared with 7 percent for non-minority women. Cervical cancer affects 20 percent of Native American women, a rate more than twice that of the US national average of 8.6 percent. The death rate for Native women from cervical cancer is also higher due to delayed diagnosis. Chlamydia rates are thirteen times higher among Native American women than for other American women.[20]

In part due to a cultural attitude of mistrust that Native people feel toward researchers, many Native Americans do not participate in research studies. Health professionals estimate that the prevalence of RTIs may be as high as 65 percent for Native Americans. The prevalence of myth, mystery, and misinformation about sexuality in Native communities presents another major challenge to the promotion of reproductive health. Alcoholism and drug abuse, as well as physical and emotional abuse, all increase the risk of RTIs. The migrant-worker status of many Native Americans also exacerbates their risk.

The high rate of diabetes on reservations is another major concern as it complicates RTIs. Diabetes is extremely common among Native American women and their pregnancies are risky. Unfortunately, there is very little research that explores the impact of diabetes on the elderly, on adolescents, and on the reproductive health of Native American women. In addition, while Native American women typically have high-risk pregnancies, the care they receive is not always adequate.

Health care is controlled by the federal government for many Native Americans. Just thirty-four Indian Health Service (IHS) clinics serve over 1.3 million Indian people nationwide, leaving 75 percent virtually without any health care. Urban Indians, the majority of all American Indians, receive less than 1 percent of the IHS budget.[21] The government's ban on traditional reproductive health care, such as midwifery, has only exacerbated the RTI-related problems.[22] Native American women with high-risk pregnancies are left with inadequate federal health care and their option for more community-based care is eroded.

The federal ban on more traditional and community-based approaches explicitly devalues alternatives to Western health care and denies Native women access to more care. The degradation of traditional health care has led to a loss of faith by the Native community in its ability to care for itself. American values have been grafted onto Native culture and have limited traditional learning.[23] Native American women's participation in self-initiated and self-controlled health care has been curtailed. IHS's population control strategy, which promotes longer term methods of contraception rather than barrier methods, leave Native women highly vulnerable to STDs and RTIs. As a result, women are often vulnerable to government care that is not only inadequate but also pervasively manipulative.[24]

Forced sterilization, with the use of Depo-Provera and Norplant, has been utilized as a form of population control. Physicians offer Norplant implants for free but charge more than $300 to have them removed. Women are pressured into a procedure that limits their reproductive capacity. Physicians take advantage of the low-income status of many women by limiting their options for reproductive health.

Oftentimes, women are not aware of the choices they have in health services. Physicians do not take the time to explain health care options, and there is little effort toward public education. Another factor that influences public awareness of health issues is education level. Because many Native American women are not high school graduates, some information that is available is not accessible due to the high reading levels required for the material.

Culturally appropriate health education material that is "tradition-inclusive" is necessary to increase public awareness of health options. Approaches that empower people in the community to take control of their health choices are also paramount. "Train the Trainer" sessions for Native American women would ensure culturally appropriate education by providing a forum for one-on-one woman-based discussions. The focus on an all-woman education group would prevent any discomfort in discussing health issues around men and/or with spouses. Ultimately, knowledge regarding health options is imperative in ensuring safe and appropriate reproductive care for Native American women.

Asian/Pacific Islander American Community

According to the US Census Bureau, Asian/Pacific Islanders (A/PIs) are the fastest growing minority group in the United States.[25] Consisting of immigrants from over twenty countries who speak more than 120 languages, this population numbered more than 10 million people in 1997.[26] The majority of this population live in urban areas, mostly in California, Hawaii, and Washington.

Despite these numbers, reliable information on the health status and needs of A/PI Americans is scarce, and much of the available national statistics on this community come from pooled data of diverse subgroups, resulting in misleading information that sometimes overlooks serious health problems, diverts health care resources to other groups, and limits A/PIs' access to health care services, according to a report published by the US Commission on Civil Rights in 1992, "Civil Rights Issues Facing Asian Americans in the 1990s."

Because much of the A/PI community is non-English speaking, mainstream health education and disease prevention efforts have had little impact on these communities, and over 11,500 new cases of sexually transmitted diseases were reported for Asian-Americans and Pacific Islanders in 1998.[27] Moreover, health care professionals have limited knowledge of the different cultures and endemic diseases from immigrants' countries of origin, and thus lack the expertise to serve immigrant clients. In addition, A/PI women often cannot afford the care that may be available.

Cultural and family influences also affect the rate of health care access. A/PI women have traditionally placed the health needs of their families at the forefront and put less emphasis on individual needs.[28] Cultural taboos surrounding the body, sexuality, and pregnancy also contribute to the low rates of health service access. Many A/PI women feel uncomfortable discussing health issues.

The misperception of Asian-Americans as a healthy and well-off "model minority" has limited the development of research studies to document any poor status in health of the A/PI community. Contrary to this stereotype, over two-thirds of Asian-American women are sexually active, but less than 40 percent always use protection against STDs.[29] One-quarter have never visited a health care provider for reproductive health services, or received education on reproductive tract infections.[30]

Linguistic, cultural, and financial barriers have had serious implications for health outcomes in A/PI communities. For example, a survey of Vietnamese women in San Francisco showed that many did not know common signs, symptoms, and risk factors for breast and cervical cancer, and a majority had never had a Pap smear test.[31] Available statistics show that Vietnamese women have the highest rate of cervical cancer in the Asian-American community.[32] A/PI women are also greatly influenced by traditional beliefs, which often result in delays in seeking services. In addition, sexuality and reproductive health are difficult topics of discussion in A/PI cultures. As a result, A/PI women receive little or no information from their families about reproductive health issues such as anatomy, menstruation, sex, or RTIs.

Nearly two-thirds of Asian and Pacific Islander Americans are foreign-born, and approximately one-third speak limited or no English.[33] Language barriers between health care providers and A/PI clients jeopardize the quality of care when access to health care is obtained.[34] Accessing health care among immigrant populations is complicated by fear of deportation, language and cultural barriers, racism, sexism, and heterosexism.[35]

One way to facilitate the provision of adequate care is through more research on nontraditional methods. It is critical for A/PI women to control their bodies, and to have influence over the care provided them. A national effort is necessary to achieve this goal and more voices need to be heard within the policy and medical arenas. Collaborative efforts to make resources known are a crucial first step.

Latina/Hispanic Community

The Latina population has many factors contributing to high risk for RTIs. Approximately 30 percent of Latinos live below the poverty line, and nearly half the poor Hispanic families are female-headed.[36] In 1995, 30 percent of the Hispanic population was not covered by health insurance.[37] Medicaid coverage for Latinos varies by state and in many states poor undocumented Latinos are ineligible for Medicaid and often cannot afford health insurance. Welfare reform has also increased the number of Latinos ineligible for publicly funded health insurance. Women who are left without care then turn to self-medication and share medicine.[38]

Latinas also underutilize available health care services. A lack of United States citizenship often deters undocumented immigrant Latinos from using public clinics and other health facilities for fear of detection and deportation. In addition, Hispanics traditionally seek family members' advice before getting professional health care, which contributes to Latinas' low or delayed utilization of health care services. In many families, women's low status impedes their ability to seek and negotiate for their own health care. Many Latinas also work in the agriculture industry which exposes workers to pesticides that place them at risk for a range of health problems, including RTIs. Hispanics are also more likely to have diabetes, placing them at greater risk for endogenous RTIs, further complicating and prolonging the treatment regime.[39]

The data available on Sexually Transmitted Diseases (STDs) among Latinas is alarming. Comprising 10.2 percent of all United States women, Latinas have a cervical cancer rate almost twice that of non-minority women.[40] Latinas are also over-represented in the number of AIDS cases among women (20.3 percent).[41] Reproductive health care, particularly for HIV-positive Latinas, is often interrupted by frequent border crossings to Central America, and extended stays in Puerto Rico.[42] Other factors limiting Latinas' access to reproductive health care include strong religious belief systems that inhibit open discussion about sexuality and safer sex practices, unequal gender relationships, and domestic violence.

High rates of cesareans and sterilization abuse cause distrust of the medical community among many Latinas. For example, according to a national fertility study conducted in 1970 by Princeton University's Office of Population Control, 20 percent of all Mexican-American women had been sterilized.[43] The disproportionate number of Puerto Rican women who have been sterilized reflects

United States government policy that dates back to 1939, when an experimental sterilization campaign was implemented. By the 1970s, more than 35 percent of all Puerto Rican women of child-bearing age had been surgically sterilized.[44]

Unfortunately, structural, cultural, and social influences often prevent Latinas from actively asserting their rights for adequate and appropriate health care services. In many cases, Latinas, particularly immigrants, do not feel they are in a position of power. Religion plays an integral role in inhibiting women from feeling confident about reproductive health needs due to the connection with sexuality. The health beliefs of many Latinas relate to their views about God as the omnipotent creator of the universe, with personal behavior subject to God's judgment. Fatalistic beliefs such as these make it difficult to establish the importance of preventive health behaviors.[45] Cultural factors also influence the spread of HIV infection and AIDS because they often are unwilling to discuss intimate and emotional matters such as illness and sex unless they are able to speak to someone in Spanish.[46]

The Black/African-American Community

The Black population in America consists primarily of African-Americans, although significant numbers of African and African-Caribbean immigrants have become part of this group in the last fifteen years.[47] Today, there are more than 32 million Black Americans in the United States, more than 12 percent of the total population, and they are currently the largest "minority" group. More than half, 17 million, are women, and many are of mixed ancestry, including people with Caribbean, Indian, and European heritages.[48]

Available data on the health status of African-American women indicate that they suffer higher rates of undetected diseases, higher incidences of diseases and illnesses, and more chronic conditions, as well as higher morbidity rates than non-minority American women.[49] According to statistics, African-American women exhibit very high rates of cervical and breast cancer and reproductive track infections (RTIs).[50]

Yet, despite high rates of serious health problems within the community, far too many women have never had a Pap smear or gynecological exam. In 1995, one in four African-American women did not receive a Pap smear, and one-third failed to receive a clinical breast exam.[51] More than half of African-American women age 50 to 64 did not receive mammography screening between 1994 and 1995.[52] One in seven (14 percent) rely on emergency rooms for basic health services.[53] Obesity, a contributing factor for some cancers, is most prevalent among African-American women.[54]

Appropriate mental health services are even worse in many cases. The influence of racial and gender oppression as it relates to depression, substance abuse, physical abuse, access to quality education, and the availability of services is often overlooked. One of the most obvious factors affecting the rate of health care access is the availability of appropriate services. In rural areas of the United States, services geared toward African-American women are frequently non-existent.[55] The lack of health care access in both rural and urban areas has led to a gap in research regarding Black women's health, including in areas of birth control, HIV/AIDS transmission, and RTIs.

The interplay between the perception of health care provision and the actual services provided often impedes health care access. SisterSong members cited the influence of history as one impediment. Unethical research in Black communities such as the Tuskegee Syphilis Study[56] has also created a distrust of the medical industry among African-Americans. Recently, efforts by medical professionals to force women, particularly poor, Black women, into using unsolicited birth control were exposed.[57] African-American women's distrust of medical professionals sometimes prevents them from disclosing information.

External constraints also contribute to low rates of health care access. SisterSong cited inadequate incomes and social supports as factors in determining health care access among many African-American women. Further, many African-American women are disproportionately affected by welfare and immigration reform, deepening their poverty and hindering their access to health services. Another influence within the African-American community that affects service access is religious affiliation. The strong religious community often prevents openness regarding sexuality and health issues. Unfortunately, churches are institutions of incredible influence that infrequently empower women to seek information about their bodies and to take control of their own health.

The lack of appropriate services, information, and research requires holistic approaches to health care that include advocacy and education. In addition, powerful and positive women motivators from the African-American community need to guide and lead dialogue around reproductive health issues. African-American women have made significant contributions in advocating for birth control, family planning, and abortion rights. However, SisterSong's African-American members believe that organizing among African-American women on reproductive health, particularly regarding RTIs, has been insufficient.

Reconceptualizing the Human Rights Framework

Global structural adjustment policies imposed by the World Bank on developing countries have resulted in cuts in social services, fees for public services, privatization, and the removal of subsidies for food, medicines, clean water, and transportation. In the United States, welfare reform is, in effect, acting as a structural adjustment program. A high level of poverty forces thousands of girls and women to sell their bodies as a means of survival.[58] Sadly enough, even in monogamous relationships, women's sexuality becomes their only bargaining tool for survival. Violence against women also tends to increase poverty, risks of STDs, unintended pregnancies, drug and alcohol abuse, and mental illness.

The lack of effective coordinated efforts to ensure the health of women and children, and for the prevention of STDs and HIV, represents an extreme challenge to the vision of SisterSong. The need for policy changes is apparent in states where schools provide only abstinence-based sex education and where women are forced to receive spousal or parental permission for reproductive medical procedures such as abortion or contraception. A solution to many of these challenges is a reconceptualization of reproductive health in terms of human rights.

Organizations concerned with reproductive health issues in the United States are increasingly drawing inspiration and tools from the international human rights movement, and those working within a traditional human rights framework are gradually including issues related to reproductive health. Women, particularly women of color, have spearheaded this rearticulation of the human rights framework in the United States.

Through the application of human rights education, SisterSong began to reconceptualize the human rights framework in the United States, particularly in its applicability to health care problems. The organizations joined other social justice activists in demanding that the United States be held accountable to an internationally applied standard of human rights. This new generation of human rights activists has called attention to significant human rights violations committed against women of color by local, state, and federal governments as well as private citizens and institutions.

Because of inherent limits in the United States Constitution, which seeks to protect the civil and political rights of individuals, the United States lacks a sufficient legal framework within which women of color may have safe and reliable access to health care. This results from the law's denial of the importance of and obligation to achieve economic, social, and cultural human rights which emphasize group or collective needs. While individual human rights are nearly universally accepted, collective or group rights remain extremely controversial.

Liberal human rights interpretations often do not recognize that equality of opportunity is an illusion in a society based on competitive individualism in which one ethnic group (whites) has social, political, and economic advantages in relationship to other ethnic groups (people of color). Thus, individualistic rights frameworks often neglect the importance of group rights of ethnicity and culture.[59] For example, while an individual African-American may have the legal freedom and the financial means to purchase a home in any community, that potential buyer must be protected from racial discrimination against African-Americans as a group, in order to enjoy that individual right.

Parental consent laws, for-profit health care, welfare reform policies, and immigration policies impact women's health choices and detrimentally affect the quality of care available. In order to ensure access to health care and treatment, and to address the intersection of class, race, and gender that affects women of color, a comprehensive human rights–based approach is necessary.

This new and comprehensive, human rights–based reproductive health agenda challenges the traditional American liberal human rights framework, by giving economic, social, and cultural rights the same consideration given to civil and political rights. The United States government has an obligation to provide an environment in which policies, laws, and practices enable women to realize their reproductive rights, and to refrain from creating conditions that compromise or restrict such rights.

In1994, the Cairo International Conference on Population and Development (ICPD) acknowledged that reproductive rights are human rights. It called on countries to ensure the reproductive rights of all individuals; to provide the information and means to decide the number, spacing, and timing of children; and to uphold the rights to have the highest standard of sexual and reproductive health, and to make sexual and reproductive decisions free of discrimination, coercion, and violence.

The World Conference Against Racism, Racial Discrimination, Xenophobia and Related Intolerance held in South Africa in August 2001 offered an opportunity to increase awareness about reproductive health issues for women of color and to identify those human rights violations women of color face around the world. The United States government failed to significantly participate in the conference, but it also denied that its policies discriminated against women of color. Further, the United States claimed that historical patterns of racism, colonialism, and genocide have no contemporary impact on the health of women of color.

Despite this intransigence, many women of color participated in the World Conference Against Racism to help develop concrete recommendations for regional, and international measures to combat all forms of racial and gender oppression. Women of color recognized the fundamental, interlinked relationship between individual and collective human rights. They understood that individual human rights of women of color cannot be protected without the protection of the collective rights of all people of color.

There are many challenges associated with the awesome task of making domestic, regional, and international human rights mechanisms responsive to the needs of women of color in the United States. Not only has the United States denied the applicability of human rights to domestic policies, it has also prevented broad applicability and coverage of the few human rights treaties it has ratified by attaching exemptions to the treaties that prevent their justiciability in United States courts.

Opponents to women's human rights have also created an artificial dichotomy between "needs" and "rights" by claiming that a human rights–based approach to health is an elite Western imposition designed to counter a "needs-based" approach. These critics ignore the reality that rights are born out of needs: rights are legal articulations of claims upon governments to meet human needs and protect human freedoms. Instead of a rights/needs hierarchy there is, in fact, a rights/needs symbiosis.[60] Despite tremendous opposition by critics and the US government's failure time and aagain to ratify treaties linking health and human rights, women of color have not been dissuaded from continuing their advocacy. Women organizers and trainers are beginning to increase human rights awareness among reproductive rights and women's health activists around the world. In the United States, many have yet to recognize women's human rights as a framework within which reproductive rights activists can find greater solidarity.

The incorporation of human rights instruments such as the Convention to End All Forms of Discrimination Against Women (CEDAW) should be a goal for the reproductive freedom movement. For example, CEDAW recognizes the ability of a woman to control her own fertility as fundamental to the full enjoyment of her human rights, including her right to health care and to family planning. It also addresses the obligations of the United States government to proactively tackle social, cultural, or traditional discrimination against women. CEDAW defines any law that restricts women's access to a range of family planning options as discriminatory. Despite the potential it holds, CEDAW remains one of the twenty-three human rights treaties the United States has yet to ratify.

Conclusion

SisterSong has made a promising beginning by bringing together women of color to address reproductive tract infections in the United States. Grassroots groups retain a great role, allowing SisterSong to build a wide-reaching, national collective. The Ford Foundation has taken a monumental step by funding a unique collaboration like SisterSong. The creative approach of SisterSong has increased the capacity of member organizations to access educational materials, services, and programs previously unavailable.

While organizations involved in the SisterSong collective face many barriers, through collaboration the collective has increased its potential. However, there still remain many challenges. Globalization is making socioeconomic conditions worse around the world and policy makers are increasingly turning to quick fixes to complex problems. Population control efforts are back with a vengeance and many liberal feminist organizations remain focused on abortion issues only. An even more troubling trend is the collaboration between international women's rights organizations and population control organizations. As Asoka Bandarage of the Committee on Women, Population, and the Environment notes:

> As fertility control is presented increasingly as the means for women's empowerment, feminist criticisms of coercion and experimentation within family planning programs get softened; the resurgence of eugenics associated with the growth of new productive technologies gets overlooked; and the social structural roots of women's subordination and the global crisis tend to be forgotten.[61]

All these challenges make the mission of organizations like SisterSong all the more urgent. The need to highlight the inextricable link between health and human rights is pressing. This is not a battle against diseases only; it is a battle against poverty, homelessness, inadequate health care, and the denial of human rights.

1   Francesca Miller, *Latin American Women and the Search for Social Justice* (Hanover, NH: University Press of New England, 1991), 207.
2   Native American Women's Health Education Resource Center, "Focus Group Report 2: The Current Status of Reproductive Health Awareness Among Young Native American Women" (1999), 6.
3   Ibid.
4   Tomris Turmen, "Reproductive Rights: How to Move Forward?," *Health and Human Rights International Journal*, Vol. 4, No. 2, (2000), 32.
5   Leslie Doyal, *What Makes Women Sick: Gender and the Political Economy of Health* (New Brunswick, NJ: Rutgers University Press,), 77.
6   National Institutes of Health, *Women of Color Health Data Book* (1998), 79.
7   Centers for Disease Control and Prevention, Office of Women's Health (1999), www.cdc.gov.
8   Sexually Transmitted Disease Information Center, "What Teens Should Know and Don't (But Should) Know About Sexually Transmitted Diseases," *The Journal of the American Medical Association* (March 8, 1999).
9   Doyal, *What Makes Women Sick*, 75.
10   Gena Corea, *The Hidden Malpractice: How American Medicine Mistreats Women*, Updated ed. (New York: Harper Colophon Books, 1985), 79.
11   US Census Bureau, "Income and Poverty Status of Americans Improve" (1996).
12   National Institutes of Health, *Women of Color Health Data Book* (1998), 1.
13   Ibid., vii.
14   A complete listing of the member organizations of the SisterSong Collective from 1998–2001 is in the Appendix.
15   National Institutes of Health, *Women of Color Health Data Book* (1998), 20.
16   National Institute of Allergy and Infectious Disease, National Institutes of Health, "Women and HIV" (April 1997).
17   US Public Health Service Office on Women's Health, "The Health of Minority Women" (1996).
18   US Office of Occupational Safety and Health, *1993 Handbook on Women Workers: Trends and Issues* (1994).
19   "Women's Health: Choices and Challenges," *The Commonwealth Fund Quarterly*, Special issue (1996).
20   National Institutes of Health, *Women of Color Health Data Book* (1998), 75.
21   Ibid., 2.
22   Ibid., 3.
23   Ibid.
24   Native American Women's Health Education Resource Center, "SisterSong Native Women's Reproductive Health and Rights Roundtable" (2001), 13.
25   United States Department of Commerce, Bureau of the Census CB97–FS.04, 1997.
26   Ibid.
27   National Asian American Women's Health Organization, "Community Solutions: Meeting the Challenge of STDs in Asian Americans and Pacific Islanders" (2000), 7.

28   Ibid., 13.
29   Ibid., 11.
30   Ibid.
31   Ibid., 15.
32   National Cancer Institute, "Racial/Ethnic Patterns of Cancer in the United States 1988–1992," NIH Pub. No. 96-4101 (1996).
33   National Institutes of Health, *Women of Color Health Data Book* (1998), 19.
34   Health Access, "Overview of Minority Health Care Concerns: Statistics" (May 2, 1994).
35   National Asian American Women's Health Organization, "Asian American Women's Health Fact Sheet" (1996).
36   National Institutes of Health, *Women of Color Health Data Book* (1998), 9.
37   Ibid.
38   Ibid., 10.
39   Ibid., 11.
40   Ibid., 75.
41   Ibid., 81.
42   Ibid., 12.
43   Angela Davis, *Women, Race and Class* (New York: Knopf, 1981), 219.
44   Ibid.
45   National Institutes of Health, *Women of Color Health Data Book* (1998), 11.
46   Ibid., 12.
47   Ibid.
48   Ibid.
49   Ibid.
50   Deborah R. Grayson, "Necessity Was the Midwife to Our Politics: Black Women's Health Activism in the "Post-" Civil Rights Era (1980–1996)," in *Still Lifting, Still Climbing: African American Women's Contemporary Activism*, ed. Kimberly Springer (New York: New York University Press, 1999), 133.
51   Ibid., 14.
52   Ibid., 62.
53   Ibid., 70.
54   "Women's Health: Choices and Challenges," *The Commonwealth Fund Quarterly*, Special issue (1996).
55   Susan F. Feiner, *Race and Gender in the American Economy: Views Across the Spectrum* (Englewood Cliffs, NJ: Prentice-Hall, 1994), 315.
56   National Institutes of Health, *Women of Color Health Data Book* (1998), iii.
57   Dorothy Roberts, *Killing the Black Body: Race, Reproduction and the Meaning of Liberty* (New York: Pantheon Books, 1997), 234.
58   Kamala Kempadoo and Jo Doezema, *Global Sex Workers: Rights, Resistance and Redefinition* (New York: Routledge Press, 1998), 17.
59   William Felice, *Taking Suffering Seriously: The Importance of Collective Human Rights* (Albany, NY: SUNY Press, 1996), 35.
60   Ibid.
61   Asoka Bandarage, "Political Environments. A New and Improved Population Control Policy" (Committee on Women, Population and the Environment, 1994).

Chapter 7

The Gendered Assault on Immigrants

Syd Lindsley

> Consider that there are somewhere near 3 million illegal immi-
> grants living in the United States. Many are having children who
> are deemed legal citizens under the present legal interpretation
> of the 14th Amendment to the US Constitution. Each is entitled
> to full welfare, education and health benefits that can easily
> amount to $250,000 during the next 18 years.
>
> This assault on our Social Security and welfare funds will
> bankrupt our present support system for those legally entitled to
> benefits. We must re-evaluate our priorities and take corrective
> action before the entire ship sinks, leaving all of us to drown.
>
> —Byron Slater, Letter to the Editor,
> *The San Diego Union-Tribune*[1]

The political climate towards immigrants in California during
the early 1990s was marked by an intense resurgence of the
anti-immigrant sentiment and activism known as nativism.
Many conservative politicians and researchers pinned the state's
economic problems on the so-called "flood" of "illegal" immigrants "invading" the state.

Earlier periods of nativism charged immigrants with flooding
the job market and thus held them responsible for displacing
"American" labor—such an argument was used to make a case for
"Operation Wetback," a period of massive deportation of Mexican
immigrants (along with many Mexican-Americans) during the
1950s.[2] The 1990s anti-immigrant assault in California took a dif-

ferent tack by targeting immigrants not as job-stealers, but as re-source depletors.[3] Immigrants, particularly so-called "illegal" immigrants and their children, were represented as depleting both California's fiscal and natural resources.

The opening quote from a letter to the editor of a prominent southern California newspaper exemplifies the way in which the alleged costs of illegal immigrant use of welfare, health, and education were portrayed as endangering the availability of these services to the rest of the population. In addition, the writer espouses "lifeboat ethics," the alarmist (and popular) notion that the consequences of immigrant use of social services threatens to sink the already overburdened welfare and social security budgets, causing "all of us to drown" if not acted upon immediately. The representation of immigrants as an immediate and dangerous threat to the availability of social services for "Americans" constituted one of the primary themes of anti-immigrant discourse in the 1990s.

Also primary to the construction of anti-immigrant discourse during the 1990s was the attack on immigrant women and their children. The letter writer's reference to the children of illegal immigrants as the cause of California's economic problems is located within a larger context of blame directed at immigrant women and their children.

I will argue that this assault is in fact an assault on immigrant women as reproductive agents. This is manifested in both the central place occupied by immigrant women's reproduction and family maintenance in restrictionist rhetoric, and in the effects of restrictionist discourse and policy on immigrant women's reproductive health, as well as the health of their children.

Throughout this chapter, I focus primarily on exclusionary rhetoric directed at Mexican immigrant women, and use the results of anti-immigrant policy for Mexican immigrant women as my primary examples. Although other groups of immigrant women of color have simultaneously been subjected to exclusionary policies, I focus on Mexican immigrant women because of the large amount of mainstream media attention towards Mexican immigration during the 1990s, as well as the prevalence of anti-Mexican sentiment in California.

In this chapter, the demographics of gender in immigration, especially the so-called "feminization of immigration," provide an important backdrop for a discussion of the gendered effects of various forms of legislation directed at immigrants during the 1980s and 1990s, including legislation aimed at restricting immigrants' access to social services. The role of welfare in regulating motherhood, both historically and currently, will be explored as an important context to the debate over immigrants' access to social services, with a focus on immigrant mothers' access. Finally, this essay will explore the current surge of nativist sentiment as the reaction to a perceived dilution of a white "American" national identity, with eugenic targeting of immigrant women's reproduction signifying an attempt to preserve the existing racial hierarchy.

The Feminization of Immigration

Contrary to popular assumptions, legal immigrant populations are usually predominantly female.[4] This pattern was disrupted during the mid-1980s with the passage of the Immigration Reform and Control Act (IRCA). The primary goal of IRCA was to control "illegal" immigration by authorizing "an increase in border enforcement and [by making] it illegal for an employer to knowingly hire an alien who does not have permission to work in this country."[5]

In addition to its employer sanction provisions, IRCA provided for the legalization of around 2.7 million people, most of them male. This gender bias was a result of several factors. First of all, men predominantly filled the types of agricultural work upon which amnesty was contingent. Cannery and packing, in which women held the majority of jobs, were specifically excluded from the amnesty provision. Also, the documentation required for amnesty, such as driver's licenses, pay stubs, and rent receipts was much more likely to be held by men than women.[6] Furthermore, a provision excluding anyone likely to become a "public charge" targeted the recipients of Aid to Families with Dependent Children (AFDC), who were primarily women.

However, by the early nineties, as legalization under IRCA was ending, the gender ratio returned to its predominantly female status.[7] While some female immigrants may come to the United States through employment-based immigration laws, the vast majority of women immigrants come through family-based immigration laws, which allow for spouses and other close family relatives to join citizens or legal permanent residents.[8] In fact, seven out of ten legal immigrants come to join close family members.[9]

Increases in Female Undocumented Immigrants

Demographic analysis suggests that women constituted a majority of the undocumented Mexican immigrant population by the early 1990s.[10] The increase in female undocumented immigrants has been caused by a number of factors, including the passage of IRCA in 1986, the globalization of production, and the increased participation of middle-class women in the United States labor force encouraged by second-wave feminism.

Part of the increase in the ratio of female to male undocumented immigrants is linked to gender bias in IRCA. Since IRCA, in effect, discriminated against women in its legalization provisions, many previously undocumented men became citizens or legal permanent residents, while many undocumented women did not qualify. In addition, fearing that IRCA signified that the "door [was] closing" and hoping that they too might qualify for legalization under IRCA, some women may have come to the United States without documents to join their husbands or family members.[11]

Female undocumented migration to the United States is also linked to (and predicated on) the globalization of production, and women's paid employment in manufacturing. Saskia Sassen describes a complex process through which globalized production processes induce the formation of a pool of female migrant workers: Export agriculture and manufacturing in developing countries pull large segments of the population into wage labor. Export manufacturing relies very heavily on the labor of young women, a sector of society previously excluded from paid employment. However, employment practices and the mental and physical fatigue associated with export-manufacturing jobs lead to high rates of turnover in such jobs.

These newly unemployed women face a difficult impasse. As Sassen asserts, "incipient westernization among zone workers and the disruption of traditional work structures combine to minimize the possibilities of returning to communities of origin."[12] These conditions lay the foundation for women's immigration.

Sassen goes on to argue that emigration is further based on linkages between industrializing countries and the countries from which the industrial capital originates:

> [T]he massive and concentrated foreign presence facilitates the emergence of emigration as an option. This would be far less likely in an "isolated" country, one lacking a massive foreign presence and the resulting structural and ideological links with the West.[13]

Thus, the country to which one chooses to emigrate is directly correlated to the origins of direct foreign investment in export-oriented development. The United States accounts for almost half of all direct foreign investment worldwide, most of which is export-oriented.[14] This factor alone is a key contributor to the emergence of emigration to the United States as an option. The option to migrate becomes even more appealing when combined with other factors, such as the perception of the United States as a land of immigrants, and the general liberalization of United States immigration policy after 1965.

Thus, in Sassen's view, migration to the United States is a highly complex process, one that is increasingly bound up in US foreign investment policy. Contrary to popular belief, the United States is by no means the passive recipient of the world's poor, but is an active agent in shaping the formation of a migrant workforce. Furthermore, the feminization of undocumented migration should be viewed as directly linked to the employment practices of American corporations and export policies in developing countries.

The rise of second-wave feminism and its effect of increasing middle-class women's participation in the labor force have also had a major effect on the demand for undocumented women's labor in the United States. Professional women have increased the needs for low-cost child-care and housekeeping—positions increasingly held by immigrant women. An article published by the National Council for Research on Women states:

While recent US Department of Labor statistics show a shrinking pool of domestic workers—from 942,000 in 1983 to
755,000 in 1991—they also show a rise in the number of women
working. In 1991, nearly two-thirds of all women age 16 and
over were in the labor force; in 1992, more than 16 million
mothers with pre-school children worked full-time. Such figures
beg the question: Who is home cleaning the house, making the
meals, and taking care of the kids?[15]

According to the available information, a partial answer to the
question lies in the hidden realm of undocumented women's labor.
While not all working women can afford to hire domestic help,
many middle-class women do rely on immigrant women's domestic labor. More than 350,000 undocumented immigrant women
worked as domestics in the United States labor market as of 1994,
according to an estimate by the International Labor Office.[16]

Undocumented women domestic workers are usually paid less
than their legal counterparts: for example, "legal nannies can cost
up to $600 per month, compared to $175 for illegal ones."[17] Also,
most domestic work is paid for under the table. In 1993, only 25
percent of household employers paid Social Security taxes for
maids, nannies, or other domestic workers, further decreasing the
costs to the employer.[18]

Thus, the feminization of immigration is marked by inequality:
between documented and undocumented women, and more dras-
tically, between middle-class professional women and the immigrant domestic workers they hire. This inequality is marked by a
hierarchy of motherhood where white women hire domestic workers to care for their children, often at the expense of the domestic
workers' own (non-white) children. I will return to this topic towards the end of the chapter in a more in-depth discussion of reproduction and racial exclusion in the United States.

Gendered Legislation

Since the mid-1980s, immigration legislation has had a differential impact on male and female immigrants. The legislative bias
towards male immigrants in IRCA's amnesty legalization provision
is one example of gendered immigration legislation; other recent

legislation has also had gendered effects. Whether or not the authors of the legislation intended these gendered effects, their impact has been clear. Post-IRCA immigration legislation can be roughly organized into two categories: policies restricting spousal immigration, and policies limiting access to social services by both documented and undocumented immigrants.

Restricting Spousal Immigration

Several pieces of federal legislation have included provisions to make it harder to sponsor family members, especially spouses. The Immigration Marriage Fraud Amendment of 1990 was specifically designed to curb phony marriages for immigration purposes, despite the fact that marriage fraud was not a significantly common phenomenon. The fear of such marriages was tied to fears of immigrants' dishonesty and manipulation, particularly on the part of immigrant women, as the primary beneficiaries of the arrangement.

In effect, this act has made it harder for legal immigrants to sponsor their legitimate spouses. In 1998, the provisions of the Immigration and Nationality Act, which had made it possible for spouses to stay in the United States while the approval of their residency status was pending, were allowed to expire; family members who apply for residency now face being forced to return home while they wait for their applications to be approved, a process which in some cases can take a decade or more. In addition, the Illegal Immigration Reform and Immigrant Responsibility Act of 1996 raised the income level required to sponsor family members to 125 percent of the poverty line, which amounts to $24,675 for a family of four. Most immigrant families' incomes fall far below the poverty line.

These provisions affect women disproportionately, because most women immigrants who gain legal residency do so through a spouse or other family member, whereas men are more likely to use other methods, such as employer-based admissions.[19] Also the income requirement affects women who are already US residents—since women, on average, have lower incomes than men, it is harder for women to sponsor relatives than it is for men.

Restricting Access to Social Services

Perhaps the most overt assault on immigrant women in recent years has been legislation aimed at diminishing the availability of social services to immigrants, especially undocumented immigrants. Undocumented immigrants were never eligible for most types of welfare and Medicaid, although public education and some health and social services were available. Recent legislation has attempted to reduce the few services available to immigrants even further.

Proposals for this type of restriction began surfacing in the early 1990s. In 1991, Elton Gallegly, a congressman from California, proposed a constitutional amendment that would deny citizenship to children born in the United States to undocumented parents. As Santiago O'Donnell of the *Los Angeles Times* observed, Gallegly's argument was based on the assumption that the amendment "would save taxpayers millions of dollars in welfare payments. He estimated that illegal immigrants receive $5.4 billion a year in social services nationwide, and cited Los Angeles County statistics that two-thirds of the babies born in county hospitals are children of illegal immigrants."[20] Gallegly's figures were highly questionable. Though Gallegly's proposal has not yet made its way into legislation, it turned out to be the first in a string of proposals designed to cut the use of social services by people born outside of the United States.

In April of 1992, California Congressman Dana Rohrabacher proposed to abolish federal health and welfare benefits for illegal immigrants. Describing his frustration with stories about newcomers using subsidized medical care, Rohrabacher said "if Pedro's not here legally, he's not going to get $50,000 for that heart-bypass operation."[21] He asserted, "People are coming from across the world in order to get their hands on this free package of benefits we offer.... Unless you take away the incentives, there's no way to keep them out.... We simply have to have the intestinal fortitude in saying no in giving away the taxpayers' dollars to people here illegally."[22] Rohrabacher argued that allowing immigrants to come into the United States would lead to "our own social services breaking down, our criminal justice system breaking down.... The fabric of our society ... fraying."[23]

Rohrabacher's statements are not only racially charged (his derogatory use of the name "Pedro" reveals whom he thinks is illegal), they are based on the false premise that immigrants come to the United States in order to receive health and welfare benefits, even though undocumented immigrants are largely ineligible for such benefits. Even Rohrabacher himself admitted that his proposal's underpinnings were "mainly anecdotal."[24] Indeed, a 1996 University of California at Irvine study on the reasons undocumented Latinas come to live in the United States found that "those who are not here legally came for work, not welfare."[25]

Still, Rohrabacher's claims about the magnet of health and welfare benefits for undocumented immigrants formed the basis for much of the subsequent debate and legislation. In the fall of 1992, Californians voted on Proposition 165, a welfare reform measure that would have cut AFDC grants, based welfare payments to teen mothers on their school attendance, required teen mothers to live with their parents in order to receive welfare, and denied women on welfare benefits for children they give birth to while receiving welfare. While the actual legislation was not directed at immigrants, proponents argued that the measure was necessary because "California is being crippled by its obligations to the needy, especially as immigrants flow into a state that offers some of the nation's highest welfare benefits."[26] Although California voters ultimately defeated the proposition, discourse about immigrants' use of social services did not cease.

By the time California's Proposition 187 appeared on the 1994 ballot, arguments about immigrants' use of public services were commonplace. Proposition 187 harnessed Californians' fears about crime, the budget deficit, and the crisis of education and health care systems in the state. The opening text of the proposition reads:

> The People of California find and declare as follows: That they have suffered and are suffering economic hardship caused by the presence of illegal aliens in this state. That they have suffered and are suffering personal injury and damage caused by the criminal conduct of illegal aliens in this state. That they have a

right to the protection of their government from any person or persons entering this country unlawfully.[27]

Proposition 187 would have prohibited local and state agencies from providing publicly funded social services, education, welfare, and non-emergency health care to any person whom they did not verify as a US citizen or lawfully admitted alien. Furthermore, it would have required government agencies to report any applicant suspected of being an illegal immigrant to the INS. Although Proposition 187 was passed by California voters, it has since been declared unconstitutional, and was never put into effect.[28]

Critics have noted that the proponents of Proposition 187 stressed the ban on public support for prenatal care for undocumented women. The "official estimate" that two out of three babies delivered at Los Angeles county hospitals were born to undocumented women, cited by Gallegly in 1991, became an oft-quoted statistic in the Proposition 187 campaign. However, this statistic is dubious; legal scholar Dorothy Roberts contends that the number is probably inflated, due to "county officials' unscientific survey methods and confusion of legal and illegal immigrants."[29] In any case, Proposition 187 proponents clearly placed little value on undocumented women's reproductive health, as well as the health of their children.

Other aspects of Proposition 187 were also directed at women's reproduction, in slightly more subtle ways. For example, the proposed ban on public education funds for undocumented children would have permanently excluded these children from integration in American society. In addition, it would have had profound affects on the entire family's ability to integrate and survive in the United States, and would have placed a severe strain on immigrant women as advocates for their children.

Just two years following Proposition 187, Congress passed a bill that accomplished many of the same goals, this time on a national level. The bill was the Personal Responsibility and Work Opportunity Reconciliation Act of 1996 (PRWORA), popularly known as the welfare reform act. The act had a significant impact on the way both documented and undocumented immigrants may use public services.

Before PRWORA, services provided by the US Department of Health and Human Services, with the exception of AFDC and Medicaid, were available to anyone residing in the United States, with eligibility based on need rather than immigration status. PRWORA barred *legal* immigrants from receiving food stamps, and left it up to individual states to determine whether legal immigrants are eligible for Temporary Assistance for Needy Families (TANF), the program which replaced AFDC. In addition, non-refugee immigrants were banned from receiving "Federal means-tested public benefits" including Medicaid, TANF, and the Children's Health Insurance Program, for the first five years of their residency. "Non-qualified aliens," including non-immigrants (such as students and tourists) and undocumented aliens are also barred from receiving "Federal Public Benefits." The act denied undocumented immigrants access to thirty-one Health and Human Services programs, including programs for alcohol and drug abuse and for the disabled.[30]

Immediately after the enactment of PRWORA, former California governor Pete Wilson made prenatal care the first target of his campaign to enact the federal law's ban on state and local assistance to illegal immigrants. The *Los Angeles Times* reported:

> Among the first targets, Wilson vowed, would be prenatal care—a service universally acclaimed as vital to fetal and maternal health, and to averting astronomical emergency room and intensive-care costs. While not disputing the health benefits, Wilson says California taxpayers simply cannot afford the $70-million-dollar-a-year cost and should not "simply say we will take all comers, whether they are citizens or not."[31]

Wilson's callous disregard for the health of undocumented women and their children cannot be simply written off as an attempt to cut California's budget expenditures. At its most basic level, the edict reflects assumptions about the value of immigrant mothers in United States society. In fact, the attacks on immigrant women's ability to reproduce and maintain their families form the root of the recent assault on immigrants, especially through policies regulating immigrants' use of public services. The attacks should be seen as an attempt to regulate and control immigrant women's mothering.

Regulating Motherhood

Attacks on immigrant women's eligibility for welfare and other social services are no accident. Rather, the way in which welfare is legislated reflects the relationship between welfare, motherhood, and the state. Contemporary attempts to reform welfare have very little to do with economics, and everything to do with governmental control over the lives of poor women, particularly over their roles as reproducers and nurturers—that is, mothers. This is nowhere more true than in the discourse about immigrant women and welfare. This section will situate the contemporary assault on immigrant women's use of social services within a broader historical context of the use of welfare to regulate poor women's lives.

Welfare, particularly programs such as AFDC (now TANF), has its historical roots in programs designed to foster governmental involvement in single mothers' lives. The formation of mothers' pension programs (early precursors to AFDC and TANF) was based on the notion that women needed protection from waged labor, since "family life in the home is sapped in its foundations when the mothers of young children work for wages."[32] Mothers' pensions were a way for the state to "preserve the integrity of motherhood" in the absence of a male breadwinner.[33]

Based on the formulation of women as dependent on the state in the absence of their husbands, mothers' pensions paved the way for governmental regulation of motherhood.[34] In the twentieth century, the ability to both grant and deny welfare to single mothers through Aid to Dependent Children (ADC) continued to be a site through which the state could regulate the morality of motherhood. For example, "suitable home" and "fit parent" policies gave the social workers at federal and state agencies wide discretion as to their interpretation of these policies, discretion which often resulted in the denial of aid to working-class women, women of color, and immigrant women.[35] Moreover, some states also used "employable mother" rules which disqualified able-bodied women with school-age children, especially Black women, from receiving welfare, on the grounds that they should work.[36]

Mimi Abramowitz, author of *Regulating the Lives of Women: Social Welfare Policy from Colonial Times to the Present*, discusses how the construction of the "family ethic" was used to distinguish between women "deserving" of public assistance, and those who were "undeserving."[37] Abramowitz describes the family ethic as the ideology that "articulates expected work and family behavior and defines women's place in the social order."[38] The lynchpin of the family ethic is the assignment of homemaking and child-care responsibilities to women, based on the belief in gender roles as biologically determined. By taking a biologically determinist view of society, the family ethic plays into myths of biological difference between the social behavior of different sexes, races, and classes. This conception of the biology of difference provides a clear link to eugenic ideas about superiority, inferiority, and fitness.

As previously established, the welfare system has played a prominent role in determining the meaning of "fitness." Abramowitz contends that compliance with the terms of the family ethic theoretically entitles a woman to the "rights of womanhood," including claims to femininity, protection, economic support, and respectability. Non-compliance, however, leads to denial of the rights of womanhood. Poor and immigrant women and women of color, who, due to greater levels of poverty, were more likely than middle-class white women to seek paid labor outside of the home, were thus seen as outside the bounds of the family ethic. Thus, their claims to the rights of womanhood, including the economic support of welfare, were suspect. As Abramowitz writes:

> [T]he rules and regulations of social welfare programs ... treat women differently according to their perceived compliance with the family ethic. Indeed, conforming to the ideology of women's roles has been used to distinguish among women as deserving or undeserving of aid since colonial times. Assessing women in terms of the family ethic has become one way the welfare state could mediate the conflicting demands for women's unpaid labor in the home and her low paid labor in the market, encourage reproduction by "proper" families, and otherwise meet the needs of patriarchal capitalism.[39]

Indeed, by reinforcing racial and class-based divisions among women, the welfare state has helped facilitate the funneling of certain "undeserving" women into the low-wage job market, while preserving the role of full-time mother for upper-middle-class white women. Although most middle-class white women now hold jobs outside the home, the mythology surrounding the full-time mother still idealizes middle-class white women's lives.

The dichotomy between "deserving" and "undeserving" women allows for the simultaneous exploitation of the wage labor of poor women, immigrant women, and women of color with the privileging of white women's motherhood and the white middle-class family. Indeed, the 1996 welfare reform bill defined all poor women as undeserving of aid, pushing them into the low-wage jobs that form a critical base of the new service economy.

The discourse around the rights of documented and undocumented Latina immigrants hinges on the issue of the worth of their reproductive labor versus their productive labor. Proponents of increased restrictions on immigration and on undocumented immigrants' access to public services often appeal to the perception of undocumented immigrants as lawbreakers. Indeed, the very term "illegal" immigrant suggests that undocumented persons are criminals by their very presence in the United States.

References to illegal United States-Mexico border crossings as evidence of criminal activity are frequent. As one Proposition 187 supporter put it, "I think people are fed up that people can break the law (entering the country illegally) and then get on the welfare roll."[40] Several years later, in 1997, California governor Pete Wilson defended his plan to ban prenatal care for undocumented women by saying that federal law requires that "we cease the provision of taxpayer-funded benefits to those who broke our laws in entering the country."[41] Others defended the denial of public education to undocumented children on the basis of their illegal border crossing, illustrated in this 1996 letter to the editor: "We have no obligation to educate those who cross our borders illegally, any more than educating them in their own country."[42]

The final quote reflects a common assumption in much of the contemporary public anti-immigrant discourse in California: Since illegal immigrants broke the law, they are not entitled to the basic rights guaranteed to US citizens and legal permanent residents. Indeed, as lawbreakers, they are portrayed as undeserving of public aid. "We must choose whether California will be the Golden State or a welfare state. It can't be both," stated Governor Pete Wilson in his surprisingly blunt 1995 inaugural speech. During the speech, Wilson called on Californians to be prepared for "dramatic change" in the structure of California's welfare system.[43]

While Wilson's speech only touched on issues of immigrant welfare use, welfare debates in California have frequently hinged on questions of immigrant welfare use, and the role of welfare in encouraging or discouraging immigration. Between 1992 and 1996 numerous studies were conducted that tried to establish a link between immigration status and welfare use. Major newspapers reported on such studies with sensational headlines such as: "Welfare Numbers Up Most in Valley: Officials Attribute the 59% Increase to a High Concentration of Poor Immigrants ... and to the Weak Economy,"[44] "Illegal Immigrants Tab for Emergency Care: $61 Million,"[45] "Why Immigrants Get More Welfare: Family Size a Key Factor, Study Says,"[46] and "Study Backs Fears About Immigrants: Report Shows Higher Welfare Dependence."[47]

Many have disputed these claims. It is important to note that undocumented immigrants are barred from participating in most welfare programs including AFDC or TANF, although some undocumented parents may ˙ receive welfare support for their US-born children. A study at the University of California at Irvine based on telephone interviews with 160 undocumented Latinas revealed that only 3 percent of the undocumented Latinas in the study reported receiving AFDC for their US-born children.[48] Numerous studies have reported that poor Latino immigrants are less likely to receive benefits than low-income US-born people.[49]

Claims that immigrants have higher rates of welfare use are usually accompanied by the argument that welfare acts as a magnet for illegal immigration. Or, as California congressman Dana Rohrabacher asserted, "If [Proposition 187] doesn't pass, the flood of illegal immigrants will turn into a tidal wave, and a huge neon sign will be lit up above the state of California that reads: 'Come and get it.' "[50] The implication is that illegal immigrants are coming to the United States intending to exploit the availability of public benefits. The implicit (or sometimes explicit) characterization of undocumented immigrants is that they are lazy, sneaky, greedy, and willing to travel great distances in order to avoid work and get on welfare. Such a characterization fits in well with stereotypes about Latinos already prominent in the mainstream—stereotypes that Latinos are lazy, selfish, and pleasure-oriented.[51]

Certainly, Proposition 187, as well as other anti-immigrant welfare reform measures, owes much of its success to the widespread acceptance of such negative stereotypes about Latinos. These stereotypes also form the basis for the exclusion of immigrant women from welfare programs. If immigrant women are trying to get themselves and their children on welfare because they are selfishly trying to take advantage of United States taxpayers, or because they are too lazy to get a job, then they can be classified as "undeserving" and denied benefits.

Laziness and criminality are thus rhetorically pinned on immigrant women and used to prove their lack of compliance with the family ethic. Indeed, these qualities represent the antithesis of the ideal American motherhood: a hardworking and diligent homemaker, a selfless, eternally giving parent. At a more basic level, however, their very status as lawbreakers is enough to deny undocumented immigrant women assistance. What's more, by rejecting an immigrant's claim on the rights of motherhood, her claim to the rights of female citizenship is simultaneously rejected.

Motherhood and Citizenship

The debate about the accessibility of social services and benefits for immigrants, legal and illegal, touches on profound racial fears for many white citizens. Immigrant women of color and their children are targeted because of white anxieties about a racially pluralized society. Whereas Mexican immigrant men have been perceived as temporary laborers, the presence of Mexican women and children suggests permanence, and the full integration of Mexican-American communities into society.[52] Mexican immigrant women, both by their activities in consolidating settlement and by their linkage to raising and reproducing children, are key to their families' process of integration with US society. Therefore, the mythologized foundations of the American (white) national identity are profoundly shaken by the presence of Mexican and other non-white immigrant women.

Contemporary welfare reform directed at immigrants is rooted in an attempt to exclude non-white immigrant women from US society. The historical roots of welfare reform, deeply implicated in the racialized process of distinguishing between "deserving" and "undeserving" motherhood, provide an important context to the underlying purpose of contemporary welfare reform. Mothers' pensions were conditional on a woman's certification as "a proper person, physically, mentally, and morally fit to bring up her children."[53] These conditions functioned as a racialized form of quality control, a political eugenics whereby "the value of maternal work hung on women's contributions to the 'racial welfare.' "[54] Thus, the exclusion of poor women, immigrant women, and women of color from receiving mothers' pensions represents not only the loss of material benefits, but also the devaluation of their worthiness as mothers in the process of social reproduction.

The depreciated worth of non-white immigrant mothers is reflected in their work as child-care providers for upper-middle-class, mostly white women's children. While many non-white immigrant women are paid to care for other women's children, they are often simultaneously faced with a lack of desirable day care options for their own children. The situation reflects the societal prioritization of upper-middle-class and white children's interests, and the devaluation of the children of poor, non-white immigrants.

Contemporary attempts to exclude immigrant women from welfare accomplish a similar objective. Attacks on legal and illegal immigrants' rights to public services, including prenatal care, schooling for immigrant children, AFDC, and non-emergency health care, are all targeted at immigrant women's ability to have and raise children. As Dorothy Roberts notes,

> The right to bear children goes to the heart of what it means to be human. The value we place on individuals determines whether we see them as entitled to perpetuate themselves in their children. Denying someone the right to bear children—or punishing her for exercising that right—deprives her of a basic

part of her humanity. When this denial is based on race, it also functions to preserve a racial hierarchy.[55]

Roberts goes on to argue that although recent legislative attacks on immigrants "have a very concrete impact on the health and status of immigrant children, they send an equally powerful message about their humanity and inclusion."[56] This is political eugenics in its purest form. It is an attempt to control who may be considered American and to exclude undocumented immigrants, particularly Mexicans, from the rights bestowed on citizens.

Moreover, the denial of full citizenship rights to Mexicans in the United States is a way to address the tension between the temporary surplus labor that capitalism wants/needs and the desire of a dominant white class to maintain its central location in the US national identity. Capital wants labor, but doesn't want to bear the costs of reproducing it. In an ideal union between capitalism and white supremacy, immigrant women and men of color can continue to provide cheap, surplus labor, while remaining comfortably outside the realm of full citizenship. Thus, capitalist development can be preserved while the imagined white national identity can remain intact.

Conclusion

The gendered assault on immigrants in California during the 1990s was directed primarily at women, particularly at their reproductive and maternal work. The focus of policy and rhetoric on illegal immigration placed an additional strain on the undocumented, even as the numbers of undocumented women immigrants increased due to IRCA's gender bias, the uprooting of women in developing countries through globalized production practices, and the increasing demand for low-paid female immigrants to work in the domestic realm.

While contemporary anti-immigrant forces are working to exclude and marginalize recent (predominantly non-white) immigrants, immigrant women play an essential role in fostering the permanent settlement of their families, thus integrating their families and communities into the fabric of American society. Thus, immigrant women present a formidable foe to the purposes of contemporary immigration "reformers."

Whether or not the attack on immigrant women was a conscious strategic choice on behalf of anti-immigrant forces, immigrant women, particularly undocumented immigrant women, came under fire from the anti-immigrant establishment in the 1990s. When immigrant women could not be excluded from the United States altogether, anti-immigrant legislation sought to set them and their families in a class apart from the rest of American society. Undocumented women were portrayed as greedy, lazy, and criminal, in order to mark them as undeserving of public services. Most significantly, the denial of public services to undocumented immigrants, especially women and children, was an attempt to exclude them and their children from integration with United States society. The underlying message is clear: "they" are not welcome in "our" society.

The attacks on immigrant women and children are an attempt to solve the fundamental paradox of the simultaneous desire to exclude non-white foreigners from US citizenship, and to continue to enjoy the benefits from their underpaid labor. The recent legislative attacks represent a move to create a sub-class of immigrant workers who would remain decidedly outside of the United States citizen class and outside the realm of rights, being denied access to the benefits and rights of equality. This move towards creating a caste-like class system perpetuates a racial hierarchy in which Mexicans and other non-white foreigners are exploited by the dominant white class.

At the root of the attacks are racist theories about white superiority, and eugenic ideals of the perfect white society. Thus, eugenics, and its obsession with race and reproduction, is alive today and continues to inform contemporary political debate about immigration reform. It has not disappeared; it has simply changed its strategies, and put on a different mask. It shows no signs of disappearing.

1   *The San Diego Union-Tribune*, March 13, 1996.

2   Gilbert Paul Carrasco, "Latinos in the United States: Invitation and Exile," in Juan F. Perea, ed., *Immigrants Out! The New Nativism and the Anti-Immigrant Impulse in the United States* (New York; London: New York University Press, 1997), 197.

3   Grace Chang, *Disposable Domestics: Immigrant Women Workers in the Global Economy* (Cambridge, MA: South End Press, 2000).

4   US Department of Justice, Immigration and Naturalization Service, and US Department of Labor Bureau of International Labor Affairs, *The Triennial Comprehensive Report on Immigration* (Washington, DC: 1999), 20.

5   Ibid., 1.

6   Karen Judd and Anannya Bhattacharjee, *Immigration Opposition Primer* (Port Chester, NY: Pro-Choice Resource Center, 1999), 2.

7   US Department of Justice, *The Triennial Comprehensive Report on Immigration*, 20.

8   Judd and Bhattacharjee, *Immigration Opposition Primer*, 1.

9   National Immigration Forum, "Fast Facts" (February 1999).

10 Jeffery S. Passel and Karen A. Woodrow, "Post-IRCA Unauthorized Immigration to the United States: An Assessment based on the June 1998 CPS," *Unauthorized Migration to California: IRCA and the Experience of the 1980s* (Washington, DC: Urban Institute Press).

11 Pierette Hondagneu-Sotelo, *Gendered Transitions: Mexican Experiences of Immigration* (Berkeley, CA; Los Angeles, CA: University of California Press, 1994), 26.

12 Saskia Sassen, *The Mobility of Labor and Capital* (Cambridge: Cambridge University Press, 1988), 97.

13 Ibid., 117–118.

14 Ibid., 101.

15 National Council for Research on Women, "Immigration: Women and Girls, Where do they Land?" *Issues Quarterly*, 1:3 (1995), 3; Peter Stalker, *The Work of Strangers: A Survey of International Labor Migration* (Geneva, Switzerland: International Labor Office, 1994), 149.

16 Marc Linder and Larry Norton, "Nanny Tax Lets Poor Pay, Rich Profit," *New York Times*, November 13, 1994.

17 Stalker, *The Work of Strangers: A Survey of International Labor Migration*, 149.

18 Linder and Norton, "Nanny Tax Lets Poor Pay, Rich Profit."

19 Immigration law includes provisions enabling the family members of US citizens and legal permanent residents, including spouses, minor children (under 21 years old) unmarried and married sons and daughters (21 years old or more), and brothers and sisters to apply for legal immigration. Employment-based admissions are another category of admissions, and include provisions for both "skilled" workers with advanced degrees and "unskilled" workers.

20 Cited in Santiago O'Donnell, "Angry Latino Voters Decry Gallegly Proposal," *Los Angeles Times*, October 26, 1991.

21 Cited in Eric Bailey, "Latinos Blast Rohrabacher for Position on Benefits,"

Los Angeles Times, April 17, 1992.
22 Ibid.
23 Ibid.
24 Ibid.
25 "Work, Not Welfare Lures Latinas," *Los Angeles Times,* September 15, 1996.
26 "Proposition 165: Welfare, Benefits," *The San Diego Union-Tribune,* October 11, 1992.
27 *1994 California Voter Information: Proposition 187.* Text of proposed law.
28 *League of United Latin American Citizens, et al., Plaintiffs, vs. Pete Wilson, et al., Defendants;* US District Court for the Central District of California, November 14, 1997, Decided.
29 Dorothy Roberts, "Who May Give Birth to Citizens?" in Juan F. Perea, ed., *Immigrants Out!,* 207.
30 US Dept of Justice et al., *The Triennial Comprehensive,* 153.
31 Patrick McDonnell and Timothy Williams, "Prenatal Caregivers Caught Between Edict and Oath," *Los Angeles Times,* August 31, 1996.
32 Cited in Gwendolyn Mink, "The Lady and the Tramp: Gender, Race, and the Origin of the American Welfare State," in Linda Gordon, ed., *Women, the State, and Welfare* (Madison, WI: University of Wisconsin Press, 1990).
33 Ibid.
34 Ibid.
35 Ibid.
36 Mimi Abramowitz, *Regulating the Lives of Women: Social Welfare Policy from Colonial Times to the Present* (Cambridge, MA: South End Press, 1988), 318.
37 Ibid., 318–319.
38 Ibid., 36.
39 Ibid., 39–40.
40 Quoted in Leonel Sanchez, "Supporters of Immigration Issue Dug In," *The San Diego Union-Tribune,* October 31, 1994.
41 Quoted in Aurelio Rojas, "Judge Blocks Prenatal Care Ban," *San Francisco Chronicle,* December 20, 1997.
42 Fisher, H. Lee, "US has no obligation to educate illegal immigrants kids," *Los Angeles Times,* Letters to the Editor, June 8, 1996.
43 Dave and Bill Stall. "Wilson Sworn In: Bluntly Warns of Welfare Shake-Up," *Los Angeles Times,* January 8, 1995.
44 Tracy Kaplan, "Welfare Numbers up Most in Valley," *Los Angeles Times,* September 13, 1992.
45 Gabe Martinez, "Illegal Immigrants Tab for Emergency Care: $61 Million," *Los Angeles Times,* November 2, 1994.
46 Ramon G. McLeod, "Why Immigrants Get More Welfare," *San Francisco Chronicle,* April 8, 1995.
47 Jonathan Marshall, "Study Backs Fears About Immigrants," *San Francisco Chronicle,* February 26, 1996.
48 "Work, Not Welfare Lures Latinas," *Los Angeles Times.*
49 See McDonnell and Williams (1996); James Bornemeier, "Study Paints Positive Picture of Immigration," *Los Angeles Times,* December 11, 1995.

50   Quoted in Martinez, "Illegal Immigrants Tab for Emergency Care: $61 Million."

51   For a detailed discussion of the formation of these racial stereotypes of Mexicans in California, see Thomas Almaguer, *Racial Fault Lines: The Historical Origins of White Supremacy in California* (Berkeley, CA: University of California Press, 1994).

52   Hondagneu-Sotelo, Gendered Transitions: *Mexican Experiences of Immigration.*

53   Mink, "The Lady and the Tramp: Gender, Race, and the Origin of the American Welfare State," *Women.*

54   Ibid.

55   Roberts, "Who May Give Birth to Citizens?," *Immigrants Out!*

56   Ibid., 215.

Chapter 8

Put in Harm's Way

The Neglected Health Consequences of Sex Trafficking in the United States

H. Patricia Hynes and Janice G. Raymond

Trafficking in women for prostitution and related forms of sexual entertainment is so widespread yet so invisible. Its invisibility is anchored in two foundations: the traditional view of gender inequality which instrumentalizes women's bodies for sexual and reproductive use; and the more liberal view which redefines certain forms of sexual exploitation such as prostitution as work, legitimates the selling of sexual "services" as commerce, and reconstructs the female body as a commodity. The "invisible hand"[1] of the gendered market further assures that male sexual consumption is optimized in the buying and selling of women's bodies.

Macroeconomic policies promoted by international lending organizations such as the World Bank and the International Monetary Fund, which mandate "structural adjustments" in many developing regions of the world, have helped push certain countries to export women for labor (the Philippines), making them vulnerable to trafficking; or to develop economies based on tourism (Thailand), with a huge dependence on sex tourism. Male demand, female inequality, and economies in crisis—among other factors—lie at the nexus of sex trafficking.

Researchers differ on the numbers of women trafficked internationally. United Nations (UN) reports estimate that 4 million women have been trafficked. United States reports cite 700,000 to

2 million women and children internationally trafficked each year into the sex industry and for labor.[2] All estimates, however, are preliminary and do not include trafficking within countries. The most prevalent forms of sex trafficking are for prostitution, sex tourism, and mail-order bride industries. Women and children are also trafficked for bonded labor and domestic work, and much of this trafficking concludes with their being sexually exploited as well.

Defining the Problem

Currently, there is an international debate about the definition of trafficking and whether to separate trafficking from prostitution. We use the definition of trafficking from the new UN Protocol to Prevent, Suppress and Punish Trafficking in Persons, Especially Women and Children, supplementing the UN Convention Against Transnational Organized Crime that became open for member nations' signatures in Palermo in December 2000. Thus far, the protocol has been signed by at least eighty countries.

> (a) "Trafficking in persons" shall mean the recruitment, transportation, transfer, harbouring or receipt of persons, by means of the threat or use of force or other forms of coercion, of abduction, of fraud, of deception, of the abuse of power or of a position of vulnerability or of the giving or receiving of payments or benefits to achieve the consent of a person having control over another person, for the purpose of exploitation.
>
> Exploitation shall include, at a minimum, the exploitation of the prostitution of others or other forms of sexual exploitation, forced labour or services, slavery or practices similar to slavery, servitude or the removal of organs;
> (b) The consent of a victim of trafficking in persons to the intended exploitation set forth in subparagraph (a) of this article shall be irrelevant where any of the means set forth in subparagraph (a) have been used.[3]

Exploitation, rather than *coercion*, is the operative concept in this definition. A definition of trafficking, based on a human rights framework, should protect all who are trafficked, drawing no distinctions between deserving and undeserving victims of trafficking, that is, those who can prove they were forced and those who cannot. Any definition based on the victim's consent places the burden of proof on the victim and offers a loophole for traffickers to use the alleged consent of the victim in their own defense.

Other definitions have focused on consent. However, the 1949 United Nations Convention for the Suppression of Traffic in Persons and of the Exploitation of Prostitution of Others, and Article 6 of the United Nations Convention on the Elimination of All Forms of Discrimination against Women are representative of a consensus in international law, that human trafficking is the recruitment and transport of persons for the purpose of sexual exploitation, regardless of whether or not they have "consented" to their trafficking. The new UN Protocol on the Trafficking in Persons is continuous with this international consensus.

A Global Problem

Countries as diverse as Vietnam, Cuba, and those in Eastern Europe and the former Soviet Union—all beset by acute financial crises while becoming market economies in varying degrees—are witnessing a tremendous increase in trafficking and prostitution. Mail-order bride industries capitalize on the trafficking of Russian and Asian women, particularly to men in industrialized countries who want foreign wives they deem to be pliable and exotic.

In the Asian region alone, 200–400 Bangladeshi women are illegally transported into Pakistan monthly and 7,000 to 12,000 Nepali women and girls are sold yearly into the brothels of India. The trafficking of girls from Nepal to India is probably the most intensive sexual slave trade anywhere in the world. In 1992, more than 62.5 percent of total "entertainers" (a code word for prostitution) in Japan were Filipino—92 percent of them undocumented. In Asia, millions of women and girls have been led into systems of prostitution such as street prostitution, sex entertainment clubs, sex tourism, and brothels that may literally be cages or, conversely, luxury establishments. Brothels in Bombay and Delhi receive trafficked women from Bangladesh and Nepal and are often the transit point for moving women to Europe and North America.[4]

International women are trafficked from economically unstable countries to economically stable ones; from developing countries to industrialized countries; from rural to urban centers within developing countries; from developing countries to adjacent ones with sex industries; through developed countries and regions, such as Western Europe and Canada, to the United States; and within the United States. Both international and domestic women are domestically trafficked within their countries of destination or origin, respectively.

Trafficking Into and Within the United States

Until recently, trafficking in the United States was rarely acknowledged. It was not until Russian and Ukrainian women began to be trafficked to the United States in the early 1990s that governmental agencies and many non-governmental organizations (NGOs) began to recognize the problem. As many critics, including ourselves, have pointed out, Latin American and Asian women were trafficked into the United States for many years prior to the influx of Russian traffickers and trafficked women. The fact that it took blond and blue-eyed victims to draw governmental and public attention to trafficking in the United States gives the appearance, at least, of racism.

Trafficking of women into the United States by transnational sex industries is beginning to be increasingly researched, estimated numerically, and compared with the drug and weapons smuggling industry by the US Immigration and Naturalization Service (INS). The US government estimates that 45,000 to 50,000 women and children are trafficked annually from Southeast Asia, Latin America, Eastern Europe, and the newly independent states of the former Soviet Union to the United States for the sex industry, sweatshops, domestic labor, and agricultural work.[5]

However, the documented incidents of sex trafficking in the United States have, until recently, been published in isolation and usually in newspaper articles following an enforcement crackdown and prosecution. These accounts have generally lacked an analysis of the structures that account for women being trafficked into prostitution, namely, the global sex industry, the subordination of women, the gendered labor market, and the multiple economic crises and inequalities that underlie women's lives.

Many factors—including death threats to themselves and their families at home; conditions of isolation and confinement; the high mobility of the sex industry; fear of deportation; the lack of acknowledgement within many human rights and refugee advocacy service organizations who are struggling with a range of other problems; and the lack of "safe houses" and shelters—make it nearly impossible for trafficked women to seek assistance and to testify against traffickers and other exploiters.[6]

Further, the limited legislation, light penalties, and long, complicated nature of investigations for trafficking convictions tend to make trafficking cases unattractive to many US attorneys, according to a recent government report.[7] Additionally, the current immigration and criminal justice system in the United States is weighted against trafficked women. The current system hampers undocumented victims of trafficking from coming forward for fear of deportation and the lack of INS assurance that victims will be allowed to remain in the country if they choose.

This overview and analysis of the trafficking of women in the United States for sexual exploitation has had to rely, therefore, on indirect and secondary sources, including federal government estimates, as well as a minimal but growing body of primary sources, chief among which are interviews with trafficked women conducted by the Coalition Against Trafficking in Women. The authors have pieced together a composite picture of the scope and methods by which immigrant women, migrant women with temporary visas, and women lumped into the INS categories of "undocumented aliens" and "illegal aliens" end up exploited in prostitution in the United States.[8]

As for delineating the harm suffered by trafficked women, we draw from three sources: studies of prostituted women which document the health effects of prostitution including the harm from violence; the literature on the health burden of violence against women; and our interviews conducted recently with trafficked Russian women. Everything learned in this investigation of sex trafficking directs us to a policy of prevention of trafficking through alternatives for women, protection for trafficked women, and prosecution of traffickers and other exploiters.

Public health and environmental protection agencies—once they have documented human health and environmental threats—typically respond with intervention and protection programs for those at risk, coupled with enforcement mechanisms to punish and deter violators. Prevention is generally late upon the scene and inadequate for the need. In documenting the trafficking of women for sexual exploitation, we have concluded that three fronts of response to this grievous abuse of human rights are equally vital: namely, investing in women's economic development and women's human rights to create alternatives for women, while exposing the sex industry and the harm to women; providing services and protection from deportation for trafficked women; and aggressively punishing the crime of sex trafficking, not by criminalizing the women but by punishing the recruiters, traffickers, pimps, and buyers.

Migration: The Nexus of Individual Necessity, Country Policy, Post-Colonial Development, and Industry Opportunism

In the mid-1990s, nearly two percent of the world's population, or about 125 million people, were international migrants, that is, people living outside their country of origin, the highest number in history. International migration in 1995 was estimated to be up to 4 million people annually, with about one-half of these entering the United States and Canada as permanent and temporary migrants, refugees, and undocumented migrants. No one international or national data source identifies all of the people moving across national borders, but all data sources tracking refugees and migrant labor suggest that the numbers are on the increase.[9]

Determinants of Migration

"Push" and "Pull" Forces

It is commonly held that the factors influencing migration are the push of poverty and underemployment at home and the pull of employment elsewhere, the push of civil strife and persecution, and the pull of family networks abroad. In the case of recruitment for work abroad, labor recruiters and smugglers actively seek, and entrap in some cases, a supply of people in the sending country. They are "an important but under-studied factor in today's international migration networks," especially because recruiters and smugglers indenture migrants seeking labor abroad for the equivalent of anywhere from one-quarter to all of a year's salary or even a few years' salary.[10] Undocumented immigrants are more vulnerable to abuse and coercion by smugglers, traffickers, and employers, out of fear of deportation. Furthermore, recent US anti-immigrant legislation, subjecting even legal immigrants to harsh and discriminatory practices, increases the vulnerability of all immigrants.

Labor for Export

The pull of employment elsewhere is augmented by the sending country's policy, implicit and explicit, to export labor for remittance because of numerous, well-documented factors: exorbitant national debt, high unemployment, the displacement of agricultural workers with the industrialization of agriculture, and imposed re-structuring of national economies by the World Bank and International Monetary Fund,[11] both dominated by US influence. The economic development policies of many countries are locked into repaying foreign loans, often to industrialized countries that have freely plundered the resources of the very nations that are in debt bondage. Many countries encourage their citizens to leave the country for work so that the payments, which workers send back to families, can stimulate and stabilize the economy.

In 1995, 15.3 percent of the Philippine labor force (or an estimated 4,200,000 women and men) migrated for labor, making the Philippines the largest Asian exporter of labor and making workers the Philippines' largest export.[12] Remittances sent home by overseas workers have been growing annually by 35 percent since 1992, reaching $7.1 billion in 1996; and they are relied upon by the government to reduce the country's deficit.[13] Sixty percent of all overseas contract workers leaving the Philippines are now women,[14] a trend referred to as the *feminization of labor,* with 2000 women leaving the Philippines per day.

The trend in labor export and labor emigration in developing countries will continue with the global trend in *production for export*, a development policy propounded and imposed on these countries by international lending agencies and free market advocates.[15] The mechanization of agriculture for export and consequent migration from rural to urban areas is another major factor in rural unemployment and migration for work. Between 1950 and 1990, the percent of the world working in agriculture dropped from 65 percent to 50 percent, and in developing countries from 80 percent to 40 percent.[16] Tens of millions of displaced rural farmers and their children move to cities looking for work, where they are vulnerable to labor recruiters and traffickers with schemes of employment abroad. In some cases, families sell their daughters to recruiters, wittingly and unwittingly, for prostitution.[17]

Postcolonial Policy

Other factors have been cited as influencing the recent wave of immigration from Asia, the Caribbean, and Latin America, namely, powerful US political, economic, and military involvements since the 1960s that created linkages between the United States and numerous developing countries that, in turn, stimulated a flow of labor into the United States. Furthermore, the emergence of global cities, including New York and Los Angeles, as centers of international finance, culture, and business services, has resulted in an informal economy of low-paying service and sweatshop jobs which has shaped the face and locus of current immigration. Immigrants to the United States cluster in a few US regions and in large metropolitan areas; and a growing majority are women.[18] "International migrations, in other words, are embedded in larger social, economic, and political processes,"[19] which generate the "push" and pull" factors so neatly packaged by migration analysts.

The globalization of labor or the flow of labor across borders has accompanied the internationalization and global circulation of finance and capital, particularly in recent times. Sociologist Saskia Sassen argues that the specific forms of internationalization of capital in the last twenty years "have contributed to mobilizing people into migration streams," citing particularly the "implantation" of

Western development models and Western education.[20] Western development promoted replacement of small and internal agriculture and industry in developing countries with export-oriented agriculture and manufacture. Postcolonial networks and relationships, coupled with the "Pax Americana"[21]—a catch-all for US foreign policy including recent "wars for democracy," direct foreign investment, and the creation of export-processing zones—have further fueled the flow of high finance, capital, information, high-tech services, elite personnel, *and migrant poor* to a "global grid of cities."[22] In these transnational cities, the elite settle into urban zones of glamour and luxury while the migrant poor, who provide service and labor for the urban elite, reside at the urban edges in low-income, internationally diverse neighborhoods.

The "transnationalization of labor,"[23] Sassen suggests, is more accurate terminology than the older discourse of immigration to describe the modern phenomenon of labor following capital and finance transnationally. Although we do not support an increasing tendency to redefine and legitimate prostitution as "sex work," and sex trafficking as "migration for sex work," we do believe that trafficking is an industry. Thus, we refer to the transnationalization of the sex industry.

Opportunism of the Sex Industry

Globalization of the world economy has been accompanied by globalization of the sex industry. Sexual exploitation moves freely across local and national borders in the same circulation patterns as drugs, weapons, finance, information, goods and services, and labor. In what becomes a predacious cycle, the growth of the transnational sex industry—with its unique profit potential from the reuse and resale of women, compared to the one-time sale of drugs and weapons—entices governments facing economic crisis to promote women for export within the global sex industry in order to attract a flow of remittances back to the sending country; or to directly and indirectly promote local sex industries to bring money into the country.

Sex trafficking into and within the United States is opportunistically bound up with migration for labor; that is, it preys on the fact that women are migrating across borders, as well as within their countries, in unprecedented numbers for purposes of labor and income. Moreover, as the Internet sprawls into one massive (cyber-)mall, the growth in the transnational sex industry is spurred by the immense promotion and marketing of women and children for sex tourism, as electronic mail-order brides, and in pornography. The virtual trafficking in women and children along the information cyber-highway mimics the migration routes of sexual exploitation by air, land, and sea across the globe.[24]

The Structure of Trafficking of Women in the United States

Economic Pull Factor Embedded in Sexual Inequality

In countries such as Thailand, Australia, and certain European countries, prostitution and sex entertainment are imputed and institutionalized parts of the formal economy, making use of the media, airlines, hotel chains, international communications and travel agencies, and banks. The sex industry is so pervasive in Thailand that it accounts for up to 14 percent of the gross national product (GNP).[25] To view trafficking for prostitution only through an economic lens, however, is to omit other key considerations.

The economic reasons why individual women enter prostitution and/or are trafficked are fairly straightforward. Not well spotlighted are the gendered facts that prostitution or sex entertainment is generally the only form of work that allows many women to make more money than they could in other circumstances; and that prostitution is overwhelmingly the selling of *women's* and *girls'* bodies to men for the sex of prostitution. An economic analysis is necessary but insufficient for explaining the business and the buyers of prostituted women. It leaves unaddressed the tolerated and/or accepted "natural law" of male sexuality—that men's alleged innate sexual needs must be satisfied and therefore, that prostitution is inevitable.

Methods of Recruitment and Initiation

Traffickers recruit women in their countries of origin for service and entertainment industries abroad through ads and informal or organized recruitment networks. Passports, visas, and letters of employment are commonly obtained for women by the traffickers; often the passports and visas are fraudulent. Often, large fees are charged for procuring the documents, the alleged job, and airline tickets, fees so exorbitant that women can be indentured to the traffickers for years. Many traffickers use itineraries with multiple stop points and non-surveilled entry ports into the United States, employing paid accomplices along the way. Corrupt travel agencies, embassy officials, and inspection police facilitate trafficked women's exit of and entry to countries without inspection.[26]

Once in the United States, trafficked women are frequently seasoned into their plight through repeated rape, threats to their lives and those of their family members, and the withholding of their legal or illegal travel documents. Initially housed at staging points, they are then moved frequently to brothels in a circuit of cities. The frequent moving serves many purposes: male customers are assured of a fresh supply of exotic women, women have little time to establish contacts who could assist them, and enforcement agencies are more easily eluded.

One case that is particularly illustrative of the patterns of sex trafficking in the United States, and the ways in which women are moved quickly from place to place, occurred in Atlanta, Georgia in March 1998. Original reports indicated that FBI agents had raided a house in Atlanta in which they found eight girls, ages 15 and 16, being held in prison-like conditions. The brothel turned out to be only one in a nationwide network operating in fourteen states. Later reports indicated that 500 to 1,000 trafficked women from Asian countries between the ages of 13 and 25, many of them minors, passed through Atlanta. The average time they spent in the city was two weeks, after which they were moved to other locations. Since the brothels made, on average, $100 a "trick," the cost of flying the women from state to state when other brothel owners bought out the women's contracts was insignificant.[27]

The sex businesses operated in houses, apartments, and townhouses with barbed wire fencing often enclosing the houses and land. Hundreds of sex acts later, some of the women were able to purchase their freedom but, as undocumented and thus illegal, had nowhere to go. Ultimately, some of these women became madams who were put in charge of other women in brothels.[28]

Those trafficking women into the United States include organized crime groups from Russia, Eastern Europe, Latin America, and Asia, particularly from China and Vietnam, groups which are both small and sometimes family-based with loosely connected crime networks, as well as large criminal syndicates. Cases investigated by the United States government have revealed that trafficking in women is tightly linked with other criminal activities, including bribery, forgery of documents, extortion, money laundering, and more.[29] Traffickers secure their operations by victimizing women, often from their own racial and ethnic groups, and sometimes restricting and controlling the male clientele.[30]

Profits From Industries

Many trafficked women have become indentured for up to $50,000, a debt accrued from a string of inflated charges for passport, travel tickets, lodging, meals, alleged job, a "jockey" who accompanies them to the United States, and the trafficker's fee. If sold to a brothel owner, a woman is further indebted. Women are kept in cheap, crowded conditions to maximize industry profits and often they have to buy back their travel documents.

Thai traffickers made an estimated $1.5 million in fifteen months in a New York–based operation that enslaved Thai women; and Mexican traffickers made $2.5 million in a period of two years from Mexican women and girls they procured for prostitution where customers paid $22 for fifteen minutes of sex.[31] The Atlanta brothel in the trafficking operation cited earlier grossed $1.5 million in two and one-half years[32] while the women were kept in debt bondage and as virtual prisoners. A continuous supply of women and girls enables traffickers and brothel owners to maximize their profits by requiring women to see multiple male customers per day, paying them at will or denying them health care, and discarding them when sick, injured, diseased, or disfigured.

The Health Effects of Trafficking in Prostitution

Women trafficked in prostitution are uniquely vulnerable to

being physically harmed and traumatized by gender-based violence. While we have a limited set of interviews documenting the health effects of violence against women trafficked in prostitution, we can also extrapolate from other research. There is a substantial yet limited-in-scope set of studies on the health effects of prostitution and a larger body of international studies on the extensive health consequences of violence against women that help characterize, if not yet quantify, the harm. If anything, we surmised, the injury and harm could be more egregious because trafficked women are sexual chattel, ultimately expendable, often "illegal aliens" who do not speak English, and without recourse to law enforcement, health, and social services. The men who sexually traffic them are linked directly and indirectly with criminal networks and explicitly set out to exploit the trafficked women. The conditions are ripe—with few social controls on the men and no social protections for the women—for gender-based violence, abuse, injury and infection, and medical neglect.

The Health Burden of Violence Against Women

Gender-based violence preponderantly involves men harming women. While interpersonal in nature, it is socially rooted in unequal power relationships between men and women and condoned by patriarchal ideology and institutions.[33] Women victimized by male violence suffer bodily injury, disability, homicide, and suicide; severe stress and psychological trauma; substance abuse; a plague of sexually transmitted diseases, infections, and non-infectious diseases; and unwanted pregnancy, miscarriages, abortions, and infertility.[34] A World Bank study has estimated that women worldwide between the ages of 15 and 44 lose as many years of healthy life to the above-cited consequences of rape and domestic violence as they do to each of the following disease conditions high on the agenda of the World Health Organization: HIV/AIDS, tuberculosis, maternal sepsis, cardiovascular diseases, and all cancers.[35] Rape survivors are nine times as likely to attempt suicide and suffer severe depression as non-victims.[36]

The World Bank estimates of healthy years lost by women due to male violence have been calculated within cultural and medical contexts that have historically condoned, denied, ignored, and trivialized violence against women. In the United States, for example, researchers have estimated that greater than 1 million battered women per year seek medical care for injuries (still a fraction of those battered); yet "of those seeking medical care only one in ten is officially identified as a battered woman by health care professionals."[37] Moreover, even when battering has been identified, most medical professionals have trivialized or denied it. Woman battering—which causes up to an estimated one-third of female trauma injuries—had no priority as a medical health issue, according to studies conducted through the late 1980s.[38]

The Health Burden of Prostitution

Women in prostitution are particularly at risk of gender-based violence—including physical, psychological, and economic harm—from pimps, buyers, police, and boyfriends. In some cases, police are buyers, and boyfriends/husbands are women's pimps and traffickers.[39] Yet, historically, the overriding preoccupation of medical and public health practitioners regarding prostitution has been *prostitutes as vectors of disease.* Their research has fixated on the prevalence of sexually transmitted (STD) and infectious diseases in prostituted women and the women's role in the web of disease causation, to the exclusion of documenting the injuries and other-than-STD illnesses suffered by women in prostitution.

Medical and public health remedies—including regular and mandatory surveillance for sexually transmitted diseases, routine antibiotic treatment, and promotion of condoms—have functioned to monitor and control women in prostitution, but rarely, if ever, to medically monitor, challenge, control, or reform the more numerous male purchasers of sex. These remedies also do not address the more powerful sex industry. Studies conducted to characterize and document the full health impacts of prostitution on the women involved (impacts such as injury and trauma, in addition to sexually transmitted and communicable diseases) for the sake of intervention and advocacy that benefits the women, are a rarity.

One unique and telling source, *Prostitutes in Medical Literature,*[40] provides a comprehensive annotated bibliography of studies on women in prostitution published in international medical literature from 1900 through 1990. By far the preponderance of studies conducted in the late nineteeth and twentieth centuries were preoccupied with the epidemiology of sexually transmitted diseases. Numerous case control studies found that women in prostitution have significantly higher rates of sexually transmitted diseases or infections, hepatitis B, and HIV/AIDS; higher risk of cervical cancer; decreased fertility; and a higher abortion rate.[41] However, the absence of studies on the physical violence and psychological trauma that prostituted women suffer at the hands of pimps, purchasers, police, and boyfriends confirms that health professions have largely ignored and not documented nor studied the full scale of gender-based harm in prostitution.

The lack of documentation on the harm of prostitution and trafficking, and its health burden, may in large part be due to the fact that prostitution has not been categorized as a form of violence against women, and the ambivalence on the part of many researchers, NGOs, and governments to view prostitution as a violation of women's human rights. This professional disregard parallels the earlier and common medical response to battered women, a response increasingly documented and characterized by health researchers over the last twenty years.[42]

Women in the sex industry who have been trafficked and prostituted suffer the same kinds of injuries as women who are battered, raped, and sexually assaulted. However, when women are subjected to these same injuries in the context of prostitution, the violence is ignored or redefined as "sex." "Rough sex," sadism and rape—for women in prostitution, whether trafficked there or not—are often accepted or tolerated as "occupational hazards." When women are made to endure unwanted sexual behavior on the job, it is called sexual harassment. When men in a sex club or brothel pay to enact the same behavior, it is accepted as commercial "sex work."

Studies by Service Organizations for Women in Prostitution

Only recently, as survivors of prostitution are organizing alternatives for women in prostitution and as international NGOs are

confronting the expanding trafficking in women and girls for purposes of sexual exploitation, are studies being undertaken to document the full health impacts of prostitution and trafficking on
women and girls in this industry. A 1994 survey conducted with
sixty-eight women in Minneapolis/St. Paul, who had been prostituted for at least six months in varied contexts from the "street" to
massage parlors and escort services, found that 62 percent had
been raped by a john; half the women had been physically assaulted
by their purchasers; and a third of these experienced purchaser assaults at least several times a year. Twenty-three percent were
beaten severely enough to have suffered broken bones; two were
beaten into a coma.[43] In another survey of fifty-five victims/survi-
vors of prostitution who used the services of the Council for Prostitution Alternatives in Portland, Oregon, 78 percent reported
being raped by pimps and male buyers on average forty-nine times
a year. Eighty-four percent were the victims of aggravated assault,
often requiring emergency room treatment; 53 percent were sexually abused and tortured; and 27 percent were mutilated.[44]

The emotional consequences of prostitution reported include
severe trauma, stress, depression, anxiety, self-medication through
alcohol and drug abuse, and eating disorders. Ninety-four percent
of the women in the Minneapolis/St. Paul study categorized themselves as chemically addicted. Crack cocaine, marijuana, and alcohol were used most frequently, with most women taking up crack
cocaine after being in prostitution. Virtually all of the women (93
percent) had been in drug treatment programs, an average of three
times each; they reported, however, resorting to drugs during prostitution. Ultimately, women in prostitution may be at extreme risk
for self-mutilation, suicide, and homicide. Forty-six percent of the
women in the Minneapolis study had attempted suicide, many repeatedly; and 19 percent had tried to mutilate and harm themselves
physically in other ways. Rates of suicide attempts did not vary
among women with different prostitution experiences (that is,
street, massage parlors, and escort services) nor age of initiation.
"Most notably, drug abuse and violence were virtually universally
present in all the women's lives, regardless of age, race, or
type/amount of prostitution."[45]

Most of the women interviewed in the Twin Cities study had some type of medical coverage and access to health care (a situation which is likely very different from trafficked women whose status in the United States may be "illegal alien"). One-third of the women disclosed their experience in prostitution to their health providers, while the majority did not out of feared repercussions, namely social stigma, threats from abusive pimps and partners, loss of children, and being reported to authorities.

HIV/AIDS

The dawning recognition that the etiology of HIV/AIDS in most women is sex with infected men has begun to realign the dominant view of prostituted women as vectors of sexually transmitted disease. The 12th World AIDS Conference held in Geneva in July 1998 and World AIDS Day in December 1998 provided a lens through which to frame one of the most lethal (and growing) health impacts of male trafficking in women and girls for purposes of prostitution. The most recent data on the prevalence rates and geographical and gender-specific spread of this modern-day plague reveal that "men drive the AIDS epidemic" by their self-interested sexual promiscuity. The epidemic in HIV/AIDS among women is driven, in particular, by male use of prostitutes and infected men's transmission of the virus to their wives, sexual partners, and sexual prey. Women and girls, consequently, are contracting HIV primarily from men and at a faster rate than men and boys.[46] Of an estimated 33 million people currently with HIV, approximately 43 percent are women and girls.

Prostituted women are highly susceptible to this "new" sexually transmitted disease because of the nature of the disease transmission, the exploitative nature of sex in prostitution, and the web of social and economic factors that exacerbate disease and injury for women in prostitution. Women contract HIV more easily than men in heterosexually-penetrative sex because the genital tract of women allows the virus to pass through the bloodstream relatively easily. Researchers estimate that women contract HIV up to ten times as easily as men, with the risk being driven up further by factors of powerlessness, ill health, and economic vulnerability of the female vis-à-vis the male.[47] When sexual intercourse is frequent, hurried, or non-consensual, women have an increased likelihood of infection. Most prostituted women are required to service multiple customers per day. Studies have documented that women in prostitution have had to service dozens of men per day, orally, vaginally, and anally.[48] Sexually transmitted diseases of the lower and upper reproductive tract, including syphilis, genital herpes, chancroid, trichomoniasis, chlamydia, and gonorrhea further increase the HIV transmission rate in women two- to ten-fold.[49]

HIV/AIDS is both a stark disease burden and also a biomarker of the gendered condition of women and of male sexual consumption. The highest rates in the world today exist in centers of sex tourism, in the military, and in societies and subcultures that condone male sexual exploitation, male sexual promiscuity, and female subordination.[50] When these landscapes of sexual politics are further riven by economic collapse and conflict, we see—as in Africa, South and Southeast Asia, and the Newly Independent States (NIS) of the former Soviet Union—the rise of trafficking in women and girls for prostitution and the emergence of new and the re-emergence of "old" sexually transmitted diseases.[51]

Retrograde Public Health Response

Despite the known etiology of HIV/AIDS, the public health response to prostitution as codified in the Contagious Diseases Acts of the nineteenth century—medicalize the women to protect the men—has little changed in the modern health campaigns to check the HIV epidemic. Promoting policies which are distinctly imitative of population control, AIDS-prevention advocates are targeting prostituted women—not male customers and transmitters—for disease control, even though epidemiologists have documented that the epidemic is now driven largely by male-to-female viral transmission and male use of prostituted women. Potentially infected women, not the sexual consumption of infected or potentially infected men, is the focus of control. Working within that framework, one Worldwatch analyst describes married men who are prostitute users as "a bridge between high- and low-risk groups" and advocates targeting condom programs to the "high-risk" group, women in prostitution.[52] The role and responsibility of men who act recklessly in their sexual lives is neutralized and safeguarded, by suggesting that men are mere passive thoroughfares over which HIV/AIDS migrates from culpable "high-risk" women to "innocent" low-risk women. (Indeed, mosquitoes that contract the West Nile encephalitis virus from infected birds and then bite and infect humans are treated with more surveillance and control!)

Interviews with Women Trafficked in the United States

In 1999, the Coalition Against Trafficking in Women (CATW) received funding from the Ford Foundation to study the health effects of migrant sex trafficking. The project is being conducted in selected countries of three major areas of the Coalition: Asia, Latin America, and North America. In these regions CATW is analyzing female migration and the health effects of sex trafficking in the contexts of the globalization of markets and capital, the globalization of the sex industry and the internationalization of patterns of sexual exploitation. Coalition partners have designed a survey which is being used to interview 150 trafficked women for the purpose of documenting: the injuries and infections suffered by these women in prostitution; the sexual and reproductive consequences of being trafficked into prostitution; and the women's perspectives on the traffickers and the buyers and on the viability of prostitution as so-called "work" for women. Since the project is ongoing, only preliminary results of a subset of questions regarding the health effects of prostitution will be presented here.[53]

A Russian NGO partner has translated the CATW survey into Russian and interviewed numerous Russian women who were trafficked for prostitution, both before and after entering the United States. We report here on the results of interviews during 1999–2000 with seventeen women.

Recruitment, Conditions, and Buyers

The women interviewed were recruited into prostitution through a variety of means: ads in Russian print media for dancers, babysitters, waitresses, and secretaries; by a boyfriend, a family member, a neighbor, an acquaintance, strangers, a US pen pal; and by immigrant husbands in the United States. Eight of the seventeen women had been in prostitution in Russia, and it was mainly they who were recruited or pressed into prostitution by boyfriends, acquaintances, and family members once they were in the United States working in low-paying jobs or unemployed.

In prostitution in the United States, most of the women were moved frequently by pimps and traffickers and placed in bars, massage parlors, and brothels in cities, rural areas, suburban sites, and immigrant areas. The men who purchased sex were described by the women as "all kinds" of middle-aged businessmen and blue-collar truck drivers from the United States and of various other nationalities, with some brothels being frequented especially by Russian and Azerbaijani businessmen. Women were made to service multiple "customers" per day and do group sex; one woman reported an average of ten to thirty male buyers per day.

Health Effects

In response to the question of what injuries they suffered from clients while in prostitution in the United States, the women interviewed reported an extremely high incidence of bruises, bleeding, and mouth and teeth injuries. Twelve of seventeen women (71 percent) suffered bruises, with the majority answering that they were bruised often. Seven (41 percent) reported mouth and teeth injuries; ten (59 percent) had vaginal bleeding; seven (41 percent) had "other bleeding"; eleven (65 percent) reported suffering internal pain; four (24 percent), head injuries; and two (12 percent) broken bones.

Virtually all (94 percent) reported seeing other women injured in prostitution by male buyers and brothel owners. When asked about specific injuries that other women in the brothel suffered, twelve of the sixteen (75 percent) who responded to the question reported even higher incidence of injury than they reported about themselves. Some women found it harder to talk about injuries they had seen other women endure than what had happened to themselves, while others who could not speak about their own did answer questions about other women's injuries. For this reason, the composite of what they experienced and of what they witnessed other women experience is important to document in order to capture the full scope of male violence and female injury in prostitution.

So-called "safety policies" in brothels did not protect women from harm. Even where brothels supposedly monitored the "customers" and utilized "bouncers," women stated that they were injured by buyers and, at times, by brothel owners and their friends. Even when someone intervened to control buyers' abuse, women lived in a climate of fear. Although 60 percent of women reported that buyers had sometimes been prevented from abusing them, half of those women answered that, nonetheless, they thought that they might be killed by one of their "customers."

Condom Use

In response to a series of questions about condom use, the women revealed that buyers willing to use condoms ranged from 30 percent to 80 percent of men. With those buyers not willing to use condoms, women employed whatever strategies they knew to try to convince them, often unsuccessfully. Where buyers were allegedly required to use condoms, this requirement did not deter them from offering to pay more for sex without a condom. Twelve of the seventeen (71 percent) interviewees said that male buyers offered to pay more for sex without a condom. The prostituted and trafficked women's physical and economic vulnerability could easily render any "policy" on condom use ineffective.

In answer to the question, "Did the condoms ever break," an astoundingly high eleven out of sixteen (69 percent) replied "yes," with the number ranging from one time to at least ten times.[54] This extraordinarily high rate of condom breakage, together with reported vaginal irritation and bleeding from multiple condom use, raises serious questions about the validity of relying on public health policy that mainly emphasizes condom use in the name of protecting women in prostitution from sexually transmitted infections, including HIV/AIDS.

Integrative Public Health Response Needed

Public health programs which promote "safer sex" and condom use in the sex industry are more likely to protect male prostitute users than to protect women from men who engage in "risky" sex. Ultimately, they insure a healthier supply of prostituted women for male buyers. Safer sex intervention programs do not protect women against condom breakage during intercourse,[55] nor against latex allergies and vaginal abrasions from frequent sex with multiple customers—and, most importantly, against the high incidence of physical and psychological harm women in prostitution have reported. Condom programs in prostitution are like gun locks in gun safety programs: they do save some lives; they don't eliminate the source of the harm.

Promoting Alternatives Versus Risk Reduction

A fuller public health response to the harm of prostitution for women could draw by analogy from the Principle of Precautionary Action, proposed by environmentalists to guide industrial activities and prevent harm to human health and the environment. The "Precautionary Principle" breaks out of the now normative school of risk assessment, which is commonly employed in environmental health decision making and program design. Risk assessment is the process of estimating the amount of damage or harm that may occur or can be reduced if an activity under consideration takes place. (For example, if 95 percent of buyers purchasing women in commercial sex can be made to use condoms, and condoms have a certain breakage rate, what is the predicted rate of new HIV infection cases among the prostituted women in a particular sex tourism area?) According to scientist and critic Mary O'Brien, risk assessment concerns itself with "How much damage or harm is safe and tolerable, rather than how little damage is possible?"[56]

Risk-based regulatory systems, like those of cost-benefit analysis, assume that there is a "safe" amount of harm that can be tolerated, that we can set limits to control irreversible harm, and that we know enough about the causes of harm to take risks.[57] Risk reduction programs (such as safety training for pesticide applicators; warning labels on toxic substances; and controlling the access of minors and pregnant women to toxic substances or activities) are generally promoted by those who have a stake or interest in the risky business.[58]

In the case of prostitution industries into which women are trafficked, it is the sex industry that has sought legitimacy through its public relations campaign of alleged condom promotion in the brothels. They set the parameters of condom use and, often, when condom distribution is allowed, it is the brothels—not the women—who receive them directly. NGO advocates who promote and distribute condoms in the brothels are also restricted in what they can mention to women in prostitution. For example, HIV educators in Bombay report that they were only given permission to enter the prostitution areas when they agreed to the traffickers' directives mandating that they could promote condom usage only if they would not discuss "social issues," and if they would ignore the rampant child prostitution.[59] Condoms could only be promoted by not challenging the brothel keepers and by not discussing with the women alternatives to prostitution.

A precautionary approach asks different, yet commonsensical, questions in designing a public health response to a high-risk activity such as prostitution: "What are the alternatives to this ... activity that achieve the desired goal?" and "Does society need this activity in the first place?"[60]

Politicizing Health

Some "safer sex" policies and programs for women in prostitution join condom use with holding out hope for an AIDS vaccine.[61] However, relying on a magic molecular bullet to remove the risk of AIDS in prostitution treats disease as an individualized body-based event rather than as "the outcome of multiple conditions arising from changes not only in cell nuclei but also in social, economic, and ecological conditions."[62] An interdisciplinary team of researchers at Harvard University, who are studying the emergence of "old" and "new"' communicable diseases, affirms the view that the causation of epidemics and pandemics "must be understood in the broad sense as residing in much larger wholes than are usually considered by the microbiological or clinical paradigms."[63] Thus, epidemiological models and public health responses to the emergence of new disease epidemics such as AIDS must become socialized, politicized, and gender-based.

A politicized and structurally-based public health response to the risks of prostitution—risks which HIV/AIDS have drawn the world's attention to—would heed the lessons that integrated and social epidemiology have learned from the reemergence of old diseases, such as tuberculosis and hepatitis, and the emergence of new diseases, including AIDS. Diseases evolve and come about within a complex interaction that includes social and economic inequality and ecological changes, as well as pathogens, vectors, and hosts. A fuller public health response would advocate for the health and safety of women within the sex industry, at the same time that it seeks to dismantle the sex industry. When "safe sex" advocates for women in prostitution, as well as reproductive health activists, are as willing to confront the sex industry as they are to challenge the pharmaceutical industry and other multinationals, this will be an enormous step forward.

As early as 1987, one survivor of domestic trafficking and prostitution in the United States noted the limitations and hypocrisy of condom promotion not accompanied by other legal and structural solutions.

> We don't believe for one moment that politicians are concerned that prostitutes will die from AIDS: they're not concerned that we're bought and sold like cattle...they're not even concerned when we're killed off one by one, or en masse by serial murderers. Why would we believe that they'd be frantically concerned about us dying off from a virus? We think perhaps they're frantically concerned about their own well-being and maintaining their ability to traffic in women without any health risks to themselves.[64]

Her conclusion: women who have been trafficked and prostituted don't mainly need condoms but "civil remedies to fight the traffickers." Disease prevention strategies, such as condom promotion for women in prostitution, will only be effective in protecting women if they embrace recognition and active promotion of women's human rights—most importantly, the right not to be trafficked into the sex industry.

Public Policy Recommendations

There has been a recent trend to separate international sex trafficking from domestic sex trafficking and prostitution. This directly contradicts the United Nations Convention for the Suppression of the Traffic in Persons and of the Exploitation of the Prostitution of Others, which recognized the inconsistency of isolating the international problem of sex trafficking from the various forms of commercialized sex within nation-states. The international experts came to the conclusion that the principal factor fostering international traffic in women from the East, for example, was the existence of both illegal and licensed houses of prostitution already operating on a national level in the East.[65]

Our final policy recommendations are based on the necessity to rejoin trafficking with prostitution. There is an urgent need for courage and for the political will to act against this global exploitation of women and children. The challenge for governments today is to recognize that prostitution is a massive and growing industry, while not ratifying prostitution as a job. The challenge for governments today is to provide rights and protections for women in conditions of sex trafficking and prostitution, while acknowledging that sex trafficking and prostitution violate women's rights and bodily integrity. The challenge for governments today is to punish the growing numbers of sexual exploiters—traffickers, pimps, procurers, and buyers—while not penalizing the women who find themselves in conditions of sex trafficking and prostitution.

Although it is not within the scope of this article to explain at length the debate over legalization of prostitution, legalization vs. decriminalization, and recognizing and redefining prostitution as "sex work," and sex trafficking as "migration for sex work," it is necessary to understand some of this background with reference to the policy dimensions. Legalization means that the state, whether through regulating health, size of brothels, and/or working conditions for those in the sex industry, recognizes prostitution as work and provides a legal framework within which the sex industry may operate. At the same time, the state taxes brothels and other sex-related enterprises and thus, as some would say, becomes the pimp and lives off the earnings of women in prostitution.

Decriminalization, on the other hand, means that those in the sex industry are not arrested, charged, or prosecuted for prostitution-related offenses because they are not criminally liable. Many groups, such as COYOTE in the United States and the Global Alliance Against Trafficking in Women internationally (GAATW) want the entire industry decriminalized. They argue that prostitute users ("customers" or johns) should be decriminalized and that women have the right to contract with third parties, now known as pimps, redefining them as "third party business agents" for women in the sex industry. Other NGOs, such as the Coalition Against Trafficking in Women and the International Human Rights Network, want the women decriminalized, and prostitute users and pimps subject to prosecution. For many years, the sex industry has lobbied for legal and economic recognition of prostitution and related forms of sexual entertainment as "sex work." Now, some women's groups and other NGOs are doing the same kind of advocacy under the banner of women's human rights.

It is our contention that state recognition of prostitution as work, or state regulation of the sex industry as an economic sector, institutionalizes the buying and selling of women as commodities in the marketplace. Legalization and state regulation of prostitution further removes women from the economic mainstream by segregating prostituted women as a class set apart for sexual service and servitude. Legalization and decriminalization of the entire industry reinforces the definition of woman as sexual object, and as a provider of sexual services, thereby eroticizing and perpetuating gender inequality. Furthermore, legalization and decriminalization of the buyers and pimps legitimizes and strengthens men's ability to put the bodies of women at their disposal.

Rather than accept the unexamined premise that some women need prostitution to survive economically, we question why prostitution is the only place where mostly women can turn when all else fails. It is a gendered reality that prostitution may be the best of the worst economic options that many women face. However, the fact that there are often no better income opportunities for women should not function as a new economic law turning many women's desperate economic plights against them by institutionalizing their exploiters as entrepreneurs. In our framework, this is to surrender the political battle for women's right to sustainable work, and to tolerate women's bodies being increasingly bought for sex and used as merchandise in the marketplace.

Some will say that women's choices should be respected and that if women consent to entering and remaining in the sex industry, that is their right. We think that this argument confuses compliance with consent. Nor do we doubt that a number of women "choose" to enter prostitution. However, we do not think that choice should be the issue or the governing standard. We can "choose" to be exploited and we can "choose" to enter into conditions that may harm us.

The political questions are: "Should governments confer legal legitimacy on the sex industry, and foster legal conditions that legitimate exploitation of and harm to women in the name of fostering choice? Whose choice is really promoted in this argument?" Distinctions between "forced" and "consensual" prostitution promote the view of prostitution as the individual act of an individual woman and conceal the role of an enormous global industry that propels women and children into prostitution. The sex industry makes no distinctions between "forced" and "free" prostitution, while encouraging others to do so.

We, therefore, encourage governments to use the following elements in implementing policy, and in drafting national, regional, and international legislation addressing sex trafficking and prostitution: that governments protect and promote women's rights, while they are still in conditions of sex trafficking and prostitution, and at the same time aggressively eliminate the causes; reject any policy or law that legitimizes sex trafficking or prostitution or that legalizes or regulates prostitution in any way, including as a profession, occupation, entertainment, or an economic sector; decriminalize the women in conditions of sex trafficking and prostitution, at the same time as they penalize the traffickers, pimps, procurers, and promoters of prostitution, as well as those who buy women for sexual acts (johns or customers); adopt legislative and other measures to prohibit sex tourism and to penalize those who organize and advertise tourism for the purpose of sexual exploitation as practices of the procuring and promoting of prostitution; use appropriate publicity to warn of prosecution for sex tourists; prohibit persons or enterprises from promoting, profiting from, or engaging in any business involving the matching of women in marriage to foreign nationals, as in mail-order bride sales and pseudo-marriages.

Women in conditions of sex trafficking and prostitution have the right to sexual integrity and sexual autonomy, and should therefore be able to sue for sexual harassment, assault, and rape. Consent of the woman procured for sex trafficking and prostitution should not be recognized as a defense for pimps, procurers, and buyers, nor as a rationale for state-sanctioned institutionalization of prostitution as work. Sociocultural practices of temporary marriage honor or written contracts should not be used to justify or defend against any act of sexual exploitation.

Women should receive fair, sustainable, and, if necessary, legally mandated compensation as waitresses, receptionists, dancers, singers, bar workers, entertainers, artists, "GROs" (guest relations officers)—but not as "sex workers"—so that the economic pressure to engage in the prostitution often cloaked by these terms is reduced. Women should be able to keep and control any money they receive, and no third party should profit from the earnings of women in conditions of sex trafficking and prostitution.

Most importantly, governments and non-governmental organizations must put resources at women's disposal such as credit, micro-lending programs, enterprise training, and other needed services; and provide medical care, shelter, voluntary counseling, and educational programs for women who have been harmed by sex trafficking and prostitution. A woman's prior sexual history, or status as an illegal immigrant or stateless person should not be used against her. Trafficked women should be provided with refuge, visas, refugee status, protection from traffickers, and voluntary repatriation whether, as victims of sex trafficking, they have entered a country legally or illegally. Under no circumstances should governments construe these above recommendations in a manner to prevent women from migrating or traveling abroad.[66]

Governments and non-governmental organizations can acknowledge that there are women and girls attempting to survive in conditions of sex trafficking and prostitution without normalizing prostitution as work. Governments and non-governmental organizations can acknowledge that women have the right to do what they can to mitigate these conditions until they can live in a society which no longer supports or tolerates the mass male consumption of women and children who have been trafficked and prostituted.

Governments and non-governmental organizations have tended to emphasize short-term solutions for women in sex industries that encourage women to stay in the industry, such as negotiating for safe sex, condoms, and HIV/AIDS testing. However, it is important to advocate for such measures within a context of other proposals, which provide women with alternatives to sex trafficking and prostitution. We believe that women have the right to humanitarian assistance to help them out of prostitution rather than humanitarian assistance to keep them in it.

1   The Scottish economist Adam Smith promulgated the "invisible hand" in society as the underlying principle that when each individual acts in their own self-interest, the society will achieve an optimum level of economic welfare. This principle, which fortifies market capitalism, has been widely critiqued by feminist and environmental economists. Marilyn J. Waring, *If Women Counted* (San Francisco, CA: HarperCollins, 1988); Herman E. Daly and John B. Cobb, *For the Common Good* (Boston, MA: Beacon Press, 1989).

2   Amy O'Neill Richard, "International Trafficking in Women to the United States: A Contemporary Manifestation of Slavery and Organized Crime," (Washington, DC: Central Intelligence Agency, 1999).

3   The Protocol to Prevent, Suppress and Punish Trafficking in Persons, Especially Women and Children is a wide-ranging international agreement to address the crime of trafficking in persons, especially women and children, on a transnational level. It creates a global language and legislation to define trafficking in persons, especially women and children; assist victims of trafficking; and prevent trafficking in persons. The trafficking in persons protocol also establishes the parameters of judicial cooperation and exchanges of information among countries. Although the Protocol to Prevent, Suppress and Punish Trafficking in Persons, Especially Women and Children anticipates accomplishing what national legislation cannot do on its own, it is also intended to jumpstart national laws and to harmonize regional legislation against the trafficking in women and children.

4   The Bangladeshi-Pakistan and Nepal-India estimates come from the "Fact-Finding National Workshop on Trafficking in Women and Children" (Dhaka, Bangladesh: Centre for Women and Children Studies, May 23-25, 1997), 33. However, a report from the Lawyers for Human Rights and Legal Aid (LHRLA), "Trafficking of Women and Children in Pakistan: the Flesh Trade Report 1995–96," puts the figure higher at 100–150 Bangladeshi women per day trafficked into Pakistan. The Philippines to Japan numbers come from Irene F. Daguno, "Migration and Trafficking of Filipino Women for Prostitution," in *Halfway Through the Circle: the Lives of Eight Filipino Women Survivors of Prostitution and Trafficking* (Manila: Women's Education, Development, Productivity and Research Organization, 1998).

5   Richard, "International Trafficking in Women to the United States."

6   Janice G. Raymond, Donna M. Hughes, and Carol A. Gomez, "Sex Trafficking of Women in the United States: International and Domestic Trends," funded by the US National Institute of Justice (2001). Available online at www.catwinternational.org.

7   Richard, "International Trafficking in Women to the United States."

8   Coalition Against Trafficking in Women, "Women in the International Migration Process: Patterns, Profiles and Health Consequences of Sexual Exploitation," funded by the Ford Foundation (2002).

9   Philip Martin and Jonas Widgren, "International Migration: A Global Challenge," *Population Bulletin*, Vol. 51, No. 1 (April 1996), 1–48.

10   Ibid.

11 Irene L. Gendzier, "Labour Exodus: Market Forces and Mass Migration," *Global Dialogue* (Summer 1999), 89-101.

12 Women's Education, Development, Productivity and Research Organization (WEDPRO), *Halfway Through the Circle.*

13 Ibid.

14 Philippines National Statistical Office, Survey of Overseas Workers (1994).

15 Gendzier, "Labour Exodus." *Global Dialogue,* 89–101.

16 Martin and Widgren, "International Migration," *Population,* 1–48.

17 Human Rights Watch, *A Modern Form of Slavery: Trafficking of Burmese Women and Girls into Brothels in Thailand* (New York: Human Rights Watch, 1993), 46–52.

18 Saskia Sassen, *Globalization and Its Discontents* (New York: The New Press, 1998).

19 Ibid., 55.

20 Ibid., Note 12, xxxvi.

21 Ibid.

22 Ibid., xxxi.

23 Ibid, xxx.

24 More than 40,000 sex-related sites exist on the Internet, and it's commonly known that pornography sites have the highest user demand, bring in the most revenues, and literally, *drive the Internet.* "Adult materials account for 69 percent of the $1.4 billion pay-to-view online-content market, far outpacing video games (4 percent) and sports (less than 2 percent)." Brendan Koerner, "A Lust for Profits," *US News and World Report* (March 27, 2000), 36–42. Indeed, one analyst concludes that the growth of the Internet has been spurred by the immense sex consumption taking place on the Internet, especially at pornography, sex tourism, and mail-order bride Web sites. Donna Hughes, *Pimps and Predators on the Internet: Globalizing the Sexual Exploitation of Women and Children* (North Amherst, MA: Coalition Against Trafficking in Women, 1999).

25 S. Tunsarawuth, " 'Thailand's $44 Billion Underworld Prostitution Heads List of Lucrative Businesses,' Says Study," *Straits Times*, December 3, 1996.

26 Richard, "International Trafficking in Women to the United States."

27 Michael Ellison, "Atlanta Police Smash Sex Slave Ring," *Guardian,* August 21, 1999.

28 R. Robin McDonald, "Human Contraband: Asian Women Expected Jobs, Not Prostitution," *The Atlanta Constitution,* August 31, 1999.

29 Richard, "International Trafficking in Women to the United States."

30 Ibid., 17.

31 Ibid., 19–20.

32 Ellison, "Atlanta Police Smash Sex Slave Ring," *Guardian.*

33 United Nations Population Fund, *Violence Against Girls and Women: A Public Health Priority* (New York: 1998).

34 Lori Heise with Jacqueline Pitanguy and Adrienne Germain, "Violence Against Women: The Hidden Health Burden," World Bank Discussion, Paper 255 (Washington, DC: The World Bank, 1994).

35 Ibid., 17.

228   Policing the National Body

36 Ibid., 19–20.

37 Wendy Taylor and Jacquelyn Campbell, "Treatment Protocols for Battered Women," *Response*, Vol. 14, No. 4 (1991), 16.

38 Ibid. This body of research and the professional activism of feminist health care providers has resulted in more recent written policy and protocols for medical providers in clinic, office, and emergency room settings to assess injured women for battering, to document the physical findings, to inform the woman of her rights, and to give her referral information for counseling and shelters.

39 Raymond, Hughes, and Gomez, "Sex Trafficking of Women in the United States."

40 Sachi Sri Kanta, *Prostitutes in Medical Literature* (Westport, CT: Greenwood Press, 1991).

41 Ibid., 173–176.

42 Taylor and Campbell, "Treatment Protocols for Battered Women," *Response*, 16–21.

43 Ruth Parriott, *Health Experiences of Twin Cities Women Used in Prostitution: Survey Findings and Recommendations* (1994), Available from Breaking Free, 1821 University Ave., Suite 312, South, St. Paul, Minnesota 55104.

44 Council for Prostitution Alternatives, 519 Southwest Park Avenue, Suite 208, Portland, Oregon 97205.

45 Parriott, *Health Experiences of Twin Cities Women Used in Prostitution*, 21. These studies are cross-sectional interviews based on self-reporting and recall in a select groups of women survivors. They are not case control studies like those cited in the significant body of medical literature on prostitution and sexually transmitted diseases amassed by Kanta. Historically, health professionals have designed case control studies which single-mindedly envisaged prostituted women as vectors of sexually transmitted disease. The health intervention designed from the findings of those studies prescribed a regimen of antibiotics for prostituted women. Other harm and trauma were ignored, and prostitution was "protected" for the buyers.

46 Martin Foreman, "A Global Epidemic Driven by Men Puts Women at Risk," *The Gazette* (Montreal), November 28, 1998, B1.

47 Gena Corea, *The Invisible Epidemic* (New York: HarperCollins, 1992).

48 Kanta, *Prostitutes in Medical Literature*.

49 Jodi Jacobson, "Women's Reproductive Health: The Silent Emergency," *WorldWatch*, Paper 102 (Washington, DC: Worldwatch Institute, June 1991).

50 Mary Caron, "The Politics of Life and Death," *WorldWatch* (May/June 1999), 30–38.

51 Ibid.; *Southeast Asian Population in Crisis* (New York: UNFPA, 1998); Murray Feshbach, "Dead Souls," *The Atlantic Monthly* (January 1999), 26–27.

52 Caron, "The Politics of Life and Death," *Worldwatch*, 34.

53 Coalition Against Trafficking in Women, *Women in the International Migration Process: Patterns, Profiles and Health Consequences of Sexual Exploitation*, funded by the Ford Foundation (2002).

54 One interview was discounted for this question because of a contradictory response.

55 Sharon Edwards, "Condom Breakage in Brothels," *International Family Planning Perspectives*, Vol. 20, No. 1 (March 1994), 2.

56 Mary O'Brien, *Making Better Environmental Decisions: An Alternative to Risk Assessment* (Cambridge, MA: MIT Press, 2000).

57 Ibid.

58 Ibid.

59 Robert I. Friedman, "India's Shame: Sexual Slavery and Political Corruption are Leading to an AIDS Catastrophe," *The Nation* (April 8, 1996), 4.

60 Environment and Research Foundation, "The Precautionary Principle," *Rachel's Environment and Health Weekly*, No. 586 (February 20, 1998), 3. Questions attributed to Joel Tickner.

61 Caron, "The Politics of Life and Death," *Worldwatch*; Geoffrey Cowley, "Fighting the Disease: What Can be Done," *Newsweek* (January 17, 2000), 38.

62 Richard Levins, et al., "The Emergence of New Diseases," *American Scientist*, Vol. 82 (January-February 1994), 52–60.

63 Richard Levins, "Toward an Integrated Epidemiology," *Trends in Ecology and Evolution*, Vol. 10, No. 7 (July 1995), 304.

64 Sarah Wynter, "Prostitutes, Politicians & Prophylactics," *WHISPER Newsletter*, II, 3, (Summer 1987), 2.

65 *Report of the Special Body of Experts on Traffic in Women and Children*, League of Nations Document (1927) and *Report to the Council of the Commission of Inquiry into Traffic in Women and Children in the East*, League of Nations Document (1932).

66 Janice G. Raymond, "Trafficking for Prostitution," in Eve Landau, ed., *Women in the 21st Century*, (Paris: UNESCO, 2002).

Chapter 9

Superpredator Meets Teenage Mom

Exploding the Myth of the Out-of-Control Youth

Anne Hendrixson

There are an unprecedented number of young people in the world today—the largest generation of youth in history. Of the 6 billion (and counting) world population, over half are under the age of 25, the majority of whom live in less developed countries.[1] Youth are a hot topic: demographers analyze them, the United States military monitors them, and population and reproductive rights agencies rally around them. But the preoccupation with youth doesn't stop there. The justice system seeks to control them, while journalists stereotype them, and non-governmental organizations (NGOs) and government agencies attempt to modify their sexual behavior.

The focus on youth is not solely in response to population size. Adolescents in the United States are subject to speculation and discussion as readily as their counterparts in the global South, although the American youth population is smaller than the aging Baby Boomers. It is the prominent role that young people play in determining the future that commands attention, rather than their size. While there is no question that this generation of youth will strongly affect the world's future, the question of how youth will shape the future remains.

The impact of young adults is seen as a particular concern in two areas: security and reproduction. Policy-makers and analysts depict youth as violence prone and predisposed to irresponsible motherhood, and this view has caught the attention and imagination of the popular press. Take for example, the depiction in the *Business Week* article, "Teens: Here Comes the Biggest Wave Yet":

> For all their appeal as consumers ... this generation of teens has some wrenching problems. In the past 30 years, the birthrate among unmarried women 15 to 19 years old has almost tripled, to 45 births per 1,000. Crime statistics are equally disturbing: 104,137 juveniles were arrested in 1992 for violent crimes, up 57.1% from 1982.[2]

Stereotypes and generalizations dominate the portrayal of youth violence and reproductive behavior in the United States and in other parts of the world. Two distinct stereotypes emerge: ruthless, criminal young men and potential young mothers in whose hands population growth lies. Consequently, youth are framed as a generation in need of control. (It is ironic that even as youth are heralded as a new generation, and harbingers of change, they are subject to classic gender roles—young men as warriors, young women as mothers.)

In this essay, I look at the depiction of young men as potential criminals and revolutionaries in security discourses, and the portrayal of young women as mothers in reproductive health discourse both in the United States and in the developing world. In both discussions, I examine the situation in the South and then compare it to that in the United States. While the prevailing literature treats the youth discourses around the world as separate, this article argues that there are many similarities and draws parallels between youth depictions worldwide.

Overview of The Youth Population

The youth population is not spread evenly throughout the world. Consistent with overall world population distribution, the majority of the under-25 population live in less developed countries. Youth in the South outnumber older generations. In 1998, children under the age of 15 accounted for up to one-third of the population in the South, with even greater proportions in some regions.[3] This demographic distribution creates a pyramid effect when graphed—85 years of age and older are the apex of the pyramid at under 5 million, 15 years of age and younger make up the wide base at over 500 million.[4]

The reason for the large and growing youth population in the South is classic demographic transition. The South is undergoing the process that occurs when the trend of high birth and death rates (minimal population growth) is interrupted by a long-term decline in mortality rates primarily associated with improved health care and sanitation. Continued high birth rates, coupled with low mortality rates, result in rapid population growth. After a time, birth rates also begin a long-term decline until they reach the same level as mortality rates. When birth and death rates reach similarly low levels, population growth stabilizes. The process of demographic transition is not the same for every country and region. Economics, politics, and history of colonialism, among other factors, lead to unique trajectories for different countries.

Like the current "bulge" of youth in the Southern population, the United States also experienced a bulge in youth populations during the process of demographic transition—the Baby Boom of 1946 to 1964. Europe and North America, as well as a number of other areas, began the process of demographic transition in the nineteenth and early twentieth centuries and many Northern countries are now approaching levels of fertility where parents are having the number of children to replace themselves in the population. This is known as "replacement fertility." In the United States, birth rates dropped following the Baby Boom, but have not yet reached replacement fertility levels; thus, the young population is slowly increasing. Still, the Baby Boomers continue to be the largest population. In contrast to the pyramid-shaped population graph of the South's population, the graph of population age distribution in the North illustrates that there are a proportionally smaller number of youth, with the population bulge appearing in the age range of 35 to 55.

Due to concern about rapid population growth in developing countries, and consequently, the growing population of young people, a distinct set of youth-related problems are usually attributed to the South. However, even though the growth of the United States youth population is slowing and is smaller than the Baby Boomers, similar concerns about young people in the United States abound, also based on fears about population size. For example, the United States military views globally Southern young men as a generation of disaffected, potential revolutionaries, while United States criminology views American young men as potential "superpredators."

The "Youth Bulge" in the South

The United States military and academics consider the large youth population in the South a "youth bulge." Geographer Gary Fuller defines the term "youth bulge" as "an anomaly in a country's population age structure that occurs when the country has a disproportionately large number of young adults." Fuller holds that "when the fourth and fifth age cohorts (that is, those aged 15–19 and 20–24) represent 20 percent or more of a country's population, political unrest almost certainly occurs.[5] Fuller created his "youth bulge hypothesis" in 1985 as a tool for predicting unrest and uncovering potential national security threats. He believes that "the youth bulge hypothesis is a useful tool to assist busy intelligence analysts in organizing and prioritizing their work."[6] Thus the "youth bulge" hypothesis seeks to correlate youth populations with the threat of violence.

Analysts embrace the youth bulge hypothesis and position the youth bulge as a national security threat. Personified as a discontented, rebellious teenage boy, almost always a person of color, the youth bulge is portrayed as an unpredictable, out-of-control force in the South with the potential to catalyze uncontainable conflicts that would spill over into neighboring countries and even other areas of the world, including the United States. For academics, the youth bulge hypothesis functions as an indicator of social unrest and a subject demanding further study.[7] But whether it is used as a tool to predict unrest or a subject of academic inquiry, the concept of a youth bulge generates population alarmism and racist imagery. Population alarmism is an oversimplified concept, reliant on the false premise that population is the cause of development problems, resource scarcity, and political instability, and the idea that youth are particularly prone to violence. It is also a popularly accepted concept, one that has greatly impacted past and current defense policy.

Historically, the United States has viewed youth in the South as a threat to national security. After World War II, when overall perceptions about population were beginning to shift in this country, the United States military defined the growing number of youth in the South as a problem.[8] Some analysts suggest that this fear of youth in the South coincided with growing United States interest in Southern raw materials to supply industry. For the United States, access to raw materials depended on good relationships with Southern governments. However, at the time anti-colonial nationalism was on the rise, and American national interests were threatened by this trend. Betsy Hartmann, author of *Reproductive Rights and Wrongs*, notes:

> The success of the Chinese Revolution, Indian and Indonesian nonalignment, independence movements in Africa, economic nationalism in Latin America—all these contributed to growing US fears of the Third World. Population growth, rather than centuries of colonial domination, was believed to fuel nationalist fires, especially given the increasing proportion of youth.[9]

Though political trends have shifted since that time, the United States has continued to characterize youth as a threat and has created "appropriate" defense policy in response. In the absence of a single competitor or enemy in the post–Cold War era, the military has redirected its defense efforts toward new threats including the youth bulge. Lieutenant General Patrick M. Hughes, director of the Defense Intelligence Agency, contends that "in much of the world, there still exists a potentially explosive mix of social, demographic, economic and political conditions which run counter to the global trend toward democracy and economic reform."[10] He further argues:

Global population will increase some 20 percent between now and 2010, with 95 percent of that growth occurring in the developing areas that can least afford it. Many of these states will experience the "youth bulge phenomenon" (a relatively high percentage of the population between 18 and 25 years of age), which historically has been a key factor in instability.[11]

On March 15, 2000, in his testimony before the House Armed Services Committee, General Anthony C. Zinni, commander in chief of the United States Central Command, commented:

Population growth is also increasing, dramatically putting pressure on natural resources, specifically water, and economic systems. This has resulted in instability, especially in countries experiencing this "youth bulge." Certain areas of this dynamic volatile Central Region offer a fertile environment for extremists to recruit, train, and conduct terrorist operations. These extremists pose a significant and growing threat to US personnel around the world and to their own people and governments.[12]

The scapegoating of population as the cause of political insecurity is mimicked in the popular press. An article in *US News and World Report* reads, "Who's the Enemy? The answer, it turns out, is not Russia or China or Iraq. It's demographics." The article declares the enemy "will be young, and restless: A 'youth bulge.' "[13]

The position that the youth bulge represents a security threat is based on the idea that population pressures cause resource scarcity. Resource depletion in the South will supposedly force youth to compete for employment, land, and educational opportunities, and when their needs are not met, youth will then supposedly react with violence against the nations that have failed them. J. Brian Atwood, the former administrator for the US Agency for International Development (USAID), remarked, "the human social and economic costs of failed nation states are immense and many of these conflicts have been propelled, in part, by populations of disaffected youth."[14] Thus, youth are characterized as having the potential to send a nation into a state of chaos.

Given that the United States military and academics define the youth bulge an explosive force that holds great power over nation-states, the military feels it must be equipped to handle sudden unrest. The urgency of the youth bulge serves as a rationale for defense buildup and strategy. As Lieutenant General Martin R. Steele, deputy chief of staff for plans, policies, and operations of the US Marine Corps, comments, "The end of the Cold War also means that defense is no longer a subject that excites the American people. We in the military are victims of our own success."[15] In order to justify continued military spending, the creation of new enemies has therefore become critical. Sustaining the myth of a dangerous youth bulge thus bolsters the importance of the military.

The myth of this restless, potentially violent youth population also helps further United States military presence in resource rich parts of the world, particularly those areas endowed with oil. As General Anthony Zinni put it, "primary among US interests ... [are] the promotion of regional stability and the insurance of uninterrupted secure access to Arabian Gulf energy resources."[16] As previously noted, Zinni considers the "Central Region," including the Arabian Gulf, as a potential hotbed of youth bulge terrorist unrest.

Analysts link predicted youth unrest in the Central Region with the spread of Islam. In *Clash of the Civilizations and the Remaking of World Order*, Samuel Huntington argues that "Population growth in Muslim countries, and particularly the expansion of the fifteen-to twenty-four-year-old cohort provides recruits for fundamentalism, terrorism, insurgency, and migration."[17] He further contends, "The Islamic challenge is manifest in the pervasive cultural, social, and political resurgence of Islam and the accompanying rejection of Western values and institutions."[18] For Huntington, challenges to "Western values and institutions" are synonymous with American loss of control over the most valuable natural resource in the world. Huntington continues to study "youth unrest" as part of the Olin Institute Studies.

The potential threat of migration of Southern youth to the United States is another component of the youth bulge theory. It is assumed that due to resources and job scarcity, youth from the developing world will infiltrate the United States. In "World Population Growth and US National Security," Alex de Sherbinin posits,

> Just as the young age structure and unemployment problems in
> many developing countries create a large pool of potential mi-

grants to the United States, analysts argue that it also increases the likelihood of social or political unrest. One estimate shows that by 2025, the number of job seekers in Africa will triple to 14.7 million, resulting in personal tragedy and "a social and political time bomb ready to explode."[19]

Many Americans fear the United States will be overrun by immigrants who will steal "our" jobs and land and "overpopulate" the country. They are also anxiety-ridden about the potential transformation of the American racial landscape from majority white to brown. Nobel Laureate and economist Amartya Sen calls this anxiety the "Fear of Being Engulfed."

> That fear translates into worries of various kinds in the North, especially the sense of being overrun by the South. ... It is easy to understand the fears of relatively well-off people at the thought of being surrounded by a fast growing and increasingly impoverished Southern population. As I shall argue, the thesis of growing impoverishment does not stand up to much scrutiny; but it is important to address first the psychologically tense issue of racial balance in the world (even though racial composition as a consideration has only as much importance as we choose to give it.[20]

The angst surrounding the youth bulge thus has underlying assumptions about race. I would argue that one of the main reasons that the youth bulge is thought to be highly volatile, in addition to population alarmism about resource scarcity, is because the youth bulge consists largely of people of color. That fact alone is enough to make the youth bulge a threat to many. Although not overtly discussed, racism infects the stereotypes of young men in youth bulge discourse. Euphemisms like "poor countries" and the "South" usually substitute for direct references to race and ethnicity:

> The poorest and fastest growing countries are characterized by a bottom-heavy population profile: they are nations of young people, the ones that yield the sad images of barefoot children with automatic rifles. Their political instability may be in part a result of their demographic structure; and in their relations with other states they seem likely to confirm the prophecy that "teen-age populations are unlikely to be easy to negotiate with."[21]

These militant young men are stereotyped as violent, bending the rules of "civilized society." In an article entitled "The Coming Anarchy," journalist Robert Kaplan popularized the racist depiction of Southern youth, even among liberal policy-makers. He forecast that the growth in youth population would lead to a state of political chaos. Kaplan characterized the young men he encountered in West Africa as "hordes" and cautioned that they were "like loose molecules in a very unstable social fluid, a fluid that was clearly on the verge of igniting."[22]

Hardly anywhere in the literature is the youth bulge depicted positively. Youth bulge activity is most often treated as the supposed breeding ground for violence. For instance, Gary Fuller has identified student movements as evidence of instability and crisis and a prime example of "classic youth bulge activity."[23] He argues that if student uprisings last over time, youth bulge activity—such as student demonstrations—can become "institutionalized."[24]

While Fuller acknowledges that students usually respond to real problems, he ignores young people's legitimate right to influence policy and voice their opinions. He writes, "The youth bulge throughout the Third World is a generation in transition between a village society and a true national society. Its presence is literally explosive, as collectively it demands a greater say in national policies."[25] The term "explosive" suggests that Fuller views youth as revolutionaries who are bypassing proper channels for government participation, and disrupting legitimate business.

In "Youth Bulges in Asia," Fuller remarks that South Korean student organizing "was not a case of sowing discontent; discontent was already rife. Rather, it was a case of channeling anger in the direction that student activists wanted."[26] Fuller does not remark on whether the students' response effected constructive changes. This failure to acknowledge youth as a legitimate force in society obscures their historical role in facilitating important social change. It ignores the important political changes that student and youth movements have contributed around the world. For instance, student uprisings in Indonesia forced President Suharto's resignation in 1998. In one journalist's words, "Indonesian students have traditionally been center stage during periods of cataclysmic change ...

students have been seen as protectors of the people, avenging angels, avatars of change."[27]

Stereotypical references to youth as a generation of unpredictable, potentially dangerous young men, is robbing them of their dignity and potential. Without recognition that this generation can, and will, contribute to the advances of society and development, discussions on this generation strip it of self-respect, underestimate its potential, and leave it devalued. The alarmist youth bulge rhetoric is clearly in the interest of those who advance it and not in the interest of supporting the next generation of youth. Unfortunately, this is also the case in the United States. In US internal security discussions, youth are framed in much the same way as youth in the South.

Superpredators: The Criminalization of Youth in the United States

As in the developing world, youth in the United States are also considered dangerous. Although American youth are not perceived as political rebels like those in the South, they too are feared for safety and security issues. Young men in the United States are believed to prey on communities as criminals. The discourse on youth usually exempts young Americans from the youth bulge theory, primarily because the youth population in the United States is proportionately smaller than that in the South. As Fuller remarks, "long-lasting and high-percentage youth bulges characterize Third World countries. Western countries have brief, modest youth bulges if they have them at all."[28] I will argue that despite the demographic distinctions between the groups of youth, the language and concepts used to describe the threat of United States youth are similar to that used to define youth bulges—ruthless and violent young men.

In his article "The Coming of the Super-Predators," Princeton Professor John J. DiIulio, Jr. draws from the images of demographic alarmism. He claims, "all of the research indicates that Americans are sitting atop a demographic crime bomb. And all of those who are closest to the problem hear the bomb ticking."[29] And he declares:

[T]he youth crime wave has reached horrific proportions from coast to coast.... But what is really frightening everyone from DAs to demographers, old cops to old convicts, is not what's happening now but what's just around the corner—namely, a sharp increase in the number of super crime-prone young males.[30]

In DiIulio's view, not only is the number of young, mostly male, criminals on the rise, but the type of crimes they commit is becoming more serious. Why are young men becoming more and more "super prone" to crime? DiIulio's answer: "more boys begets more bad boys."[31] That is, an increase in the number of young men automatically creates a proportional increase in the numbers of young criminal men. DiIulio refers to those super crime-prone young males with the hyperbolic label "superpredators."[32]

The exaggerated term "superpredator" applied to American youth is similar to descriptives like the word "explosive" often used to refer to youth in the South. These labels have given rise to the idea, often with instigation from conservatives, that today's youth are far more dangerous than youth in prior generations.[33]

In reality, the number of juvenile arrests in the United States has declined. In "Dispelling the Myth: An Analysis of Youth and Adult Crime Patterns in California over the Past 20 Years," authors Mike Males and Dan Macallair find that youth today are no more crime prone than the generations before them.[34] Moreover, "the declining violent crime rates during the middle and late 1990s occurred while the teenage population was rising by more than half a million."[35] This fact has led supporters of the "superpredator" theory to admit that the threats predicted did not materialize. James Q. Wilson, formerly a proponent of the "superpredator" theory, admits, "So far, it clearly hasn't happened.... That is a good indication of what little all of us know about criminology."[36]

Although the crime statistics do not support the "superpredator" theory, the "cohort hypothesis," which understands population size as an indicator of crime, is a commonly accepted theory among criminologists. Darrell Steffensmeier, Cathy Striefel, and Miles D. Harer, explain the arguments behind the cohort hypothesis in "Relative Cohort Size and Youth Crime in the United States, 1953–1984":

> In large cohorts, too many young people compete for jobs and education, and they feel the world is a less hospitable place then they were led to believe as children.... Especially in a society already undergoing rapid social changes, the growth of large juvenile cohorts complicates adult society's attempt to reorient the self interests of youth to the adult community interests (i.e., to civilize those barbarians) and encourages the development of youth subcultures and generational conflict.[37]

The cohort hypothesis attributes the same motivation to youth crime as is given for youth bulge unrest—resource scarcity. Steffensmeier and Harer conclude that the cohort hypothesis is too simple a diagnostic, and a more complex analysis that accounts for variables such as income and community responses to youth crime, in addition to cohort size, is needed to fully comprehend youth crime.[38]

The notion of the "superpredator" has changed the way the United States deals with youth. One consequence has been the rise in the number of young adults channeled into the criminal justice system, despite the decrease in youth crime. A study of juvenile crime conducted by the Human Rights Watch notes:

> With frequent references to "juvenile predators," "hardened criminals," and "young thugs," US lawmakers at both the state and federal levels have increasingly abandoned efforts to rehabilitate child offenders through the juvenile court system. Instead, many states have responded to a perceived outbreak in juvenile violent crime by moving more children into the adult criminal system. Between 1992 and 1998, at least forty US states adopted legislation making it easier for children to be tried as adults.[39]

The Violent Youth Predator Act of 1996, for instance, mandates prosecution of children as young as 13 years old as adults. The Juvenile Crime Initiative of California's Proposition 21[40] requires "children as young as 14 to be tried in adult courts when accused of murder and other serious crimes. It also transfers authority from the court system to prosecutors, enacts stricter probation rules ... and overhauls the juvenile court system."[41] Proposition 21 is facing fierce opposition from activists. The ACLU of Northern California, the League of Women Voters of California, the Children's Advocacy Institute, and Coleman Advocates for Children and Youth are bringing a lawsuit challenging the constitutionality of the law. Young people are also responding to what they see as a "War on Youth." *ColorLines* Magazine explains:

> By putting Prop 21 on the ballot, Pete Wilson and his conservative colleagues sowed the seeds of a movement. Youth organizations and other movement-building institutions across California successfully used the initiative to build the momentum against the War on Youth.[42]

The Violent and Repeat Juvenile Offenders Accountability and Rehabilitation Act of 1999 is another example of punitive juvenile law. The ACLU has opposed this bill, because, among other things, "it urges the states to prosecute children as young as 10 years-old as adults ... and it would remove the requirement that states receiving federal funds address disproportionate rates of minority confinement in detention facilities."[43] Furthermore, the ACLU expects the act to "disproportionately increase the number of minority children in both the state and federal systems."[44]

Minority children are already overrepresented in the criminal justice system. M.A. Bortner of Arizona State University remarks,

> Young people are being locked up to reassure a fearful public that the cause of social unrest has been identified and that politicians and government have taken action to restore order and provide safety.... Incarcerated youth are disproportionately poor, male, and people of color. Although minorities comprise about 32 percent of the youth population, they are the majority, about 68 percent, in prison.[45]

Similarly, Mike Males, author of *Framing Youth: 10 Myths about the Next Generation*, suggests that race is a powerful influence on the understanding of youth crime and the image of young men.

> Fear of racial transition appears [to be] a powerful factor.... In most of America's big cities, white elders govern non-white kids. In California, two-thirds of the elders are Euro-white;

three-fifths of the youths are non-white or Latino. As California
and the cities are, so America is becoming."[46]

Here, Males's argument runs parallel to Amartya Sen's sentiment
about the "Fear of Being Engulfed." Males carries his argument
even further:

> Racial fear is building at a time when racism is impolitic to openly
> express…. Thus, New Democrats led by President Clinton have
> developed racialist code words such as "youth violence" and
> "teen pregnancy," which are modernized versions of 1960s "law
> 'n' order" and pre-'60s "Negro question" ("nigger-baiting," or
> "niggering," in plain stump talk) employed by traditional south-
> ern politicians. The function of modern crypto-racism is more re-
> fined than that of its cruder past: to simultaneously flatter
> majority constituencies, avoid antagonizing key minority groups,
> and avail aging America's fear of the rising population of
> non-white youth. Because racial coding cannot be admitted to-
> day, it is hidden behind a false image of an entire generation out of
> control, from meanstreet to megamall.[47]

Just as the image of the "explosive" youth in the South provides a rationale for United States defense strategy, the stereotype
of the "superpredator" in the United States legitimizes the need for
a more punitive criminal justice system. The "superpredator" provides a rationale for channeling youth—particularly youth of
color—into the prison industrial complex. Although youth criminal behavior has decreased, youth incarceration has escalated. The
promotion and institution of the "superpredator" stereotype reinforces the United States military's stereotype of the youth bulge.

The Critical Generation: Young Women in the South

In much the same way that young men are branded
"superpredators" and "explosive" threats, young women are also
perceived as a potentially dangerous population in need of regulation. However, it is not the potentially violent behavior of young
women but their reproductive potential that has analysts worried.
International family planning and development organizations,
population agencies, and aid organizations all focus on young
women's reproductive capacity in order to curtail the "alarming"

population growth in the developing world.

USAID, for instance, recognizes youth as the "critical generation" largely because their reproductive choices will determine the
future rate of population growth. In its report, "Youth: The Critical
Generation," the agency warns that "the world is facing a daunting
challenge" and that "[m]ore than one billion young men and
women aged 15–24—the largest generation in history—are entering their childbearing years."[48] As with the youth bulge, "the critical generation" refers to youth in the South largely because of the
demographic distribution of youth. More specifically, it refers to
young women. Young men are also included in the discourse, but
as secondary players—the discussion focuses on young women
and their reproductive choices. "Youth" in this context refers to
those entering their childbearing years, up to about 20 years old.
The United Nations Fund for Population Activities (UNFPA)
agrees with USAID. In a recent paper, it justifies the necessity for a
youth focus by citing birth rates.[49] Youth are once again the focus
of attention due to their numbers and their potential to increase the
world's population.

How should the world respond to the challenge posed by the
"critical generation"? Most international family planning and population organizations agree that the best strategy is to provide
young women with birth control. The Alan Guttmacher Institute
echoes this argument:

> Even though the world's population growth rate appears to be
> slowing down, the world's population promises to continue to
> grow significantly over the coming decades as the largest cohort
> in history enters its reproductive years. The greater the degree to
> which women's increasingly prevalent and ever-stronger desire
> for smaller families can be addressed today, especially through
> better access to effective contraceptive services, the more likely
> that world population will stabilize at fewer than 10 billion peo-
> ple by the middle of the next century.[50]

The emphasis on population size, seen here and throughout
the discourse on the critical generation, is problematic. The focus
on numbers, rather than on young women, reinforces demographically driven population messages, even though it does not specifi-

cally promote them. Development organizations do focus on meeting the needs of young women, however, the underlying motivation is to reduce numbers of births.

Organizations advocate for providing the critical generation with forms of support besides birth control, borrowing the language and ideas from the International Conference on Population and Development's "Programme of Action" developed at Cairo.[51] UNFPA's "A Time to Empower Girls to Delay Pregnancy Until Physical and Emotional Maturity," quotes the ICPD "Programme of Action" under the heading "Meet the Needs of Young Women":

> The International Conference on Population and Development endorsed these objectives: "To meet the special needs of adolescents and youth, especially young women, with due regard for their own creative capabilities, for social, family and community support, employment opportunities, participation in the political process, and access to education, health, counseling and high-quality reproductive health services."[52]

Another objective, not mentioned above, is helping young women to achieve equal rights with men.[53] As with birth control, the implementation of these objectives would serve to lower birth rates, while improving young women's lives.

> The combined efforts of better education and better reproductive health services are tremendous. In poorer countries, people will live longer, have fewer but healthier children, and young people will be a smaller but more educated part of the population. The population momentum can be slowed significantly if young people are enabled and encouraged to have children later in life. For individual adolescents, reproductive health care protects both health and future.[54]

While the ICPD objectives aim to improve young women's status and lives, lowering birth rates remains a motive behind the objectives. The feminist ideals of empowering young women are promoted hand in hand with a demographically driven population message. The message is muted, compared with the alarmist messages common before ICPD, however, the message persists: It is necessary to curb young women's birth rates for the welfare of the world. It is sometimes unclear whether ICPD's main priority was to lower birth rates, or to empower women.[55]

Most discussions on young women and population promote the ICPD ideals and show the same mixed message about priorities. In fact, the literature on youth and reproduction varies very little across organizations. It seems that the Cairo consensus has resulted in a common population language and consensus of theory as well. I call this the "lullaby of Cairo." The ICPD objectives for lowering birth rates are almost universally accepted and repeated as the "solution" to population problems. However, while they offer positive steps, they do not provide the final answers to population issues. Repeating the objectives without critical analysis becomes a lulling, soothing response to difficult issues, without resolving them. Within this framework, the potential of young women to increase population momentum is a problem and the ICPD objectives are the solution to that problem. Of course there are dissenting voices. The Catholic Family and Human Rights Institute for instance, disagrees with the ICPD's emphasis on birth control for young, unmarried women. Instead it wants to focus on abstinence.[56] However, ICPD's position is the dominant paradigm.

For instance, the World Population Foundation and the Communications Consortium Media Center, with editorial assistance from United States NGOs in Support of the Cairo Consensus, published the widely circulated paper "Youth and Population Momentum."[57] The paper is posted on a number of nonprofit and NGO websites, including those of Zero Population Growth and the Center for Development and Population Activities (CEDPA). It employs alarmist youth population statistics, then switches to language on the critical necessity to address young peoples' needs. It contends, "The reproductive behavior of these young people will determine the planet's future. If they are enabled to realize their potential, they will be a real 'demographic bonus'—an unprecedented bulge of human resources for future development."[58] Interestingly, the World Population Foundation and the Communications Consortium Media Center collaborated on the equally schizophrenic "Day of 6 Billion" campaign, in consultation with UNFPA. On the one hand, the campaign supports the reform efforts of ICPD, while on the other hand, it promotes alarmist images and messages based on "overpopulation."[59]

Despite its preoccupation with population reduction, ICPD's model has positively affected the discourse around young women's reproduction. In notable contrast to the negative stereotypes of young men and the youth bulge as security threats, young women are often portrayed positively in development discourses, as a generation capable of rational choice and worthy of respect and trust:

> When young people have access to private and confidential services, they are better able to protect themselves against sexually transmitted diseases (STDs), avoid unwanted pregnancy, care for their reproductive health and take advantage of educational and other opportunities that will affect their lifelong well being…. Young people need comprehensive information and access to services. They have a right to privacy, confidentiality and respect.[60]

The discussion centers on girls, emphasizing the need to empower them with education and equal rights. "At 1.04 billion, today's is the biggest-ever generation of young people between 15 and 24, and this age group is rapidly expanding in many countries. The world has an unprecedented opportunity to benefit from their energy and ambition."[61] The emergence of such a positive presentation of young women is a result of feminist inclusion by organizations such as ICPD. The increased participation of feminists in youth discussions and policy will undoubtedly help reframe young people's depiction in a more positive light.

In addition to an emergence of positive characterizations of young women, a number of organizations are also soliciting young women's input into their programmatic and policy work. Young women are given a voice in determining their futures. (This presents a sharp contrast to how young men in the South are depicted as interfering with proper government function, when they seek a voice in policy.) For example, the Margaret Sanger Center International placed a full page ad in *Earth Times* recently, where the caption above a young woman's picture reads "Listen. In our own voices: Worldwide youth speak out on sexual and reproductive rights." The ad reads:

We need comprehensive sexuality education that respects our ability to make decisions rather than programs focused only on reducing problems or limiting our opinions. We also need to be involved in designing programs and policies that affect us. We are 1 billion strong and we have the right to be heard. Listen to us.[62]

UNFPA has a similar view on including youth in programming. "In light of the complexity of issues facing adolescent reproductive health programming, it is crucial that young people be involved in all aspects of programming. They should be the subjects and not the objects of programmes."[63] While the motive behind youth inclusion in programming is not always clear, the approach of recognizing youth as subjects rather than objects has led to a more realistic depiction of youth. Youth programs view the critical generation young women as a generation with many faces, many stories to tell. I would argue that the inclusion of youth voices has served to counterweight crude stereotypes of youth. However, these positive images of young women in the South do not carry over to the United States, where negative stereotypes of young women and their sexual behavior prevail.

Babies Having Babies: Teenage Moms in the United States

While positive depiction of young women is increasing in the development context, the picture has been far from positive for young women in the United States. The federal government, the media, and many conservative nonprofit groups have narrowed the discussion on youth and reproduction and have primarily focused on the "epidemic of teenage pregnancy." Though it is widely acknowledged that teenage birth rates are currently declining and there is no "epidemic," United States policy and nonprofit activity continue to define teen pregnancy as a pressing problem among adolescent girls.

The discussion surrounding teen pregnancy almost entirely focuses on young women as potential mothers, and casts a negative moral judgment on teen motherhood. Like the dominant discourse on the "critical generation," the discussion on "teens" in the United States is almost exclusively about young women; teen parenthood is not the focus, teen motherhood is. Furthermore, the phrase "teen mother" often refers to Black and Latina teens, without mentioning race overtly. Kristin Luker contends that, "The debate, in centering on teenagers in general ... permitted people to talk about African-Americans and poor women (categories that often overlapped) without mentioning race or class."[64]

The role of men in teen pregnancy is addressed only sporadically. Young women are held entirely responsible for their pregnancy even though two-thirds of teenage births are the result of sexual relations between men over the age of 20 and adolescent girls.[65] Despite the role of an adult father—a fact often overlooked—the pregnancy is still referred to as "teenage pregnancy."

Is teenage pregnancy a problem? Even before birth rates began declining eight years ago, birth rates among teens were lower than in the 1950s, when teenage birth rates peaked in this country.[66] Dorothy Roberts comments:

> The public's concern about teenagers having babies has depended much more on the politics of sexuality, abortion, family values, and welfare than on numbers. When people refer to the "problem" of teenage pregnancy they may mean one or a combination of several concerns—teenagers having sex, teenagers getting pregnant, teenagers raising children, teenagers having babies out of wedlock, and teenagers having babies at public expense.[67]

The "problem" of teenage pregnancy, then, represents much more than young women having babies.[68]

The federal government views teenage pregnancy as a major factor in United States population growth. In a 1996 report, the President's Council on Sustainable Development maintained, "growth adds another Connecticut in population each year, and another California each decade. Only a handful of countries, all of them developing, contribute more to their populations annually." It cited resource scarcity as the reason why the United States cannot accommodate such significant growth. It claimed "the United States is already severely challenged by the need to provide better opportunities for millions of disadvantaged citizens, and continued population growth will exacerbate those challenges."

Who is to blame for United States population growth? According to the President's Council, poor teen mothers and immigrants are the primary culprits.[69] Believing that the elimination of "unintended" pregnancies will significantly lower the population growth rate, the report suggests targeting young women and poor women for contraceptive dissemination.[70] In effect, the report advocates for lowering the population growth rates of poor teenage mothers of color specifically.

Drawing on stereotypes and misinformation, the report states, "the costs of adolescent pregnancy in the United States are incalculable: in impaired health of the teen mothers and their infants; in the stunted lives of the families created; and in lost educational, economic and social opportunities." In fact, there are several studies which dispute these assertions about the failure of teen mothers.[71] Further, the recommendation is based on the erroneous belief that teen birth rates are on the rise. It seems the recommendation is based on assumptions about the "cost" of teenage motherhood, rather than on accurate accounts or numbers.

The cost of teenage motherhood, which receives the most attention in the report, is its cost to the welfare state. The report immediately makes links between unintended births and welfare. "More than half the teens who give birth receive welfare within five years—although not all of these are unintended births."[72] In short, the report suggests that preventing teenage births would not only lower population growth rates, it would also lower the number of welfare recipients.

This focus on teenage mothers and welfare is not surprising. The United States government has a number of initiatives to keep teen mothers from reproducing and receiving welfare benefits. For instance, twenty-three states have adopted "family cap" measures that punish women who have additional children while receiving welfare, by denying them benefits.[73] The Department of Health and Human Service has also initiated what it calls "A National Strategy to Prevent Teen Pregnancy." This initiative was developed to support welfare reform policies targeting teen mothers. It aims to reduce the numbers of teen moms, thereby reducing the number of women and children on welfare.

Recognizing teen mothers and their children as an undue burden on the government, the Strategy has launched a two-tiered response: preventing out-of-wedlock teen pregnancies and promoting abstinence.[74] Financial assistance and other services to teen mothers have been replaced by moral lessons in "American" ideals, such as marriage and self-sufficiency. This shift is clear in this quote from the Department of Health and Human Services comment on the role of the Personal Responsibility and Work Opportunity Reconciliation Act of 1996 (PRWORA) in preventing teen pregnancy:

> Along with the $50 million allocated to states for abstinence-only education efforts, the law replaced the Aid to Families with Dependent Children (AFDC) program with a new block grant, Temporary Assistance for Needy Families (TANF). Several provisions within TANF target or influence teens, particularly teen parents. These provisions send a clear message to teens that personal responsibility, self-sufficiency, education, and work are priorities—and that welfare assistance is time-limited.[75]

The government's shift from supporting teen mothers to sermonizing at them suggests that the furor around teen mothers has little to do with economic realities, and everything to do with fear about social change in United States society. Kristin Luker writes that "the sexual behavior and reproductive patterns of white teenagers were beginning to resemble those of African Americans and poor women—that is, more and more whites were postponing marriage and having babies out of wedlock."[76] I would suggest that the "mainstreaming" of teenage pregnancy and the discomfort surrounding teenage sexuality intensifies the government's drive to place moral controls on teenage girls.

Unfortunately, a rhetoric of morality is not the only form of controlling teenage fertility. Ironically, even as abstinence education takes precedence over sex education, both Norplant and Depo-Provera are advocated as the answer to reducing teen pregnancy for poor teens of color. Like punitive welfare reform measures, targeting poor women for long-term, provider-controlled contraceptives is another form of population control in the United

States.[77] Contraceptives such as Depo-Provera are now "viewed as the magic bullet to reduce teen pregnancy rates (primarily among women of color)."[78]

Characterized as the cause of out-of-control population growth and leeches on the welfare system, teenage girls become menaces who threaten the moral underpinnings of the nation, and contribute to economic ruin with pregnancy. Young welfare moms of color are the female counterpart to the "superpredator" man of color. While "superpredators" threaten violence, Black teen welfare moms are held responsible for "poverty, school dropouts, child abuse and neglect, welfare dependence, despair, and crime."[79]

Not all agencies use such exploitative language and agenda to describe teens. A number of US nonprofits promote programs for teen girls similar to those for young women in the global South. Many of these nonprofits portray young women positively. For instance, Planned Parenthood Federation of America (PPFA) sponsored a full-page ad in the July 2000 issue of *Vogue Magazine*, similar to the one the Margaret Sanger Foundation placed in *Earth Times*. The ad depicts a young woman with the words, "there's power in your voice ... USE IT!" urging young women to contact Congress to advocate for "sexual and reproductive freedom." Clearly, nonprofits in this country are engaged in important work to amplify young women's voices and empower them to make decisions. However, although teen girls' sexuality is portrayed positively by many US nonprofits, the same questions about youth programming apply here as they do to youth programming in the South.

Conclusion

Images of youth as superpredators and superbreeders that dominate policy discourses are spurious. Such stereotypes mask the complexity of young people and deny their ability to exercise rational thought. They are associated with violence, crime, terrorism, irresponsible sexuality, and moral decay. With the exception of some reproductive rights and population organizations, like UNFPA, most agencies continue to understand today's youth as a generation in desperate need of control. This perceived necessity to control young people leads to extreme punitive measures in the criminal system, in military strategies, and in social policy. Alarmist images of youth do not serve any positive purpose, especially in the lives of youth. Instead of asking how to control volatile youth, we should be asking "Why are today's adults willing to sacrifice the next generation of youth to their own fears?"

1   United Nations Population Fund, "UNFPA and Adolescents" (April 19, 2000), www.unfpa.org/icpd/round%26meetings/ny_adolescent/reports/adoles.htm.

2   Marti Benedetti, Jonathan Berry, Alice Z. Cuneo, Sandra Jones, Kate Murphy, and Laura Zinn, "Teens: Here Comes the Biggest Wave Yet," *Business Week*, 3366 (April 11, 1994), 76.

3   Alene Gelbard, Carl Haub, and Mary M. Kent, "World Population Beyond Six Billion," *Population Bulletin*, 54.1 (1999), 19.

4   Ibid., 18.

5   Gary Fuller and Robert B. Hoch, "Youth Bulges in Asia," (unpublished document, 1998), 2.

6   Ibid., 48.

7   The Olin Institute for Strategic Studies, in Cambridge, Massachusetts is beginning a project on "how youth bulges in various countries around the world might lead to internal and external instability that could ultimately affect global stability and US national security."

8   See Betsy Hartmann, *Reproductive Rights and Wrongs* (Cambridge, MA: South End Press, 1995).

9   Ibid., 102.

10 Lieutenant General Patrick M. Hughes, "A DIA Global Security Assessment" (February 1997), www.defenselink.mil/speeches/1997/dr1217.html.

11 Ibid.

12 General Anthony C. Zinni, commander in chief of the US Central Command, Prepared Testimony, Federal New Services, Inc. (2000).

13 Richard J. Newman, "Are We Still Getting Ready for the Wrong War?," *US News and World Report* (May 1997), www.usnews.com/usnews/issue/970512/12quad.htm .

14 J. Brian Atwood, Excerpts from Administrator Atwood's remarks at the University of Texas Law School, Austin, TX (February 1998). Printed in *Environmental Change and Security Project Report 5* (Summer 1999).

15 Lieutenant General Martin R. Steele, "Deep Coalitions and Interagency Task Forces" (Winter 1999), www.nwc.navy.mil/press/Review/1999/winter/art1-w99.htm.

16 Zinni, Prepared Testimony.

17 Samuel Huntington, *The Clash of Civilizations and the Remaking of World Order* (New York: Simon and Schuster, 1996), 103.

18 Ibid., 102.

19 Alex de Sherbinin, "World Population Growth and U.S. National Security," *Woodrow Wilson Environmental Change and Security Project Report 1* (Spring 1995), 32.

20 Amartya Sen, "Population: Delusion and Reality," *New York Review* (1994), 63.

21 Donald Kennedy, et al., "Environmental Quality and Regional Conflict: A Report to the Carnegie Commission on Preventing Deadly Conflict" (Carnegie Corporation of New York, 1998), 36.

22 Robert Kaplan, *The Coming Anarchy* (New York: Random House, 2000), 5.

23 Fuller and Hoch, "Youth Bulges in Asia," 26.

24 Ibid., 26.

25 Gary Fuller and Forrest R. Pitts, "Youth cohorts and political unrest in South Korea," *Political Geography Quarterly*, Vol 9, No. 1 (1990).

26 Fuller and Hoch, "Youth Bulges in Asia," 26.

27 Suzanne Charlé, "Banning is Banned," *The Nation* (October 5, 1998).

28 Fuller and Hoch, "Youth Bulges in Asia," 25.

29 John J. DiIulio, Jr., "The Coming of the Super-Predators," *The Weekly Standard*, Vol. 1, No. 11 (1995), 23.

30 Ibid.

31 Ibid.

32 Ibid.

33 For instance, John DiIulio co-authored *Body Count: Moral Poverty ... and How to Win America's War Against Crime and Drugs* (New York: Simon and Shuster, 1996) with former drug czar William J. Bennett and John P. Walters, former deputy director for Supply Reduction, Office of National Drug Control Policy.

34 Daniel Macallair and Michael Males, "Dispelling the Myth: An Analysis of Youth and Adult Crime Patterns in California Over the Past 20 Years" (San Francisco, CA: Justice Policy Institute, May 2000), www.cjcj.org/themyth/index.html.

35 Ibid.

36 Michael Bochenek, "No Minor Matter: Children in Maryland's Jails" Human Rights Watch, (1999).

37 Darrell Steffenmeier, Cathy Streifel, and Miles D. Harer, "Relative Cohort Size and Youth Crime in the United States, 1953–1984," *American Sociological Review*, 52.5 (1987), 702.

38 Ibid., 708.

39 Michael Bochenek, "No Minor Matter."

40 Proposition 21 was voted into California Law in 2000. For more information on the law, see the California Legislative Analysts Office web site, www.lao.ca.gov/initiatives/2000/21_03_2000.html.

41 "ACLU Challenges CA Juvenile Justice Initiative," American Civil Liberties Union Freedom Network, www.aclu.org/news/2000/n060700a.html.

42 For more information, see *ColorLines* at www.colorlines.com/waronyouth.

43 "ACLU urges coalition on Juvenile Justice," ACLU Freedom Network, www.aclu.org/news/1999/n031099a.html.

44 "ACLU opposes S. 254, the Violent and Repeat Offender Accountability and Rehabilitation Act of 1999," ACLU Freedom Network, www.aclu.org/congress/1031099a.html.

45 M.A. Bortner, "America's War on Youth," *ColorLines* (Fall 1998), 23.

46 Michael Males, *Framing Youth: 10 Myths About the Next Generation* (Monroe, ME: Common Courage Press, 1999), 8.

47 Ibid., 9.

48 Center for Population, Health and Nutrition, "Youth: The Critical Generation," POP Briefs (Washington, DC: US Agency for International Development, 1999).

49   United Nations Population Fund, "UNFPA and Adolescents."

50   Susan A. Cohen, "A Response to Concerns about Population Assistance" (The Alan Guttmacher Institute, 1997), www.agi-usa.org/pubs/ib15.html.

51   The UN International Conference on Population and Development took place in 1994, in Cairo. The purpose was to further the "consensus" developed in earlier meetings, that development is key to reducing birth rates.

52   United Nations Population Fund, "UNFPA and Adolescents."

53   United Nations Population Fund, "Safeguarding a Future of Promise," www.unfpa.org/modules/intercenter/time/safeguarding.htm.

54   Ibid.

55   See Betsy Hartmann's chapter in this anthology for a critique of ICPD.

56   Catholic Family and Human Rights Institute, "UNFPA Releases Annual Ideological Look at 'State of the World's Population,' " 3.44 (2000).

57   World Population Foundation and Communication Consortium Media Center, with editorial contributions from the US NGO's in Support of the Cairo Consensus, "Youth and Population Momentum," www.zpg.org/Reports_Publications/Reports/report25.html .

58   Ibid.

59   See "Opposition to 'Day of Six Billion': the Campaign," www.cwpe.org, under Population Control.

60   United Nations Population Fund, "UNFPA and Adolescents."

61   United Nations Population Fund, "Safeguarding a Future of Promise," www.unfpa.org/modules/intercenter/time/safeguarding.html.

62   Advertisement, Margaret Sanger Center International, *Earth Times* (March 16, 2000), 15.

63   United Nations Population Fund, "UNFPA and Adolescents."

64   Kristin Luker, *Dubious Conceptions: The Politics of Teenage Pregnancy* (Cambridge, MA: Harvard University Press, 1996), 86.

65   Males, *Framing Youth*, 189.

66   Luker, *Dubious Conceptions*, 8.

67   Dorothy Roberts, *Killing the Black Body: Race, Reproduction, and the Meaning of Liberty* (New York: Pantheon Books, 1997), 116.

68   See Luker, "Constructing an Epidemic," in *Dubious Conceptions*, for an in-depth discussion on why teen pregnancy is considered a problem.

69   President's Countil on Sustainable Development, "Population and Consumption," (1996), www.whitehouse.gov/PSCD/Publications/TF_Reports/pop-chap1.html.

70   Ibid.

71   Males, "Myth: Why Teen Moms are Ruining America," *Framing Youth*.

72   President's Council on Sustainable Development, "Population and Consumption," (1996).

73   See Betsy Hartmann's chapter in this anthology.

74   Department of Health and Human Services, "A National Strategy to Prevent Teen Pregnancy" (1996), www.aspe.os.dhhs.gov/hsp/teenp/intro.html.

75   Ibid.

76   Luker, *Dubious Conceptions*, 86.

77   "Provider controlled" contraceptives are those administered by a provider (like a Depo-Provera shot, which is given by a doctor every three months) as opposed to birth control controlled by the user (like condoms).

78   Sara Littlecrow-Russell, "Time to take a Critical look at Depo-Provera," *Different Takes*, No. 5 (Amherst, MA: Hampshire College Population and Development Program).

79   Editorial, *Cincinnati Enquirer*, December 8, 1996, E02.

Chapter 10

The Changing Faces of Population Control

Betsy Hartmann

What's in a word? Plenty when it comes to population terminology. Demographic language is often freighted by controversial associations with geopolitics, sex, power, gender, race, religion and personal rights.

> *Population control* is a prime case in point. The term is now out of favor with experts in the field because it implies force—a negative thing to most. To some it evokes men trying to control women, industrialized nations trying to weaken the power of developing nations' increasing numbers, or whites trying to reduce the future numbers of people of color.... To stress the voluntary nature of the actions sought, experts use terms like "stemming," "stabilizing" or "slowing" population growth.[1]

So states an instruction sheet for journalists covering the United Nations's population conference Cairo+5 in 1999. But despite the change in language, is population control really passé? Unfortunately, the answer is no. The belief that human numbers must be controlled because overpopulation is a major, if not the major, cause of poverty, environmental degradation, and political instability is alive and well. This belief not only distorts family planning and health policies, but serves as a powerful ideological glue that binds liberals to conservative causes. It rationalizes inequality, reinforces racism, and blames the fertility of poor women, not only for their own poverty, but for the ecological destruction of the entire planet.

This belief in overpopulation persists and gathers strength even though population growth rates are declining worldwide more rapidly than anticipated even a few years ago. Since 1965, the world's annual population growth rate has fallen from 2.04 percent to 1.33 percent. According to the UN's medium projection, world population will reach 8.9 billion people in 2050 and then will start to level off, stabilizing at about 10 billion after 2200.[2]

The lingering perception that we are still experiencing a population explosion stems from the fact that a large proportion of the population in Southern countries is comprised of men and women entering their reproductive years. Barring major catastrophes, an inevitable demographic momentum is built into our present numbers, even as birth rates decline. The challenge is to plan effectively for the addition of 3 billion more people in the next fifty years.

Instead, too often the response is an apocalyptic "demographic alarmism," rooted in racial fears that Southern masses are going to overwhelm and destroy "our" Northern paradise. For example, the December 1994 cover of the *Atlantic Monthly* featured a lone white middle-class male barbecuing hot dogs in his backyard while a mass of dark faces watched him from just behind the fence. "Whether it's racist fantasy or realistic concern, it's a question that won't go away," states the cover blurb. "As population and misery increase, will the wretched of the earth overwhelm the Western paradise?" Such alarmism draws less on absolute population numbers than on population distribution. Eighty percent of the earth's people live in the South, and this figure is likely to rise to 90 percent in 2050.[3]

The fear of overpopulation has real consequences for women's lives, especially poor women of color. Since the mid-1960s, the US government has been one of the main actors funding, designing, and organizing population control efforts in the Third World. Many of these efforts have treated poor women of color as targets in a war against population growth. The goal of family planning programs has been to reduce birth rates as fast and cheaply as possible through the mass provision of long-lasting contraceptive methods such as Depo-Provera and Norplant, without attention to their health risks, or in some cases through coercive sterilization.

Not surprisingly, these methods have met with resistance from many quarters: from local people themselves, health and human rights advocates, and reproductive rights activists concerned about the quality of care and extent of contraceptive choice in family planning programs. Anti-choice forces against birth control and abortion have also voiced their own criticisms of population control. Because of mounting opposition, population control has had to keep changing faces over time.

This essay takes a look at its current "feminist" face internationally, and its more openly punitive face in the United States. Part One analyzes the impact of the 1994 UN International Conference on Population and Development (ICPD) in Cairo, heralded as a great victory for women's rights. The conference generated a new "consensus" about international population policy, in which governments endorsed women's empowerment and reproductive health as the solution to the population problem, instead of narrow family planning programs designed to drive down birth rates. Was this victory more semantic than real? To what extent has it led to reform of population policies and changes in budget allocations?

The United States government and private foundations played a major role in forging the "Cairo consensus," yet it has made little positive impact within the United States. Part Two addresses population control at home, where an increasingly punitive state threatens the reproductive rights, and basic human rights, of poor women. The United States is also home to a well-funded and orchestrated population-environment propaganda machine, which perpetuates negative myths and stereotypes of poor women overseas and immigrants at home.

Finally, Part Three anticipates future developments, focusing on genetic research. Only by understanding how population control changes faces with the times will feminists and other progressive activists be able to mount an effective resistance. The first step is to awake from the complacency which has set in since Cairo.

Talk the Talk, Walk the Walk: The Contradictions of Cairo

In embracing women's empowerment and reproductive health as the new centerpiece of population policies, the Cairo consensus is a step forward. However, it essentially leaves intact the old understanding of population growth as a principal drain on social, economic, and environmental resources. It is firmly situated within the neoliberal model of development, with its emphasis on the free market, privatization, and dismantling of the state's social welfare functions. Specifically, the Cairo plan of action adopted at the conference calls for more efficient government, more foreign investment, and greater reliance on the private sector and non-governmental organizations (NGOs) for service delivery.[4]

The Cairo consensus is thus a strange brew of feminism, neoliberalism, and population reductionism. Because of its attention to gender issues, it appears progressive, inspiring a certain "you can have your cake and eat it too" syndrome—you can be for women's rights and population control at the same time. This complacency, though convenient, obscures the fundamental contradictions at the heart of the consensus.

On the positive side, Cairo has opened up space for reform of international family planning. On the rhetorical level at least, many population agencies have now adopted a more voluntary approach, abandoning sterilization incentives, coercion, and fixed targets for how many women should "accept" a given contraceptive method. In principle family planning is supposed to be integrated into broader reproductive health services in which women have access to pregnancy care, sexuality education, and the prevention and treatment of sexually transmitted diseases (STDs). Cairo also broke ground in terms of advocating for adolescent services and greater male responsibility for contraception, though its language on abortion is weak.

Cairo has no doubt strengthened the hand of reformers in population agencies and governments who want to resist traditional population control policies but are still dependent on international funding.[5] Nevertheless, most observers agree that the actual implementation of its agenda has been disappointing.[6] The Cairo agreement itself still favored financing family planning over reproductive health by a margin of two to one, and most of the proposed funding for reproductive health has not materialized. Two years after Cairo, the Unites States government still devoted over half of its population assistance to family planning, and just a third to basic reproductive health.[7] Funding is only the tip of the iceberg, however. Far deeper economic and political obstacles stand in the way.

Globalizing Inequality

Cairo's commitments to women's health and empowerment ring hollow in a period of intensive economic polarization and marginalization associated with the globalization of advanced capitalism. The statistics are glaring: According to the UN Human Development Report, in 1960 the one-fifth of the world's people who lived in the North had thirty times the income of the poorest one-fifth; now they have eighty-two times as much. The 225 people who comprise the "ultra-rich" have a combined wealth of over $1 trillion, equivalent to the annual income of the poorest 47 percent of the world's people.

Despite improvements in infant mortality, life expectancy and literacy rates, almost one-third of the people in the South still live below the income poverty line of $1 per day. Over half lack access to sanitation, nearly a third to safe water, and almost one-third of children under age five are underweight.[8] Maternal death rates remain unconscionably high in many places.

At the Cairo conference, and at Cairo+5, these basic economic facts of life were largely avoided since they would call into question the whole neoliberal enterprise. Since poverty in the South is the main cause of ill health, reproductive and otherwise, this "oversight" means that the Cairo plan can never fully succeed. As the Eritrean government pointed out at Cairo, even the most enlightened population policy will not dramatically improve people's lives until there is a fairer international economic order and a sustained internal development.[9]

And what does "women's empowerment" mean in this context? The Cairo consensus mainly regards women's empowerment as a means to reduce population growth rather than as a worthy end in and of itself. Hence, empowerment has come to mean education for girls and family planning services for women since these ostensibly have the strongest correlation with fertility decline.

Many of Cairo's proponents pay little attention to important issues of economic justice such as unionizing women workers or transforming legal and land tenure systems to give women greater control over resources. Instead, micro-credit programs are promoted as a one-size-fits-all panacea for women's poverty.

Also missing from the Cairo picture are poor men, who arguably need more power too. In terms of education, critics point out that the Cairo focus on girls' education obscures the wider gap in access to education by socioeconomic status. Demographers John Knodel and Gavin Jones argue that except for South Asia and the Arab states, the gender gap in primary and secondary education is closing, and the main determinant of access is income level. "By placing almost sole emphasis on gender inequality," they write, "demographers risk aligning themselves with a reactionary perspective that fails to emphasize the urgent need to remove obstacles to greater socioeconomic equity in access to schooling."[10]

"Empowerment" may sound nice, but it is essentially a passive and patronizing term, implying that power is given rather than struggled for. The power neoliberalism is willing to give to poor women is the power to make the "right" choices: to have fewer children, to become mini-entrepreneurs or low-wage workers, to buy more consumer goods. And more important than what neoliberalism gives is what it does not deliver. This includes the basic human right to decent health care.

"Health for All"—Who Can Pay

Among neoliberalism's most destructive legacies are the structural adjustment programs imposed by the World Bank and the International Monetary Fund in the 1980s and 1990s. Structural adjustment deepened the health care crisis in many Southern countries through cuts in public health services, imposition of user fees for previously free services, dramatic increases in pharmaceutical prices, and overall deterioration of living standards among the rural and urban poor.[11] As the main caretakers of their families, women were especially hard hit.

Structural adjustment also intensified the AIDS crisis, especially in sub-Saharan Africa. While AIDS was spreading rapidly in the region during the period, international aid agencies and financial institutions pressured governments to slash health expenditures and devote more attention to controlling population growth. AIDS was largely cast as a problem of Africans' sexual promiscuity, neglecting the transmission role played by unsterile needles and infected blood supplies in the (deteriorating) health services, as well as the role of poverty in general.[12]

The result of this unbenign neglect has been a massive increase in death rates. It is now projected that sub-Saharan Africa will face a "demographic catastrophe," with a quarter of its population likely to die of AIDS.[13] In Botswana, over one-third of the adult population is already infected, and in Zimbabwe a quarter.[14]

Today structural adjustments continue under the mantle of "health sector reforms." Ostensibly designed to improve the efficiency and accessibility of health services, these reforms often place them outside the reach of poor people. The introduction of user fees in Nigeria, Kenya, and Ghana led to a 50 percent decline in attendance at clinics and hospitals after a few weeks; in Nigeria user fees for emergency admissions are one of the factors cited for the increase in maternal mortality.[15] "Like all other adjustment policies in the social sector, health sector reforms have defined efficiency without taking into account the enormous human cost of coping strategies adopted by the poor, women in particular."[16]

Building a reproductive health program on top of a nonexistent or deteriorating health system—and in many countries in the context of a rapidly escalating AIDS epidemic—is like building a house on a foundation of sand.[17] Hence, reproductive health itself has become a problematic concept.

Reproductive Health: Pro-Women or Women-Centered?

Clearly, reproductive health is an extremely important part of medical care, but should it be the centerpiece of a women's health strategy? As Indian public health analyst Imrana Qadeer writes, the current concept of reproductive health "is not necessarily pro-women, only women-centered."[18] It puts too much focus on women as mothers and reproducers, neglecting the other aspects of their lives such as their health in childhood and old age and debilitating illnesses like malaria and tuberculosis.

Qadeer points to how the concept glosses over differences in women's health issues by region and social class in favor of a universal, homogenous agenda. Moreover, it tends to ignore the structural constraints in poor women's lives, both within the family and within the larger community, and women's own priorities in terms of meeting basic survival needs.

In terms of implementation, reproductive health is often watered down to consist of technical, cost-effective "packages" of services, rather than the broader vision advocated by women's groups.[19] Typically, many programs provide a limited range of contraceptives, some basic maternal and child health (MCH) services, and prevention and treatment of sexually transmitted diseases.

In many population programs, reproductive health is limited even further to family planning/population control. This occurs on the programmatic level where reproductive health services provide contraception and nothing else, and on the ideological level where the concept targets women's high fertility as the cause of their own ill health as well as the nation's underdevelopment.

Population agencies such as the US Agency for International Development (USAID) have long rationalized their narrow focus on contraception with the justification that family planning itself is one of the most effective health interventions to reduce infant and maternal mortality. While family planning has many other benefits, this truism is in fact not true. What saves lives is access to decent health services, clean water, and nutrition.[20]

Tanzania provides an example of the deployment of this defective logic. USAID's 1997–2003 Strategic Plan for Tanzania claims that high fertility is the single most important risk factor in low birth weights and infant death, and a significant cause of maternal depletion and poor health. This claim, political scientist Lisa Richey writes, "is based on ideology, not evidence."[21] Instead, poverty is the main risk factor: the outcome of a high-risk pregnancy or birth is largely determined by a woman's socioeconomic status and whether or not she can access decent health services.

In the same document, USAID also blames high fertility for

contributing to Tanzania's rapid population growth, which undermines the country's development efforts. Family planning thus becomes the key not only to reproductive health but economic and social progress, with poor women's bodies at the strategic center of policy. The challenge is to get these women to change their irrational high fertility behavior and to use modern contraception to save themselves, their children, and the country.

Since direct methods of population control are no longer so acceptable, the rhetoric of reproductive health is used instead.[22] This version of reproductive health fits well with neoliberal prerogatives, not only because it helps to obscure their negative effects—Tanzania, after all, has been hit hard by structural adjustment and economic crisis—but because it draws on the neoliberal ideology of the individual economic actor making rational choices in the free marketplace. The individual woman makes rational contraceptive choices in a fantasy world where poverty and oppression are no constraint.

Driving Birth Rates Down

Accepting Cairo rhetoric at face value, many people now believe that international family planning programs have been "fixed" to make them more voluntary and responsive to women's rights. While there is some progress in this direction, rhetoric does not match reality in many places. Bureaucratic inertia is partly to blame. Despite edicts from the top, it takes a long time to transform local systems and reeducate family planning workers previously trained to meet numerical targets of contraceptive "acceptors" or else risk losing their jobs.

The main barrier to improving services, however, is the population control imperative that remains central to the Cairo consensus. International agencies such as USAID, the UN Fund for Population Activities (UNFPA), and the World Bank still pressure countries to reduce population growth through results-driven family planning programs. USAID's population assistance programs, for example, are "driven solely by the need to 'reduce the rate of population growth.' "[23] USAID and the World Bank also have a long history of making other forms of development assistance contingent on a country's population performance.

Although the Cairo consensus discourages contraceptive acceptance targets at the local level, it does not challenge national level targets to reduce population growth rates by a certain percentage in a given (usually unrealistically short) amount of time. These national level targets open the door to sterilization and contraceptive abuse. In Peru, for example, the right wing Fujimori government, well known for human rights violations, set a target of reducing fertility from 3.2 births per woman in 1996 to 2.5 by the year 2000. USAID noted the challenges of achieving such an ambitious target in "a quality way," but was willing to fund the population program anyway. Its grant agreement with the Peruvian government states:

> USAID policy in family planning places equal weight on access and quality.... If services have to be rationed because of resource constraints, on the basis of equity priority should be given to such at-risk populations as rural and peri-urban dwellers, people who have not been able to benefit from much formal education and people of low income. Accordingly, equilibrium should be sought at which services meeting a minimum threshold of quality can be offered to the greatest number of at-risk people.[24]

USAID failed to take into account the political reality that those same "at-risk" populations were precisely the ones most vulnerable to sterilization abuse by a right wing government eager to prove its efficiency to USAID and other international donors. In 1997, Peru's reproductive health and family planning program began to emphasize female sterilization over other forms of birth control, holding "contraceptive fairs" in mainly poor and indigenous areas where female sterilization clients were recruited without adequate informed consent procedures or attention to medical quality. Mandatory quotas for family planning workers also resulted in forced sterilizations.[25] In 1997, state doctors in Peru performed 110,000 female sterilizations, compared to 30,000 in 1996 and 10,000 in 1995.[26] When women died from botched operations and the scandal finally broke in the international press, USAID pleaded ignorance and was quick to distance itself from the government's program. But the fact remains that by supporting Fujimori's population reduction targets, USAID helped create the context in which such abuses could occur.

Peru is a particularly dramatic example, but in many other countries smaller scale mistreatment is routine, built into the institutional structure of family planning programs designed to reduce birth rates as fast and cheaply as possible. Typical of these programs are lack of contraceptive choice; promotion of more "effective" but riskier provider-controlled, long-acting contraceptives such as Norplant, Depo-Provera, and the IUD; neglect of safer barrier methods; refusal to remove Norplant and the IUD on demand; the absence of adequate counseling, screening, and treatment of contraceptive side effects; and the omission of other reproductive health measures.[27] The fact that contraceptive "choice" remains heavily weighted toward non-barrier methods is especially problematic given the prevalence of HIV/AIDS and other STDs. Moreover, there is growing concern that contraceptives like Depo- Provera which are based on the hormone progestin may actually increase the risk of acquiring HIV/AIDS.[28]

Incentives—typically, payments to sterilization "acceptors" and recruiters, or to communities who achieve family planning targets—also remain in vogue in many places, especially South Asia. India is already reneging on its commitment to abandon its notoriously abusive sterilization incentives and targets by allowing states like Andhra Pradesh to use coercive methods to pressure poor people to be sterilized after one or two children.[29]

In the glow of post-Cairo complacency, contraceptive and sterilization abuse issues tend to be glossed over or forgotten entirely. Mexico, for example, is now touted as a model for reducing birth rates, with enthusiastic reports in the US press about the success of its voluntary family planning program.[30] Yet a 1999 study revealed that many poor women in Mexican public hospitals have been sterilized under pressure during unnecessary cesarean sections.[31] In the private maquiladora sector, Human Rights Watch has documented how women workers must submit to mandatory pregnancy testing as a condition for getting a job, and in some cases must show their soiled sanitary pads to company employees as proof of menstruation. Many of the factories involved are US-owned, and the Mexican government is complicit in these practices.[32]

The Mexican case points to the need to monitor population control abuses not only within government services, but in corporate, non-governmental, and philanthropic sectors as well. The privatization of abuse is likely to accelerate in coming years, as health and family planning services become more market-based and NGO-based and less subject to public scrutiny and regulation.

The fact that over 100,000 women have been subjected to potentially dangerous quinacrine chemical sterilization without any official regulatory approval or oversight is damning evidence of this development. The money of one of the world's richest financiers—US multibillionaire Warren Buffett—is greasing the machine in a particularly stark example of the merger between corporate power and population control. A population control advocate, Buffet has provided Family Health International with two million dollars to do laboratory tests on quinacrine in the hopes that the method will gain FDA approval. Without the money, it is doubtful quinacrine research would have moved forward. [33]

Depoliticizing the Women's Movement

Cairo has proved to be a double-edged sword in terms of transnational women's organizing. On the one hand, it opened up space for many women's groups to organize and pressure governments on reproductive rights concerns. On the other, it concentrated power in the hands of a few well-funded, mainly US-based organizations and blunted the critical analysis of the global women's health movement,[34] ultimately helping to depoliticize it.

Many women's groups, including the Committee on Women, Population, and the Environment (CWPE), were wary of the compromises involved in endorsing the Cairo consensus. Although they participated in the Cairo process, they constantly highlighted how political economy issues such as structural adjustment, the debt crisis, and globalization were being left out of the picture, and how population control was still a central objective despite the language of reproductive health.[35]

More mainstream groups, however, argued that Cairo was not the time to talk about development; it could wait until the UN Social Summit of 1995 in Copenhagen. They contended that the main threat to reproductive rights was religious fundamentalism, and Cairo provided an opportunity to ally strategically with population agencies against the Vatican.

While religious fundamentalism was, and is, a major threat to women's rights, it was no justification for dropping development issues from the Cairo agenda or minimizing the continuing impact of population control. Indeed, one can argue that silence on these issues helped cede the moral high ground to the fundamentalists —for example, at Cairo the Vatican painted itself as the great defender of poor people's rights.

Now, belatedly, there is some recognition of this mistake. According to Rosalind Petchesky, the failure of the Cairo Women's Caucus to make a strong case for social development stemmed from preoccupation with the threat of fundamentalist forces and thus reluctance to jeopardize alliances with mainstream population and family planning groups and government delegations (from the United States and the European Union) committed to market-oriented macroeconomic policies. This reluctance made it difficult to take a strong, uncompromising position on structural transformations and redistributive policies as the basis for implementing a broad approach to reproductive and sexual health.[36]

Petchesky describes the divisions between women's groups on this issue as "more strategic than political,"[37] but in fact they were political to the core. Not only were more critical groups marginalized for not going along with the consensus, but the collusion that ensued opened the door for many women's groups to participate in the neoliberal agenda.[38]

Five years later at the Cairo+5 NGO Forum in the Hague, "partnership" was the new buzzword, shorthand for the neoliberal social contract in which "civil society," in the form of undifferentiated NGOs, forms partnerships with the state and the private sector to usher in a new age of women's empowerment. Enlightened elites, meanwhile, will manage the nasty side effects of globalization and protect the "marginalized sectors" with a few safety nets.

There are many problems with the notion of partnership. First, it masks inequalities in power. NGOs, the state, and the private sector are not all equal partners in terms of who gets to determine actual policy. If they are not careful, NGOs can be used to give a rubber stamp of approval to repressive and/or regressive social agendas. Moreover, through partnering with Northern-based NGOs, Southern NGOs can lose their autonomy and become beholden to foreign patrons. Second, partnerships not only include, but also exclude. Social movements, for example, seem to have dropped out of the concept of "civil society"—perhaps because they are occasionally uncivil and political in demanding their rights. Third, partnerships can turn participating NGOs away from political advocacy work towards service delivery. For example, many women's NGOs now face the choice of whether to accept funding to run direct reproductive health programs. In so doing, they may provide better services to women than the state, but at the cost of becoming the agents of the increased privatization of health care and neglecting their advocacy work. Moreover, the scope of their work is necessarily limited—they cannot replace the state in terms of serving large populations. They can all too easily become the "showcase," the positive example used to mask the dearth of quality services nationwide.

These dilemmas are not easy to resolve, and many women's groups are searching for ways that they can provide services but continue their grassroots advocacy and political work. Ultimately, they face the question of accountability—are they most accountable to the government, international funders, or the constituencies of women they are supposed to represent?[39]

Lastly, and related to all of the above, partnerships can silence once critical voices. In Peru, for example, a National Population Commission was formed in 1997, which included women's groups, other NGOs, the UNFPA, and the Fujimori government. One of the requirements for participating in this commission was agreeing to discuss controversial issues with the other members before making them public. "Therefore," writes health advocate Mabel Bianco, "NGOs and women's groups are often called upon to play a new role and postpone denouncing government actions in order to retain the possibility of having an impact on policies."[40]

In Peru, the perils of such postponement became clear at once. One of the main women's organizations in the country, Manuela Ramos, initially remained silent about Fujimori's coercive sterilization campaign because of its collaborative work with the government. This "quiet diplomacy" ultimately proved ineffective.[41] Considerable public pressure from the outside was needed to change Fujimori's policy. In her analysis of the implications of the Peru case for the women's movement, Martha de la Fuente concludes that "the worst reaction to these painful events is silence."[42]

As a result of the partnership process, many of the same women's groups that played a prominent role in forging the Cairo consensus are now part of a new reproductive health establishment in alliance with more liberal actors in the population field. This establishment is definitely an improvement over old-guard population control hardliners, and has had some success in reforming population policies—but within, not outside, a neoliberal framework. Their language and actions bear the hallmark of this constraint. They are not going to rock the boat.

Who is going to rock the boat? Has Cairo undermined the global women's health movement as a social movement, turning it more into a loose collection of professional NGOs, dominated by Northern funders? If so, where is new leadership to come from? Are there strategic ways to engage in the politics of reform—to seize the institutional spaces Cairo has opened up—while still advancing a radical critique of neoliberalism? These hard questions have no easy answers, but fortunately, there are still many grassroots women's health and rights activists who have refused to stop fighting for fundamental social and economic transformation. For them the contradictions of Cairo were always apparent.

Contradictions or Logical Outcomes?

Because the Cairo agenda was more part of the neoliberal framework than a challenge, it is not surprising that it has generated so many contradictions and unfulfilled promises. While in some cases it has proved a useful instrument for feminist reform of population policy, in others it has advanced a new phase of neoliberal disciplining of the poor, especially poor women. Seen through this darker lens, the Cairo consensus reinforces the belief that economic and environmental "scarcities" are caused by population growth, not by a highly unequal, unstable, and unjust global capitalism. It rationalizes the continuing assault on public health by prioritizing family planning over reproductive health, and reproductive health over primary health care, as well as promoting the privatization of services. And it uses gender as a way to obscure class inequalities. The consensus also defines women's empowerment in narrow terms designed to incorporate them into the industrial economy as semi-educated, low-wage, non-pregnant workers who do not need maternity benefits, and exchanges the coercive population control methods of the past for a notion of self-disciplined female reproductive behavior through the correct "choice" of modern contraception.

The irrationality of advanced capitalism—its unpredictability, gluttonous resource use, high profit margins, and unwillingness to invest in social reproduction—demands ever more "rational" reproductive behavior from women, including low fertility. If the neoliberal state refuses to provide social services to poor populations, then the only way to reduce poverty, the logic goes, is to reduce the number of poor people being born. Cairo's proponents would like women to manage their fertility voluntarily and preferably through the invisible hand of the free market, but if the project fails, the heavy, not-so-invisible hand of state coercion could once again come down hard. The one power the neoliberal state refuses to relinquish is the power of repression. The heavy hand is already coming down hard on poor women in the United States.

Back in the United States: Of Earth Mothers and Welfare Queens

One of the great ironies of the Cairo period was the disjuncture between the Clinton administration's actions abroad and in the United States. Before, during, and after the Cairo conference, the Clinton administration vocally championed international women's rights. With the support of the private population lobby, the media, and major foundations, the US government played a key role in orchestrating the Cairo consensus,[43] while at the same time it prepared to launch a brutal war against poor women at home.

Shortly after coming into office in 1992, Clinton began using the language of his right wing foes, extolling "family values" and blaming single motherhood for many social woes. In 1996 he literally signed onto the conservative agenda, putting his signature to welfare "reform" legislation that ended sixty years of guaranteed federal aid to poor families, most of whom are women with children in single-parent households. This legislation sets unrealistic time limits and work requirements for receiving aid, restricts food stamp and Medicaid eligibility, slashes funding of anti-poverty programs, and shifts responsibility for administering welfare to the states.

The legislation also endorses population control disincentives that run counter to the administration's commitments at Cairo. It permits states to enact "child exclusion" or "family cap" measures that deny additional benefits for children born to women already receiving welfare. Twenty-three states now have such a provision. These measures are based on the popular myth that high fertility rates among poor (mainly Black) women are the cause of their poverty and that welfare encourages them to overbreed. In reality, women on welfare have two children on average, and the longer they are on welfare, the less likely they are to have more children.[44] Since women of color are overrepresented in the welfare population, these measures disproportionately impact them. They "are predicated on the degradation of Black motherhood and serve to perpetuate the welfare system's historical racism and the long-standing stereotypes of women of color, with devastating consequences."[45]

Of course, the United States has never been a welfare state in the sense of European countries such as France, Sweden, and the Netherlands, which have made investments in public health, education, and social services a high national priority. Now the United States is above all a punitive state, where imprisonment is viewed as the main solution to the social problems generated by poverty. In poor communities of color, even pregnancy itself is becoming criminalized.

Why is there such a disconnect between the Clinton administration's liberal Cairo rhetoric and its willingness to endorse, if not actively promote, this repressive population control agenda at home? Part of the reason lies in the difference between the foreign policy establishment and domestic policy-making. Early in the administration, Clinton abandoned his commitments to universal health care and a strong affirmative action platform in the United States. Foreign policy was less affected by his strategic shift to the right, and liberal internationalist appointees enjoyed considerable power in the State Department, especially during the Cairo period.

These appointees, notably Timothy Wirth, former under secretary of state for global affairs, actively sought alliances with women's groups around Cairo in order to create a united front against conservative forces opposed to population assistance and abortion. The alliance was effective in advancing the Cairo consensus, but the focus was overseas, despite all the rhetoric about "bringing Cairo back home." Blinded by the bright lights of power, many US women's groups ignored how the foundations of a punitive state were being carefully laid. This is not surprising given the mainstream reproductive rights movement's long history of neglecting issues faced by poor women and women of color. Especially for white middle-class groups, it is much easier to sound progressive on the international stage than to do the hard work of multiracial network building at home. In the end, the rhetoric of Cairo served to mask the perpetuation of population control both overseas and in the United States, in another variation of the liberal/conservative tango. This dance has been carefully choreographed over the years to win over more constituencies to the population control cause. While rationales shift according to the political climate, one which has proved particularly resilient is the supposed threat population poses to the environment.

Have They No Shame?

On July 16, 2000, an ad appeared in the *New York Times Magazine* sponsored by PLANet, a population and environment campaign funded by the David and Lucile Packard Foundation, now the nation's second largest private philanthropy.[46] Underneath the caption "FAMILY PLANNING CHANGES EVERYTHING" are two pictures, one of a degraded tropical forest on fire, the other of the same forest lush and green. The ad then states:

> Amazing as it may seem, providing people in developing nations access to family planning is a critical first step in saving much of the 40 million acres of tropical rainforest being lost each year. Forests that are being cut down to create cropland to feed the world's ever-growing population. Forests that are home to many near-extinct animal and plant species. In places where family planning programs already provide voluntary contraception, health care and sex education, most women are choosing small families. This, in turn, eases the intense pressure on the environment's natural resources.[47]

This ad is not only misinformation, but disinformation. Surely, its creators are not so ill informed that they do not know that the destruction of tropical forests has much more to do with the activities of large-scale commercial farming, ranching, logging, and mining than the bodies of poor women. The main cause of deforestation in the Southern countries is demand for wood and paper, and nearly half that wood and three-quarters of that paper is used in industrial countries.[48] Have they not considered the fact that the destruction of the Amazonian rain forest has accelerated in Brazil at the same time that birth rates have dramatically declined?[49] The ad is also deeply insulting to women, equating them with nature in a new post-industrial essentialist mythology that stands the Earth Mother on her head. If women's bodies are too fertile, the forest disappears. But when they have fewer babies, it magically grows back again. Unfortunately, this particular ad is just one example of a whole genre of propaganda which blames over-population for environmental destruction. In the immediate aftermath of Cairo, this propaganda died down for a while, but now it has come back with a vengeance.

From personal conversations with people in the population and environment field, I know that many find these messages problematic but some nevertheless insist that the ends justify the means—the only way to get Americans to support international family planning assistance, which is under threat from congressional conservatives and now the Bush adminstration, is to stoke fears of overpopulation in the Third World. Media focus groups tell them that fear sells, women's rights do not.[50] Others truly believe what they preach, suffering from that peculiarly American proclivity to ignore the destructive role of our own institutions, whether government, corporate, or military, in the rest of the world and to blame the victim instead.

Some deep ecologists subscribe to an even more dangerous dualism. People are bad (except for a few enlightened environmentalists like themselves), nature is good.[51] This can lead to a more apocalyptic and draconian view of population growth. Some even believe that the more people who die from diseases like AIDS, the better (as long as they are not yourself and your friends).[52]

While this may seem an extreme position, the attitude and inaction towards the AIDS crisis in sub-Saharan Africa has been influenced by population control thinking. Even attempts by US intelligence analysts to study the likely trajectory and impact of the disease in the late 1980s met with resistance. A military official at the US National Intelligence Council was reported to have told one of the analysts that the impact of AIDS "will be good, because Africa is overpopulated anyway."[53]

In a cynical twist, the prominent environmentalist Lester Brown of the Worldwatch Institute now blames the AIDS crisis in Africa on what he calls governments' "demographic fatigue." African governments are just too worn down by struggling with the consequences of rapid population growth to respond to new threats like AIDS. He also blames the genocide in Rwanda and other ethnic conflicts in Africa on overpopulation and demographic fatigue.[54] Brown's main solution to just about all the problems the world faces is population control, with two-child family limits if necessary. He embraces the idea of countries adopting a national optimal population policy, ignoring the legacy of Nazi Germany in this regard. The policy recommendations he makes point to the considerable dangers of linking family planning to environmental concerns.

The PLANet campaign advocates voluntary family planning, but the end product of its propaganda efforts could be to convince people that the environmental crisis is so dire that involuntary measures are justified. It could well help set the ideological stage for initiatives further to the right. These include "the greening of hate," the attempt by conservative anti-immigrant groups, such as Carrying Capacity Network, Population-Environment Balance, Negative Population Growth, and the Federation for American Immigration Reform (FAIR), to use population and environment issues as a political wedge to win over liberal environmentalists. The crux of their argument is that immigrants, by contributing to US population growth, are destroying our environment.[55]

Another worrying trend is the linking of population and environment to national security concerns.[56] The Rand Corporation's *Population Matters* series recently published a report on "The Security Dynamics of Demographic Factors," funded by the Hewlett, Packard, and Rockefeller foundations and the US Army. Some of its findings hearken back to the bad old days of the Cold War. For an instance:

> Some high-fertility developing states contain radical political movements on the fringes of their political spectra. In these states, the emergence of high structural unemployment at a time when the national age pyramid is highly skewed in favor of 18- to 24-year-olds may result in many of the youthful unemployed coming to support the radical political alternatives. If the elites in these radical political movements can effectively mobilize these youths, then a full-scale revolution may occur.[57]

The report contains a strange mix of policy recommendations. Side by side, it calls for US family planning aid for governments "that wish to take the direct approach of reducing their fertility rates outright," and better military technologies, such as unmanned aerial surveillance vehicles and body armor, to improve the performance of US troops in urban warfare.[58]

The goal of the Population Matters project is to raise awareness of the importance of population policy issues among policy-makers and the public, in order, no doubt, to increase international family planning assistance. But is it really in women's best interest to have contraceptives mentioned in the same breath as body armor, and to have their fertility viewed as a matter of strategic concern to military and intelligence agencies? Reproductive rights are important rights in and of themselves — we do not have to accept the myth that poor women's fertility is destroying the environment, facilitating the spread of AIDS, or fomenting political violence in order to support their rights to abortion and birth control. Using these myths as scare tactics to increase family planning assistance is political opportunism of the worst kind.

What's Next? From Genetic Surveillance to Eugenic Social Policy

The technological revolution in plant and human genetic engineering will likely shape the forms population control takes in coming years. Ideologically, fears of overpopulation already serve as spin control for seed biotech companies which claim their mission is to feed the hungry masses, rather than to reap huge profits from monopolizing the market for agricultural inputs. "Worrying about starving populations won't feed them," the US-based Monsanto Corporation has declared. "Food biotechnology will."[59]

A disturbing new development in the population field is the linking of social science demographic research and biological testing, which raises the prospect of bio-prospecting on a large scale. The Demographic Health Survey (DHS), financed by USAID, has collected data for the last two decades on family planning and health issues in Southern countries. In a recent initiative, called "DHS+," survey workers are also collecting blood samples from women and children in order to determine the prevalence of iron-deficient anemia. So far, this data has been gathered in Kazakhstan, Uzbekistan, Kyrgyz Republic, Madagascar, Peru, and Bolivia.[60]

This practice raises a number of serious ethical issues. One is the very real possibility of inadequately trained and equipped survey workers spreading HIV and other blood-borne diseases through unsterile technique and the generation of biohazardous waste. The manual designed for DHS+ anemia testing notes that: "Unfortunately, in most areas where the population-based surveys are implemented, it will not be possible to arrange to use health facilities for proper hazardous waste disposal," nor will commercial waste containers be available. It recommends a time-consuming procedure for burning and burying the waste locally.[61]

It is questionable whether local people will benefit from the testing—current protocol is that those people diagnosed with anemia receive simple dietary recommendations and instructions to seek medical care. Of course they probably wouldn't be anemic in the first place if they had proper access to health services and nutritious food.[62]

Blood collection on this scale raises a red flag in terms of possibile use/abuse in genetic testing and bio-prospecting. A paper on the challenges of combining biological and demographic research notes the "potential for genetic testing" in the future:

> We must remain attuned to the ethical debates in the northern hemisphere regarding genetic screening. As with other areas of biological and clinical data collection, the challenges genetic testing pose are likely to be even more daunting in LDCs [less developed countries] than in more developed countries.[63]

Will informed consent and confidentiality be assured? Who will own and store the information? Will blood samples be used for purposes other than those initially proposed?

The use of satellite global positioning data in such research opens up the possibility of a new genetic geography. Even if surveys cover extensive areas and large populations, satellite data can potentially pinpoint not only communities but households and individuals where specific blood samples have been collected.[64] Without adequate oversight, population research could become the vehicle for a new strategy of genetic surveillance.

As population growth rates continue to decline around the world, attention is starting to shift away from absolute population quantity to population age composition and "quality." Already, we are witnessing the rebirth of eugenics, the "science" of producing superior offspring, which was one of the hallmarks of Nazi ideology. The belief that social problems such as poverty and criminality are inherited and often racially based traits led to the first wave of eugenics in the early twentieth century and the compulsory sterilization of thousands of poor Americans.

Now the punitive climate towards poor women of color, combined with the religion of the free market and consumer choice, is leading to a new eugenics that operates at two different levels. For the so-called underclass, reproductive punishments, though not strictly eugenic in nature, help set the stage for social acceptance of a truly eugenic program. According to Dorothy Roberts, punishments such as the criminalization of pregnancy or coercive Norplant insertion

> are not eugenic because they are not based on the belief that criminality is inherited.... They are based, however, on the same premise underlying the eugenic sterilization laws—that social problems can be cured by keeping certain people from having babies and that certain groups therefore do not deserve to procreate.[65]

With increased genetic screening, and the search for genes linked to anti-social behaviors, a negative eugenics could once again become part of the population control agenda. For the white, able-bodied, heterosexual middle and upper classes, however, the eugenics program will appear positive. The language will be one of consumer choice; the technologies cloning and germline engineering; and the goal genetic enhancement to create perfect (read white, non-disabled, athletic, talented, straight, intelligent, beautiful—in other words, Aryan dream) offspring.[66]

In the techno-eugenicist vision, the rich will have access to the technologies of genetic enhancement, and the poor will not, leading to what Princeton geneticist Lee Silver describes as a species division between the "GenRich class" and the "Natural class." The GenRich will control the economy, media, and the knowledge industry, while the Naturals work in low-wage service and manual jobs.[67] Thus Silver points to the possibility of a new stage of eugenic capitalism, where inequality is reproduced not just in the economy and culture, but bred right into our genes.

In reality, it is highly unlikely that biologically such a world would come to pass since genes alone do not determine behavior and there is too much complexity and unpredictability in human reproduction to assure such an outcome. What Silver's vision does is to legitimize existing social hierarchies through a pseudoscientific biological determinism. Already both negative and "positive" eugenics are serving to redefine social norms away from the ideal of a liberal, pluralist democracy to a bifurcated polity of citizens free to make consumer choices and non-citizens stripped of even the basic choice to reproduce.

Outside the Safety Zone

Population control will not go away as long as it is a useful ideological rationale for racism and inequality. In an era where both are intensifying, feminists must remain particularly vigilant about its new faces. This is not only a question of waking up from post-Cairo complacency, but of speaking up and speaking out, even if this means jeopardizing funding sources.

In the United States, many reproductive rights organizations receive funding from foundations which also believe strongly in population control. Today, several of these larger foundations are beginning to dominate the field, eclipsing the power of funders such as the Ford and MacArthur foundations, which shifted much of their portfolio out of narrow population programs to reproductive and sexual health and rights. This development could give literal truth to the old adage that silence is golden: silence means money. Better to play it safe.

Better to play it safe, too, the argument goes, given the strength of the anti-abortion movement. Any criticism of population control plays into their hands because at least population agencies are in favor of family planning. Yes, but what kind of family planning, and for what purposes? Shouldn't we be the ones seizing the moral high ground against coercion?

We need to move outside the safety zone of liberal feminism if we are ever going to build a reproductive rights movement strong enough to defend both women's right to terminate a pregnancy and to bear a child, if we are ever going to confront the racism both inside and outside the movement. Outside the safety zone are many possibilities for alliances with other social movements—immigrant rights, human rights, labor, economic justice, prisoners' rights, and environmental justice among them. Feminists can help

bring reproductive rights and gender analysis into these movements, at the same time that they take back into their own organizations a deeper understanding of class and race.

Perhaps the hardest task of all will be to dismantle the parochi-
alism and prejudice that run so deep in American culture that even
schoolchildren are taught to believe that overpopulation is the
main cause of the planet's ills. Population fundamentalism is a
crude article of faith in a popular religion where church is not separate from the state. As long as people are convinced that poor
women's fertility is destroying the rainforest, they will fail to notice
the corporate chain saws cutting down the trees and ripping apart
the social fabric. Ignorance is not bliss, it is dangerous.

The Changing Faces of Population Control   285

1   "Journalist's Notebook: What's in a Word?" December 1998. (A handout at a conference.)

2   Population figures are taken from UN Population Division, Department of Economic and Social Affairs, *Population Newsletter*, No. 68 (December 1999), 1–6.

3   Ibid.

4   Betsy Hartmann, "Cairo Consensus Sparks New Hopes, Old Worries," *Forum for Applied Research and Public Policy*, Vol. 12, No. 2 (1997), 33–40.

5   In Tanzania, for example, Lisa Richey contends that the government may be able to use the Cairo agenda to push for more funding for social sector programs other than family planning, using the argument that these programs will ultimately help reduce population growth. See Lisa Richey, "Family Planning and the Politics of Population in Tanzania: International to Local Discourse," *Journal of Modern African Studies*, Vol. 37, No. .3 (1999), 457–487.

6   See, for example, Women's Environment and Development Organization (WEDO), "Risks, Rights and Reforms: A 5 Country Survey Assessing Government Actions After the International Conference on Population and Development" (New York: 1999); Rosalind P. Petchesky, "Reproductive and Sexual Rights: Charting the Course of Transnational Women's NGOs," *UNRISD Occasional Paper*, No. 8 (Geneva: UN Research Institute for Social Development, 2000); Karen Hardee, et al., "Reproductive Health Policies and Programs in Eight Countries: Progress Since Cairo," *International Family Planning Perspectives*, 25, Supplement (1999), S2–S21; and Shepard Forman and Romita Ghosh, eds., *Promoting Reproductive Health: Investing in Health for Development* (Boulder, CO: Lynne Reiner Publishers, 2000).

7   Center for Reproductive Law and Policy (CRLP), "Cairo+5: Assessing US Support for Reproductive Health at Home and Abroad" (New York: 1998), 7.

8   United Nations Development Program (UNDP), *Human Development Report 1998* (New York: Oxford University Press, 1998).

9   Rather than "a compartmentalized and piecemeal approach," what is required "is a much bolder and holistic approach that addresses and tackles the real causes of underdevelopment." "The Statement of the Government of Eritrea," excerpt reprinted in Betsy Hartmann, *Reproductive Rights and Wrongs: The Global Politics of Population Control* (Cambridge, MA: South End Press, 1995), 152.

10 John Knodel and Gavin W. Jones, "Post-Cairo Population Policy: Does Promoting Girls' Schooling Miss the Mark?" *Population and Development Review*, Vol. 22, No. 4 (1996), 683–702. It is also important to look at the negative impact of rapid economic changes on male identities. See Margethe Silberschmidt, *Women Forget that Men are the Masters: Gender Antagonism and Socio-Economic Change in Kisii District, Kenya* (Somerset, NJ: Transaction Publishers, 1999).

11 For an in-depth picture of the neoliberal assault on basic health, see Jim Yong Kim, Joyce V. Millen, Alec Irwin, and John Gershman, eds., *Dying for Growth: Global Inequality and the Health of the Poor* (Monroe, ME: Common Courage Press, 2000).

12 Stephen F. Minkin, "Medical Research on AIDS in Africa–Comments," *Social Science and Medicine*, Vol. 33, No. 7, (1991), 786–790.

13 Barton Gellman, "US Targeting AIDS as a Security Threat," *International Herald Tribune*, May 2, 2000, 1.

14 Barton Gellman, "West Refused to Heed Early Warnings of Pandemic," *International Herald Tribune*, July 6, 2000, 1–2.

15 PANOS, "Diagnosing Challenges: Health and the New Millennium," *PANOS Briefing*, No. 36 (London: 1999).

16 WEDO, "Risks, Rights and Reforms," 11.

17 For concrete country case studies of the difficulties of implementing reproductive health programs in the context of declining health budgets and health sector reforms, see Forman and Ghosh, *Promoting Reproductive Health.*

18 Imrana Qadeer, "Reproductive Health and Rights: A Public Health Perspective," in Centre of Social Medicine and Community Health, *Reproductive Health in India's Primary Health Care* (New Delhi: Jawaharlal Nehru University, 1998), 11.

19 For a discussion of the current state of reproductive health, see *Reproductive Health Matters*, Vol. 7, No. 14 (1999), which is devoted to "Access to Reproductive Health: A Question of Distributive Justice."

20 For a discussion of these issues, see Betsy Hartmann, *Reproductive Rights and Wrongs*, 237–239.

21 Lisa Richey, "Development, Gender and Family Planning: Population Politics and the Tanzanian National Population Policy," PhD dissertation, (Chapel Hill, NC: University of North Carolina Political Science Department, 1999), 311.

22 Ibid., 310.

23 CRLP, "Cairo+5," 6. See also Judith E. Jacobsen, "The United States," in Forman and Ghosh, *Promoting Reproductive Health.* Jacobsen is more optimistic about progress towards implementing the Cairo agenda at USAID, but notes that program success is still largely measured in terms of reductions in fertility rates.

24 USAID, "Coverage with Quality," *Limited Scope Grant Agreement 527–0375*, signed in Lima, Peru, September 26, 1996, 4. This agreement can be found as an appendix to Elizabeth Liagin, "USAID and Involuntary Sterilization in Peru" (Bethesda, MD: Information Project for Africa, Inc., n.d.).

25 Latin American and Caribbean Committee for the Defense of Women's Rights (CLADEM), CRLP, and Estudio para la Defensa de los Derechos de la Mujer, "Women's Sexual and Reproductive Rights in Peru: A Shadow Report" (New York: CRLP, 1998).

26 Calvin Sims, "Using Gifts as Bait, Peru Sterilizes Poor Women," *New York Times*, February 15, 1998, 1.

27   Hartmann, *Reproductive Rights and Wrongs*. For a description of this process in Tanzania, see Richey, "Development, Gender and Family Planning."

28   See Dr. C. Sathyamala, *An Epidemiological Review of the Injectable Contraceptive, Depo-Provera* (Delhi: Medico Friend Circle and Forum for Women's Health, 2000).

29   Celia W. Dugger, "Relying on Hard and Soft Sells, India Pushes Sterilization," *New York Times,* June 22, 2001, 1. For an historical analysis of sterilization incentives in India, see Hartmann, *Reproductive Rights and Wrongs*.

30   See, for example, John Ward Anderson, "6 Billion and Counting—but Slower," *Washington Post,* October 12, 1999, A16.

31   Arachu Castro, "The Impact of the Epidemic of Cesarean Sections in the Fertility Decline in Mexico," paper presented to the Population Association of America Conference, panel on Fertility and Family Planning in Latin America (New York: March 26, 1999).

32   Human Rights Watch, Mexico, "A Job or Your Rights: Continued Sex Discrimination in Mexico's Maquiladora Sector," Human Rights Watch Report, Vol. 10, No. 1(B) (1998).

33   On Buffett's involvement, see Marie McCullough, "Polarization on Sterilization," *Philadelphia Inquirer,* February 28, 2000.

34   For an analysis of the Global Women's Health Movement, see Norma Swenson, "Global Health Movement," in Cheris Kramarae and Dale Spender, eds., *Encyclopedia of Women* (New York: Routledge, 2000).

35   See Jael Silliman, "Introduction" and "Expanding Civil Society, Shrinking Political Spaces: The Case of Women's Nongovernmental Organizations," in Jael Silliman and Ynestra King, eds., *Dangerous Intersections: Feminist Perspectives on Population, Environment and Development* (Cambridge, MA: South End Press, 1999).

36   Petchesky, "Reproductive and Sexual Rights," *UNRISD*, 51.

37   Ibid.

38   See Silliman, "Expanding Civil Society, Shrinking Political Spaces," *Dangerous Intersections*.

39   See Petchesky, "Reproductive and Sexual Rights," *UNRISD*, for an interesting discussion of this dilemma.

40   Mabel Bianco, "Monitoring Implementation of the Cairo Program of Action as a Women's Citizenship Practice in Five Latin American Countries," edited draft (Latin American and Caribbean Women's Health Network, November 9, 1998), 7.

41   Petchesky, "Reproductive and Sexual Rights," *UNRISD*, 41–42.

42   Martha De la Fuente, "Peru: Call for a Re-evaluation of the National Reproductive Health Program," *Women's Global Network for Reproductive Rights Newsletter,* No. 3 (1998), 7.

43   See Hartmann, *Reproductive Rights and Wrongs*, 131–155.

44   Randy Abelda, et al., *The War on the Poor: A Defense Manual* (New York: The New Press, 1996).

45 NOW Legal Defense and Education Fund and the Illinois Caucus for Adolescent Health, "Caught in the Crossfire," report of the Illinois Roundtable on Welfare, Reform, Women of Color and Reproductive Health (Chicago, IL: October 13, 1999), 1.

46 The Packard Foundation poured $13 million into the first year of the campaign, a five-year effort coordinated by the National Audubon Society, CARE, Communications Consortium Media Center, Planned Parenthood Federation of America, Population Action International and Save the Children. See Ken Strom, "Welcome to PLANet," *National Audubon Society Population and Habitat Newsletter*, 12.4 (2000), 1–2.

47 The ad can be viewed on www.familyplanet.org.

48 UNDP, *Human Development Report 1998*.

49 Hartmann, *Reproductive Rights and Wrongs*.

50 This parallels the mainstream abortion rights movement's decision to adopt more conservative messages to win public support. See William Saletan, "Electoral Politics and Abortion: Narrowing the Message," in Rickie Solinger, ed., *Abortion Wars: A Half Century of Struggle, 1950-2000* (Berkeley, CA: University of California Press, 1998).

51 For a critique of deep ecology, see Joni Seager, *Earth Follies: Coming to Feminist Terms with the Global Environmental Crisis* (New York: Routledge, 1993).

52 See Ramachandra Guha, "Radical American Environmentalism and Wilderness Preservation: A Third World Critique," *Environmental Ethics*, 2.1 (1989).

53 Gellman, "West Refused to Heed Early Warnings of Pandemic," *Herald Tribune*, 1.

54 Lester R. Brown, Gary Gardner, and Brian Halweil, *Beyond Malthus: Nineteen Dimensions of the Population Challenge* (New York: W.W. Norton, 1999). For a critique, see Lisa Richey, "Why 'Demographic Fatigue' Contributes Little to Our Understanding of Contemporary Africa," *Different Takes Issue Paper*, No. 3 (Amherst, MA: Hampshire College Population and Development Program, 2000).

55 See Rani Bhatia's essay in this anthology (chapter 11).

56 See Hartmann, "Population, Environment and Security: A New Trinity," in Silliman and King, eds., *Dangerous Intersections*.

57 Brian Nichiporuk, *The Security Dynamics of Demographic Factors* (Santa Monica, CA: Rand Corporation, 2000), xix.

58 Ibid., xx-xxi.

59 Quoted in Sarah Sexton, "Ten Reasons Why Genetically Engineered Food Won't Feed the World," *Different Takes Issue Paper*, No. 1 (Amherst, MA: Hampshire College Population and Development Program, 1999).

60 "DHS+ Measures Anemia Prevalence," DHS+ Dimensions, (n.d.), 9.

61 Almaz Sharmanov, *Anemia Testing Manual for Population-Based Surveys* (Calverton, MD: Macro International, Inc., January 2000).

62 Elizabeth Holt, Ties Boerma, and Robert Black, "The Challenges of Biological and Clinical Data Collection in Large-Scale Population-based

Surveys in Less Developed Countries," paper presented at the Conference on Biological and Clinical Data Collection in National Surveys—Potential and Issues, National Academy of Sciences (Washington, DC: January 24–25, 2000).

63 Ibid., 6.

64 See ibid., 4 for a discussion of satellite data and issues of confidentiality.

65 Dorothy Roberts, *Killing the Black Body: Race Reproduction and the Meaning of Liberty* (New York: Pantheon Books, 1997), 200.

66 For an interesting discussion of the differences between modern and post-modern control of reproduction, and the understanding of the body, see Adele Clarke, "Modernity, Postmodernity and Reproductive Processes ca. 1890-1990," in Chris Hables Gray, ed., *The Cyborg Handbook* (New York: Routledge, 1995). Also see for more information on genetic technologies: Corner House, "If Cloning is the Answer, What was the Question?," Briefing No. 16 (October 1999). Available at www.icaap.org/ Cornerhouse/.

67 Marcy Darnovsky, "The New Eugenics: The Case Against Genetically Modified Humans," *Different Takes Issue Paper*, No. 4 (Amherst, MA: Hampshire College Population and Development Program, 2000). Lee Silver lays out this scenario in *Remaking Eden: Cloning and Beyond in a Brave New World* (New York: Avon, 1997).

Chapter 11

Greening the Swastika

Nativism and Anti-Semitism in the Population and Environment Debate

Rajani Bhatia

For nearly a decade the Committee on Women, Population and the Environment[1] has kept a watchful eye out for anti-immigrant racism, nativism, and eugenics emerging at the population-environment nexus.[2] Still largely unnoticed, this agenda advances behind the neutral pretense of mainstream rhetoric on population and the environment. A complex web of organizations and individuals, backed by ultraconservative funders, has oriented programs concerning population and the environment within a nativist framework. Taking advantage of the mainstream alarm regarding population growth, this lobby exploits the construct singling out population size as a primary cause of environmental degradation.

An examination into the way the radical right conceptualizes population and environment reveals ideological underpinnings which resonate from Nazi discourse on these concepts. Through both its ideology and policies, Nazi Germany set a precedent and predisposed future ideas of population and the environment to fascist interpretations.

The Nazis understood population in the context of a social Darwinist struggle between races for survival and power. They viewed population as an aggressive force, a means by which races compete against each other to occupy and control space and land. They depicted population pressures from Eastern Europe as a threat to German *Lebensräume* or living spaces.[3] Current right-wing rhetoric on population in the United States portrays the presence of immigrants as a threat to "American" culture. In this conception, "culture" replaces "race" as the primary category of division among peoples, but the idea of population as a hostile force by which one group generatively competes against another remains the same.

Since population is not understood in a strict numerical sense as a conglomeration of individuals, it is entirely relevant which people make up population. The right-wing conception of population borrows much from the mainstream projection of an absolute "overpopulation" in the global South. For half a century, international population control policies stemming from the United States and the United Nations have sought to control the fertility rates in the so-called Third World, primarily through the scientific development and administration of birth control.

The global "overpopulation crisis" as projected by the mainstream produced images of illiterate, poor, dark-skinned masses, breeding indiscriminately to the point where they would spill beyond their country's borders. Since white people from the North are not perceived as part of the population problem, the notion of population itself does not connotatively encompass them. The people who make up population, therefore, are "foreign," "alien," teeming masses of poor people of color from the South.

If white Americans are not conceived of as part of population, where do they fall in the population-environment link? The Nazi conception of the environment, through the notion of an intimately bound "blood and soil," projected the German people as part of the environment or landscape. Nazi ideologues posited an exclusive, even mystical connection of the German people to the land or environment. Not only were Germans thought to have a higher propensity than others to care for the environment, the mere presence of the "superior" race enhanced rather than degraded it. Similarly, the anti-immigrant, radical right interpretation of the link between population and environment in the United States views "American" culture as an integral part of an environment enclosed by the US borders. In this conception, environment is not treated as global in scope. Protecting the environment translates foremost into protecting white, American culture, or the "European derived" peoples.

Similar to an environmental campaign to protect an endangered species, the right wing focuses on protecting "American" culture. In concrete terms, this means a rejection of multiculturalism, diversity, bilingualism, and immigrant rights coupled with intensive immigration and fertility controls. The extreme right wing position on population and the environment is not a study of the way humans interact with the non-human environment. Instead, the assertion "population growth is a primary cause of environmental degradation" unleashes nativist impulses in defense of "American" culture and heritage against increases in non-"American" population. Moreover, "Americans" are absolved of responsibility for environmental problems. As part of the environment, they cannot contribute to the population-environment tension which results in environmental degradation.

An examination of Nazi ideas of policy on population and the environment underscores not only the possibility but also a tradition of fascist interpretation and application of these concepts in socially regressive ways. Current right-wing trends on population and the environment in the United States exhibit these very racist and nativist impulses. Broad-based, mainstream discourse on population and the environment has largely served to mask the radical right orientation of this movement. However, the construction of a neofascist manifestation of these concepts has in some cases become increasingly explicit.

National Socialist Preoccupation with Population

The term population already has significant associations with the Nazi period in Germany, given the epitomization of genocide through the Holocaust. Yet, the extent to which population sciences and prominent demographers of the time fueled the system of hate and assisted in defining and locating peoples who were subsequently deported and annihilated remains under-acknowledged.

In their book *Berechnung und Beschwörung* (my translation: *Calculation and Conjuration*), historian Susanne Heim and filmmaker

Ulrike Schaz trace the population problems outlined by demographers and economists just prior to the Second World War. At the 1935 International Conference of Population Science in Berlin, Friedrich Zahn, Friedrich Burgdörfer, and Felix Boesler presented calculations of losses to German "Volkskapital" or human capital caused by falling birth rates, "racial alienation" amid the growing presence of immigrants, and welfare paid to the mentally and physically disabled.[4] They treated "population" not only in the abstract numerical sense used by statisticians, but in the explicit market terms of supply and demand for a raw material or product, and in terms of profit and loss to the state's budget.

Susanne Heim and Ulrike Schaz describe the process beginning at the end of the First World War in which German population experts produced dire warnings of "population pressures" from the East, conjuring fears of immigration by Jewish and Slavic peoples. Falling birth rates in Germany alongside rising birth rates in Eastern and Southern Europe bred perceptions of "infiltration" or population "pressure." Harold Callender, writing in a *New York Times* article in 1933, described population growth rates in the countries of Eastern and Southern Europe as a source for political instability in Western and Northern Europe. "One of the main reasons for Germany's very genuine apprehension regarding her Eastern frontiers is the fact that the Poles, while less than half as numerous as the Germans in the Reich, multiply at more than twice the rate of the Germans."[5] Callender quotes Dr. Hans Harmsen, member of both the German Academy and the German Society of Population Sciences who proclaimed, "The danger for Germany and Austria, is that both face, in the east and south, extremely prolific peoples."[6]

A clear intersection between anti-immigration and anti-Semitism is revealed in an illustration stemming from a 1934 slide series prepared by the Race Policy Office of the Nazi party. It depicts thirteen migrant women, men, and children entering Germany from the East. Some carry belongings slung in bags over their shoulders and walking canes. Superimposed over a small map of Germany, their bodies are disproportionately large in size and appear to be covering the map. The caption reads, "Daily 13 Jews!

Immigrated from 1910 till 1925 from Eastern Europe into Germany."[7] Erich Rosenthal, in his study on trends in Jewish population in early twentieth century Germany, reported that the German Statistical Office used results from the 1933 census in Germany to classify the Jewish population by both nativity and citizenship in order to build "a further basis upon which Jews could be classed as aliens."[8] Current anti-immigrant messages arising from experts in the population field, therefore, have notable historical antecedents.

According to Susanne Heim and Ulrike Schaz, many of the experts concerned with population made recommendations prior to the war's beginning, which read like a handbook for German occupation policy later. Prior to Germany's occupation of Poland in 1939, for example, a school of influential economists and demographers from the Königsburg Institute for East European Economy and Institute for Population Sciences defined Poland's population problems and proposed solutions. In 1935, an influential book by Theodor Oberländer, director of the Königsburg Institute, depicted excess rural population, which he presumed to number from 4.3 to 7.1 million people, as the central problem of Poland's economy.[9]

According to Oberländer, the weight of Poland's rural population inhibited its agrarian sector from producing surpluses, which in turn, prevented the development of industry needed to absorb population excess. Oberländer also published ratios of productive workers to "mere mouths" in the agrarian sector of Romania (1:0.6), Bulgaria (1:0.7), and Yugoslavia (1:1.09).[10] From the same institute in 1938 appeared a 700-page book by Peter-Heinz Seraphim, which blamed "overpopulation" in Poland and elsewhere in Eastern Europe on the predominance of Jews in industrial, urban areas.[11] Seraphim justified anti-Semitism on the basis of "economic" reasons, arguing that "for years young generations of farmers' sons of the native folk have been prevented by the Jewish element to make a living in the cities. The cities were 'blocked' by the Jews! Now, the moment has come to break this monopoly!"[12]

In 1939, the Economics Ministry of the newly set up Occupation Government in central Poland announced a policy of dissolving Jewish shops and businesses, in order to provide work for "excess rural population" and reduce "agrarian overpopulation."[13] As the Nazis invaded eastward into the Soviet Union, they implemented policies of selective pro-fatalism. "Existence worthy" workers would be "Germanized" (taught discipline and a faster work tempo), while "undesirables" or "excess" populations would be resettled on the periphery or eliminated. Heim and Schaz argue that German Nazis developed techniques of war not simply to subjugate or gain military victory through an attack, but to depopulate areas under their control. Depopulation was not an end in itself, but a means to free up raw materials and food.[14] The German military isolated urban areas from rural, in order to cut off their food supply. In this way they planned the systematic death by starvation of millions of people. Four weeks prior to the attack on the Soviet Union, a German military officer gave this directive:

> Ten millions of people will become ... superfluous and will die or be forced to emigrate to Siberia. Attempts to save these peoples from starvation through provisions from the Schwarzerdezone (a particularly fertile agrarian region of the Ukraine) can only succeed at the expense of sustaining Europe. They will weaken Germany's ability to hold out during war."[15]

Whether or not population and war policy actually converged, concepts stemming from the population field, such as "pressure," "superfluous," or "excess" became intrinsic parts of Nazi thinking and annihilation policy.

Susanne Heim and Ulrike Schaz also describe the policies of selective anti-natalism among forced labor in Germany. Pregnant French workers were given extra provisions and allowed to return home, while expectant Russian and Polish workers were not only denied these protections but also forced to continue working under particularly harmful conditions, causing many to miscarry.[16]

Leonardo Conti, the health minister of the Reich, dictated the policy of exploiting East women laborers urgently needed for arms production, while preventing their reproduction. In "East Workers and Population Policy," Conti wrote that anyone who thought that miscarriages or abortions among East European women went against the German interest for a future supply of workers was completely off the mark and showed little understanding of population policy.[17] Heim and Schaz document the application of a host of other eugenic and population control policies, forced sterilizations, and birth control campaigns alongside rigorous pro-natalist campaigns among German women.

How exactly did population experts at that time perceive "population"? Gunther Ipsen, a colleague of Oberländer and Seraphim at the Institute for Population Sciences in Königsburg, defined population in 1933 not merely as the sum of individuals, but as the pressure by which a race actively fills its area of rule and proves the power of its existence. Ipsen viewed population as divided into unified groups ("folk" or "race"), which could be differentiated on the basis of presumed common, generative behavior.[18] Ipsen also invoked the idea of "living space" occupied by races into a central category of his theory.

From this framework, Ipsen interpreted population problems of his time, echoing his contemporaries. To him, the building of an industrial Europe was a struggle of races, and he blamed falling birth rates in Germany on the system of Versailles, which destroyed the will of the German race to resist and survive. He depicted the "German population question as primarily a question of the German East…. Corresponding to the direction of pressure from overpopulated to underpopulated areas, the German folk are almost everywhere on the defensive, while an attack from the East advances."[19] In today's right-wing conceptualization of population, "culture" replaces "race" as the primary category of division among peoples, and cultures are likewise depicted in a constant state of competition and conflict.

William Seltzer's study on the role of statistical systems in carrying out the Holocaust evaluates the potential for abuse of different types of data collection. According to Seltzer, frequently updated registries with information on Jews, more so than traditional censuses, aided Holocaust operations. His examination of these systems in Germany, Poland, France, the Netherlands, and Norway during the Second World War reveal similarities:

> In all these countries there was an initial classification and count early in the process, a continuing interest in data to describe the

size, structure, and conditions of the Jewish population, and the use of unprotected microdata (that is, data that permit the identification of individual persons) to aid in rounding people up for internment and deportation.[20]

Seltzer's comparative study notes that the highly acclaimed and comprehensive Dutch registry consequentially led to higher Jewish mortality. Seventy-three percent of Dutch Jews were killed, in comparison with 40 percent of Belgian Jews, and 25 percent of French Jews.[21] The 1939 census in Germany was among the resources used by the Gestapo to compile deportation lists. Friedrich Burgdörfer, professor of statistics and population policy at the University of Munich and director of the German Statistical Office, wrote the instructions to identify "racial" Jews.[22]

In addition to his work on this census, Burgdörfer proposed the "Madagaskar-Plan," which envisioned the transport of Europe's Jews to Madagascar.[23] Dr. Roderich Plate, who headed the entire census activity, served directly under both Himmler and Eichmann, two of the highest ranking leaders in the Nazi hierarchy, and "appears to have provided Eichmann with the population statistics used at the Wannsee Conference," where the final solution was conceived.[24]

Dr. Richard Korherr, Himmler's inspector of statistics in 1943, had earlier participated in the 1935 and 1937 International Population Conferences held in Berlin and Paris. In 1938, as Director of Statistics for the municipality of Würzburg, he hosted the annual meeting of the German Statistical Society attended by Roderich Plate, Friedrich Burgdörfer, and Friedrich Zahn. Under Himmler's order, Korherr prepared a statistical report, dated March 23, 1943, with comprehensive data on the Jewish population, and its changes over time, in Germany. It reported on the number of Jews "evacuated," in ghettoes, in concentration camps, in prisons, and in forced labor.[25] Hitler saw a condensed version of this report. In the preliminary remarks to the report, Korherr blamed any inaccuracies on

> the character and development of Judaism, its definition, the many thousand years of restless wandering, the numerous conversions to and from Judaism, the efforts toward integration,

the miscegenation with the native population and above all the efforts of the Jews to avoid registration.... [As a result,] errors of classification tend to vary in inverse proportion to the amount of Jewish blood.[26]

Korherr, like many other well-established demographers of his time, unambiguously served the operation of genocide.

National Socialist Preoccupation with the Environment

National Socialism's preoccupation with environmental themes was partially born out of a populist tradition from nineteeth-century Germany known as the *völkisch* movement. Significant impulses of the *völkisch* movement included ethnocentrism and racism alongside agrarian mysticism, and obsession with naturalism and purity. The movement has also been described as essentially romantic, anti-urban, and anti-rational.[27] In this developing conception of environment, the German *Volk* or people became an intrinsic part of the landscape, believed to have organic ties to the land and forests.

The notion of "blood and soil" expressed rootedness, purity, and a mystical connection specifically between German people and German land. Such depiction laid the groundwork for discontent with anything foreign.

For the enthusiasts of Blut and Boden [blood and soil], the Jews especially were a rootless, wandering people, incapable of any true relationship with the land. German blood, in other words, engendered an exclusive claim to the sacred German soil.[28]

Environment articulated in terms of sacredness, nature worship, nature reverence, holism, harmony, and interconnectedness alludes not only to the romanticism of the period, but to the fundamentalism which began developing in response to the real displacements of modernity. Völkisch thinking enjoyed continued expression during the early twentieth century, culminating in the 1920s through a back-to-nature, youth movement known as "Wandervögel," and conservationist nature protection organizations. Peter Staudenmaier draws on the example of a 1923 call for recruitment from the League for the Protection and Consecration of the German Forest to demonstrate the extent to which German ethnocentrism and environmentalism were bound together.

> In every German breast the German forest quivers; ... in all German souls the German forest lives and weaves with its depth and breadth, ... it is the source of German inwardness, of the German soul, of German freedom. Therefore protect and care for the German forest for the sake of the elders and the youth, and join the new German "League for the Protection and Consecration of the German Forest."[29]

Indeed, extracting German national ethos from this ad would fundamentally alter its pro-environmental content.

From Ernst Moritz Arndt's 1815 article, "On the Care and Conservation of Forests," to Ludwig Klages's 1913 essay, "Man and Earth" and thereafter, early contributors to environmental thought in Germany have at the same time been implicated for their extreme racist, nationalist, and socially regressive ideas.

Yet, some of them continue to receive uncritical recognition in today's green circles. The German zoologist, Ernst Haeckel, for example, who coined the term "ecology," establishing it as a science in the 1860s, also introduced social Darwinism to Germany. He promoted the idea of "natural law" determining racial hierarchy, Nordic racial superiority, and eugenics. His particularly German variant of social Darwinism conceived of the "fittest" not in terms of an individual, but rather in terms of race.[30] Therefore, from its very inception, scientific ecology incorporated ideas of biological determinism and eugenics.

This range of ideas, from agrarian romanticism to social Darwinism, intimately bound to the study of how organisms interact with their environments, found resonance in National Socialist ideology. National Socialism elicited some policies familiarly environmental. Especially during the early years after their rise to power, the Nazis institutionalized and spread methods of organic farming, established the first ecological preservation sites in Europe, and implemented programs of reforestation and animal and plant species protection. They also promoted ecologically responsible industrial development and technology. The 1935 *Reichsnaturschutzgesetz* (nature protection law), an accomplishment of Nazi ecologists, established rules of special protection for flora, fauna, and undeveloped lands.[31] Staudenmaier muses on the ecological outlook of leaders in the Nazi hierarchy:

> Hitler and Himmler were both strict vegetarians and animal lovers, attracted to nature mysticism and homeopathic cures, and staunchly opposed to vivisection and cruelty to animals. Himmler even established experimental organic farms to grow herbs for SS medicinal purposes. And Hitler, at times, could sound like a veritable Green utopian, discussing authoritatively and in detail various renewable energy sources (including environmentally appropriate hydropower and producing natural gas from sludge) as alternatives to coal, and declaring "water, winds and tides" as the energy path of the future.[32]

While the Nazi record on the environment may at first appear redeeming, it is crucial to understand that this program was intimately linked in ideology and in practice to some of the worst crimes against humanity. There were several prominent leaders in the "Green Wing" of the Nazi Party. Richard Walther Darre, a leading Nazi ecologist, served as minister of agriculture. In spite of writings replete with anti-Semitic sentiments (Darre referred to Jews as "weeds"), his implementation of broad-based organic farming practices and ecologically sound land use planning has continued to impress some contemporary Greens.

Staudenmaier addresses the apparent contradiction between Nazi agrarian predilections and the rapid industrial expansion which took place during their twelve-year rule. Even those in charge of modernization processes like the construction of the "Autobahn" or highway did so along green lines. According to Minister Fritz Todt, for example, "The fulfillment of mere transportation purposes is not the final aim of German highway construction. The German highway must be an expression of its surrounding landscape and an expression of the German essence."[33] In addition to the "Green Wing" Nazi leadership, the base membership of the party included a significant proportion of environmental activists. By 1939, 60 percent of the membership of Weimar-era nature protection organizations had joined the Nazi Party.[34]

At the same time, green views in the Nazi party elicited policies of expansion and extermination. Richard Walther Darre, as minister of agriculture, led significant aspects of the implementation of the anti-urban agenda. Darre recalled the idea of "blood and soil" to instigate and justify expansionist policy in the East. "The concept of Blood and Soil gives us the moral right to take back as much land in the East as is necessary to establish a harmony between the body of our Volk and the geopolitical space."[35] Darre's statement along with the following from Himmler, which stems from a 1942 decree on the treatment of the Eastern territories, reveal the interwoven ideas at the crux of ecofascist thought: preoccupation with living space needed to realize an exclusive (superior) racial connection to nature. Himmler's decree stated:

> The peasant of our racial stock has always carefully endeavored to increase the natural powers of the soil, plants, and animals, and to preserve the balance of the whole of nature. For him, respect for divine creation is the measure of all culture. If, therefore, the new *Lebensräume* (living spaces) are to become a homeland for our settlers, the planned arrangement of the landscape to keep it close to nature is a decisive prerequisite. It is one of the bases for fortifying the German *Volk*.[36]

Himmler not only reiterates the idea of connectedness between the German "Volk" and the landscape, but also asserts that Germans, on account of their supposedly advanced culture, are naturally inclined to better care for and preserve the environment. He suggests that by expanding and occupying new territories, Germans do the environment a favor.

Alfred Rosenberg, a chief Nazi ideologue and ecologist, in his 1938 book *The Myth of the 20th Century*, expressed fear of encroachment on "living spaces" and urban resentment. "Today we see the steady stream from the countryside to the city, deadly for the *Volk*. The cities swell ever larger, unnerving the *Volk* and destroying the threads which bind humanity to nature; they attract adventurers and profiteers of all colors, thereby fostering racial chaos."[37]

The anti-urban and anti-modern aspects of Nazi environmentalism were invoked in Darre's plans as minister of agriculture to "reagrarianize" land under Nazi control. The fact that Jews largely inhabited urban areas became "proof" of their supposed inability to relate to nature.[38] The idea that non-Germans did not innately hold a bond to nature, were not considered part of nature's totality, or worse, were considered part of the destructive forces on nature, reflects the twisted logic that can be implicated in leading to policies of annihilation. Therefore, the National Socialist imperative to restore nature fueled anti-Semitism and incited "solutions" necessitating the "removal" of Jews and other non-Germans from the revered landscape. The constrictions of "natural order" or contemplation of environmental problems in the absence of a social context prevented any alternative.

Current Dangerous Population-Environment Trends

The examination of Nazi preoccupation with population and the environment highlights that these concepts are not immune from deployment by the radical right to serve an ethnocentric, racist agenda. While the role each term played in Nazi Germany was evaluated separately, thrown into the current rise of right wing interpretations of population and environment is the connection established between the two concepts three decades ago.

As the presumed threat of "overpopulation" to the world's food supply became increasingly discredited, environmental degradation emerged as a legitimization for global population control.[39] In the late 1960s and 1970s, mainstream organizations concerned with population first promoted the idea that "overpopulation" threatens the environment, which soon gained a foothold in mainstream environmental organizations such as the Sierra Club and the National Audubon Society.[40]

During the last decade, a new lobby of organizations focusing on the United States began to produce a particularly reactionary take on the population and environment connection.[41] In this scenario, just as in the Nazi interpretation, environment refers increasingly to "American" society and culture, in addition to the physical ecosystem enclosed by United States boundaries. It is not global in orientation.

Increasingly detached from international development discourse, the reactionary interpretation of population encompasses a worldview in which people, divided primarily along race and ethnic lines, compete with each other for power and survival. In this struggle, immigration and fertility can be used as demographic ammunition to encroach upon a "host" society. "Host" or "native" societies refer to white people from the North, while population itself is personified by the "overbreeding" poor, and people of color from the South. The political ramifications of the by now well established construct, "population growth degrades the environment," become clearer, especially when population growth is understood mainly as rising rates of "foreign" immigration and fertility.

The right-wing population and environment lobby comprises a complex network of organizations, key individuals, and foundations, which articulate opposition to immigration in the context of a broader set of conservative goals. Following a brief encapsulation of key figures involved in the right-wing population-environment lobby, and main points of their agenda, the lobby's theories on environment and population are examined to reveal an ideological orientation which mirrors Nazi conceptualizations of these themes. The essay examines why these dangerous trends remain cloaked by popular, depoliticized conceptions of population and the environment.

The Lobby and Network

Garrett Hardin, professor of human ecology at University of California, Santa Barbara, and Virginia Abernethy, professor of psychiatry at Vanderbilt University School of Medicine, are leading advocates of the anti-immigrant, environmental movement. They steer a host of organizations that embrace right-wing environmentalist thought and promote anti-immigrant racism. These include Federation for American Immigration Reform (FAIR), Carrying Capacity Network (CCN), Population-Environment Balance (PEB), Californians for Population Stabilization (CAPS), California Coalition for Immigration Reform (CCIR), and Negative Population Growth (NPG). Abernethy sits on the board of directors for both CCN and PEB, while Hardin presides in various steering and advisory roles for CAPS, PEB (as honorary chairman and advisory board member), and FAIR. The Weeden, and S.H. Cowell

Foundations, which fund NPG, FAIR, CCN, PEB, and CAPS, also fund the "English Only" movement, another nativist impulse in the United States. There are many intersections between these movements. For example, FAIR's founder, John Tanton, also founded the anti-bilingual group US English.[42] FAIR receives funding from the Pioneer Fund, which has a history of supporting eugenics research.

Founded in 1937, the first president of the Pioneer Fund, Harry Laughlin, wrote the Model Eugenic Sterilization Law, enacted by twenty-seven states in various versions. It resulted in the forced sterilization of over 60,000 people.[43] The fund supported South Africa's system of apartheid and opposed desegregation in the United States. It finances the work of numerous "professors of hate," some with clear ties to white supremacist and Nazi activities, and many who attempt to "prove" genetic inferiority of people of color.[44]

The research of Garret Hardin, J. Philippe Rushton, and Richard Lynn, all recipients of Pioneer Fund grants, figures prominently in current right wing conceptualizations linking population and the environment. A notorious eugenicist, Rushton teaches psychology at the University of Western Ontario, and is known for his theory on racial differences, based on what he sees as an inverse relationship between sex organs and brain size.[45] Richard Lynn is a psychology professor at the University of Ulster in Northern Ireland. Lynn advocates eugenics, classifying the poor and sick as "weak specimens whose proliferation needs to be discouraged in the interests of the improvement of the genetic quality of the group, and ultimately of group survival."[46] The writings of Rushton, Lynn, and Hardin are featured on pro-eugenics websites.

Relatively new on the scene is Kevin MacDonald, professor of psychology at California State University at Long Beach. Recently he testified on behalf of David Irving, who denies the existence of gas chambers at Auschwitz and disputes the number of Jewish victims of the Holocaust. Irving accused Deborah Lipstadt of libeling him in her 1993 book, *Denying the Holocaust: The Growing Assault on Truth and Memory*. MacDonald is currently the editor of *Population and Environment*, a peer-reviewed journal published by Kluwer Aca-

demic/Human Sciences Press. Virginia Abernethy edited the journal prior to MacDonald for eleven years until July 1999. She
continues to sit on the journal's advisory board alongside Garrett
Hardin and J. Philippe Rushton.

The Agenda

Common campaigns of the population-environment extreme
include opposition to multiculturalism, bilingual education, affirmative action, dual citizenship, citizenship rights to children born to undocumented parents, and welfare rights for elderly and disabled
immigrants. Some of these are echoed in the following excerpt from
Carrying Capacity Network's 1999 report on the decade, under the
heading, "American Culture and National Unity":

> Mass immigration is fueling the widening gap between haves
> and have-nots, balkanization, "identity politics" and multicul-
> turalism that threaten to tear our country apart.... CCN believes
> strongly that social cohesion is a cornerstone in building a sus-
> tainable society. Thus, we are increasing our effort to support
> educational reform and oppose racial preferences, bilingual edu-
> cation, multiculturalism, and dual citizenship.[47]

Beyond mere rhetoric, CCN articulates a clear platform and set of
objectives, some of which were echoed in legislation during the last
decade (for example, Propositions 187 and 209 in California and
federal welfare and immigration "reform" laws in 1996).

The right-wing network has also impacted more moderate environmental organizations and publications in terms of policy and
agenda setting. In a highly organized effort in 1998, PEB, FAIR,
and the Sierrans for US Population Stabilization (SUSPS) came
close to successfully lobbying Sierra Club members to vote for a
call for net reductions in immigration as part of a "comprehensive
population policy for the United States," known as Alternative A.[48]
Sixty percent of the Club membership voted instead for Alternative B, which not only affirmed the Club's neutral policy on immigration, but also called instead for women's empowerment, human
rights, and environmentally responsible consumption to address
the root causes of migration and global population problems. Dis-

turbingly, only a few months after the vote, proponents of Alternative B were taken off the Club's National Population Committee and the Sierra Club Board of Directors changed Club policy to advocate for population reductions in the United States and the world. In her analysis of these changes, Betsy Hartmann writes, "the recent policy shift from population stabilization to population reductions reflects the disenfranchisement of those who supported the Alternative B approach to population issues as well as the growing power of anti-immigrant opponents."[49]

E Magazine has recently featured articles replete with alarmist rhetoric on population and the environment. In an article on US population, the magazine's editor, Jim Motavalli, gives ample voice to Abernethy, PEB, NPG and others, as he argues that US population growth primarily fueled by immigration will devastate the environment and ends by asking, "If there's one thing that Americans can agree on, it's that we need to hold onto our dwindling natural heritage. And what chance is there of doing that if, as predicted, the US population doubles to 500 million by 2100?" Motavalli's use of "Americans" and "heritage" appeals unambiguously to a sense of nativism.[50]

In her exploration of recent anti-immigration environmental trends, Syd Lindsley draws attention to the number of mainstream environmental organizations signing onto ASAP (Alliance for Stabilizing America's Population), a PEB initiative begun in 1997. ASAP calls on the President and Congress to institute immigration moratoriums, do away with amnesty programs, step up deportation of undocumented immigrants, and even repeal citizenship rights to their children.

> About half of ASAP's signatories are groups working primarily on land and wildlife protection and restoration issues including: Earth First! (LA), the Gaia Institute, the Inland Empire Public Lands Council, the International Society for the Preservation of the Tropical Rainforest, Northwest Environmental Advocates, and many more.[51]

On the question of why ASAP appeals to well-intentioned environmental advocates, Lindsley contends that a "lack of social anal-

ysis leaves such organizations open and vulnerable to racist
scapegoating messages cloaked in the language of sustainability."⁵²

Unlike mainstream organizations concerned with "overpopulation," the population-environment right prioritizes anti-immigration
stances over fertility reduction schemes involving the development
and dissemination of birth control. The right wing views individuals
as prone to fertility behavior genetically determined by their race or
ethnicity. Garrett Hardin, for example, rejects contraception as a
primary means for reducing population. "Better technology is always welcome, of course, but improvements in reproductive control will not, by themselves, keep the human race from 'trashing'
the environment that supports it."⁵³ For the anti-immigrant, population-environment lobby, birth control can only marginally affect
population growth rates. Therefore, their main response to population and environmental problems is to prevent "the highly fertile" from entering United States borders.

The Ideology—On Environment

For this anti-immigration contingency, "culture" or ethnicity
has replaced "race" as the primary category of division between
peoples. Janet Biehl observes this phenomenon in her account of
ecofascism in today's Germany, where ideas about the organic
connections between German *Volk* (people), *Heimat* (homeland),
and *Lebensräume* (living spaces) have begun to reassert themselves
not only in neofascist organizations and parties, but in green and
new age circles.⁵⁴ "Most often, the far right claims to be defending
cultures rather than races; if the Nazis persecuted those who practiced '*race* mixing' and sought to preserve '*racial* purity,' today's fas-
cists say they oppose *cultural* mixing and seek to preserve their
culture."⁵⁵ Indeed, European and Anglo-American "culture" is
treated as an imperiled species close to extinction, and ever threatened by an "onslaught" of immigrants and "overpopulation."

Ecofascist trends on both sides of the Atlantic refer to their
primary culture of concern as part of the environment, part of that
which needs protection. Other non-"native" cultures, on the other
hand, belong to the degrading elements, those which destroy the
environment. For example, according to Herbert Gruhl, a founder

of the right wing Ecological Democratic Party in Germany, European culture will "perish not because of the degeneration of its own people, as previous high civilizations have, but because of physical laws: the constantly overflowing mass of humanity on an earth's surface that remains constant."[56]

Similarly, in the United States, perceptions of environment include treatment of the white "American" culture as a species on the verge of extinction. For example, American white supremacist Tom Metzger notes, "it seems to me that as we are becoming more aware of our precarious state, the white man, the white woman's state in the world, being only about 10 percent of the population, we begin to sympathize, empathize more, with the wolves and other animals."[57] Similar to the predicament of an endangered environment, both Gruhl and Metzger describe their cultures as "perishing" or in a "precarious state."

Like the "blood and soil" connection established by Nazi ideologues, the rhetoric of the right-wing, population and environment lobby views an organic bond between "American" culture and "American" land or environment. It bemoans the loss or corruption of "American" culture and values, blaming this on theories of "cultural alienation" caused by immigration of non-"European-derived" cultures.

The Ideology—On Population

In the radical right's perception, population does not refer to a mere statistical conglomeration of individuals. Population represents, as in the Nazi antecedent, the threat of a culture, which can assert its power in demographic terms, encroaching on the space of a "host" society. In this case, population has come to denote the expanding presence of poor people of color from the South in a white, "host" society in the North. Mainstream organizations preoccupied with global "overpopulation" often fuel this conception of population by leaving whites out of alarmist images and metaphors used to depict population problems.

Interestingly, current right-wing thinkers on population do not entertain the idea of development. In this matter they distinguish themselves clearly from the mainstream population field. Hardin and Abernethy, for example, reject outright and blame foreign aid and welfare for fueling rapid population growth. They denounce the idea that development can bring to the countries of the South a demographic transition (the transition to low fertility and low mortality rates) as experienced in the North. Not only are development schemes ineffective in reducing population quantity, Hardin contends that they compromise population "quality."

> Consider the matter of charity. When one saves a starving man, one may thereby help him to breed more children…. Every time a philanthropist sets up a foundation to look for a cure for a certain disease, he thereby threatens humanity eugenically."[58]

Without development, the extreme right-wing population-environmentalists forgo an international reception to their ideas. This is reflected in their inward looking agenda, which promotes United States nativism in opposition to multiculturalism.

The anti-immigrant population-environment lobby displays a particular contempt for multiculturalism and diversity, which it says will ultimately lead to balkanization, and "race or culture wars." This mirrors the social Darwinist divisions and struggles between races depicted in Nazi discussions on population. For example, Hardin notes that "the blessings of 'diversity' evaporate when we try to meld many cultures into one. Recurrent violence in the Balkans and in the Near East indicates that the most dependable outcome of 'multiculturalism' is the violence of civic disorder."[59] This theme is further developed by Kevin MacDonald, who assumes that ethnic conflict is something natural, having "deep biological roots."[60] He relies on theories which describe ethnicity and ethnic conflict as either a product of human biological predisposition or "evolved psychological adaptation." According to MacDonald, these theories establish the primacy of ethnicity or culture over class-based divisions in society. Outward signs of ethnic group membership including "physical features, religion, and, not uncommonly, clothing or other obvious markers of group membership," he claims, ultimately begin in the genes.[61] MacDonald posits that ethnic groups, when not involved in violent conflict, engage in ethnic competition via migration and fertility:

> Immigration policy and group differences in fertility influence
> political power within and between societies, often with explo-
> sive results. Demographic expansion has often been an instru-
> ment of ethnic competition and is an important source of
> conflict in the contemporary world.[62]

MacDonald contends that this type of demographic encroachment
sets off the "social identity mechanisms" of the "host" society,
which in the extreme can lead to various forms of ethnic cleansing.

Not surprisingly, MacDonald interprets both immigration and
fertility as forms of aggression on "European-derived" peoples,
harkening back to the combative notion of population prominent
during the Nazi era in Germany. He warns, "It is noteworthy that
minority groups, especially African-American and Latino groups,
have already developed strong ethnic identities in the United
States. These movements often have militant, racialist over-
tones…. Latino ethnic activists have a clearly articulated policy of
'reconquering' parts of the United States via immigration and high
birth rates."[63]

Virginia Abernethy echoes this idea in an editorial in *Population
and Environment*, "The root causes [of the Kosovo conflict] are the
combination of immigration and the much higher fertility rate of
Albanians, who are mostly Muslim."[64] She suggests that a similar
secessionist conflict will arise in the United States, due to high immigration and fertility of Latinos. Mexicans, in particular, she
points out, are planning an irredentist movement, called *Aztlan*, to
reconquer the states of California, Arizona, New Mexico, Texas,
and southern Colorado.

Moreover, Kevin MacDonald's views on immigration and fertility are linked to his primary work on Judaism stemming from a
three-volume work, presently under investigation by the
Anti-Defamation League.[65] In this trilogy, Kevin MacDonald depicts Judaism as a "group evolutionary strategy," a genetic blue-
print of behavior, which predicts that individual Jews across the
Diaspora will engage in positive eugenics and form cohesive and
exclusive groups, in order to ensure their primacy in a social Dar-
winian struggle for power and survival. MacDonald claims that
Jews had an ulterior motive in initiating and carrying out promi-

nent intellectual and political movements of the past century. In his view, these movements, which include the Boasian school of anthropology, psychoanalysis, and leftist ideology and activism, primarily serve Jewish interests, or "evolutionary group strategy."

MacDonald views United States immigration and fertility rates among ethnic minorities within this overall framework of a larger conspiracy by Jewish communities around the world to protect themselves and their interests. Population problems manifest in immigration levels and fertility rates, he claims, have somehow benefited Jewish ethnic interests at the expense of non-Jewish "natives." MacDonald's analysis recalls the popular *völkisch* sentiment during the 1920s in Germany, which imagined a Jewish world conspiracy behind all the social problems stemming from modernization.[66] MacDonald's techniques of scapegoating may have evolved in complexity from classical Nazi fascism, but the similarities are far from remote. Therefore, the influence of MacDonald's perspectives on US immigration policy and fertility lend an ever more explicit, neofascist interpretation to population-environmentalism.

A Neofascist Interpretation of United States Immigration Policy

In his essay, "Jewish Involvement in Shaping American Immigration Policy, 1881–1965: A Historical Review," Kevin MacDonald claims that Jews plotted to liberalize restrictionist immigration legislation from the 1920s and succeeded with the Immigration Act of 1965. Jewish organizations, determined to break the homogeneity and hegemony of white Protestant culture, advocated not only for liberal immigration policy but also for the secularization of United States society and a foreign policy based on internationalism. Motivated by a leftist ideology and his strong identification as a Jew, according to MacDonald, Franz Boas pioneered a whole new school of anthropology to replace biological explanations of race and human behavior differences with cultural or environmental explanations.

This "ideology of racial equality," as MacDonald refers to the Boasian view, was "an important weapon" in Jewish efforts to break down immigration restrictions. MacDonald repeatedly invokes differences between ethnicities and races as inherent.

> In the real world, ethnic groups differ in their talents and abilities; they differ in their numbers, fertility, and the extent to which they encourage parenting practices conducive to resource acquisition; and they differ in the resources held at any point in time and in their political power.[67]

MacDonald regrets what he sees as the dominance of "Boasian cultural determination" over "biologism" in the human sciences.

In addition to instigating a revolution in academia, MacDonald further claims that Jews led a highly organized effort to turn the United States into a multicultural society. So as not to reveal the Jewish interest in their endeavor, Jews developed pro-immigration arguments "couched in terms of universalist humanitarian ideals" and recruited non-Jews to serve as "window dressing" for their battles.[68] Jews even employed the memory of the Holocaust. Although MacDonald's testimony in the Irving case did not touch on his own view of the Holocaust, he has described it as:

> an instrument of Jewish ethnic interests not only as a symbol intended to create moral revulsion to violence directed at minority ethnic groups… but also as an instrument to silence opponents of high levels of multi-ethnic immigration into Western societies.[69]

According to MacDonald, Jewish interests in liberalizing immigration laws were threefold. Apart from securing the entry of Jews themselves into the United States, open immigration would lead to a pluralistic society, which, MacDonald asserts, safeguards Jewish cohesive cultural characteristics against pressure to integrate into the mainstream and decreases the chance that Jews will be singled out as scapegoats by a hostile majority. In pluralism, Jews would be just one among many minority groups. "Indeed," MacDonald writes in his conclusion, "lowering the political and demographic power of the European-derived peoples of the United States has clearly been the aim of the Jewish political and intellectual activities discussed here."[70] With this, MacDonald returns to his theory of ethnic group competition.

What is the consequence of this Jewish plot to subvert the power of the "European-derived" peoples through liberal immigration policy? Ultimately, the "morality," "altruism," and "self-sacrifice," of the "host" white Protestant culture will run low. "I rather doubt such altruism will continue to occur if there are obvious signs that the status and political power of the European-derived group is decreasing while the power of other groups increases as a result of immigration and other social policies."[71] MacDonald predicts ethnic warfare, because multiculturalism for him is really a code word for ethnic separatism, which has led to balkanization and ethnic cleansing most recently in Yugoslavia and Rwanda. MacDonald foresees a United States "heading down a volatile path—a path that leads to ethnic warfare and to the development of collectivist, authoritarian, and racialist enclaves."[72] MacDonald's views on fertility likewise build on his theory of biological determinism and his racist academic discourse.

Neofascist Interpretations on Fertility

According to Adam Miller, author of "Professors of Hate," J. Philippe Rushton:

> [C]laims that less evolved organisms—such as blacks—fight for survival by coupling promiscuously, flooding the environment with offspring for whom they provide little care and many of whom die. He says more evolved forms—such as Asians—wage their battle through monogamous relationships, producing few children upon whom they lavish care and many of whom survive.[73]

Rushton believes that races have evolved distinct reproductive strategies. Similar to Rushton, Kevin MacDonald depicts two fundamentally different kinds of human fertility behavior: "K-selected species," those adults who have few, but well cared for children, and "r-selected species," those who have many, but poorly cared for children.[74]

These differences evolved in response to ancestral environments, MacDonald argues, expressing in evolutionary terms a particular (one would infer superior or inferior) level of "biological fitness." Simply by virtue of their genes, for example, "K-selected species" are friendlier to the environment, because, "while r-selected species tend to overshoot their resource base, adversity selected and K-selected species remain within the carrying capacity of the environment."[75] MacDonald writes of the presence of both "genetic proclivities," as developed over time, and "environmental triggers," which can induce a particular style of parenting. He claims that variables such as age of the onset of puberty, age of first sexual intercourse, and especially intelligence determine the outcome of fertility behavior, and are heritable.

With regard to the political and social movements of the 1960s and that decade's effect on reproductive behavior and fertility, MacDonald suggests that the years prior to 1965 were characterized by low levels of "illegitimacy" and single parenting maintained through "powerful social controls embedded in the religious and legal framework of Western societies."[76] The cultural changes of the 1960s, which challenged and removed these social controls, resulted in increased rates of single parenting, teenage sexual activity, pregnancy, and out-of-wedlock births. Once again, MacDonald implicates Jews for these developments.

> My personal experience at Wisconsin during the 1960s was that the student protest movement was originated and dominated by Jews and that a great many of them were "red diaper babies" whose parents had been radicals.... These students had very positive attitudes toward Judaism as well as negative attitudes toward Christianity, but perhaps surprisingly, the most salient contrast between Judaism and Christianity in their minds was in attitudes toward sexuality. In line with the very large Freudian influence of the period, the general tendency was to contrast a putative sexual permissiveness of Judaism with the sexual repression and prudery of Christianity, and this contrast was then linked with psychoanalytic analyses that attributed various forms of psychopathology and even capitalism, racism, and other forms of political oppression to Christian sexual attitudes.[77]

Following MacDonald's line of argument, Jews are responsible for initiating a "sexual revolution." This led to "irresponsible" sexuality, childbearing, and higher rates of fertility, but not across board for all races and ethnicities. Based on evidence from *The Bell Curve*, MacDonald attests that these rates remained relatively unchanged for white women with high IQ, and therefore, he concludes, "the erosion of traditional Western controls on sexuality have had far more effect on those who are genetically inclined toward precocious sexuality."[78]

MacDonald compares the birth rates in the United States in 1995 among women aged 15 to 44 by race/ethnicity (white, Black, and Hispanic), and contends that differences in fertility rates exist, "even in response to the same environmental context." Yet, his assumption of "same environmental context" blatantly disregards the historical and current realities of race, gender, and class exploitation and oppression. He invokes race and ethnicity only to define members of racial and ethnic minorities as having low intelligence, being lazy, irresponsible, overly fertile, and oversexed. In a reference to the work of eugenicist Richard Lynn, MacDonald writes:

> [L]ow-IQ individuals who engage in low-investment parenting under contemporary conditions may be low on the personality trait of Conscientiousness and therefore less able to defer gratification, engage in sustained work, use birth control consistently, persevere in long term goals, etc.[79]

Steeped in covert racism, MacDonald weaves together his views on fertility and immigration, and then situates them within the framework of ethnic group conflict. He depicts the combination of high immigration and high fertility as an onslaught by minority groups on white "natives."

According to MacDonald, the net effect of immigration of ethnic groups with high fertility is to further suppress the already low fertility of the native population. This represents "natural selection against the genes of the native population.... Given that 90 percent of recent immigrants to the United States are non-European, this implies selection differentials against European peoples."[80] He estimates that "US women are foregoing over one million births per year as a result of immigration,"[81] and suggests that this supports the predictions of early-twentieth-century eugenicist and immigration restrictionist Madison Grant, who authored *The Passing of the Great Race* in 1916.[82]

Like his colleague, Virginia Abernethy, MacDonald views conflict in Yugoslavia as another example of demographic competition between ethnic groups.

> Demography may be destiny, but from an evolutionary perspective it is not surprising that the destiny of groups with a high reproductive rate to rule the areas where their numbers come to eclipse other groups may be hotly contested by the groups being eclipsed. In theoretical terms this may often be a conflict between r-strategists, relatively speaking, and K-strategists. By definition, r-strategists in this case the Albanians, out-reproduce K-strategists, but K-strategists may use other means of competition, including warfare, "ethnic cleansing" via expulsion, and genocide.[83]

MacDonald casually invokes the most violent crimes against humanity, genocide and ethnic cleansing, and does not seem to acknowledge them as crimes at all. Indeed, MacDonald has depicted ethnic cleansing as "a rather clear rationale," adding in an academic afterthought, "obviously in the perceived ethnic interests of the group doing the cleansing."[84] He views these forms of violence as simply another means of ethnic competition, a legitimate evolutionary psychological reaction of one group, whose presence and power is ostensibly threatened by the demographic expansion of another. Since he presupposes the inevitability of ethnic conflict, he suggests that the most horrific means by which ethnic groups compete might always come into play.

MacDonald naturalizes "ethnic cleansing" and "genocide" as legitimate behavior in a world he characterizes by power and survival struggles between ethnic groups and cultural areas. Furthermore, reverting to Nazi style fascist ideology, MacDonald uses a sophisticated form of scapegoating to implicate Jews for his prediction of impending cultural warfare.

The Mask

"We are neither left nor right, but up front."[85] This popular slogan among contemporary German Greens may at first seem like a noble attempt to overcome political differences, in order to promote a clean environment for the common good of all. However, such a slogan has contributed to the popular misconception that pro-environment stances are by definition progressive and void of any particular political orientation. In a March 1998 editorial in *Population and Environment*, Virginia Abernethy applauds a defense of the environment, which likewise attempts to diffuse different ends of the political spectrum. Abernethy gives an account of an environmental conference she attended through the eyes of a pet parrot brought along by one participant. "At the conference, handicapped by a crippled foot and battered wing, African Grey Moishe perched on the dais while his companion spoke of the symbolic importance of USA-187[86] to unite the left and the right as Environmental Patriots, with the goal of preserving Land for Creatures and Country." In this context, left and right "uniting" actually translates into the nullification of the left under a "common" nativist and anti-immigrant umbrella. Therefore, the idea that environmentalism ought to be pursued without the "interference" of politics can be fallacious.

In a very powerful argument, Peter Staudenmaier refers to the dangers of denying a political orientation to environmental movements:

> Environmental themes can be mobilized from the left or from the right, indeed they require an explicit social context if they are to have any political valence whatsoever. "Ecology" alone does not prescribe a politics; it must be interpreted, mediated through some theory of society in order to acquire political meaning. Failure to heed this mediated interrelationship between the social and ecological is the hallmark of reactionary ecology.[87]

Janet Biehl concurs stating, "the politicization of ecology is not only desirable but necessary," especially given the very real ecological crisis, which ought to be urgently addressed.[88] Therefore, to dismiss ecofascism as feigned environmentalism ignores the ideological traditions of an ecology movement from the far right. The link between population and environment can lend itself to a particularly reactionary, "blood and soil" interpretation, which leads to politics of fear and scapegoating. Yet, these politics remain masked by depoliticized and liberalized notions of population and environment, which are married to the concept of development.

The titles of the latest mega-events on population and environment, the UN Conference on Environment and Development (Rio de Janeiro, 1992), and the International Conference on Population and Development (Cairo, 1994), indicate how automatic the coupling of each idea with development has become in international policy discussions. Development has a potent ability to retain its comforting perception of promise and progress, even in the face of egregious failure in reducing gaps between rich and poor, and the high social and environmental price tag attached to some of its schemes. Development's perennial optimism is not only very self-sustaining, it has seeped into and fundamentally altered our thinking on other terms, playing an intrinsic role in development discourse, particularly population and environment.

By conjuring perceptions of emergency or crisis, which call for management or control on the global level, population and environment give to development a further justification for interventionism. At the same time, development "sanctifies" interventions in the name of population and environment, by imparting them with its undying quality of best intentions. Whatever their premise, whatever worldview they may harbor, and whatever policies they may elicit, population and environment, it is most often assumed, act on behalf of the greater common good. Therefore, names like Population Environment Balance and Carrying Capacity Network, combined with the largely neutral-sounding population and environment rhetoric serve to mask the right wing's anti-immigrant and nativist agenda.

Conclusion

On the one hand, neofascist interpretations of the population and environment nexus exploit perceptions of population already developed through the heavy alarmism used by mainstream organizations involved in international discourse on population. This projects global "overpopulation" as exclusively a problem of the Southern hemisphere. Population has come to personify teeming millions from the Third World. Add to this conceptualization a worldview in which cultures are depicted in constant competition.

Then, the numerical expansion via migration and fertility of one culture relative to another will be perceived as a threat, and result in an outbreak of conflict. Population itself comes to connote the encroachment by people of color from the South into the territory occupied by a white "host" in the North.

During Nationalist Socialist Party rule in Germany, a similar perception of population led to the fear of encroachment by peoples from Eastern Europe, and significant intersections between anti-Semitism and anti-immigration. On the other hand, the right wing connection between population and the environment significantly alters the concept of environment used in conjunction with international development discourse. Environment has been reduced from its global reach, but broadened conceptually to include not just the geophysical environment within the US borders, but also white American culture. This development reflects a "blood and soil"-type connection, which Nazi ideologues described as an innate and exclusive bond between the German race and land.

When the above conceptions of population and the environment are combined, as they are in mainstream international discourse, then expressions like "population growth threatens the environment," or "population growth is a primary cause of environmental degradation," take on a significantly changed meaning. The millions from the Third World entering US borders are perceived of as a threat, not only to the physical environment, but also to the "American" culture. Immigrants are easily scapegoated for a variety of population/environmental problems. Consequently, the lobby has developed a broad conservative and nativist agenda to promote "American" culture and values, the English language, and immigration restrictions or moratoriums, while campaigning against immigrant rights, multiculturalism, and diversity.

Given the increasing influence of the right-wing population-environment lobby among mainstream US environmental organizations, it is essential to re-examine the predominant, popular notions of population and environment, and how these mask racist and dangerous ideology and politics. Actions and campaigns mobilized in the name of population and environment stem from all points along the political spectrum. It is important to identify the ideological underpinnings of these movements, so that they can be situated within a broader political framework, and evaluated for socially regressive content.

1   The Committee on Women, Population and the Environment (CWPE) is an alliance of feminist scholars, activists and health practitioners, which since 1991, has produced feminist analysis on population, environment, and development issues.

2   Nativism refers to a sociopolitical agenda which favors the interests of established inhabitants over those of immigrants, while eugenics refers to the study and practice of outbreeding "undersirable" or "unfit" persons from society through selective immigration restrictions as well as coercive sterilization.

3   Susanne Heim and Ulrike Schaz, *Berechnung und Beschwörung: Überbevölkerung Kritik einer Debatte* (Rote Strasse, Berlin: Schwarze Risse, 1996), 53, 63.

4   Ibid., 40–41.

5   Harold Callender, "Europe's Population Trends: A Cause of Great Uneasiness," *New York Times,* June 11, 1933, xxiii.

6   Ibid., 6.

7   Printed in Heim and Schaz, *Berechnung und Beschwörung,* 38.

8   Erich Rosenthal, "Trends of the Jewish population in Germany, 1910–1939," *Jewish Social Studies,* Vol. 6, No. 3 (1944), quoted in William Seltzer, "Population Statistics, the Holocaust, and the Nuremberg Trials," *Population and Development Review,* Vol. 24, No .3 (September 1998), 516.

9   Heim and Schaz, *Berechnung und Beschwörung,* 47.

10 Ibid., 59.

11 Ibid., 50–51.

12 Translation my own, quoted in Heim and Schaz, *Berechnung und Beschwörung,* 61.

13 Ibid., 56.

14 Ibid., 63.

15 Translation my own, quoted in ibid., 62.

16 Ibid., 66.

17 Ibid., 67.

18 Ibid., 53.

19 Translation my own, quoted in ibid., 53–54.

20 Seltzer, "Population Statistics, the Holocaust, and the Nuremberg Trials," *Jewish Social Studies,* 515.

21 Ibid., 540.

22 Ibid., 516.

23 Heim and Schaz, *Berechnung und Beschwörung,* 56–57.

24 Seltzer, "Population Statistics, the Holocaust, and the Nuremberg Trials," *Jewish Social Studies,* 517.

25 Ibid., 529.

26 Quoted in ibid., 529.

27 Peter Staudenmaier, "Fascist Ideology: The 'Green Wing' of the Nazi Party and its Historical Antecedents," in Janet Biehl and Peter Staudenmaier, eds., *Ecofascism: Lessons from the German Experience* (San Francisco, CA: AK Press, 1995), 7.

28 Ibid., 18.

29 Quoted in Staudenmaier, "Fascist Ideology," *Ecofascism,* 13.

30 Ibid., p. 7.
31 Ibid., 19–23.
32 Ibid., 15–16.
33 Quoted in Staudenmaier, "Fascist Ideology," *Ecofascism*, 21.
34 Ibid., 17.
35 Ibid., 19.
36 Ibid., 16.
37 Ibid., 15.
38 Ibid., 7; Heim and Schaz, *Berechnung und Beschwörung*, 51.
39 Tim Dyson, *Population and Food: Global Trends and Future Prospects* (London: Routledge, 1996).
40 Betsy Hartmann, *Reproductive Rights and Wrongs: The Global Politics of Population Control* (Cambridge, MA: South End Press, 1995), 141.
41 Syd Lindsley, "The Greening of Hate Continues," *Political Environments: A Publication of the Committee on Women, Population and the Environment*, Vol. 8 (Winter/Spring, 2001), 15; Betsy Hartmann, "To Vanquish the Hydra," *Political Environments*, 1 (Spring 1994), 5; Betsy Hartmann, "Dangerous Intersections," *Political Environments*, Vol. 2 (Summer 1995), 4–5.
42 Syd Lindsley, "Discourses of Blame: Race and Reproduction in the 1990s Anti-Immigrant Agenda in California," (Division III, Social Science, Hampshire College, May 2000), 69.
43 Michael Ollove, "The Lessons of Lynchburg," *The Baltimore Sun*, May 6, 2001, 6F.
44 Adam Miller, "Professors of Hate," *Rolling Stone*, 693 (October 20, 1994), 110–111.
45 Ibid., 109.
46 Quoted in Tony Ortega, "Witness for the Persecution." *The New Times Los Angeles*, April 20, 2000.
47 Lindsley, "Discourses of Blame," 74.
48 China Brotsky, "A Defeat for the Greening of Hate," *Political Environments*, Vol. 6 (Fall 1998), 1.
49 Betsy Hartmann, "What's in a Word? The Sierra Club Moves Right and Away from Democracy," *Political Economy*, Vol. 7 (Fall 1999/Winter 2000), 18.
50 Jim Motavalli, "Balancing Act: Can America Sustain a Population of 500 Million—Or Even a Billion—by 2100?" *E Magazine* (November/December 2000), 33.
51 Syd Lindsley, "The Greening of Hate Continues," *Political Environments*, 19.
52 Ibid.
53 Forward by Garret Hardin, in Virginia Abernethy, *Population Politics: The Choices that Shape Our Future* (New York: Plenum Press, 1993), ix.
54 Janet Biehl, "'Ecology' and the Modernization of Fascism in the German Ultra-Right," in Biehl and Staudenmaier, eds., *Ecofascism*, 53.
55 Ibid., 59.
56 Quoted in ibid., 63.
57 Ibid., 64–65.
58 Quoted in Miller, "Professors of Hate," *Rolling Stone*, 112.

59   Foreword by Garrett Hardin, in Abernethy, *Population Politics*, xi.

60   Kevin MacDonald, "The Numbers Game: Ethnic Conflict in the Contemporary World," *Population and Environment*, Vol 21, No. 4 (March 2000), 421.

61   Ibid.

62   Kevin MacDonald, "An Evolutionary Perspective on Human Fertility," *Population and Environment*, Vol. 21, No. 2 (November 1999), 223.

63   Ibid., 423.

64   Virginia Abernethy, "Secession, Good for the Goose but Not for the Gander?" *Population and Environment*, Vol. 20, No. 5 (May 1999), 394.

65   Tony Ortega, "Witness for the Persecution," *The New Times Los Angeles*, April 20, 2000.

66   Biehl, "'Ecology' and the Modernization of Fascism in the German Ultra-Right," *Ecofascism*, 33.

67   Kevin MacDonald, "Jewish Involvement in Shaping American Immigration Policy, 1881-1965." *Population and the Environment*, Vol. 19, No. 4 (March 1998), 348.

68   Ibid., 311.

69   MacDonald, "The Numbers Game," *Population and Environment*, Vol. 21, No. 4, 420.

70   MacDonald, "Jewish Involvement in Shaping American Immigration Policy, 1881-1965," *Population and Environment*, 348.

71   Ibid., 350.

72   Quoted in Tony Ortega, "In the Hot Seat," *The New Times Los Angeles*, May 25, 2000.

73   Miller, *Rolling Stone*, 109.

74   Kevin MacDonald, "An Evolutionary Perspective on Human Fertility," *Population and Environment*, 225.

75   Ibid.

76   Ibid., 233.

77   Kevin MacDonald, *The Culture of Critique: An Evolutionary Analysis of Jewish Involvement in Twentieth-Century Intellectual and Political Movements* (Westport, CT: Praeger, 1998).

78   MacDonald, "An Evolutionary Perspective on Human Fertility," *Population and Environment*, 234.

79   Ibid., 235.

80   Ibid., 237.

81   Ibid.

82   Ibid.

83   Ibid., 238.

84   MacDonald, "The Numbers Game," *Population and Environment*, 415.

85   Staudenmaier, "Facist Ideology," *Ecofascism*, 26.

86   "USA-187" echoes Prop 187 in California. It refers to a call for a complete moratorium on immigration to the United States.

87   Staudenmaier, "Fascist Ideology," *Ecofascism*, 25.

88   Biehl, "'Ecology' and the Modernization of Fascism in the German Ultra-Right," *Ecofascism*, 64–65.

Afterword

Reflections on
Post-September 11 America

An Interview with Angela Y. Davis

Anannya Bhattacharjee and Jael Silliman

A few months after the September 11 attacks on the World Trade Center, we asked Angela Davis about the significance of that day and the US response. We asked her how the recent political and cultural developments speak to the issues of criminalization, surveillance, and racism discussed in this anthology. Her responses provide a post-September 11 context for the anthology—a context that colors most discussions today.

Editors: In the wake of September 11, how has the environment changed for civil liberties of communities of color and immigrant communities? Is it more of the same or is it a historically new context?

Angela Davis: First of all, I want to say what an honor it is to do this interview with you on the occasion of the publication of your new book, *Policing the National Body*. Your book makes an invaluable contribution to contemporary theories and practices of resistance. I am sure that, like myself, all of your readers will be enlightened, transformed, and inspired. As someone who is often referred to as a veteran activist, I want to thank you for sharing your ideas on surveillance, policing, and violence, practices that have become even more pervasive in the aftermath of September 11.

Looking back at the popular understanding that appeared to emerge immediately and spontaneously—that nothing would ever be the same after September 11—we can now interpret this as a dangerous preparation for the enormous erosion of civil liberties in the following months. The notion that nothing would ever be the same was repeatedly pronounced by government officials, rehearsed by the media, and seemed to capture the popular sentiment that the country was prepared for a drastic shift in the way we live our lives, including the increased surveillance and policing represented as necessary to defeat terrorism. As has so frequently been the case in United States history, racist assumptions were mobilized to define the enemy, and within a matter of days, the already repressive conditions experienced by immigrant communities increased astronomically. Thus, practices of racial profiling that have long been a target of anti-racist activism were more intensely deployed against Arab, Middle Eastern, South Asian, and Muslim communities. The swift passage by Congress of the USA Patriot Act, with its repressive provisions for deportation, detention, and surveillance, has brought about a drastic curtailment of civil liberties, which will be extremely difficult to reverse.

Of course, the current situation is not without historical precedent. There are, for example, sinister parallels with the McCarthy era. And those of us who have been active in the anti-prison movement for the last decade or so have noticed a striking resemblance between the representation of the terrorist and the representation of the criminal. In many ways, the public was already prepared for the mobilization of nationalist emotions based on fear of a racialized enemy. This had already occurred in connection with the so-called war on crime and the emergence of a vast prison industrial complex, which not only promoted the popular ideological assumptions that safety and security were a function of the imprisonment of vast numbers of people of color, but also, in the process, criminalized undocumented immigrants. The expansion of the INS as an apparatus of policing and imprisonment was, as we can now see, a dangerous rehearsal for the present moment.

Editors: How do you think the issues of poor women—such as poverty, HIV/AIDS, erosion of reproductive rights, increasing number of women in prisons—will be affected by the Bush administration's response to September 11?

Angela Davis: Ironically, Laura and George Bush have positioned themselves as principal advocates of women's liberation in relation to Afghan women, thus utterly ignoring the fact that the international campaign on behalf of Afghan women has a long history, one that dates back to the period when the United States supported the Taliban against the former Soviet Union. The United States government's call for women's rights in central Asia as a component of the so-called war against global terrorism is actually part of a larger strategy that promotes violence against women throughout the world. Once again, the United States government is vying for increasing global superiority—economic, military, and ideological superiority. The support available to poor women—whether in the southern region or in the capitalist countries—will continue to decline under the impact of the onslaught of capital. Resources that ought to be available to address urgent health issues such as HIV/AIDS are being devoured by both the military and prison industrial complexes. Against the backdrop of the rapid expansion of the prison industrial complex, for example, women constitute the fastest growing sector of the imprisoned populations. To support these new prison infrastructures, resources that should be used to promote reproductive rights, health, and economic well-being are being used to promote oppression, disease, and destruction. This is a pattern that was already in place before September 11, and one that undoubtedly will be intensified during the coming period.

Editors: For some time now, there have been complaints about the fragmentation of social justice movements. What are the possibilities for multi-issue organizing? Has September 11 extended or impeded these possibilities?

Angela Davis: In the aftermath of September 11, social movements have an even greater responsibility to propose radical critiques of the government—not only to organize visible protests, but to help change the popular discourse that equates the actions of the government with the interests of the people. The patriotism that emerged as a marketable commodity in the aftermath of the attacks, allowing the American flag to adorn every imaginable aspect of daily life, did not cause the ubiquitous fear to wane, but rather established an array of enemies to be feared as intensely as people learned to fear the possibility of another attack. While some "enemies" became obvious immediately—Middle Eastern, South Asian, Arab, and Muslim communities—other "enemies" such as, immigrant rights organizers, anti-racist, and other social justice organizations, are also on the agenda. This means that political reconfigurations after September 11 (for example, the dangerous reluctance of congresspersons, with the single exception of Barbara Lee, to speak out against war) have resulted in a more generalized conservatism. This conservatism makes the work of radical organizations (some of which have exercised self-censorship) far more difficult. A powerful mandate for global solidarities and intersectional approaches to social justice organizing was created by the NGO Forum of the United Nations World Conference Against Racism, which was unfortunately overshadowed by the events of September 11. Many groups that are taking up the contemporary challenge recognize how important it is to build bridges across many divides.

SISTERSONG MEMBER ORGANIZATIONS 1998–2001

Native American

Moon Lodge Native Women's Outreach, Riverside, CA (anchor)
Wise Women Gathering Place, Oneida, WI
Minnesota American Indian AIDS Task Force, Minneapolis, MN
Native American Women's Health Education Resource Center,
Lake Andes, SD

Asian/Pacific Islander

National Asian American Women's Health Organization, San
Francisco, CA (anchor)
Asians and Pacific Islanders for Reproductive Health, Oakland, CA
The Clinic for Women—Asian Health Project, Los Angeles, CA
Kokua Kalihi Valley Comprehensive Family Services, Honolulu, HI

Black/African-American

SisterLove Women's AIDS Project, Atlanta, GA (anchor)
Project Azuka Women's AIDS Services, Savannah, GA
California Black Women's Health Project, Los Angeles, CA
National Center for Human Rights Education, Atlanta, GA
African American Women Evolving, Chicago, IL

Latina/Hispanic

Casa Atabex Ache, New York, NY (anchor)
Grupo Pro Derechos Reproductivos, San Juan, Puerto Rico
The Women's House of Learning, Oxnard, CA
National Latina Health Organization, Oakland, CA

Index

A

Abernethy, Virginia, 304, 306–7, 310–11, 318

abortion: access to, 94, 105–7, 109–10, 115–17, 119n13; laws on, 104, 107–9, 112, 119n11, 120n30; mifepristone (RU486), 111, 119n13; movements about, 104–7, 110–11, 116–18, 148–53, 271; "partial birth," 112–13, 120n30, 121n31; polls on, 116; poverty and, 12–14, 103–4, 106–8, 114–17, 119n11–12, 121n33; women of color and, 12–14, 113–16, 121n33, 139–40, 146n90, 151–53; young people and, 103–4, 107, 114–16. *See also* reproductive rights

Abramowitz, Mimi, 186–87

Afghanistan, 327

AFL-CIO, 40

Africa, 238, 239, 264–67, 278

African-American community: criminalization of, xv–xvi, 44–45, 56, 62–63, 69; health care access, 166–68; history of, xvii, 55, 73; incarceration surge, xiii–xv, xvi, 4, 56–57, 66–69; population control of, xvii, 63–64; profiling of, xvii, 42; social destruction and, 70–71; unequal treatment of, xv, 20, 56, 58–60, 67–69; voting rights lost, 69, 79n105. *See also* war on drugs; women of color

African-American Task Force, 46

AIDS. *See* HIV/AIDS

Alan Guttmacher Institute, 245

Alliance for Stabilizing America's Population, 307

American Civil Liberties Union (ACLU), 20, 29, 148, 243

American Friends Service Committee (AFSC), 10, 24, 26, 40, 47

Amnesty International, xv, 20–21, 27, 30

anti-choice. *See* abortion: movements about

Anti-Defamation League, 311

anti-Semitism, 294–99, 301, 302–3, 312–16

Anti-Terrorism and Effective Death Penalty Act, 7

anti-violence movement. *See* women's anti-violence movement

Aptheker, Herbert, 141–42

Arbourezk, James, 126

Arndt, Ernst Moritz, 300

Asian and Pacific Islander community (A/PI): activists from, 157; domestic violence, 16, 47; health issues, 159–60, 163–64; labor exploitation of, 32; language barriers, 164; profiling of, 42; sex trafficking, 199–200, 207–8. *See also* women of color

Asian Women's Shelter (AWS),
16, 47
Atlantic Monthly, 260
Attico, Burton, 135
Atwood, J. Brian, 236
Australia, 206

B

Balone, Celine, 135
Bandarage, Asoka, 172
Bangladesh, 137, 199, 226n4
Barnett, Don, xxi
Barnett, Roger, xxi
Barr, Mary, 43
Bay Area Police Watch, 10
Beijing Women's Conference
(1995), 118, 149
Bell Curve, The (Herrnstein and
Murray), xxiii, 316
Bellanger, Pat, 127
Bennett, William, 59
Berechnung und Beschwörung (Heim
and Schaz), 293
Biehl, Janet, 308, 318
birth control. *See* contraception
Blacks. *See* African-American
community
Blacks for Life, 152
Boas, Franz, 312–13
Boesler, Felix, 294
Border Patrol. *See* Immigration
Naturalization Service (INS)
Bortner, M.A., 243
Boycott Crime Coalition, 33
Boyz N the Hood, ix
Brandy (prisoner), 83, 86, 87, 89,
91–93
Bratton, William, 5
Brewster Heights Packing Plant,
34

Brightman, Lehman, 127
Brown, Lester, 278
Buffett, Warren, 270
Burgdörfer, Friedrich, 294, 298
Bush, George H., 58–59
Bush, George W., xiii, 153, 327,
328
Bush, Laura, 327
Business Week, 232

C

Cairo +5 conference (1999), 259,
263, 271
Cairo plan. *See* International
Conference on Population and
Development (ICPD)
California, 176, 182–85
California Coalition for
Immigration Reform (CCIR),
304
Californians for Population
Stabilization (CAPS), 304–5
Callender, Harold, 294
Canada, 140, 200, 202
caregivers. *See* mothers
Carrying Capacity Network
(CCN), 279, 304, 306, 319
Catholic Charities, 153
Catholic Family and Human
Rights Institute, 247
Center for Development and
Population Activities
(CEDPA), 247
Chandler, Cynthia, 86, 100n3
Chideya, Farai, 60
Child Custody Protection Act,
112
Children Requiring a Caring
Kommunity (CRACK), 63, 64,
76n53, 131

Children's Advocacy Institute, 243
Children's Health Insurance Plan, 185
China, 208, 236
Choice USA, 116
Christian Coalition, 152
CIA (Central Intelligence Agency), 70–71
Claremore, Oklahoma, 127, 128
Clash of the Civilizations and the Remaking of World Order (Huntington), 237
class. *See* poverty
Clemon, U.W., xiii
Clinton, William, 66–67, 244, 274–76
Coalition Against Trafficking in Women (CATW), 201, 215, 222
cocaine. *See* war on drugs
Coleman Advocates for Children and Youth, 243
Coles, Claire, 62
Collins, Patricia Hill, 125
ColorLines, 243
"Coming Anarchy, The" (Kaplan), 239
"Coming of the Superpredator, The" (DiIulio), 240
Committee on Women, Population, and the Environment (CWPE), xxiv–xxvi, 172, 270, 291
Communications Consortium Media Center, 247
Concord Feminist Health Center, 110
Contagious Diseases Acts, 214
Conti, Leonard, 296

contraception: abuse of, 114, 135–40, 162, 269; Dalkon Shield, 144n48; Depo-Provera, 63, 131–35, 137–38, 162; IUD, 155, 269; Norplant, 13, 63, 131, 136–40, 162, 252; quinacrine, 117, 270; tubal ligations, 127, 129, 140, 144n23. *See also* sterilization
Correa, Sonia, xi
COYOTE (Call Off Your Old Tired Ethics), 222
crack. *See* war on drugs
criminal justice system, 82–84, 90–91, 93, 97–98; expansion of, x, 1–2, 6–8, 45–46, 326; gendered analysis of, 1–2, 17–18; interagency cooperation, 8, 45–46
criminalization: of caregivers, xi, 33, 45, 150; of communities of color, x, 3, 8, 22, 43, 56; drug use and, xi, xvi, 6, 62–63, 66–67; of immigration, 8, 43; of institutions, 9; of poverty, xiii, 43, 56, 84, 90–91, 101n17; of work, 39, 43; of youth, xxiii, 8, xxviii(n30), 240–43. *See also* criminal justice system
Crow Service Unit, 138
Cuba, 199

D

Dangerous Intersections (Silliman and King, eds.), xxv
Darre, Richard Walther, 301, 302
Davara (prisoner), 83, 86, 87–88, 90–91, 94, 96–97
David and Lucile Packard Foundation, 276, 279

Davis, Angela, 325–28
Democratic Party, 116
Demographic Health Survey, 280–81
Denying the Holocaust (Lipstadt), 305
Depo-Provera, 63, 131–35, 137–38, 162, 252–53
Detention Watch Network, 22
DHS+ initiative, 280–81
Diallo, Amadou, xv
DiIulio, John D., Jr., xxiii, 240–41
Dimmock Community Health Center, 47
Dinkins, David, 65
"Dispelling the Myth" (Males and Macallair), 241
Doe vs. Bolton, 119n12
domestic violence: in the Asian and Pacific Islander community, 47; enforcement violence and, 11, 29–30; gender entrapment, 14–16, 84; health impacts, 209–10
Donohue, John, 115
Donziger, Steven, 61
drugs. *See* war on drugs

E

E Magazine, 307
Earth First!, 307
Earth Times, 248
Ecological Democratic Party (Germany), 309
Ehrenreich, Barbara, xv
Eichmann, Adolf, 298
Einstein Medical Center, 62
Ella Baker Center for Human Rights, 10, 23
Emory University, 133

enforcement accountability movements: concerning immigration, 10, 22–24, 38, 43; by mothers, 33, 37–38; of police, 5–6, 10, 25–26, 31–33, 47; for prisoners, 10, 20–22, 27, 29, 36–39; women of color and, 29–31, 46–48
enforcement violence: gendered analysis of, 2–3, 10–11, 17–18, 23, 26; immigrants and, 9–11, 19–20, 22–25, 30–32, 34–35; sexual assault and, xxvii(n3), 24, 26–28, 39, 41–42; toward caregivers, 29–30, 33, 37–38, 45; work and, 39–40, 43
environment, 150, 276–80, 291, 299–303. *See also* population-environment right-wing movement
Esteves, Luis Santiago, 24
eugenics: concerns about, 191–93, 280–83; definition of, 322n2; support for, 114, 187, 305

F

Family Health International, 270
family planning, 172, 260–62, 266–70, 277, 279. *See also* abortion; population control; reproductive rights
Family Violence Prevention Fund, 15
FBI (Federal Bureau of Investigation), 5, 132, 138, 144n48, 207
FDA. *See* United States Food and Drug Administration
Federal Anti-Drug Abuse Act, 67
Federation for American

Immigration Reform (FAIR), 279, 283–84, 304–5, 306
feminism, xi–xii, 2, 172, 178–79, 246–49, 283–84
feminization of labor, 177–80, 203–4
Ferguson vs. City of Charleston, xvi
Fishman, Mark, 60
Fitzgerald, Mary, 39
Ford Foundation, 157, 172, 215, 283
Foucault, Michel, xiv
Framing Youth (Males), 243–44
Fujimori, Alberto, 268, 269, 272–73
Fuller, Gary, 234, 239

G

Gaia Institute, 307
Gallegly, Elton, 182, 184
Gauntlet Magazine, 41
genetics, xix–xx, 280–83. *See also* eugenics
genocide, 126, 141–42, 151, 296. *See also* contraception; population control; sterilization
Georgia Citizens' Coalition on Hunger, 153
Georgia Supreme Court, 77n82
Germany. *See* Nazi Germany
Ghana, 265
Gideon, Patrick, 134–35
Giuliani, Rudolph, x, 5
Global Alliance Against Trafficking in Women (GAATW), 222
globalization: of labor, 178–80, 192, 198–200, 202–5; neoliberalism and, 262, 264, 267, 272–74; poverty and,

263–64; structural adjustment, 168, 197, 203, 264–65, 270–71
Goddard, Jaime, 132
Going Up the River (Hallinan), xiv
Grady Clinic (Emory University), 133, 134, 139
Grandparent Caregiver Advocacy Project, 33
Grant, Madison, 316–17
Gruhl, Herbert, 308–9

H

Haeckel, Ernst, 300
Haiti, 137
Hallinan, Joseph, xiv
Hamilton, Ellen, 140
Hardin, Garrett, 304–6, 308, 309, 310
Harer, Miles D., 241–42
Harlem Legal Services, 46
Harmsen, Hans, 294
Harris, Barbara, 131
Harris, Stanley S., 79n93
Hartmann, Betsy, 235, 307
Hartouni, Valerie, xx, xxii–xxiii
Harvard University, 219
Hatcher, Robert, 133
Hay, Jeremy, 41–42
Heim, Susanne, 293, 294, 295, 296, 297
Heller, Simon, 121n31
Hernandez-Avila, Ines, 123
Hewlett Foundation, 279
Himmler, Heinrich, 298, 301, 302
Hispanics. *See* Latino community
Hitler, Adolf, 298
HIV/AIDS: factors in spread of, 136, 213–15, 269, 280; in prison, 81–82, 84–87, 93–94, 100n5–6, 101n24; prostitution

and, 211, 213–15, 218–20;
public health response to, 214,
219–20; high risk communities
for, 160–61, 165–67, 265, 278
Hughes, Patrick M., 235
Human Laboratory, The (Cadbury),
136–37
human rights: health care and,
154, 168–72; movement for,
24, 40; sex trafficking and, 198,
202, 211, 221–25; war on drugs
and, 57, 71–72. *See also*
reproductive rights
Human Rights Watch, 36, 71,
242, 269
Humphreys, Lori, 16
Huntington, Samuel, 237
Hyde Amendment, 108, 109,
119n11, 139

I

ICPD. *See* International
Conference on Population and
Development
Illegal Immigration Reform and
Immigrant Responsibility Act
(IIRAIRA), 4, 5, 7, 181
immigration: enforcement
accountability movements, 10,
22–24, 26, 38, 43; enforcement
violence and, 9–11, 19–20,
22–25, 30–32, 34–35; family
issues and, 34–37, 176, 181,
184, 186–88, 190–93;
feminization of, 177–80,
203–4; health care and, 175,
177, 180–85, 188–93; labor
exploitation, 39–41, 177–80,
188, 192–93, 203–5; legislation
against, 4–5, 7, 177–78,

180–85, 192–93, 194n19;
movements against, 193, 279,
306–8, 312–14, 316–17. *See also*
Immigration Naturalization
Service
Immigration and Nationality Act,
181
Immigration Law Enforcement
Monitoring Project (ILEMP),
24, 26
Immigration Marriage Fraud
Amendment, 181
Immigration Naturalization
Service (INS): abuses by, 11,
15, 27, 30, 39; Border Patrol, 5,
8, 10–11, 24, 30; deportation
and, 34–35, 37, 201; detention
system of, 4–6, 8–9, 21, 27, 33;
expansion of, xx–xxi, 1, 5–6,
326; interagency cooperation,
5, 8, 15, 18, 23; movement
against, 10, 22–24, 27, 33, 38;
raids by, 6, 19–20, 30, 34–35,
40–41; sex trafficking report,
200; war on drugs, 30, 70–71
Immigration Reform and Control
Act (IRCA), 177, 178, 180–81,
192
India, 137, 199, 269
Indian Health Services (IHS), 109,
126–31, 137–39, 161–62
Indians. *See* Native American
community
Indigenous Women's Network,
141
Indonesia, 239
Inland Empire Public Lands
Council, 307
INS Watch, 23
Institute on Violence, 46–47
International Conference on

Population and Development
(ICPD) (Cairo, 1994):
development and, 319;
empowerment of women and,
246–49, 261, 263–64, 274;
family planning, 246–48,
260–62, 266–70, 277, 279;
health care and, 261–66, 271,
274; neoliberalism and,
262–65, 270–71, 273–74;
NGOs and, 271–73;
reproductive rights and, 118,
170, 271; United States policies
and, 261, 274–76; women's
movements and, 149, 270–71
International Convention on the
Elimination of All Forms of
Racial Discrimination (CERD),
71
International Human Rights
Network, 222
International Labor Office, 180
International Monetary Fund
(IMF), 124, 197, 203, 264
International Society for the
Preservation of the Tropical
Rainforest, 307
International Women's Health
Coalition (IWHC), 154
Internet, xix, 206, 227n24
Inuit, 140
Ipsen, Gunther, 297
Iraq, 236
Irving, David, 305
Irving, Lawrence, 68

J

Jackson, Andrew, 124
Jackson, Keith Timothy, 58
Jannett, Raymond, 135

"Jewish Involvement in Shaping
American Immigration Policy,
1881-1965" (MacDonald), 312
Jews, 294–99, 301, 302–3, 312–16
Jimenez, Maria, 40
Johnson, Darlene, 13
Johnson, Jennifer, 63
Johnson vs. State, 63
Jones, Gavin, 264
Justice Now, 82, 83
Justice Works, 10, 39

K

Kaplan, Robert, 239
Kaw, 127
Keels, Renee Wormack, 38
Kennedy, Anthony, 66
Kenya, 265
Killing the Black Body (Roberts),
xvii
King, Martin Luther, Jr., 152
King, Rodney, xv
Kingery, Carol, 86, 87, 100n3
Klages, Ludwig, 300
Knapp, Whitman, 78n93
Knodel, John, 264
Koppel, Ted, 27
Korherr, Richard, 298–99
Krome Detention Center
(Florida), 38
Ku Klux Klan, 73n10

L

La Raza Centro Legal, 23
labor: exploitation of, 39–41,
177–80, 188, 192–93;
feminization of, 177–80,
203–4; globalization of, 192,
198–200, 202–5

Latina Roundtable on Health and
    Reproductive Rights, 157
Latino community: enforcement
    violence, xxi, 10–11, 19–20,
    23–24, 30–31, 35; family issues,
    xxi, 181, 184, 186–88, 190–93;
    health issues, 157, 160, 165–66;
    incarceration and, xiv–xv; labor
    exploitation of, 39–43, 177–80,
    188, 192–93; nativism against,
    175–76; profiling of, 20, 42;
    public services and, 177,
    180–85, 188–93; sterilization
    of, xvii; war on drugs, 63–64,
    70. See also women of color
Laughlin, Harry, 305
law enforcement. See criminal
    justice system
League of Women Voters, 243
Lebensräume (living spaces), 292,
    302, 308
Lee, Barbara, 328
Legal But Out of Reach, 107
Legal Services for Prisoners with
    Children, 10, 33, 37
Legalized Abortion and Crime (Levitt
    and Donohue), 115
legislation: on abortion, 104,
    107–9, 112, 119n11, 120n30;
    gender bias of, 180–81,
    184–88, 190, 191–93, 214; on
    immigration, 4–5, 7, 177–78,
    180–85, 192–93, 194n19; on
    war on drugs, 66–68,
    77n81–82; welfare reform,
    114–15, 184–85, 188, 252; on
    youth, 112, 242, 243
lesbians, 23, 25–26, 28–29, 33
Levitt, Steven, 115
Life Dynamics Inc., 110
Lindsley, Sid, 307

Lipstadt, Deborah, 305
Los Angeles Times, 182, 185
Luker, Kristin, 250, 252
Lynn, Richard, 305, 316

M

Macallair, Dan, 241
MacArthur Foundation, 283
MacDonald, Kevin, 305, 306, 310,
    311, 312–17
Males, Mike, 241, 243–44
"Man and Earth" (Klages), 300
Margaret Sanger Center
    International, 248
Marin, Leni, 15
Martinez, Theresa, 81
Masaki, Beckie, 16, 47
Matheson, Scott M., 126
Medicaid, 125, 165, 182, 275
Melbourne, Audrey, 78n93
Metzger, Tom, 309
Mexican community. See Latino
    community
Mexico: border issues, 11, 19–20,
    24, 30, 40; border vigilantes,
    xxi; illegal immigrants, 188;
    population control, 269–70
Miller, Adam, 314
Miller, Francesca, 148
Model Eugenics Sterilization Law,
    305
Mollen Commission, 65, 76n65
Mollen, Milton, 65
Monsanto Corporation, 280
Motavalli, Jim, 307
mothers: citizenship and
    immigration issues, 190–92;
    enforcement issues, 11, 29–30,
    33, 37–38, 45; policies against,
    186–90, 251–52, 275; in prison,

14, 19–21, 36–37, 57, 63, 85;
stigmatization of, 121n37,
187–88, 190–91, 249–50,
252–54; teenage, 249–53; war
on drugs and, xi, xv–xvi, 20,
57, 61–64; women of color as,
32–36, 38–39, 44–45, 186–88,
190–93. *See also* reproductive
rights
Mothers for Freedom, 33, 38
Murray, Charles, 121n37
Myth of the 20th Century, The
(Rosenberg), 302

N

Nadelmann, Ethan, 6
National Abortion Federation,
151
National Abortion Rights Action
League (NARAL), 148, 151
National Asian Women's Health
Organization, 149
National Audubon Society, 303
National Black United Front, 149
National Black Women's Health
Project (NBWHP), 133, 134,
149, 150
National Clearinghouse for the
Defense of Battered Women,
15
National Coalition of
Anti-Violence Programs,
25–26
National Coalition on Police
Accountability (NCOPA), 10
National Council for Research on
Women, 179–80
National Institute of Drug Abuse
(NIDA), 68, 74n18, 78n89

National Institutes of Health, 157,
160
National Intelligence Council, 278
National Latina Health
Organization, 134, 149
National Network for Immigrant
and Refugee Rights (NNIRR),
10
National Network of Abortion
Funds, 105, 107
National Organization for
Women (NOW), 148
National Population Commission
(Peru), 272
National Right to Life
Committee, 13
National Welfare Rights
Organization, 149
National Women's Health
Network, 131, 132, 133–34
Native American community:
abortion and, 109, 114,
139–42, 146n90; contraceptive
abuse, 134–39; criminalization
of, 3; health issues, 160–62;
Indian Health Services (IHS),
109, 126–31, 137–39, 161–62;
population control, 123–27;
prisons and, 28; sterilization of,
xvii–xviii, 126–31, 141. *See also*
women of color
Native American Women's
Health Education Resource
Center (NAWHERC), 134,
137, 138, 141, 149
nativism, 175, 293, 307, 310,
322n2. *See also*
population-environment
right-wing movement
Nazi Germany: demographic
science, 293–94, 297–98;

environment focus, 299–303;
immigration, 294–95;
population control, 278,
296–97; racism, 295–96, 303;
social Darwinism, 291–92, 300
Negative Population Growth
(NPG), 279, 304–5, 307
"Negro Cocaine 'Fiends' Are A
New Southern Menace"
(Williams), 57
neoliberalism, xi, 262, 264, 267,
272–74. *See also* globalization
Nepal, 199
Nevas, Alan, 78n93
New Orleans Times-Picayune, 60
New York City: corruption in, 65;
media, 60; militant policing in,
x, 5, 8, 11, 42–43
New York City Police Watch,
6–7, 10, 25
New York Times, x, 57, 276, 294
New Zealand, 134
Nigeria, 265
Nightline, 27
nongovernmental organizations
(NGOs): neoliberal agenda
and, 262, 270, 271–73; sex
trafficking issues and, 200, 215,
219, 222
Norplant: population control, 63,
131, 140, 162, 252; safety/side
effects of, 13, 136–39
Northwest Environmental
Advocates, 307

O

Oberlörlander, Theodor, 295
O'Brien, Mary, 218
O'Donnell, Santiago, 182
Ohio Reformatory for Women

(ORW), 21
"On the Care and Conservation
of Forests" (Arndt), 300
Operation Rescue, 152
Operation Wetback, 175
Organization of American States
(OAS), 20
Osthoff, Sue, 15

P

Packard Foundation, 276, 279
Pakistan, 199, 226n4
Palafox, Jose, xxi
Paltrow, Lynn, xvi, 19
Parents Against Police Brutality,
33
Partnership for a Drug-Free
America (PDFA), 59–60,
74n20–21
Passing of the Great Race, The
(Grant), 316–17
Persian Gulf War, 124
Personal Responsibility and Work
Opportunity Reconciliation
Act of 1996 (PRWORA)
(welfare reform bill), 114–15,
184–85, 188, 252
Peru, 268–69, 272–73, 280
Petchesky, Rosalind, xi, 271
Pharmacists for Life, 111
Philadelphia Inquirer, 131
Philippines, 197, 203
Pioneer Fund, 305
PLANet, 276, 278, 288n46
Planned Parenthood Federation
of America (PPFA), 148, 151,
253
Plate, Roderich, 298
Poland, 294, 295
police. *See* criminal justice system;

enforcement violence
Population and Environment, 305,
311, 318
population control:
contraceptives and, 114,
135–40, 162, 252–53, 269;
empowerment of women and,
248–49, 261, 263–64, 274;
environment myths, 150,
276–80, 291; family planning,
172, 260–62, 266–70, 277, 279;
genocide, 126, 141–42, 151,
296; overpopulation myths,
124, 260, 292, 303; poverty
and, 114, 131, 274, 305; racism
and, 12–13, 63–64, 123–25,
259–60, 303; youth and,
244–48. *See also* contraception;
population-environment
right-wing movement;
sterilization
Population-Environment Balance
(PEB), 279, 304–7, 319
population-environment
right-wing movement:
description of, 304–6;
ecofascism of, 308–9, 318–19;
Nazi parallels to, 292–93, 303,
309–10, 320; neofascist
tendencies of, 312–17; politics
of, 291, 306–8, 310, 318–21.
See also Nazi Germany
Population Institute, 124
Population Matters, 279
poverty: abortion and, 12–14,
103–4, 106–8, 114–17,
119n11-12, 121n33; in
communities of color, 85, 164,
167, 260; criminalization of,
xiii, 43, 56, 84, 90–91, 101n17;
exploitation of, 39–41, 177–80,
188, 192–93; globalization and,
7, 263–66; migration and,
191–92, 202, 205; motherhood
and, 33, 36, 117, 186–88;
movements against, 148–49,
152–53; population control
and, 114, 131, 252–53, 267,
274, 305
Powell, Sharon, 124
Powers, Mary, 25, 42, 51n54
Precautionary Principle, 218
Princeton University, 165
prison: enforcement
accountability and, 10, 20–22,
27, 29, 36–39; HIV/AIDS,
81–82, 84–87, 93–94, 100n5–6,
101n24; incarceration surge,
xii–xv, 56–57, 66–69; inmate
activism, 81–83, 85–86, 88,
95–96; pregnancy and
motherhood issues, 14, 19–21,
36–37, 57, 63; prison industrial
complex, xiv, 8, 83, 85, 87, 327;
sexual assault, 10, 22–23,
26–28, 93–94, 102n40;
victimization, 82, 84, 91–93,
98; women of color and,
20–22, 27–28, 36–39, 84–85,
90–91
pro-choice. *See* abortion:
movements about
Pro-Choice Public Education
Project, 116
"Professors of Hate" (Miller), 314
Proposition "21," 242–43
Proposition "165," 183
Proposition "187," 183–84, 188,
189, 190
Prostitutes in Medical Literature
(Kanta), 210–11

prostitution: health issues,
208–11, 213, 217–18; policy
solutions, 202, 220–24; sexually
transmitted diseases, 210–11,
213–15, 217–20, 228n45;
transgendered people and, 25,
42; violence and, 41–43, 92,
207, 210–12, 216–17. *See also*
sex trafficking
Public Health Service, 160
Puerto Rico, 165–66

Q

Qadeer, Imrana, 265–66
quinacrine, 117, 270

R

Race and the Education of Desire
(Stoler), 123
racism: anti-Semitism, 294–99,
301, 302–3, 312–16; history of,
55, 73n10, 123–25; population
control and, 12–13, 63–64,
123–25, 259–60, 303;
reproductive rights and,
123–25, 151–52, 170;
September 11 and, 326–28; war
on drugs, 56–60, 64–65, 67–68,
71–72. *See also* eugenics;
nativism; Nazi Germany
Rand Corporation, 279
rape. *See* sexual assault
Ravenholt, R.T., 124–25
Real War on Crime, The (Donziger),
61
Rebecca (prisoner), 83, 86, 89, 90,
93–98
Regulating the Lives of Women
(Abramowitz), 186

Rehnquist, William, 66
Reiman, Jeffrey, 64
"Relative Cohort Size and Youth
Crime in the United States,
1953–1984" (Steffensmeier et
al.), 242
religious right wing. See abortion:
movements about
Reproductive Coalition for
Abortion Rights, 148
reproductive health. See health
care
reproductive rights: definition of,
12, 114–18, 140–41, 168–72,
262–66; empowerment of
women and, 248–49, 261,
263–64, 274; family planning,
172, 260–62, 266–70, 277, 279;
links to other movements,
x–xii, 14, 22, 26, 148–53;
movement for, 148–53, 157,
270–73; racism and, 123–25,
151–52, 170; RTIs and, 154–57
Reproductive Rights and Wrongs
(Hartmann), 235
reproductive tract infections
(RTIs): activism on, 157–59;
African Americans and,
166–68; Asian and Pacific
Islanders and, 163–64; Native
Americans and, 161–62; report
on, 159–60; reproductive rights
and, 154–57; sexually
transmitted diseases (STDs),
155, 156, 161–65, 209, 269
Republican Party, 116
*Rich Get Richer and the Poor Get
Prison, The* (Reiman), 64
Richie, Beth, 15
right wing. See abortion:
movements about; Nazi

Germany;
population-environment
right-wing movement
Roberts, Dorothy: on abortion
issues, 13, 121n33; on
immigation, 184, 191–92; on
population control, xvii, 282;
on teen pregnancy, 250
Rockefeller Drug Laws, 7
Rockefeller Foundation, 279
Roe vs. Wade, 108, 119n12
Rohrabacher, Dana, 182, 183, 189
Romo, Jesus, 30
Roosevelt, Theodore, 57
Rosenberg, Alfred, 302
Rosenthal, Erich, 295
Ross, Luana, 3, 28, 29
Rushton, J. Philippe, 305, 306,
314
Russia, 199, 200, 208, 215–16,
236

S

Sanchez, Maria, 129
Sassen, Saskia, 178–79, 204, 205
Schaz, Ulrike, 295, 296, 297
School for Me, A, 135
Scully, Judith, xiv
Selders, Larry, 24
Seltzer, William, 297–98
Sen, Amartya, 238, 244
Sentencing Project, 4
September 11, xx, 153, 326–28
Seraphim, Peter-Heinz, 295
Serena, Norma Jean, 129
sex education, 112, 115, 152, 168,
247, 252
sex trafficking: causes of,
199–200, 202–6; children and,
198–99, 206, 213, 219, 221;

health impacts, 210–15,
217–20; Internet and, 206,
227n24; mail-order brides, 198,
199, 206, 224; policy solutions
to, 202, 220–24, 226n3; tacit
support for, 205, 206, 221, 225;
UN protocols and conventions
on, 198–99; violence and,
41–43, 201, 207, 209, 212,
216–17; women as a
commodity, 199, 205, 206, 222,
226n4
sex work. *See* prostitution; sex
trafficking
sexual assault: abortion and,
139–40; by African-Americans,
myth, 57; effects of, 209;
enforcement violence and,
xxvii(n3), 24, 26–28, 39, 41–42;
in prison, 10, 22–23, 26–28,
93–94, 102n40; prostitution
and, 207, 210–12, 216–17
sexually transmitted diseases
(STDs), 155, 156, 161–65, 209,
269. *See also* HIV/AIDS;
reproductive tract infections
S.H. Cowell Foundation, 304–5
Shaylor, Cassandra, 28
Sherbinin, Alex de, 237
Sierra Club, 303, 306, 307
Silent Warriors, 38
Silver, Lee, 282–83
Singleton, John, ix
SisterSong Women of Color
Reproductive Health Project,
xviii–xix, 154, 157–60, 167–69,
172
60 Minutes, 62, 75n39
slavery, xiii–xiv, 55–56, 60, 198,
199
Sleders, Larry, 24

Slepian, Barnett, 104, 119n6
Smith, Adam, 226n1
Smith, Justine, 141
Sobel, Solomon, 132, 133
social Darwinism, 291–92, 300, 310, 311, 317
Soderbergh, Steven, ix
South Africa, 305
South Korea, 239
Stannard, David, 124
Stanton Yellowknife Hospital, 140
Staudenmaier, Peter, 299–300, 301, 318–19
Steele, Martin R., 237
Steffensmeier, Darrell, 241–42
Stenberg vs. Carhart, 113, 121n31
Stephens vs. State, 77n82
sterilization: abortion and, 139–41; contraceptive abuse, 114, 135–40, 162, 269; Depo-Provera, 63, 131–35, 137–38, 162; in India, 269; in Mexico, 269; of Native Americans, 126–31; Norplant, 13, 63, 131, 136–40, 162, 252; in Peru, 268–69, 272–73; quinacrine, 117, 270; tubal ligations, 127, 129, 140, 144n23; United States and, 125, 165–66, 305; of women of color, 12, 63–64, 94, 126–31, 260
Stoler, Ann, 123
Streifel, Cathy, 241–42
Strom, Lyle, 78n93
structural adjustment, 168, 197, 203, 264–65, 270–71
Suharto, 239
superpredators, xxii–xxiii, xxviii(n30), 69, 240–44, 253

T

Tanton, John, 305
Tanzania, 266–67, 285n5
Tate, Preston, 102n34
Temporary Assistance for Needy Families (TANF), 185, 186, 189, 252
Thailand, 197, 206
Third World: fear of immigration, 309, 319–20; labor migration, 197–98, 203–6; neoliberalism and, 264; population control, 260, 278, 292; poverty and, 263; sex trafficking, 199–200; sterilization abuse, 124–25, 137; youth bulge, xxiii, 239
Todt, Fritz, 301
Traffic, ix
Tuskegee Syphilis Study, 167

U

Ultimate Test Animal, The, 132, 138, 139
United Nations: Cairo +5, 259, 263, 271; Conference on Environment and Developement (Rio, 1992), 319; Convention Against Transnational Organized Crime, 198; Convention for the Suppression of the Traffic in Persons and of the Exploitation of the Prostitution of Others, 199, 221; *Convention on the Elimination* of All Forms of Discrimination against Women (CEDAW), 171–72, 199; Fund for Population Activities (UNFPA), 245, 246, 247, 249,

267; population projections, 260; Protocol to Prevent, Suppress, and Punish Trafficking in Persons, Especially Women and Children, 198, 199, 226n3; sex trafficking report by, 197; Fourth World Conference for Women (Beijing, 1995), 118, 149; World Conference Against Racism, 170, 328

United States: abortion in, 104, 105, 107–9, 112, 119n11, 120n30; Aid to Families with Dependent Children (AFDC), 177, 183, 185–86, 189, 191; border issues, 11, 19–20, 24, 30, 40; Constitution, 55–56, 71, 72, 169, 175; economics and, 7, 124, 179, 180, 203; founding principles of, 90; human rights and, 169–71; ICPD conference and, 261, 274–76; immigration issues, 178–80, 184–85, 188, 202–4, 292; National Drug Control Strategy (1989), 58; population control and, xvii–xviii, 125, 260, 261; sex trafficking in, 200–202, 205–8; war on drugs, 70–72; welfare policies, 275–76; battered women in, 210; youth bulge and, 235, 249–52

United States government agencies: Agency for International Development (USAID), 124, 245, 266–69, 280; Army, 279; Central Intelligence Agency (CIA), 70–71; Commission on Civil Rights, 163; Congress, 13,

50n25, 68, 108; Customs Service, 20, 49n1; Defense Intelligence Agency, 235; Department of Health and Human Services, 185, 251; Department of Health, Education, and Welfare (DHEW), 125, 130; Drug Enforcement Agency (DEA), 58, 70; Federal Bureau of Investigation (FBI), 5, 132, 138, 144n48, 207; Food and Drug Administration (FDA), 131, 132, 133, 134; General Accounting Office (GAO), 126–29; Indian Health Services (IHS), 109, 126, 126–31, 137–39, 161–62; Justice Department, 70; Sentencing Commission, 67, 68; State Department, 70; Supreme Court, 113, 149–50. *See also* Immigration Naturalization Service (INS)

United States NGOs in Support of the Cairo Consensus, 247

University of California, 116, 183, 189

University of Chicago, 13

University of Florida, 62

Up and Out of Poverty Network, 153

Upjohn Company, 132, 133, 134, 135

Uri, Connie, 126, 127, 128, 129

US English group, 305

US News and World Report, 60–61, 236

US Prostitutes Collective (USPROS), 41, 42

V

Valley State Prison for Women
    (Chowchilla), 26–27, 28
Vatican, 271
Vietnam, 199, 208
violence. *See* domestic violence;
    enforcement violence; sexual
    assault; women's anti-violence
    movement
Violent and Repeat Juvenile
    Offenders Accountability and
    Rehabilitation Act (1999), 243
Violent Youth Predator Act
    (1996), 242
Virago, Shawna, 25
Vogue Magazine, 253
voting rights, 69, 79n105

W

Walrond, Tabitha, 35–36
war on drugs: crack, 61–64,
    67–68, 75n42, 78n89, 78n93;
    history of, 57–58;
    incarceration, xvi, 20, 56, 61,
    66–69; laws concerning, 66–68,
    77n81–82; mothers and,
    xv–xvi, 20, 57, 61–64; police
    corruption, 65–66, 76n65;
    propaganda about, 58–60;
    racism of, xvi, 56–58, 71–72;
    social destruction by, 56, 65,
    69–70; voting rights lost, 69,
    79n105
Warrier, Sujata, 16
Washington Alliance for
    Immigrant and Refugee Justice,
    10, 34, 40–41
Washington Post, 60
Weeden Foundation, 304–5

Weinstein, Jack B., 78n93
welfare: African-American use of,
    121; immigration fears and,
    175–76, 182–82, 189–92;
    mothers and, 186–90, 250, 251,
    275; Proposition "165," 183;
    Proposition "187," 183–84,
    188–89; PRWORA reform bill
    (1996), 114–15, 184–85, 188,
    252
Willeby, Rosemary, 81
Wilmott, Donna, 5, 37
Wilson, James Q., 241
Wilson, Pete, 185, 188, 189, 243
Wirth, Timothy, 276
Women In Prison, Families in
    Crisis Initiative, 47
Women of All Red Nations
    (WARN), 127, 138, 141
women of color: abortion and,
    12–14, 113–16, 121n33,
    139–40, 146n90, 151–53;
    criminalization of, x, 8, 22, 43,
    56; enforcement accountability
    movements, 14, 16–17, 29–31,
    46–48; enforcement violence
    on, 14, 20, 82, 84, 91; health
    care and, 148–50, 153–54,
    156–60, 167–71, 182–85;
    motherhood, 32–36, 38–39,
    44–45, 186–88, 190–93; in
    prison, 20–22, 27–28, 36–39,
    84–85, 90–91
women's anti-violence movement:
    domestic violence, 14–17,
    29–30, 227n38; links to other
    movements, 10–12, 26, 32,
    47–48, 82, 98
Women's Commission for
    Refugee Women and Children,
    22, 27

Women's Health Education Project, 134

Women's Positive Legal Action Network, 100n3

World AIDS Conference, 213

World AIDS Day (1998), 213

World Bank: health care crisis caused by, 264; migration and, 168, 197, 203; population control and, 124, 267; on violence against women, 209–10

World Conference Against Racism, Racial Discrimination, Xenophobia, and Related Intolerance, 170, 328

World Health Organization, 134, 209–10

World Population Foundation, 247

World War II. *See* Nazi Germany

Worldwatch Institute, 214, 278

Wright, Hamilton, 57

Wyeth-Ayerst Laboratories, 136, 137

Yugoslavia, 314, 317

Z

Zahn, Friedrich, 294, 298

Zero Population Growth, 247

Zimbabwe, 265

Zinni, Anthony C., 236, 237

Y

young people: abortion and, 103–4, 107, 114–16; criminalization of, 8, xxviii(n30), 240–43; demographics of, 231–33, 231–33; fear of immigration by, 237–38; population control of, 244–48; pregnancy of, 249–53; security concerns and, 234–37, 239–40, 279–80; as superpredators, xxii–xxiii, 69, 240–44, 253

youth bulge. *See* young people

About the Contributors

Rajani Bhatia is currently the coordinator of the Committee on Women, Population, and the Environment (CWPE). She has been involved in women's health research and activism for seven years in partnership with Forum for Women's Health (Mumbai) and the Feminist International Network of Resistance to Reproductive Technology and Genetic Engineering based in Germany. She lives in Baltimore, Maryland.

Anannya Bhattacharjee is based in New York City and is currently the program officer at the Unitarian Universalist Veatch Program. She is the former executive director of CAAAV: Organizing Asian Communities; founder and former executive coordinator of Sakhi for South Asian Women; and co-founder of the SAMAR Collective (a South Asian media resource). In 1998, she was awarded the Activist-in-Residence fellowship from the Asian/Pacific/American Studies Program and Institute at New York University, and in 1999, she became a Charles H. Revson Fellow on the Future of the City of New York at Columbia University. She writes and speaks widely on social justice work.

Sarah L. Brownlee is an expert in community organizing and lesbian and gay issues. She was formely the program director of the National Center for Human Rights Education. Brownlee is a massage therapist.

Cynthia Chandler is the co-founder and co-director of Justice Now, a nonprofit organization based in Oakland, California that provides legal services, prisoner peer education support, and community education around the needs of women prisoners. Prior to this position, she founded and directed Women's Positive Legal Action Network, an organization dedicated to reducing the suffering of women prisoners with HIV and Hepatitis C. She is active in the prisoner rights and sex worker rights communities. She is the author of numerous articles.

Dazon Dixon Diallo is a women's human rights activist and a public health expert. She is the founder and president of SisterLove Women's AIDS Project.

Marlene Gerber Fried is a long-time reproductive rights activist, most recently as the founding president of the National Network of Abortion Funds. She is professor of philosophy at Hampshire College and director of the Civil Liberties and Public Policy Program. She is the editor of *From Abortion to Reproductive Freedom: Transforming a Movement* (South End Press, 1990) and is currently working on a new book, *The Politics of Inclusion: Women of Color and the Reproductive Rights Movement*, along with Loretta Ross and Jael Silliman.

Betsy Hartmann is the director of the Population and Development Program at Hampshire College in Amherst, Massachusetts, and a core committee member of Committee on Women, Population, and the Environment. A longstanding member of the international women's health movement, she writes and speaks frequently on international population and environment issues. She is the author of *Reproductive Rights and Wrongs: The Global Politics of Population Control* (South End Press, 1995) and co-author of *A Quiet Violence: View from a Bangladesh Village* (Food First and Zed Books, 1983). She has recently published *The Truth About Fire*, a novel about right-wing terrorism (Carroll and Graf, 2002).

Anne Hendrixson is a freelance writer and editor and a member of the Committee on Women, Population, and the Environment. Currently, she is engaged in a project on youth, "A Generation Out-of-Control."

H. Patricia Hynes is professor of Environmental Health at the Boston University School of Public Health and director of the Urban Environmental Health Initiative, where she works on issues of urban environment, feminism, and environmental justice. She is the author of *The Recurring Silent Spring* (Pergamon, 1989); *EarthRight* (Prima, 1990); *Taking Population out of the Equation: Reformulating I=PAT* (Institute on Women and Technology, 1993); and *A Patch of Eden: America's Inner-City Gardeners* (Chelsea Green,

1996), which won the 1996 National Arbor Day Foundation Book Award. She is currently co-director of the Lead-Safe Yard Project.

Carol Kingery is a prisoner rights activist and a volunteer with Justice Now, a nonprofit organization based in Oakland, California. Her piece in this anthology is part of a series she is co-authoring with women prisoners and Cynthia Chandler that critically examines the reliance on prisons as a solution to sexist violence. She is currently a law student at the University of California, Berkeley.

Syd Lindsley is a feminist activist who has been involved in the immigrant's rights, reproductive rights, and queer rights movements. She has written several articles on gender and immigration, and the anti-immigrant movement. She currently works at Cornish College of the Arts and lives in Seattle.

Janice G. Raymond is professor of Women's Studies and Medical Ethics at the University of Massachusetts in Amherst. She has been visiting professor at the University of Linköping in Sweden, and visiting research scholar at the Massachusetts Institute of Technology. Raymond is also co-executive director of the Coalition Against Trafficking in Women, International. She is the author of five books the most recent of which is *Women as Wombs: Reproductive Freedom and the Battle Over Women's Bodies* (Harper, 1994).

Luz Rodriquez is an expert in women's health issues in the Latina community. She is the former executive director of Casa Atabex Ache, a women of color health organization based in the Bronx, New York.

Loretta J. Ross is the executive director of the National Center for Human Rights Education, the first human rights education organization in the United States that focuses primarily on domestic human rights violations.

Judith A.M. Scully is an associate professor at the West Virginia University College of Law, where she teaches Criminal Law; Race, Racism and American Law; Trial Advocacy; and International Human Rights Law. Prior to teaching, she practiced law in Chicago. For the past fifteen years, she has been a civil rights, human rights, and reproductive rights activist. Scully is a steering committee member of the National Conference of Black Lawyers and the Committee on Women, Population, and the Environment.

Jael Silliman is an assistant professor of Women's Studies at the University of Iowa. She is a steering committee member of the Committee on Women, Population, and the Environment, an executive committee member of the University of Iowa Center for Human Rights (UICHR), and co vice-chair of the Reproductive Health Technologies Project. She is the co-editor of *Dangerous Intersections: Feminist Perspectives on Population, Environment and Development* (South End Press, 1999) and is the author of *Jewish Portraits, Indian Frames: Women's Narratives from a Diaspora of Hope* (University Press of New England, 2001). She has written several articles and speaks extensively on social movements, and on issues of population, development, and the environment from a feminist perspective.

Andrea Smith is a co-founder of Incite! Women of Color Against Violence. She was a co-founder of the Chicago chapter of Women of All Red Nations and is assistant professor of American Culture and Women's Studies at the University of Michigan.

About South End Press

South End Press is a nonprofit, collectively run book publisher with more than 200 titles in print. Since our founding in 1977, we have tried to meet the needs of readers who are exploring, or are already committed to, the politics of radical social change. Our goal is to publish books that encourage critical thinking and constructive action on the key political, cultural, social, economic, and ecological issues shaping life in the United States and in the world. In this way, we hope to give expression to a wide diversity of democratic social movements and to provide an alternative to the products of corporate publishing.

Through the Institute for Social and Cultural Change, South End Press works with other political media projects—Alternative Radio; Speakout, a speakers' bureau; and *Z Magazine*—to expand access to information and critical analysis.

To order books, please send a check or money order to: South End Press, 7 Brookline Street, #1, Cambridge, MA 02139-4146. To order by credit card, call 1-800-533-8478. Please include $3.50 for postage and handling for the first book and 50 cents for each additional book.

Write or e-mail southend@southendpress.org for a free catalog, or visit our web site at www.southendpress.org.

Related Titles from South End Press

Dangerous Intersections: Feminist Perspectives on Population, Environment, and Development
Jael Silliman and Ynestra King, editors

Reproductive Rights or Wrongs? The Global Politics of Population Control
Betsy Hartmann

From Abortion to Reproductive Freedom: Transforming a Movement
Marlene Gerber Fried, editor

Abortion Without Apology: A Radical History for the 1990s
Ninia Baehr

Criminal Injustice: Confronting the Prison Crisis
Elihu Rosenblatt, editor

For Crying Out Loud: Women's Poverty in the United States
Diane Dujon and Ann Withorn, editors

Women Under Attack: Victories, Backlash, and the Fight for Reproductive Freedom
Susan E. Davis, editor

Women, AIDS, and Activism
The ACT UP New York Women and AIDS Book Group

Rethinking Ecofeminist Politics
Janet Biehl